SHAKESPEARE REPRODUCED

SHAKESPEARE REPRODUCED
The text in history and ideology

Edited by
Jean E. Howard
and
Marion F. O'Connor

Methuen

New York and London

First published in 1987 by
Methuen, Inc.
29 West 35th Street, New York NY 10001

Published in Great Britain by
Methuen & Co. Ltd
11 New Fetter Lane, London EC4P 4EE

Photoset by Mayhew Typesetting, Bristol, England
Printed in Great Britain by Richard Clay Ltd,
Bungay, Suffolk

Library of Congress Cataloging-in-Publication Data

Shakespeare reproduced.
Bibliography: p.
Includes Index.
1. Shakespeare, William, 1564–1616 – Political and
social views – Congresses.   2. Politics in literature –
Congresses.   I. Howard, Jean E. (Jean Elizabeth),
1948– .   II. O'Connor, Marion F.
PR3017.S57   1987   822.3'3   87–14135
ISBN 0 416 00922 0
0 416 00932 8 (pbk.)

British Library Cataloguing in Publication Data

Shakespeare reproduced: the text in history
and ideology.
1. Shakespeare, William – Criticism and
interpretation
I. Howard, Jean E.   II. O'Connor, Marion F.
822.3'3   PR2976

ISBN 0 416 00922 0
0 416 00932 8 Pbk

Contents

Introduction
JEAN E. HOWARD and MARION F. O'CONNOR   1

1 Political criticism of Shakespeare
WALTER COHEN   18

2 Power, politics, and the Shakespearean text: recent criticism in
England and the United States
DON E. WAYNE   47

3 Theatre of the Empire: "Shakespeare's England"
at Earl's Court, 1912
MARION F. O'CONNOR   68

4 Prospero in Africa: *The Tempest* as colonialist text and pretext
THOMAS CARTELLI   99

5 The Order of the Garter, the cult of Elizabeth, and class–gender
tension in *The Merry Wives of Windsor*
PETER ERICKSON   116

6 "And wash the Ethiop white": femininity and the monstrous in
Othello
KAREN NEWMAN   143

7 Renaissance antitheatricality and the politics of gender and rank in
Much Ado About Nothing
JEAN E. HOWARD   163

8 "Which is the merchant here? and which the Jew?": subversion
and recuperation in *The Merchant of Venice*
THOMAS MOISAN   188

9 Lenten butchery: legitimation crisis in *Coriolanus*
MICHAEL D. BRISTOL   207

10 The failure of orthodoxy in *Coriolanus*
THOMAS SORGE   225

11 Speculations: *Macbeth* and source
JONATHAN GOLDBERG   242

12 Towards a literary theory of ideology: mimesis, representation,
authority
ROBERT WEIMANN   265

Afterword
MARGARET FERGUSON   273

Index   285

Introduction

Jean E. Howard and Marion F. O'Connor

One way to locate this book is to say that it publishes work first prepared for a seminar on Shakespeare and ideology which took place at the International Shakespeare Congress held in West Berlin in April, 1986. In Berlin, the wall materially marks the city as the site of political contest and ideological division. But texts, too, as we argue below, are sites of ideological and political contestation, and so, in some instances, are conference sessions. In Berlin, participants in the two seminars on Shakespeare and ideology debated, with some heat, not just the political and ideological functions of Elizabethan theater in its own time, but also the functions of Shakespeare within present pedagogical, critical, and theatrical practices. Differences became very obvious: differences, for example, over whether the "playfulness" of Elizabethan theater can function as a critique of oppressive orthodoxies within the conditions for production and reception obtaining in modern middle-class theaters; differences over whether or not Shakespeare's centrality to a universalizing and overtly apolitical pedagogy implies that the study of his work had best be abandoned by those attempting a pedagogy established on other principles; differences over the possibility of merging Marxism with tenets and practices of poststructuralism.

The present volume cannot reproduce the seminar, nor, given the bizarre things occasionally said by nearly everyone at such events, would that be a good idea. Inevitably, some positions have been elided, and the whole enterprise has been shaped by the priorities of the editors. Yet what was said at Berlin, by seminar participants and by audience members, has left its mark on a great many of the individual essays. In an important sense, this book results from work collectively undertaken and refined. The editors would like to thank *all* the members of that seminar, including those whose texts are not published here, for their spirited participation in what turned out to be a strenuous intellectual encounter and for their incalculable shares in this volume.[1]

There is, however, a second way in which this volume records a collective enterprise, and there is another set of coordinates on which to map it besides those provided by the local context of a particular Shakespeare congress. The essays in this volume are obviously traversed by a variety of contemporary discourses. To acknowledge these calls in question the idea of authorial/critical originality, but also makes possible a recognition of the historical specificity of this work. A glance at the list of contributors to this volume will indicate that most are North American academics. Moreover, some scrutiny of the Library of Congress data in contributors' several books establishes that, almost without exception, they are of an age. Most of the contributors, having been students at North American universities in the 1960s and in the early years of academic employment in the 1970s, have been constructed by discourses both theoretical and political. Yet there are tensions and contradictions among these discourses. Much political activism of the 1960s remained relatively untheorized and was often premised on notions of autonomous, unified, and wholly volitional selves acting as agents of change within social formations assumed to be responsive to such agency. These common-sense premises have been put under pressure by much poststructuralist theory, with its emphasis on the discursive production of discontinuous subjectivities, on the problematic nature of the concept of agency, and on the capacity of the social order to recuperate subversive and contestatory movements. Marxism itself, the most developed political criticism in the west, has been divided by the eruption of poststructuralist challenges to traditional Marxist notions of teleological history, of agency, of ideology, and of base–superstructure relationships. This book cannot escape the contradictions occasioned by its own historicity, perhaps most clearly as it both voices the desire to change – if not the world – at least the academy, and also articulates quite forcefully the many barriers to the realization of such an ambition.

While the work in this volume articulates a number of different, and conflicting, premises about how to approach Shakespeare in history and ideology, a collective debt has been incurred to several contemporary developments in Shakespeare studies: namely, to feminism, new historicism, and various forms of Marxist criticism, including cultural materialism. As Walter Cohen argues in the opening essay, these movements, at least in the American academy, have in the 1980s facilitated the emergence of a vigorous political criticism of Renaissance drama. But intersections and abrasions among these discourses are altering them. What one sees in this volume – and not, of course, only here – are, for example, essays which adopt many of the strategies and premises of new historicist criticism (the assumption, for example, that cultural studies do not give access to some unchanging human nature, only to historically specific constructions; or the assumption that dramatic texts are intertextually connected to many "non-literary" cultural texts and practices), but which refuse the drift of much new historical scholarship toward seeing the Renaissance theater simply as an instrument of state, a site where challenges to dominant ideologies were endlessly recuperated. At the same time, many of the essays share with the work of the British cultural materialists a concern for what we might call the effective

history of the Shakespearean text: its continuing implicaiton in a variety of
cultural practices and institutions in which the authority of Shakespeare is
appropriated to serve particular political ends. Historicizing the text thus comes
to mean, not only locating it within the coordinates of Renaissance culture, but
mapping its uses at subsequent moments of reception and reproduction
(Longhurst, 1982; Dollimore and Sinfield, 1985; Hawkes, 1986). At the same
time, it is the twin pressures of historicism and materialism which most radically
are altering American feminist criticism. The necessity to historicize gender
constructions if one wishes to escape the oppressive notion of a universal human
nature, or, worse, of an eternal feminine, is increasingly apparent, as is the need
to talk about the way race and class affect constructions of the feminine and
pluralize the monolithic concept of "woman." Simultaneously, feminism
continues to lodge a powerful critique of any political mode of cultural analysis,
be it Marxist or new historicist, which fails to take account of the central role
played by the production of gender difference in the perpetuation of economic
and social oppression. In short, while the volume is affiliated with these and
other contemporary critical discourses – including the Bakhtinian discourse of
carnival and the discourse of deconstruction, which is sometimes appropriated
in this volume simply as a strategy for showing how a text differs from itself,
and sometimes elaborated as a political critique of totalizing claims – it modifies
and reconfigures them.

Genealogy, however, is less important than what is done with the space
opened up by prior work. Speaking here for themselves, and letting contributors
speak primarily through their essays, the editors of this volume intend it to
further a political analysis of Shakespearean texts and their uses in culture. By
a political analysis we mean one which examines how Shakespearean texts have
functioned to produce, reproduce, or contest historically specific relations of
power (relations among classes, genders, and races, for example) and have been
used to produce and naturalize interested representations of the real. In speaking
of "interested" representations, we do not imply that there is a conscious
conspiracy on the part of particular social groups to distort (misrepresent) reality
through dramatic fictions. Rather, we mean that reality is knowable only
through the discourses which mediate it, and that there is a constant, if subter-
ranean, struggle over whose constructions of the real will gain dominance.
Dramatic works, at their moments of production, are implicated in such
struggles; and they are reimplicated each time they are reproduced in criticism
or in the theater. (A criticism which presents Coriolanus as enemy of the people
and a criticism which presents him as victim of lower-class envy and ignorance
circulate two quite distinct constructions of what would constitute a proper social
order within the play world, and probably within *the* world as well.) There is,
in short, no way to place drama outside of ideological contestation, ideology
being understood as that inescapable network of beliefs and practices by which
variously positioned and historically constituted subjects imagine their relationship to the real and through which they render intelligible the world around
them. Ideology can never be "disinterested" because it functions to render

"obvious" and "natural" constructions of reality which, often in oblique and highly mediated ways, serve the interests of particular races, genders and classes within the social formation (Althusser, 1971, esp. 127–86).

Theater, as a social practice, is inevitably implicated in ideological production and reproduction. On a very simple level, this is illustrated by the way the geographical placement of certain North American Shakespeare festivals in lush rural settings difficult to reach by public transport results in white audiences of middle-class culture buffs, a result which both is produced by and also further strengthens tacit assumptions about who owns Shakespeare and the green fields (the nature) with which he is so insistently connected. On another level, every reading or staging of a play is implicated in ideology in that it produces the play within the codes and conventions sustaining particular, interested constructions of the real.[2] Far from distorting the "true" meaning of an unchanging text, however, such constructions *are* the text: it lives in history, with history itself understood as a field of contestation. One end of a political criticism, conse-quently, is to explore the ideological functions of texts at various historical junc-tures and in various cultural practices. A further aim of much political criticism, however, is not only to *describe*, but to *take a position on*, the political uses of texts: to challenge some critical, theatrical, or pedagogical practices involving Shakespeare and to encourage others. In short, it is a critical practice in which the critic acknowledges his or her own interested position within the social formation, rather than laying claim to an Olympian disinterestedness.

Probably more than any other figure in western culture, Shakespeare has been used to secure assumptions about texts, history, ideology, and criticism different from those outlined above. He functions, in many quarters, as a kind of cultural Esperanto, a medium through which the differences of material existence – differences of race, gender, class, history, and culture – are supposedly canceled. He is repeatedly presented as the writer who transcends such differences to get at the abiding truths of human existence, as "not for an age, but for all time."[3] Claims about Shakespeare as the bearer of universal truths serve an oppressive function when they render illegitimate readings produced outside the dominant ideologies which secure a society's understanding of what the true is. As feminists and Third World critics, among others, have suggested, when texts are said to speak for humankind, humankind often shrinks radically to include only those within a traditional pale of privilege. This volume aims to question claims of Shakespeare's universality and to reveal ways in which historically specific factors determine the "Shakespeare" produced in criticism, in the classroom, and on the stage.

Accompanying the contention that Shakespeare depicts a universal and unchanging human nature are often two further claims: first, that the meaning of a Shakespearean text is ineluctably *in* that text (and consequently never changes); and second, that the Shakespearean text resides in an aesthetic zone above ideology. One stark link among these claims is their avoidance of history. To posit an unchanging meaning *in* texts, waiting to be found by "good" readers, is to deny the historicity of the reading and theatrical practices through which a plural and opaque text is rendered variously intelligible at different historical moments and from different interested positions within the social formation. Similarly, to posit a category of self-evidently literary works, somehow above ideology, is to ignore the historicity of the very category of the literary, the way, that is, different works fall within that category at different historical moments (Eagleton, 1983, 1–16). Such a move essentializes what is socially constructed; and it arbitrarily places outside the arena of social contest certain pieces of writing and certain acts of reading. Again, the ideological function of such claims is to allow local and particular constructions of Shakespeare to enjoy the privilege of natural and unchanging truths, uncontaminated by the ''merely'' political or parochial. This volume argues against such ahistorical and overtly disinterested critical practices.

By the title, *Shakespeare Reproduced: The Text in History and Ideology*, the editors intend to signal the nature of the countercriticism undertaken in these pages. If Shakespeare is often used to reproduce (to repeat and so continuously to give new life to) certain ideas about art's transcendence of history and politics, many of the essays included here aim to produce Shakespeare *differently* (reproduction understood as refashioning or making new) by exploring the political functions of the text at specific historical junctures within specific social practices. These range from the critical practices of the North American academy in the 1980s to the theatrical practices of the public stage in the 1590s and to the practices of imperialism in nineteenth-century England. And while criticism does not have a single, unchanging purpose, currently dominant uses of Shakespeare in Anglo-American cultural and educational institutions have occasioned the critical project undertaken in this volume.

Because the editors want this book to be of *use* in changing specific practices – beginning with pedagogical practices – associated with the dissemination of Shakespeare in culture, we hope that numerous among its readers will be not only students, but particularly teachers and postgraduates planning to become teachers. In the opening essay of this volume, Walter Cohen rather optimistically states that political criticism is gaining prominence, perhaps preeminence, in Shakespeare studies. His evidence is the increasing number of books published since 1980 which fall within his definition of ''political criticism.'' But we would question whether the publication of a number of books and essays by Shakespeare scholars who are often based at elite institutions really changes much in the classroom and theaters where Shakespeare is most widely produced and consumed. Many university-press books do not get widely read. And for the few who do read such books, the practice of reading and/or writing criticism and the practice of teaching can be discrete activities, even as undertaken by a single individual. It is only too easy to read and/or write as a born-again poststructuralist/Marxist and still teach like an unregenerate New Critic.

The relative autonomy of the several spheres of academic practice can be explained in several ways. While not all academics, not even those who teach in North American universities, find it necessary to publish rather than perish, those who do publish find that publication can lead to conference invitations, to leaves of absence, to promotions, and in North America even to steep increases in salary. Given that time/energy invested in teaching tend to reap rather less substantial/visible dividends, and that the shares take much longer to mature, teaching often becomes the activity of the left hand, what is done by the easiest and most familiar patterns. In many cases this means a formalistic, ahistorical passage through the canon dispensing the "meaning" of the major plays. But perhaps of even more importance than such local instances of bad faith, thoroughly supported though they are by the reward structure of the profession, is the sheer difficulty of reconstituting the teaching of Shakespeare within an overtly depoliticized and dehistoricized curriculum which takes Shakespeare as a central warrant for its practices.

Consider the ideological implications of some of the pedagogical practices commonly associated with the study of Shakespeare in North American universities. Most strikingly, Shakespeare nearly always stands alone, the preeminent "major figure." Typically, his plays are arranged to display a developmental teleology, either in terms of his handling of the genres of comedy, history, and tragedy, or in terms of the general development of his "thought." In either case, the canon remains hermetically sealed as a discrete object of inquiry – and the inquiry finds Shakespeare being ever more true to himself and his genius. The primary forms of intertextuality are presented as existing among Shakespeare's own works or between his texts and the text of nature. In fact, in the North American academy he is often separated not only from writers contemporaneous with him, but from all but the most general historical ground. This separation goes to show that, somewhat like a Dior suit, Shakespeare never ages and eludes all historical implication. He serves to give the lie to perceptions of dizzying cultural change and to authorize a view of the humanities as the site where the appreciation of what is "classic" is taught. (Less often mentioned is the role of the Shakespeare classroom as a site where a student's position within the cultured middle class is secured.) Moreover, the typical undergraduate Shakespeare course centers on "close reading" of the plays, a process by which attention to supposedly objective aspects of their construction allows the texts to speak for themselves, without meaning being coerced or distorted by the critic. By contrast, much of this volume argues against the idea of unmediated access to anything – Shakespeare, nature, the text, truth – and attempts to shift the emphasis from letting the text "speak for itself" to examining the interests served by the discourses with which the text "is given voice."

Transforming the pedagogical practices within which the teaching of Shakespeare proceeds may be both more difficult and ultimately more important than getting academic presses to publish volumes of criticism like this one. Given the degree to which Shakespeare has become implicated in a pedagogy that effectively effaces both the historicity of the text at its moment of production and the historicity of subsequent uses and appropriations of it, some may prefer to abandon the teaching of the single-figure-Shakespeare course. An alternative is to use the Shakespeare text as the site for contesting the idea of a text "above" history and ideology. This would mean redesigning the Shakespeare course to unseal the privileged and aestheticized space within which the Shakespearean text is customarily examined, and there to make room for a great many things besides Shakespeare. The essays in this volume suggest some of the things that could be introduced into that space. For example, there is the need within Shakespeare teaching to theorize the question of how meaning is historically and ideologically produced. Unless this is done, unless students are asked to consider *how meaning is made*, the hermeneutic activities undertaken in relation to texts privileged by tradition as aesthetic masterworks will continue to seem mysterious, ineffable, and beyond contestation. Shakespeare's is by now a name which evokes reverence, and traditional pedagogical practice – with its emphasis on letting the great text speak for itself even while prodding the student to respond to that text in specific ways – invites passivity and confusion. It encourages students to recognize neither the legitimacy of their own demands upon the text nor the consequences, for their reading, of their own positioning within the social formation and their stake in the contest over meaning.

Moreover, rather than covering the Shakespeare canon, instructors might explicitly engage in uncovering the lives of specific texts in history: that is, as produced in Central Park in the 1960s or by the Royal Shakespeare Company in the 1980s, as edited by Pope, marketed by Penguin, criticized by Hazlitt, or rewritten by Bond. Such a course not only breaks the aesthetic frame provided by the "literature" classroom in that it looks at Shakespeare's use in a variety of cultural practices and at the text as cultural commodity, but it also allows one to examine specific instances of the plurality of the text's lives in history and the plurality of ideological determinants governing the text's reproduction at particular historical moments. Clearly, to argue that Shakespeare's plays always exist in ideology does not mean that there is some unchanging ideological function always performed by particular plays. Such an argument would essentialize ideology in the same way "literariness" or "meaning" have been essentialized as inhering within the artifact, rather than as qualities produced by the play's incorporation into specific discourses and social practices.

Another way radically to reconstitute the Shakespeare classroom, again an option that leads away from "coverage," is to attend to the ideological determinants of the text at its original moment of production and to place the text in history in quite a different way than is traditionally attempted. Although the curriculum in English is usually structured in terms of period courses, it is almost always only the ghost of history that hovers over that curriculum and those courses. Literature courses rarely teach either literature in history, that is, its place in a complex social formation, or even the history *of literature* conceived of as an inquiry into the politics of canon formation and period construction. In most period courses, anything which contextualizes the "text" enters by the back door, most often by means of a source book or potted history of the period which supplies the great ideas supposedly characteristic of the age and determinative of the literary productions of its greatest writers. But to place the text within history and ideology means understanding the drama, not as a passive reflector of great ideas, but as a site of social struggle conducted through discourse. To understand the Elizabethan drama in this way means, in the classroom, taking up the question of the ideological function in the Elizabethan social formation of the various discourses – of love, usury, politics, etc. – which traverse the text and taking up the question of how the theater as a material social institution intervenes in the circulation, production, subversion of those discourses.

This process differs from a traditional approach to literature in history in several ways. First, it places literature *in* history, rather than as a reflection *of* it, makes it one of a vast ensemble of cultural practices through which constructions of the real are circulated and people positioned as subjects of ideology. Second, it argues that representations and cultural practices are not politically neutral: at some level they advance particular interests. Consequently, one is interested not just in "what the Elizabethans thought and did" as reflected in their literature, but in the *uses* of ideas and practices in producing a particular social order and subjects to work within it and in enabling, as well, points of *resistance* to dominant ideologies. Third, while assuming that literature and drama cannot exist outside of ideology and history, one nevertheless recognizes that the specific material conditions connected with a cultural practice have ideological consequences. Thus, an Elizabethan tract railing against crossdressing will have different effects than a play in which a character rehearses the same position but on a stage on which male actors routinely impersonate women. Talking about the play in history thus means seeing the theater not only as affiliated to other cultural practices and as a site of convergence for competing discourses, but as a material institution whose materiality and specific location within the social formation affect its production and dissemination of ideology.

A course that attempts in this way to talk about plays in history and ideology will not "cover" the usual array of literary texts. It will, instead, be investigating a range of social texts and practices against which to assess, differentially, the specific function of the theater and of dramatic representations, and it will be preoccupied with theorizing the ground of its own undertaking. In both regards it will offer a counterpractice to those usually predominating in the teaching of Shakespeare.

The fine tuning of a counterpractice will be made, of course, to the particular practice which it counters. The preceding suggestions have been sketched out with an eye to pedagogic practices prevalent in the North American academy. Courses akin to those outlined above have been undertaken in British higher education, where institutional conditions are arguably more favourable to such enterprises than are those which obtain on the other side of the North Atlantic. In the States what goes on in classrooms is supposedly up to the instructor, and tenets of academic freedom have been devised to guarantee that no instructor is punished for espousing radical or unorthodox views. But American universities also have highly elaborate tenure systems. After six years (in some cases after eight to ten years) a candidate is judged by peers on the basis of the quality of his or her service, teaching, and scholarship. It hardly needs saying that even when everyone tries in good faith to make the system work fairly, it is often difficult to *recognize* the quality of modes of scholarship or pedagogy alien, or even opposed to, dominant practices. In a department where "Shakespeare" is a required course and most sections of the course cover thirteen plays a semester, will an instructor who teaches only three plays and an array of theoretical and nondramatic Renaissance texts, be judged as having taught Shakespeare "well," no matter what rationale he or she offers for this mode of approaching the course? There is always an implicit pressure on new instructors to conform their own practices to department and disciplinary norms. And the advice showered on new assistant professors about how to handle particular courses or teaching problems often ends up blunting whatever crucial difference a new faculty member with new ideas might make. It is through such informal practices that the academy is particularly skillful at reproducing itself. Moreover, it is increasingly true, not just at research universities, but also at liberal arts colleges, that teaching simply matters less than research when the time comes to consider tenure. After six years, whatever pedagogical habits one has developed just to get by while writing two books may be hard to break or to rethink.

By contrast, British academic staff in the early years of their careers do not operate within quite the same set of constraints. The degree of latitude allowed teaching staff in designing and teaching courses varies considerably, in part according to the sector (university, polytechnic, or college of further education) in which they are employed, and in part according to departmental organization within the employing institutions; but in many places it is considerable. Moreover, the reward structure of the academic profession in Britain gives teaching staff little or no inducement to keep their courses within established boundaries. The state-funded universities, for example, have a single pay scale: at London the scale is weighted to cover the cost of metropolitan living, and at Oxford or Cambridge a college appointment can add considerable perquisites and supplements; but the scale itself is uniform and progress along it is a matter of slow movement by automatic – up to a point – annual increments. Short of the rare promotions which go leapfrogging up the scale from lecturer to professor, the British university system offers few financial rewards for good behaviour. Nor does it often punish for bad. Relative to their North American colleagues – who spend the first five to ten years of their professional lives picking their way along the tenure track as if it were made of eggshells – British academic staff are left at liberty. Tenure is secured earlier and more easily: permanent appointments are made in the expectation that the person appointed will be confirmed in post after a probationary period of three years. With the contraction of the British educational system enforced by Thatcher's government, however, permanent appointments have become rare, and tenure is under attack. The long-range consequences for the traditional "freedoms" of British higher education are incalculable.

Moreover, certain present practices, including the British mode of examining, effectively curtail some of the pedagogical liberty noted above. In the United States the individual teachers of a course have authority and responsibility over that course from beginning to end. The extensive deployment of teaching assistants means, of course, that some teachers are deemed more responsible than others; but power over the course remains locally vested and immediately effective. In the United Kingdom, by contrast, power over a course is, because of the examination system, far more diffused. The weight which British degree results carry in determining graduates' later lives has been held to warrant examining procedures so elaborate as to astound American academics encountering them for the first time.[4] A dozen people may be involved in setting a question paper for a Shakespeare examination at Honours BA level, another half-dozen in checking the paper or assessing the answers to it. (Not all of these people will be attached to the same institution, for British universities employ each other's senior staff to watchdog examinations.) With all of these people having, in effect, veto power, the examining drift is towards a lowest common denominator – and that is usually towards precisely that set of common-sense assumptions which it is part of the business of a political criticism to challenge. Here, as a beginning, exponents of such criticism can learn from the feminist movement's gradual, but by now perceptible, achievement in getting sexist terms and phrases discredited and withdrawn from circulation. Students sitting examinations need not be addressed as if they were (or were required to pretend to be, *pro tem*) ahistorical, universal, male subjects – the position which examination questions, like most other academic discourse, tend to construct for them. Nor need they be induced to join in the fraud of presenting their carefully learned responses as spontaneous. Nor need they be offered false choices between indefensible positions. Perhaps especially in British higher education – given the importance assigned to examinations – an ongoing political critique of examination practices will be an essential part of an oppositional pedagogy.

In order to understand the particular pedagogical challenges facing Shakespeare teachers in the two academies, it is necessary to end by noting that in England Shakespeare is a cultural icon – is woven into the fabric of the nation's life – in ways which quite exceed America's investment in the Bard, great as that may be. One obvious sign of this greater investment is the fact that a student could not come into the British university system to read English without having any previous academic acquaintance with Shakespearean texts. That a North American undergraduate might begin a Shakespeare course without any such acquaintance is entirely imaginable: it is at least notionally possible to achieve a perfect score in the verbal component of the American standardized examination for university entrance, the Scholastic Aptitude Test, and score not a single one of the 800 points on Shakespeare. On the correspondent (in function, though not in kind) British examinations, however, this would be virtually impossible.[5] And where those North American students who have studied Shakespearean texts at secondary school have generally encountered them in the course of a literary survey galloping from Aeschylus to *Endgame*, British A and O-level candidates have encountered Shakespeare as an author whose characteristics are exemplified in one or two closely studied plays.

Consequently, teaching Shakespeare in British higher education often means going against the grain of reading practices already firmly in place. In the first instance, this task of clouding the transparent and making strange the familiar is a matter of foregrounding and challenging expectations derived from literary realism. Undergraduates have to be taught new skills for reading drama (as opposed to novels) and have to learn to recognize the artificial, constructed (and ideological) nature of dramatic representations. Beyond that, and getting beyond that can be very difficult, a teacher is tackling, alienating, deeply embedded operating assumptions about meaning – assumptions whereby the 'truth' of a text (the true text) is held simultaneously to be (1) determined by the recognizable intention of a self-expressive author, (2) immanent in a text, and (3) dictated by an autonomous subject encountering that text. None of these assumptions is peculiar to Shakespearean study in British higher education. Why they are perhaps hardest, and most important, to deal with in the context of such study, however, is that students so often see themselves (or perhaps a vision of themselves which they have read off their teachers and parents) in Shakespearean texts, and the high cultural status of those texts reinforces the image. Reading Shakespeare becomes a matter of looking at one's own reflection in a mirror that, being framed in gold, conveniently provides a halo. In an obvious but extremely powerful way, the idea of a timeless and infinitely valuable text guarantees the value of the student who can "appreciate" that text and guarantees, as well, his or her sense of belonging in the company of those who are truly part of the nation's culture. In such a context, a Shakespearean pedagogy aimed at revealing the plurality of the text in history and at revealing the various, sometimes oppressive, ideological ends it has served, is both deeply necessary and deeply transgressive.

The essays comprising the rest of this volume take up in much greater detail a number of problems merely glanced at in this introduction. Some read Shakespearean texts from within contemporary discourses, such as feminism or Marxism, which raise issues often ignored in an overtly apolitical, humanist criticism – issues such as the role of these texts, at specific historical junctures, in maintaining or challenging oppressive race, gender, and class relations. Some essays aim to foreground those histories – of the marginalized, or of popular culture and practice – hidden from view in dominant critical practice. And while a number of authors focus on the ideological function of the Shakespearean text at its moment of production in Elizabethan or Jacobean culture, others look at the ideological ends the plays have served in subsequent eras. Finally, some of the pieces in this volume investigate the historical specificity and the ideological implications of particular critical practices used in reading Shakespeare.

The first two essays, by Walter Cohen and Don E. Wayne, pursue the last course. Both pieces are sociological and metacritical; both reflect on the historical conditions accompanying the present emergence of a political, historical, and ideological criticism of Shakespeare; both attempt to account for the different forms this criticism has assumed in England and the United States;

and both critique aspects of its practice. Cohen is particularly interested in mapping the differences among political criticisms of Shakespeare produced by Marxists, by new historicists, and by feminists, both American and British. Wayne focuses more particularly on those factors in American academic life in this century that have led to the emergence of new historicism and to its difference from the more politicized criticism currently published in England. From different positions, each makes clear that if the Shakespearean text exists in history and ideology, so does criticism. Critical movements arise for determinate historical and political reasons, and sustaining the oppositional force of emergent critical practices remains a crucial theoretical and practical problem.

The immediately ensuing essays, by Marion F. O'Connor and Thomas Cartelli, discuss specific uses of Shakespeare in history. Cartelli looks at the afterlife of *The Tempest* in colonialist discourse and practice and in the writings of Third World authors such as Ngugi Wa Thiong'o. He makes clear that Shakespearean texts can have material consequences in the world as they become, for example, the warrant for practices such as the control or extermination of the dark-skinned other; and he demonstrates what a different ensemble of meanings is produced when a play such as *The Tempest* is read from the divergent political and historical positions occupied by a Cecil Rhodes and a Ngugi. O'Connor looks, by contrast, not at the afterlife of a particular text, but at a particular use of Shakespeare as cultural institution in turn-of-the-century England. She gives an account of the ''Shakespeare's England'' exhibition at Earl's Court, London, in 1912, an exhibition organized by Lady Randolph Churchill and designed mainly by the architect Edwin Lutyens. O'Connor identifies the cultural antecedents of the exhibition in several parallel activities of the year 1897. She concentrates on two spectacular displays in ''Shakespeare's England'' – a replica of the *Revenge* and a full, working reconstruction of the Globe Theatre – as icons which a nation approaching World War I invested with imperial meanings. She is also concerned with the class significations of the images which were marketed and enacted at ''Shakespeare's England.'' O'Connor's account uses some previously unpublished material, including photographs: ''Shakespeare's England'' has been largely forgotten because it does not fall squarely in the catchment area of any institutionalized academic discipline.

The following seven essays read particular plays in part in terms of their ideological function within the Elizabethan or Jacobean social formation. While these essays start from a number of quite different theoretical assumptions, collectively they place the Shakespearean text in relationship to Elizabethan texts other than the text of nature; and they examine the ideological function of Renaissance theatrical practices and representations in light of a range of other cultural practices. For example, Peter Erickson reads *The Merry Wives of Windsor* in relation to the ceremonies of the Order of the Garter, to Elizabeth's Petrarchan politics, and to the political uses of Renaissance pastoral. His larger concern is to show the quite different ways in which gender and class relations are represented in this play and the way in which a conservative reaffirmation of social hierarchy also becomes an ironic and troubled ratification of female power. Erickson's work relates to other essays not only as it connects the play to other practices in Elizabethan culture, but also as it self-consciously positions itself within a committed political discourse — in this instance, contemporary feminism. The strong occupation of such a discursive site not only enables a strong reading of the text in question, but also determines what aspects of the social formation are investigated in relationship to that text.

The same can be said of Karen Newman's piece on *Othello*. Writing from a strongly antiessentialist feminism, Newman investigates the discursive production of race and gender difference through the text of *Othello* and examines the way the black man and the desiring woman are linked as representations of the monstrous. Newman connects the Shakespearean text to other Elizabethan representations of blackness and femininity, but her goal is not just to locate *Othello* in relationship to racist and misogynist practices in early modern England, but to reveal stage representations *as* representations – interested constructions, not mirrors of truth – and to rewrite a canonical text in ways that contest traditional or canonical readings of it.

Jean E. Howard's essay also has a dual focus. It aims both to place *Much Ado About Nothing* in relationship to Renaissance antitheatrical discourse as that discourse provides a mechanism for managing gender and class conflict, and also to contest certain twentieth-century readings of the play, especially those which, in moralizing the play's characters and events, ignore the political implications of its representations of gender and class. Howard argues that in Elizabethan culture the public theater and transgressions of the gender and class systems were often discursively linked. She further argues that on one level it is the project of Shakespeare's play *and* the polemical antitheatrical tracts to manage and contain such transgressions, but that the material conditions of Renaissance stage production rendered contradictory and unstable *Much Ado*'s role in such a project of containment.

The difficult question of how a play's status *as* a play affects its role in ideological production is also taken up by Thomas Moisan in his essay on *The Merchant of Venice*. Like other writers in this volume, Moisan shares a concern for the relationship between the dramatic text and other contemporaneous cultural texts and practices: in this instance, Elizabethan commercial practices and tracts on usury and wealth. But Moisan insists that once we recognize such links, we have to ask if there is something specific to theater or to the play in question which would make its ideological effectivity different from that, for example, of the usury tracts. While Howard approaches this problem by focusing on the way the material conditions of Elizabethan theatrical production affect its role in the production of ideology and the creation of subjects, Moisan examines how a work such as *The Merchant of Venice* foregrounds its own radical "playfulness" and its skepticism about language's capacity to speak truth. In doing so, Moisan argues, the play opens up the possibility of the work's distance from the ideological positions it circulates.

A different set of questions is taken up in the two essays – by Michael D. Bristol and Thomas Sorge – which focus on *Coriolanus*. Using Habermas's notion of legitimation crisis as it provides a way to read the Coriolanus material, Bristol is concerned to show that the plebeians are in possession of a distinct understanding of the social order and one which differs markedly from that held by the patricians. Bristol displays these differences by showing how the patrician commitment to a rigidly vertical model of social order and its valorization of the private body is in direct contrast to the plebeian notion of a social order based on an organic solidarity, a dispersed, communal authority, and a commitment to the homeostatic processes by which a communal body renews itself. Bristol, however, moves beyond a consideration of the legitimation crisis enacted in *Coriolanus* to consider the legitimation problem of the modern state and the possibility of effective modes of opposition within that state. In arguing for a political criticism which will challenge the doxa of a pluralist academy, Bristol points to the contradictions which occur when a criticism claiming to be subversive or interventionist remains within a problematic of privatism or a commitment to a "balanced" view of the social body and the literary text.

Thomas Sorge, by contrast, uses *Coriolanus* to focus on the emergence of a new kind of critical consciousness in the early seventeenth century. Drawing on Foucault to argue that the late Renaissance saw the breakdown of analogic thinking, Sorge examines the consequences of this breakdown both for those whose authority depended on the perceived "truth" of crucial analogies and for those subject to such authority. Sorge focuses his discussion on the frequently used Renaissance analogy between the state and the human body, especially as deployed by Menenius. Sorge argues that by presenting the analogy of state to body *as a representation*, rather than an organic fact, the play opens that representation and Menenius' class position to the critical scrutiny of the citizens. Sorge argues that unlike the overt subversion of dominant ideologies found in the 1640s, Shakespeare's plays of the first decade of the seventeenth century contribute to the general historical process by which a plurality of ideological positions emerge in the public arena and invite what was historically new: the development of a critical consciousness about the interested use of representations.

Unlike most essays in the volume, Jonathan Goldberg's on *Macbeth* uses Derridean deconstruction as the enabling discourse for a political criticism. He argues that Derridean deconstruction becomes political precisely in its questioning of all modes of logocentric and metaphysical representation (including positivistic historicism) which ultimately grant ideological discourses the determinate, unified, hegemonic power they claim for themselves. For Goldberg, subversion is inevitable because hegemonic control is an absolutist or totalitarian fantasy. In reading *Macbeth* in relation to its "sources," Goldberg shows how in the intertextual space between work and sources moral differences become blurred, origins dispersed, and identity doubled and redoubled in ways that defy the control of either the monarchs *within* the play or the author *of* the play. Consequently, for Goldberg, a play such as *Macbeth* is neither simply conservative nor simply revolutionary because it differs from itself too profoundly to serve a single, determinate ideological end. Implicitly, Goldberg's essay

questions, and is questioned by, other essays in this volume which argue that
while plays are not inherently, ineluctably either conservative or subversive, it
is possible to specify circumstances in which they have served discernible, and
discernibly different, political ends.

The role of deconstruction in a political criticism is an issue also addressed,
from a different perspective, by Robert Weimann, who served as respondent at
the Berlin seminar and who, in his response, offered an overview of some of
the methodological and theoretical issues facing the development of a new
historical and materialist criticism of Shakespeare. Weimann, for example, calls
for a critique of what he sees as the unhistorical and formalist dimensions of the
poststructuralist project and urges attention *both* to the mimetic and to the
nonmimetic (signifying) dimensions of the dramatic text. His essay also
foregrounds the problem of how to take proper account of the materiality of
Renaissance theater as a social institution and as a distinct mode of production
when assessing the role of the drama in confirming or challenging hegemonic
ideologies. In a provocative conclusion, Weimann critiques the potential
puritanism lurking within any committed, political criticism which would ignore
the element of *Spass* (fun, pleasure) in Shakespearean drama.

Margaret Ferguson, in her afterword, summarizes some of the current aspects
of the debate concerning the educational apparatus as a mechanism not only for
ideological reproduction, but also for the reproduction of economic and class
relations. Outlining the views of both those who see the educational system as
impermeable to radical transformation and those who see it as a viable site for
oppositional practice, Ferguson speculates on the most effective forms of
political action available to those who are workers in American universities.
Are, she asks, the kinds of pedagogical and curricular changes outlined in this
introduction the best or the only option for action? In her call for the elaboration
of further possibilities, she invites the reader – not to quietism – but to the
difficult task of furthering and strengthening a political project which here and
elsewhere has only just begun.

On such a note it is appropriate to end this introduction and to acknowledge
that what a single writer or a single book can accomplish is inevitably limited.
Consequently, it is no disparagement of what the writers for this volume have
collectively achieved to conclude by pointing to the further work which lies
ahead. It is clear, for example, that we do not yet fully understand the
ideological function of stage plays in the Elizabethan and Jacobean social formations, nor do we yet fully understand the political uses to which they have been
put in subsequent theatrical and critical practice. The work of scholarship in
these areas is far from finished. But other work beckons, as well. We need
examinations of Shakespeare's use at *all* levels of the educational system, and
not just in colleges and universities; and we need to investigate the ideological
use of Shakespeare in other wide-reaching cultural practices such as television
and film (Holderness, 1985). But even then, we would argue, the work of a
political and historical criticism of Shakespeare will not be done. Shakespeare
is constantly reproduced in the general discourses of culture and is used to

authorize practices as diverse as buying perfume, watching Masterpiece Theater, or dispatching troops to far-flung corners of the globe (see Cartelli in this volume). We need studies which consider particular uses of the name or image of Shakespeare or of Shakespearean play titles, speeches, or snippets of verse in advertising, in popular-culture magazines, in political rhetoric. Ignoring these uses of Shakespeare as trivial or beyond our expertise means acquiescing in the separation of the academy from general culture and means ignoring, as well, much of what in our own time may be of significance to a political and historical criticism.

Notes

1. Those participating in the Berlin seminar or who sent papers for discussion were: Sandra Billington, Michael D. Bristol, Paul Brown, Thomas Cartelli, Walter Cohen, Robert Paul Dunn, Peter Erickson, Kirby Farrell, Margaret Ferguson, Elizabeth Freund, Paul Gaudet, Jonathan Goldberg, Donald Hedrick, Jean E. Howard, Dorothea Kehler, Leanore Lieblein, Thomas Moisan, Karen Newman, Marion F. O'Connor, Avraham Oz, David Pollard, Rolf Soellner, Don E. Wayne, Robert Weimann, John Westlake, and H.O. Zimmerman.
2. For further discussion of the place of the Shakespeare play *within* ideology and of the play as a *production* of ideology, see Kavanagh (1985).
3. Derek Longhurst's essay, " 'Not for all time, but for an Age': An Approach to Shakespeare Studies" (1982), discusses how and to what ends Shakespeare has been made the spokesperson for "timeless" values and universal experience. See Norris (1985) for an investigation of the paradoxical claims that Shakespeare's language is both universal and the epitome of a national identity.
4. For a political analysis of the role of Shakespeare in the British examination system, see Longhurst (1981, 1982) and Sinfield (1985).
5. Students coming to British universities to read English are expected to have passed the O(rdinary) and A(dvanced)-level examinations in English literature, and to have passed them at a good mark, usually the next to highest possible. The constant figure on the syllabuses for these examinations, which are set by some ten different boards, is Shakespeare. On a 'league table' of authors on the syllabuses of O and A level papers in English literature between 1977 and 1983 Shakespeare figured three and a half times more often than the no. 2 author, Chaucer; and in 1982, when the new G(eneral) C(ertificate of) S(econdary) E(ducation) examination was beginning to be mooted, Shakespeare was the one author whose presence on the syllabus was unanimously required (Goulden and Hartley, 1982, 6).

Works cited

Althusser, Louis (1971) *Lenin and Philosophy and Other Essays*, trans. Ben Brewster, New York, Monthly Review Press; London, New Left Books.

Dollimore, Jonathan and Sinfield, Alan (eds) (1985) *Political Shakespeare: New Essays in Cultural Materialism*, Manchester, Manchester University Press; Ithaca, NY, Cornell University Press.

Drakakis, John (ed.) (1985) *Alternative Shakespeares*, London, Methuen.

Eagleton, Terry (1983) *Literary Theory: An Introduction*, Oxford, Basil Blackwell; Minneapolis, University of Minnesota Press.

Goulden, Holly and Hartley, John (1982) " 'Nor should such Topics as Homosexuality, Masturbation, Frigidity, Premature Ejaculation or the Menopause be regarded as

Unmentionable,' " *LTP: journal of literature teaching politics*, 1, 4–20.

Grealy, Jim (1981) "School and Literature Teaching," *Red Letters*, 12, 22–32.

Hawkes, Terence (1986) *That Shakespeherian Rag: Essays on a Critical Process*, London and New York, Methuen.

Holderness, Graham (1985) "Radical Potentiality and Institutional Closure: Shakespeare in Film and Television," in Dollimore, J. and Sinfield, A. (eds) *Political Shakespeare: New Essays in Cultural Materialism*, Manchester, Manchester University Press; Ithaca, NY, Cornell University Press, 181–201.

Kavanagh, James H. (1985) "Shakespeare in Ideology," in Drakakis, J. (ed.) *Alternative Shakespeares*, London, Methuen, 144–65.

Longhurst, Derek (1981) "Reproducing a National Culture: Shakespeare in Education," *Red Letters*, 11, 3–14.

——— (1982) " 'Not for all time, but for an Age': An Approach to Shakespeare Studies," in Widdowson, P. (ed.) *Re-Reading English*, London and New York, Methuen, 150–63.

Norris, Christopher (1985) "Post-structuralist Shakespeare: Text and Ideology," in Drakakis, J. (ed.) *Alternative Shakespeares*, London, Methuen, 47–66.

Sinfield, Alan (1985) "Give an account of Shakespeare . . .," in Dollimore, J. and Sinfield, A. (eds) *Political Shakespeare: New Essays in Cultural Materialism*, Manchester, Manchester University Press; Ithaca, NY, Cornell University Press, 134–57.

1

Political criticism of Shakespeare[1]

Walter Cohen

Ideological criticism has finally had an impact on traditional areas of literary research in North America, nowhere more so, perhaps, than on Shakespeare studies. This essay concludes with a chronological list of political accounts of the playwright published in the 1980s (pp. 44–6), a list that is long and growing rapidly as the decade progresses. Fewer items might turn up in a similar compilation covering the entire first thirty-five postwar years. A comprehensive survey of recent Shakespearean scholarship would undoubtedly reveal that the majority of publications do not engage in ideological critique. Nonetheless, political interpretation has become central to work on Shakespeare; in North America this process of politicization occurred earlier than in most other fields; and the concerns and methods often pioneered in discussions of Renaissance writers and especially of Shakespeare have increasingly spread across the discipline – to the point where political approaches arguably form the cutting edge of academic criticism in the United States. The question facing sympathizers with these trends may be less how to defend a beleaguered position in an age of reaction than how to turn potentially hegemonic status within the discipline to useful political account. The following review of the causes, nature, and significance of the new writing on Shakespeare aims to begin answering that question.

A brief sketch of recent American criticism will help clarify the current situation. The dominance of New Criticism depended in part on the pervasive

WALTER COHEN teaches comparative literature at Cornell University. He is the author of *Drama of a Nation: Public Theater in Renaissance England and Spain* (Ithaca, NY, Cornell University Press, 1985).

upper-class anti-Communist offensive often localized as McCarthyism. The conjunction of the resulting theoretical vacuum with the crises of the 1960s raised the question of what sort of criticism would inherit the academy. And the answer was theory, but at least initially not a theory growing out of the politics of the 1960s, and for a very simple reason: university activists were just too young to have an immediate, decisive impact. With some distortion the deconstructive criticism developed by Paul de Man may be considered the central movement of the 1970s. Its emergence in the United States was related to the rise of a grudging internationalism – really limited to France and West Germany – bound up with both the decline of American imperial power and, in the previous decade, the expansion of foreign-language and comparative literature programs. Perhaps one can also detect an émigré biographical imprint in the work of de Man and Geoffrey Hartman – a rejection of European political conflict in favor of the stability of American society. The result in any case was a powerful theoretical position that combined radical philosophical inquiry with ambivalence about political engagement.

Why does deconstruction now seem like only one of several lively forces in American criticism? Both university expansion and campus political activism in the 1960s potentially opened scholarly organizations as well as literary curricula to new interests. In addition the generation of the 1960s gradually came to academic prominence, a process partly evident in the emergence of the political concerns of younger deconstructive critics. Finally the New Right's considerable gains during the Reagan administration have disturbed radicals and more importantly liberals, with the result that politics has acquired an urgency often absent in the late 1970s.

This is the context in which to view the new directions in Shakespeare studies. The 1980 point of departure adopted here is obviously arbitrary and would seem still more so if the bibliography also included articles, many of which date from the late 1970s. Yet books often have far greater institutional impact than essays. To this extent the beginning of the new decade marked a real shift, particularly in the United States, with the publication of the inaugural feminist (Lenz, Greene, and Neely, 1980b) and new historicist (Greenblatt, 1980) volumes on Shakespeare. In England, where leftist cultural criticism developed earlier, 1980 nonetheless represented a significant point of demarcation, with an intensified radical response to the recent victory of Thatcher, the extension of this work to Renaissance literature, and the publication of an important Marxist study of Middleton (Heinemann, 1980). The three approaches just mentioned – feminism and new historicism in the United States and Marxism in England – dominate current political work in the field. In the following pages little attention is accordingly given to psychoanalysis and to deconstruction except as methodological resources of more explicitly political theories. Third World and ethnic studies are regrettably relegated to the same subordinate role despite their obviously political thrust: a contemporary, full-length account of Shakespeare from the perspective of race and imperialism remains to be written (but see Tokson, 1982; E. Hill, 1984; Cartelli in this volume).

In this essay the "political" thus carries both a broader and a narrower sense than the one conveyed by traditional definitions of the term. On the one hand and for lack of a better word, it refers not only to government power but also to matters of race, class, and gender. On the other hand the political here polemically designates only critical or oppositional work. The vast majority of recent political writing on Shakespeare has sided with the victims of state power, class hierarchy, patriarchy, racism, and imperialism, a partisanship, it is worth asserting, not only compatible with but also necessary to a commitment to objectivity in scholarship. The narrow construal here of political criticism of Shakespeare is defined not only by the focus on oppositional work, but also by the nearly exclusive attention to feminism, new historicism, and Marxism. There are at least three justifications for these choices. Critics working from these perspectives tend most often to make political claims for their work; further, these theoretical positions do have connections with ongoing political practice; finally, and partly for this latter reason, such positions are most likely to have political efficacy. Undoubtedly this formulation indicates the subjectivity and arbitrariness unavoidable today in tracing the boundaries of the political. Yet one can concede as much and more while continuing to defend both the value of the category of political criticism and the appropriateness to contemporary Shakespearean criticism of the specific outlines of that category traced above.

A concern with political approaches to Shakespeare involves still other delimitations. Most obvious is the exclusive emphasis on Shakespeare and indeed on Shakespeare's plays, an emphasis that may have local pragmatic uses but that is difficult to justify on theoretical grounds. The inclusion of works on English Renaissance drama that do not discuss Shakespeare (e.g. Heinemann, 1980; *Renaissance Drama*, 1982; Shepherd, 1986) would not significantly change the main lines of the argument, however. Probably more important is the omission of political criticism of Shakespeare produced outside the English-language world. Among recent specimens of this work readily available in English one might mention the studies undertaken from the perspective of semiotics in Italy (Serpieri, 1985), and of Marxism in Italy (Moretti, 1982) and the German Democratic Republic (Weimann, 1985, 1986; and the essays by Sorge and Weimann in this collection). Their exclusion makes it possible to highlight the institutional shift towards political criticism in Anglo-American Shakespearean studies.

This focus requires qualification, however. Although scholarship from both sides of the Atlantic receives extended treatment, the sociological reflections concentrate on the United States – only one index of the autobiographical orientation of the essay. On the other hand interaction between British and American criticism of Shakespeare is so pervasive as to preclude any strict separation. The mutual influence of these two traditions also seems certain to grow in the coming years. More generally, political readings of Shakespeare in the United States and England belong together as part of larger ideological and social trends – not only the prominent position of both countries in the international development of feminism, but also the belated emergence on the same terrain of a substantive body of socialist, often explicitly Marxist thought. At the very time that Marxism has gone into profound crisis in the Latin countries of Western Europe and apparently lost some of its freshness in the Federal Republic of Germany, it has come into its own, as an intellectual though not as a political paradigm, in the English-speaking world, where its previous influence was far less noteworthy (Anderson, 1984, 21–31).

Yet the differences between British and North American political approaches to Shakespeare are illuminating. Since Don E. Wayne addresses those distinctions at length in the next essay, only a few preliminary remarks will be necessary here. Many of the differences follow from the far greater weight of social class in England than in the United States. Thus the apparently fuller development of an autonomous feminism, and with it of an autonomous feminist criticism, may be correlated with the relative absence of class consciousness in the former colony; conversely, the pervasive connections between feminist and historical (especially Marxist) accounts of Shakespeare reveal the visible importance of class divisions in the former colonizer. One might also note the comparative insignificance of Marxist writing and the only recent emergence of new historicism in the United States, and in England the prominence of the Labour Party and of a socialist intellectual heritage.

The formalist legacy of New Criticism may have contributed to the characteristic tendencies in American political work on Shakespeare, and not only by encouraging the close readings one often finds in new historicist and even more in feminist discussions. The emotional distance between reader and text cultivated by New Criticism, and the national and geographical distance from Shakespeare are possible sources of the felt need for historical reconstruction. By contrast, English critics inherit not only the legacy of morally committed criticism associated with Leavis, but also the tradition of using Shakespeare as national icon of conservative continuity. These experiences have led in England, by way of reaction, to a far greater orientation toward the present and toward explicitly political concerns than one finds in the United States. Similarly, the hostility towards methodological and theoretical innovation typical of mainstream British academic criticism (but not of American literary study) has produced, again as an oppositional gesture, a more pronounced theoretical turn in English Shakespeare studies, at least as far as French theory goes. Given such distinct historical situations, it is not surprising that the British rather than the Americans consistently seek to recover a usable past, a potentially progressive Shakespeare. Such an enterprise has as a logical consequence a more intense concern with the performance of Shakespeare, a tendency no doubt reinforced by the far greater prominence of theater in England. Finally and perhaps surprisingly, British political Shakespeareans neglect popular culture more than their American counterparts do.

The comments that follow seek to respect both the congruities and the divergences among the various strains of political criticism of Shakespeare. Discussion of individual writers is incidental to an elucidation of larger trends.

Previous review essays, to which these remarks are considerably indebted, have treated feminism obliquely or not at all (Goldberg, 1982; Dollimore, 1985a; Howard, 1986; Montrose, 1986). But there are encouraging signs of a more inclusive understanding of politics – for example the seminar on ''Gender and power in Shakespeare'' at the 1986 World Shakespeare Congress and the essays prepared for this volume. The strategy here will be to juxtapose the different political approaches to Shakespeare, criticizing each for its failure adequately to incorporate the theories, methods, and findings of the others. The justification for the procedure might be called anticipatory totalization. Totalization is itself a controversial ideal, one that has recently been defended (Cohen, 1985a, 21–31) and criticized (Wells, 1985, 1–19) from a Marxist perspective. It is adopted here in the hope that the disparate currents of political approaches to Shakespeare will prove fundamentally compatible. Yet totalization must be anticipatory because a genuine synthesis has not been achieved and cannot possibly be achieved within the narrow confines of Shakespeare studies. Political accounts of Shakespeare can contribute to a larger totalizing enterprise, however, especially if they are undertaken with an eye for systematic connections.

1

A development out of the women's movement that reemerged in the 1960s, feminist criticism is, with the exception of New Criticism, the most widely practiced approach to Shakespeare in the United States today. This is just a particular instance of the more general rule noted above: political activism of the 1960s lies behind the political criticism of the 1980s. In retrospect one can recognize the distortion in considering deconstruction the central theoretical movement of the 1970s in the United States. The crucial trend was not deconstruction but feminism. But the women who invented American feminist criticism were neither old enough nor established enough to reshape literary study immediately. Their individual and collective prominence dates primarily from the current decade.

Feminist accounts of Shakespeare have not drawn equally on all tendencies in American feminist criticism. The second wave of that criticism, which stresses the female literary tradition and which came to the fore after 1975, has little to offer feminist Shakespeareans. Their formation is to be located in the earlier era of feminist criticism (late 1960s to mid-1970s) concerned with images of women. Here is a summary statement from the introduction to *The Woman's Part*, the basic collection of feminist essays on Shakespeare:

> The critics in this volume liberate Shakespeare's women from the stereotypes to which they have too often been confined; they examine women's relations to each other; they analyze the nature and effects of patriarchal structures; and they explore the influence of genre on the portrayal of women.
>
> (Lenz, Greene, and Neely, 1980a, 4)

These concerns have continued to dominate feminist criticism of Shakespeare in recent years.

But one can also register the secondary influence on that criticism of several other theoretical positions, all of them prominent by the 1960s if not earlier. One thinks, for example, of the importance of psychoanalysis for Coppélia Kahn's *Man's Estate* (1981) or of New Criticism for Carol Thomas Neely's *Broken Nuptials in Shakespeare's Plays* (1985). As the only major discourse other than feminism that accords women a central position, psychoanalysis has obvious relevance. Within the narrower confines of academic literary study, New Criticism, though no longer hegemonic, has influenced nearly all contemporary critics and may remain the most widely practiced form of criticism, particularly in the classroom. Its special significance for Shakespearean feminism probably lies in the formation of feminist discourse in the late 1960s and early 1970s, before the influx of continental theories had seriously challenged the hold of New Criticism in the university.

Indeed the main accomplishments of feminist criticism of Shakespeare will emerge from a consideration of the precise way earlier approaches to literary study manifest themselves in this criticism. The crucial achievement has been to make feminist analysis stick. In numerous readings of individual plays feminist critics have shown that women are fundamental to the patriarchal world Shakespeare's characters inhabit, whether one attributes to Shakespeare patriarchal values (Erickson, 1985) or a resolute opposition to them (Dreher, 1986). This has meant among other things a psychoanalytically inspired sensitivity to the costs repeatedly exacted in the course of the plots not only from women but, given the constricting norms of male sexual identity, from men as well. Thus Janet Adelman, drawing parallels among the Midlands food riots of 1607, the hungry plebeians of *Coriolanus*, and the character of the protagonist, argues: "Thrust prematurely from dependence on his mother, forced to feed himself on his own anger, Coriolanus refuses to acknowledge any neediness or dependency: for his entire sense of himself depends on his being able to see himself as a self-sufficient creature" (Adelman, 1980, 132; see also Gohlke, 1980, 152).

The formalist heritage of New Criticism has characteristically involved an interest in the reciprocal relationship between gender and genre, a relationship often understood in terms of *Comic Women, Tragic Men* (Bamber, 1982). The etymological pun operates effectively in more local contexts as well. Kahn argues that Shakespearean comic form depends as much on "psychosexual obstacles to marriage" as on "the generic impetus to celebrate marriage" (Kahn, 1985, 16). Working even more specifically, Neely finds a connection between the ambiguity of gender roles and the ambiguity of the generic structure of *Antony and Cleopatra* (Neely, 1985, 136). A focus on this particular nexus has produced not merely new interpretations but also transvaluations of genres, of individual plays, and hence of the canon as a whole. Broadly speaking the romantic comedies, the problem plays, and the romances have received sustained, favorable treatment at the relative expense of the histories and tragedies. In criticism of the tragedies feminists' recurrent concern with *Othello* and especially *Antony and Cleopatra* has implicitly challenged A.C. Bradley's still hegemonic exclusion of the latter play from the major tragedies and his assertion that the former stands a little lower in our minds than do *Hamlet, King Lear*, and *Macbeth*. Such changes in emphasis have often been accompanied by a distinctive view of Shakespeare's development that has something in common with positions taken by the late C.L. Barber (1980), according to which the plays move away from misogyny and patriarchy toward a more equitable, humane portrayal of relations between women and men that culminates in the romances and especially in *The Winter's Tale* (Wheeler, 1981, 12–19; Sundelson, 1983, 6–7; Erickson, 1985, 9–13, 170–3; Neely, 1985, 21–2, 209).

These advances have come at a certain price, however, a price that is a consequence of the same theoretical and methodological choices underlying the gains and that takes the form of a systematic narrowness. The main problem is the inadequate exploitation of the resources of feminism itself. For example Bamber's distinction between comic women and tragic men is perhaps possible to maintain if one's attention is restricted to Shakespeare. Yet the contrast does not consistently hold across European drama or even English Renaissance drama. Bamber's work would have profited from an attempt to account for Shakespeare's atypicality. This isolating procedure, a recurrent problem in feminist approaches not only to generic questions but to Shakespeare's work in general, is one of the less fortunate inheritances from earlier Shakespearean criticism.

In psychoanalytical feminism the analogous difficlty may lie in the relative indifference to the work of Cixous, Irigaray, Kristeva, and Lacan (Evans, 1986, 168), although there are some recent exceptions (Fineman, 1985; Goldberg, 1985, and his essay in this volume; Newman, 1986). Whatever the relative merits of competing psychological paradigms, the absence of the French psychoanalytical tradition increases the danger of seeing Shakespeare's characters in unmediated fashion as real people. This theoretical weakness, which the British writer Kathleen McLuskie has attacked as "the mimetic, essentialist model of feminist criticism" (McLuskie, 1985, 91) and which is not limited to distinctively psychoanalytical forms of feminism, leads Irene Dash to assert "that Shakespeare's women are well-integrated, thoughtful portraits that have their base in reality" (Dash, 1981, 251; see also Dreher, 1986, 170). The primacy accorded to realistic characterization here harks back to the fundamental concerns of nineteenth-century Shakespearean criticism, concerns canonically expressed by Bradley, who in this respect continues to loom large in feminist studies of Shakespeare (Evans, 1986, 178–9; Hawkes, 1986, 33–42).

McLuskie's insistence on the need to take into account "the full complexity of the nature of women in Shakespeare's time or our own" (McLuskie, 1985, 91) gestures toward probably the most serious limitation of current American feminist accounts of Shakespeare – an inadequate use of historical materials, with the inevitable foreclosure of a promising mode of ideological critique within a tradition that understands its purpose to be ideological critique (French, 1981, 7–8). Although feminists stress the contemporary implications of their work, this valuable orientation usually remains implicit rather than empirical. Feminist treatments of the relationship between the plays and early modern English society face a more daunting difficulty: women's history is so new a field that both basic information and theoretical models are often lacking. Although feminist Shakespeareans regularly invoke Renaissance society, society is either an inference from formalist analysis (Erickson, 1985, ix-x), a desirable but unexplained area of investigation (Kahn, 1981, 17), or the object of sustained inquiry, but an inquiry that has the paradoxical effect of bracketing off Shakespeare's plays from most historical considerations (Neely, 1985, 8–21; Dreher, 1986, 16–39).

This last procedure deserves careful attention. The critic demonstrates the complex contradictions in ideological treatments of women during the Renaissance, in women's actual lives, and in the historical trends in the status of women. This demonstration then provides a general context for the same demonstration about Shakespeare's plays. The problem is that the Renaissance is thereby reduced to a single, synchronic movement, devoid of any discernible pattern of change. Although this assumption allows one to account for mutations in Shakespeare's career, it must find the mainspring of any systematic development in some logic internal to the man or his drama. Because there is no history of the Renaissance, there can be no history of Shakespeare. Such an approach cannot correlate changes in the course of the canon with shifts in the understanding or position of women during the two or more decades in which Shakespeare composed his extant plays. This generalizing contextualism similarly precludes the identification of the particular social phenomena to which any given play may be responding. Despite the initial attempt at historical positioning, then, the result is to render the representation of women an abstract category. Feminist criticism of Shakespeare repeatedly runs the risk of introducing reductive, allegorizing, binary oppositions: comic women and tragic men, Shakespeare's division of experience between a masculine and a feminine principle (French, 1981), the conflicts between patriarchy and mutuality or between control and emotion (Novy, 1984), the tension between domination and defiance (Dreher, 1986). The source of the trouble is the failure to explain Shakespeare's construction of gender as social product and social act in a manner responsive not only to the *Zeitgeist* but also to the specific exigencies of time and place.

One North American feminist critic of Shakespeare largely avoids this difficulty. Representing something of a new departure, her work resembles a strain in English feminist criticism of Shakespeare – to which it therefore provides an appropriate transition. Linda Woodbridge in Canada (Woodbridge, 1984), like Lisa Jardine (Jardine, 1983) and to some extent Simon Shepherd (Shepherd, 1981) in England, offers not new interpretations of the canon but "the contexts in which male and female members of the Elizabethan audience brought to the theatre a set of expectations, attitudes and beliefs about significant femaleness (and significant maleness)" (Jardine, 1983, 7). The strength of Woodbridge's *Women and the English Renaissance* lies less in any particular thesis than in the extraordinary range of materials, dramatic and nondramatic, that are coherently assembled, especially in relation to the central problematic of female transvestism. Similar claims might be made for the two British critics. Yet all three writers are weakest where the main line of American feminist work on Shakespeare is strongest: in the reading of individual plays. Though this is to fault them for failing to achieve what they do not even seriously attempt, they repeatedly interpret passages from Shakespeare out of context, paying scant attention to the formal qualities of the texts. A social contextualization here leads to an aesthetic decontextualization. In other words the scholarly findings cry out for critical appropriation. A more successful synthesis of scholarship and criticism distinguishes Peter Stallybrass's discussion of witchcraft, patriarchy, and sovereignty in *Macbeth* (Stallybrass, 1982), as well as a number of essays in the present volume.

A sociologically and ideologically sensitive feminist theorization of Shakespeare has also begun. Several years ago the American feminist critic Gayle Greene called for an alliance between Marxist and feminist approaches to Shakespeare (Greene, 1981). In England, McLuskie (McLuskie, 1985) and Catherine Belsey (Belsey, 1985b) have initiated work along these lines. Perhaps Belsey's most original, provocative insight in *The Subject of Tragedy* concerns the position of women in Renaissance discourse: ''While the autonomous subject of liberalism was in the making, women had no single or stable place from which to define themselves as independent beings. In this sense they both were and were not subjects'' (Belsey, 1985b, 150). In tragedy women's ''subject-positions are radically discontinuous'' (Belsey, 1985b, 164). Even in comedy, where women often ''are autonomous subjects'' (Belsey, 1985b, 192–3), one can discover the disruption of sexual difference, the representation of female characters who occupy ''a place which is not precisely masculine or feminine'' (Belsey, 1985a, 180, 187). Obviously, the efficacy of this suggestive approach depends on the power of the category of the subject, a category that may be evaluated by turning to the British Marxist Shakespeareans.

2

One way of registering the arbitrariness of the division between feminism and Marxism in British Shakespearean criticism is to note that the above comments refer only to the second, explicitly feminist half of Belsey's book (Belsey, 1985b) and that the entire work exemplifies a broadly defined Marxist project. The range and significance of that project suggest the value, when it comes to Marxism, of reversing the procedure adopted for feminist criticism and devoting primary attention to England rather than to North America. The common distinguishing feature of British Marxist criticism of Shakespeare is not entirely clear, however. For Malcolm Evans it ''is an acknowledged theory of the sign, the subject and ideology'' (Evans, 1986, 245–6, 248, 249). Jonathan Dollimore expands Raymond Williams's notion of ''cultural materialism'' to the point where it ''includes the considerable output of Williams himself, and, more generally, the convergence of history, sociology and English in cultural studies, some of the major developments in feminism, as well as continental Marxist-structuralist and post-structuralist theory, especially that of Althusser, Macherey, Gramsci and Foucault'' (Dollimore, 1985a, 2–3). Of these figures, perhaps Althusser has exercised the greatest influence. But the assimilation of this body of writing to Marxism should connote not a coherent, unitary position but a recurrent return to a class politics that exercises something like a gravitational force.

Belsey says that her work ''is not offered as comprehensive or definitive'' (Belsey, 1985b, 10), Evans considers his study ''necessarily indicative rather than exhaustive'' (Evans, 1986, 8), and Terence Hawkes calls his book ''the slightest series of sketches'' (Hawkes, 1986, ix). One should take seriously the repeated insistence on the provisional, even fragmentary character of this enterprise, and not simply because it eludes any simple categorization. The very purpose of many of these critics is fragmentation of the ostensibly coherent, conservative version of Shakespeare long hegemonic in both the academy and the culture at large.

Nonetheless one can plausibly follow a recent anthology in finding two main strategies in British Marxist discussions of Shakespeare: a revisionist historical analysis of the plays in their own time and a radical account of their ideological function in the present (Dollimore and Sinfield, 1985b). For the historical enterprise a Marxian narrative provides a framework in which the events of the 1640s constitute a bourgeois revolution, and early Stuart drama is seen as radical, even protorevolutionary. Christopher Hill, who here may speak for his younger colleagues, argues: ''The English Revolution is as unique as Elizabethan and Jacobean drama. Could the uniqueness of the one relate to the uniqueness of the other?'' Yes. ''The great tragedians . . . are not dealing with 'the human condition', with 'man', but with specific problems which confronted rulers and their subjects in a specific historical situation – problems which were bloodily resolved in the sixteen-forties'' (C. Hill, 1985, 4, 24). Similar comments are widespread (Barker, 1984, 11; Dollimore, 1984, 4; Belsey, 1985b, 33–4; Eagleton, 1986, 103–4; Evans, 1986, 257).

This work draws on three main theoretical tendencies: a relatively traditional Marxism, a more Foucauldian concern with the problem of the subject noted above, and a Derridean attention to linguistic deconstruction. The somewhat misleadingly termed traditional Marxists are traditional not in the sense of being oblivious to contemporary theory but in their focus on mode of production, class, and political power. These interests determine what parts of the canon are privileged. Like Marxist critics before them, they turn to Shakespeare's histories (Holderness, 1985b) and tragedies (C. Hill, 1985), and especially to *King Lear* (Aers and Kress, 1981), though often with new methods and arguments. Thus David Aers and Gunther Kress provide a sociolinguistic account of *King Lear*. And in *Shakespeare's History* Graham Holderness, through detailed readings of *Richard II*, *1 Henry IV*, and *Henry V*, effectively demonstrates the critical role of popular culture. Regrettably he all but ignores feminism, perhaps because of his very emphasis on characteristically ''male'' Marxist topics and especially on plays in which women are relegated to the sidelines. His main contention is that in the history plays Shakespeare is a bourgeois historian of a past age, of the decline of feudalism (Holderness, 1985b, 14, 30–2, 37–9). This argument works well as an account of how Shakespeare thought history worked. But perhaps because Holderness never quite acknowledges that both feudal and absolutist monarchs, rather than standing beyond or opposed to the aristocracy, belonged to that class and ultimately served its interests, his approach is less successful in explaining why Shakespeare even considers only one political arrangement, monarchy.

A more distinctively Foucauldian concern with subjectivity emerges in various ways. Dollimore's *Radical Tragedy* focuses on two dialectically related phenomena: the critique of providential religion, a matter also treated by Alan Sinfield (Sinfield, 1983, 81–128), and the decentering of the subject (Dollimore, 1984, 154). These subversive perceptions were available to Renaissance trage-dians because "the essentialist conception of man was in a vulnerable state of transition being, roughly speaking, between its Christian/metaphysical formula-tions and the later secular/Enlightenment mutations of these" (Dollimore, 1984, 155). By offering a "map of a discursive field," Belsey aims to identify a "discontinuity of meanings and knowledges, to chart in the drama of the sixteenth and seventeenth centuries the eventual construction of an order of subjectivity which is recognizably modern" (Belsey, 1985b, 4). The conflict of rival discourses, which precludes the formation of a unified subject, pits medieval against modern discourses, whether one seeks to distinguish illusionist from emblematic staging, the allegorical tradition from the internalized single voice of soliloquy, or discursive from empirical knowledge (Belsey, 1985b, 10, 32, 43–4, 64). In a slightly different inquiry Francis Barker contributes to "a political history of the body," concentrating on "the decisive reshaping of the body politic and its subjectivity that was effected in the seventeenth century" and that resulted in the "de-realization of the body" (Barker, 1984, 13, 14, 12).

In implicit opposition to much American feminist criticism of Shakespeare, these writers demystify Burckhardt's thesis of Renaissance individualism by rejecting the high valuation of the phenomenon, by denying the possibility of the unified subjectivity that individualism presupposes, and most important by demonstrating that Shakespeare's plays, unlike postrevolutionary literature and theater, reveal not the quest for an ultimately illusory coherent subject but the clash between that aspiration and earlier, often more openly religious, modes of understanding human experience (Dollimore, 1984, 174–81). More specific-ally, "Fiction, especially in the period from the sixteenth century to the present, is about what it is to be a subject" (Belsey, 1985b, x; see also Barker, 1984, 11–12; Dollimore, 1984, 249). Although these critics range well beyond Shake-speare, they draw some of their material from his plays, and especially from the tragedies. If *Othello* and *Antony and Cleopatra* are the privileged tragedies for American feminist critics, and if *King Lear* occupies a similar position for tradi-tional Marxist critics, *Hamlet*, precisely because of its evident preoccupation with the protagonist's inner life, is the site of especially stimulating work from a Marxist/Foucauldian perspective (Barker, 1984, 22–41).

Yet this work reveals an unresolved methodological problem. Foucauldian accounts of a "discursive field," especially when located within a Marxist understanding of history, often rather closely resemble broad intellectual history and hence run the risk of flattening out the specifically formal and theatrical dimensions of a play, including the contribution of popular culture. Even where this does not occur, these critics fail to overcome the larger difficulty of inadequate mediations. Although the plays are assumed to have a certain representative status, reference to the institution of the theater and to society, economics, and politics is too infrequent to make clear what the crisis of subjectivity in Shakespearean tragedy had to with the behavior of the subjects of the Tudor and early Stuart monarchs. Interestingly, one finds a careful examination of the play in its specific historical imbeddedness in a small number of essays by these and other writers that draw on Foucault more for the notions of power and surveillance than for the category of the subject, and that accordingly emphasize the conservative more than the subversive dimensions of Shakespeare (Hulme, 1981; Barker and Hulme, 1985; Brown, 1985; Dollimore, 1985b; Dollimore and Sinfield, 1985a). Such articles cut against the sometimes too eager discovery of radicalism that characterizes British Marxist work in the field. An indebtedness to American new historicism is often apparent in these essays. The obvious question with both the conservative and the subversive Foucauldian readings is whether the initial methodological orientation predetermines the political outcome of the empirical analysis.

In criticism influenced by Derrida one finds a closer attention to the text and especially to its language than in Foucauldian work. In *Signifying Nothing* Malcolm Evans argues that the valorization of speech over writing in *Love's Labour's Lost* is carried out in a linguistic medium that is ostentatiously literary (Evans, 1986, 50–65). His critique of "editorial footnotes, which generally limit polysemy in the cause of a Shakespearean text that affirms the unity of subject and sign in a serious, communicative use of words" (Evans, 1986, 158), is designed to challenge the very category of truth itself, a category that obscures the irreducibly political character of all positions. In general Evans proceeds by serial critique. Derridean deconstruction, with intermittent borrowings from Foucault, Lacan, Kristeva, and Cixous, is called into question or at least contextualized by reference to Bakhtin's and Weimann's work (Weimann, 1978) on popular culture and carnival. This latter position then leads into history, into the English Revolution, into the radical movements, and particularly into the Ranters. Yet this summary smoothes out what Evans acknowledges is a very uneven study. Precisely because of the serial approach, one never knows what the status of the superseded methodologies is. The uncertainty of the resulting analyses must be balanced against the striking responsiveness to variation.

In Terry Eagleton's *William Shakespeare*, which is characteristically full of arresting insights, subversiveness extends more systematically across the canon and its various themes.

In this sense law operates rather like money, language and desire: all of these systems involve exchange and equivalence, which is in itself a stabilizing factor; but because they are necessarily indifferent as systems to particular objects or uses, they tend to breed an anarchic state of affairs in which everything blurs indiscriminately into everything else.

(Eagleton, 1986, 57)

Here the goal of undermining organic unity issues, paradoxically, in homologous modes of resistance. This is a consummation devoutly to be wished, but perhaps one no more likely than the mirror image of absolute traditional order that it aims to dismantle.

One of Eagleton's more general formulations perhaps may be taken to apply to Evans's study as well.

Even those who know very little about Shakespeare might be vaguely aware that his plays value social order and stability, and that they are written with an extraordinary eloquence, one metaphor breeding another in an apparently unstaunchable flow of what modern theorists might call "textual productivity." The problem is that these two aspects of Shakespeare are in potential conflict with one another.

(Eagleton, 1986, 1)

One need only substitute "advertisements" for "Shakespeare" and "his plays" to see that this apparently plausible claim for the subversive power of linguistic deconstruction is in fact questionable unless one places heavy weight on "potential." Thus, even more strikingly than in much Foucauldian Marxist criticism of Shakespeare, assumptions predetermine results and historical considerations recede. Evans and Eagleton suggest how the plays might be read so as not to serve a conservative social purpose. As they seem to recognize, however, they do not demonstrate that a radical interpretation of Shakespeare is more plausible than a conservative one, or that Shakespeare is more plausibly understood as radical than is any other playwright.

Evans's study is only partially directed toward Shakespeare's texts and the contexts from which they emerged. Its primary focus is on the modern role of Shakespeare and more generally of English studies. A concern with both past and present also informs Holderness's work, which together with Evans's writing constitutes a bridge to the other main topic in British Marxist criticism of Shakespeare: the contemporary ideological function of the playwright. But an insistence on the "inherent qualities" and "authority" of the Shakespearean text (Holderness, 1985b, 6, 7) causes Holderness to distance himself from Evans's deconstructive mistrust of the category of truth and to emphasize instead the dialectical relations among historical conjuncture, ideological matrix, form, and the history of reproduction (Holderness, 1985b, 147–9), a position compatible with Barker and Hulme's (1985, 193–4) and developed in some detail by Weimann (1984). A serious reckoning with Shakespeare in both the past and the present surely requires some such framework.

The concern with reception in British Marxist criticism of Shakespeare is perhaps most striking when viewed from the other side of the Atlantic. As Evans puts it, the "studies of Shakespeare in the United States are now outdated or too unsystematic" (Evans, 1986, 11; but see E. Hill, 1984). The English work, already quite substantial, addresses a number of related issues: the critical heritage, the educational system, the larger social milieu, and performance in different media. In accounts of the critical heritage, the eminent Shakespeareans whose writings are reviewed include Johnson, Coleridge, Arnold, Bradley, Raleigh, Bridges, Eliot, Dover Wilson, Leavis, Knights, Knight, Tillyard, Bethell, Gardner, Kermode, and Harbage – a familiar list. All of them take a beating. But the point of attack is not the conventional one that no previous reader has understood the real meaning of the play. It is rather that the interpretations produced by these critics are ideologically conservative and promote dubious social ends.

A central means to such ends is the educational system. The contributions of British Marxists make it possible to construct a historical narrative of its development, in which three moments may be distinguished. The first involves the formation of English studies at the turn of the century (Hawkes, 1986, 31), the second the institutionalization of the discipline after World War I (Holderness, 1985b, 168–73; Evans, 1986, 91–4; Hawkes, 1986, 111–15), and the third the rise of progressive education in the 1960s. However paradoxically, at each moment Shakespeare has proven the guarantor of "high-cultural ideology" (Sinfield, 1985a, 153). The contribution of Shakespearean criticism and Shakespearean education to racism, militarism, and imperialism has emerged most clearly in times of world war – certainly, for example, during the early 1940s (Drakakis, 1985, 13–15; Holderness, 1985b, 177–200). But perhaps even more striking are the last stages of World War I and the immediate aftermath, which in Terence Hawkes's *That Shakespeherian Rag* reveal Shakespeare in the service of Germanophobia and anti-Bolshevism (Hawkes, 1986, 63–4, 113–4, 120–2). It would be worthwhile to pursue a similar line of inquiry for the United States, attending here, too, to the conservative political and educational conjuncture following World War I.

The consistent bleakness of this record of Shakespearean reproductions is relieved a bit by the rather more hopeful account given by British Marxist critics of Shakespeare in performance. Though harsh comments abound (Holderness, 1985a, 192–7; Holderness, 1985b, 203–13; Hawkes, 1986, 22–3), the Royal Shakespeare Company is treated ambivalently (Sinfield, 1985b), and both Brecht and antinaturalistic television and film productions are vigorously defended (Heinemann, 1985; Holderness, 1985a, 183–92, 197–200; Holderness, 1985b, 184–91, 214–20). These arguments reveal a sophisticated awareness of the difficulties (Sinfield, 1985b, 178). But they also seem to share a disillusioned literary critical conviction that since performance undermines the authority of the text, it must have something going for it. This conviction may also rest on a too easy acceptance of a Brechtian performance strategy. More generally the study of Shakespeare's contemporary social function should be understood as work in progress that is very much in need of systematic formulation and documentation.

In the far smaller field of American Marxist writing on Shakespeare, reception studies are proportionally more infrequent. Those that exist highlight the differences between the two countries. Either the dialectical process by which present meaning is made out of past texts carries an inherently positive valence from the perspective of a Habermasian "critical hermeneutics" (Wells, 1985, ix), or concern with the political impact of Shakespeare's plays on later ages is confined to the seventeenth century (Cohen, 1985a, 345–56; 1985b), or Shakespeare's views are shown not to have influenced subsequent revolutions (Siegel, 1986, 93–9), or demonstration of the conservative ideological function of Shakespeare in the present remains on the plane of intellectual history (Kavanagh, 1985). None of these critics, then, even addresses the issue that British Marxists have successfully begun to explore: the contemporary institutional force and social function of Shakespeare.

In other respects American Marxist Shakespeareans resemble the group earlier described as traditional British Marxists. One finds the same predilection for the national history play (Bristol, 1985, 180–3, 204–07; Cohen, 1985b; Wells, 1985, 36–44; Siegel, 1986, 47–92) and for *King Lear* (Bristol, 1985, 209–12; Cohen, 1985a, 327–56; Kavanagh, 1985, 156–60), though there also seems to be a vogue for *A Midsummer Night's Dream* (Bristol, 1985, 166–78; Kavanagh, 1985, 152–6; Wells, 1985, 54–60). A similar indifference to feminism or even to gender prevails. More attractive is the recourse to Bakhtin's and Weimann's work on the theory of "literary" history and on popular culture, an indebtedness shared by Holderness, Eagleton, and Evans. The overlapping is restricted to the domains of the popular and the carnivalesque, perhaps because the strong French orientation of the British critics limits the appropriation of Russian or especially German theoretical models. But even on the common terrain of popular culture, the more extensive contribution so far has been North American, especially in Michael D. Bristol's *Carnival and Theatre* (1985; see also the essays by Bristol and Moisan in this volume; Cohen, 1985a, 1985b).

Why should this be so? One possibility is that the British tendency to assimilate Bakhtin to Derrida obscures the specific class content of carnival. But this hypothesis, if correct, is double-edged. From one perspective the recovery of an obscured lower-class experience seems both historically accurate and politically valuable. But from another the assimilating procedure of the British critics may indicate an awareness of the irretrievable pastness of precapitalist, preindustrial popular culture. A concern with that culture in a contemporary North America far more cut off from the age of Shakespeare than is present-day England might then have a curious irrelevance despite its radical intentions.

3

To this difficult problem American new historicism offers a forthright solution:

that the political appeal of popular culture is illusory, since any apparent site of resistance ultimately serves the interests of power. It will be worth discovering how and why this argument emerges.

Preceding Marxism and closely following feminism into the field of Shakespeare studies, new historicism is inextricably connected to the influx of continental, and especially French, theory. Alone among these three approaches, it initially developed in relation to Shakespeare, of whom it has inspired perhaps the most consistently impressive accounts produced in recent years. When it came to prominence at the beginning of the present decade, it represented something new in North America in its combination of theory, criticism, and historical scholarship, all of them informed by a vaguely leftist sensibility. Michel Foucault's writings, particularly the work in the 1970s devoted to prisons and sexuality, stand behind the new historicism (but see Reiss, 1980), just as Foucault's practice of micropolitics suggests its activist implications. In the United States Stephen Greenblatt is at the center of this critical trend, which he is also responsible for naming (Greenblatt, 1982, 5). Since new historicism cannot possibly carry the same degree of theoretical explicitness as feminism or Marxism, and since the criticism usually assembled under its heading is quite heterogeneous, comparison with various other approaches to which it is related but from which it also consciously diverges may help define its specificity.

New historicism shares with deconstruction a questioning of the boundaries between the literary and the nonliterary, between text and context, between foreground and background, between art and society. It differs from deconstruction in its studied ambivalence toward theory (but see Reiss, 1980; Goldberg, 1985), in its emphasis on the practical productive consequences rather than the philosophical resonances of a given conceptual point of departure, and most obviously in its enthusiasm for history. It shares this enthusiasm with the old historicism, from which it parts company, however, by rejecting an often conservative intellectual history in favor of a wider cultural and social framework. In this respect new historicism has obvious similarities to Marxism. Yet unlike Marxism it does not complement a lateral or horizontal approach with a vertical one: new historicism describes historical difference, but it does not explain historical change. Finally, though its recurrent concern with gender aligns it with feminism, its subordination of gender to power leads it away from characteristically feminist concerns.

These general positionings may profit from a more systematic and extended exposition designed to demonstrate the relationship between the significant contributions of new historicism and its recurrent contradictions and blindnesses. The deconstructive impact on new historicism is most evident in the constitution of a discursive field that overrides conventional disciplinary or textual demarcations. New historicists are likely to seize upon something out of the way, obscure, even bizarre: dreams, popular or aristocratic festivals, denunciations of witchcraft, sexual treatises, diaries and autobiographies, descriptions of clothing, reports on disease, birth and death records, accounts of insanity. These areas of interest reveal the influence not only of Foucault, but also of contemporary anthropology (Montrose, 1980; Mullaney, 1987, ch. 1) and of the new social history that derives ultimately from the work of the *Annales* school in France. The strategy is governed methodologically by the assumption that any one aspect of a society is related to any other. No organizing principle determines these relationships: any social practice has at least a potential connection to any theatrical practice. Hence new historicist studies of Shakespeare have a radically unpredictable quality. This implicit commitment to arbitrary connectedness produces impressive results. Especially in the work of Greenblatt but also in the writings of Jonathan Goldberg, Louis Montrose, Steven Mullaney, Leonard Tennenhouse, and others, one regularly encounters suggestive evocations of the density, the texture of early modern society that function as "strategies of defamiliarization" (Tennenhouse, 1986, 15) to restore Shakespeare's plays to their time. These critics combine striking local insights with generalizing inferences, and in particular deploy a fineness of critical observation and stylistic expression that is rarely equaled in contemporary English studies.

Yet the commitment to arbitrary connectedness inevitably limits the persuasiveness of much new historicist work, as a brief look at some of Greenblatt's writings will illustrate. In "Invisible Bullets" Greenblatt connects the second *Henriad* to "the English form of absolutist theatricality" (Greenblatt, 1985a, 45). But in "Murdering Peasants" the rise of the Shakespearean history play entails a shift from "symbolic estate . . . to real estate," from "rank" to "property" (Greenblatt, 1983, 25). In one article the history play is aristocratic, in the other bourgeois. The relationship between power and subversion also receives contradictory formulation. In "Invisible Bullets" the "ideal image [of the monarchy] involves as its positive condition the constant production of its own radical subversion and the powerful containment of that subversion" (Greenblatt, 1985a, 30). In "Murdering Peasants" lower-class subversion is produced not by the aristocracy for its own benefit but by the lower classes for theirs: it takes the form of the Peasants' War in Germany or "the unrest and class hostility that afflicted England sporadically throughout Elizabeth's reign" (Greenblatt, 1983, 14). Again, in "Invisible Bullets" "Elizabethan power . . . depends upon its privileged visibility" (Greenblatt, 1985a, 44), but in *Renaissance Self-Fashioning* "mastery [is] invisible to the servant" and "must constantly efface the signs of its own power" (Greenblatt, 1980, 233, 234). Power is visible; power is invisible. Since each essay is a fresh start in which a particular issue is pursued to a logical extreme without the constraint of an organizing principle, contradictions between essays arise as a matter of course.

These troubling consequences of arbitrary connectedness reacquire enabling force at a higher level of abstraction, however. If an indefinitely large number of linkages define the discursive field, it follows that the theater itself is a contradictory institution. This inference separates new historicism from old. Shakespeare and his theater offered both "symbolic assimilations of potential disorder . . . and partially successful challenges to the patriarchal order"

(Montrose, 1980, 65); they were "radically unstable" (Goldberg, 1983, 230); they functioned "neither as a simple extension of . . . authority nor as a . . . subversive assault upon that authority" (Greenblatt, 1986b, 343); they provided "a site where the iconography of state power was formulated in tension with various forms of representation that contested the ideology of the Renaissance court" (Tennenhouse, 1986, 14); they were characterized, as Mullaney puts it in *The Place of the Stage*, by "ambivalence, paradox, and cultural contradiction" (Mullaney, 1987, ch. 2). New historicists thus have no dificulty in pointing to historical evidence that such apparently orthodox plays as *Richard II* and *Henry VIII* deeply troubled the Elizabethan and Jacobean upper classes (Greenblatt, 1982, 3–6; Orgel, 1982, 47; Tennenhouse, 1986, 88).

But if recognition of the contradictory quality of the theater derives from arbitrary connectedness, so too does the unsystematic nature of that recognition, the failure to specify the necessary and sufficient conditions for either containment or subversion. This failure opens the way for a sharp deflection, a deflection that leads to a very different destination from the one reached by English Marxism. Though new historicists know that the theater was at times subversive, and though they argue that it was inherently ambivalent, their readings of individual Shakespearean plays almost always demonstrate the triumph of containment (but see Mullaney, 1980). This *non sequitur* involves a certain fidelity to Foucault, whose political activity was often aimed at encouraging resistance and whose theoretical formulations allowed scope for both power and resistance, but whose historical analyses revealed the unconstrained victory of power. In new historicist accounts of Shakespeare the justification for this deflection is the category of royal absolutism, whose power is wrongly understood to be absolute. Despite the presence of internal conflict, society and especially the theater are organized down to their smallest details for the benefit of those in power. As Tennenhouse argues in *Power on Display*, drama was "a vehicle for disseminating court ideology" (Tennenhouse, 1986, 39). New historicism ends up if not with something like a totalitarian model, then at least with a sense of the almost inevitable defeat of the poor, the innocent, and the oppressed.

This position is most interesting in its method of managing conflicts. The main procedure is to restrict matters to the upper class. In *James I and the Politics of Literature* Goldberg elegantly investigates the contradictions of absolutism, limiting those contradictions, however, to the level of ideology and focusing them on their presentation in the king's own writings (Goldberg, 1983). The procedure may be extended to debates between crown and parliament or to aristocratic male resentment of a female monarch (Patterson, 1984, 58–73; Montrose, 1983, 72–5). Because only elites are involved, the conflicts need not be resolved. When the lower classes enter the picture, however, their aspirations must either be crushed (Greenblatt, 1983) or be shown to serve the interests of the state (Mullaney, 1983; Greenblatt, 1985a; Tennenhouse, 1986, ch. 1). The other procedure is to remove struggle from the terrain of social class, relocating it in a tension between theater and crown (Montrose, 1983, 86; Greenblatt,

1985b, 183) or, if the subversion is unusually powerful, in the experience of "irremediable loss" (Greenblatt, 1985b, 184). The point is that unless one is an aristocrat, there is nothing to be done.

This position is not so much wrong as one-sided. Its limits may emerge from a demonstration of its lack of grounding. In general American Shakespeareans influenced by Foucault make claims about social function in the absence of the relevant empirical evidence (e.g. Reiss, 1980, 2–3). Choosing an apparently easy case Mullaney, Greenblatt, and Tennenhouse all argue that the second *Henriad* dramatizes the conservative integration of popular culture, the celebration of royal power (Mullaney, 1983; Greenblatt, 1985a; Tennenhouse, 1986, 76–85). Each of them combines a rich evocation of the historical context with an analysis of the dramatic text. But while the effects of a play may be postulated on such bases, they can only be demonstrated by recourse to subsequent historical evidence. These critics thus commit a methodological error by deducing effect from form and context.

One can discern the problematic consequences of this procedure by looking at the fair amount of material which survives about the reception of *Henry IV* before 1660. (For a full dicussion of this material see Cohen, 1985b.) The two parts may well have been echoed or mentioned more often than any other late Tudor or early Stuart play, usually in reference to individual characters (especially Falstaff), to a few striking scenes, and to some quotable lines. Shakespeare's original name for Falstaff, Sir John Oldcastle, evoked, perhaps inadvertently, a Catholic interpretation of a Lollard and hence proto-Protestant martyr. As a result, during the theologically heterodox revolutionary years Oldcastle's name had to be defended by anxious mainstream Protestants against the imputation of sectarian religious radicalism. Falstaff also raised ideological qualms on social and political grounds. Knights are not supposed to be cowards, ruffians, or robbers; still less are they supposed to rebel. But Sir John Fastolf, from whom Shakespeare derived Falstaff's name, may have been guilty of treason. From a beleaguered Royalist perspective, moreover, it was necessary to free the life of Henry V from any taint of guilt by low-life association. Especially during the 1640s and 1650s Shakespeare's portrayal of Falstaff may have undermined notions of social hierarchy, even challenging the crown. In an age of revolution the *Henry IV* plays, far from celebrating the monarchy, generated subversive religious, social, and political ideologies, at least from the perspective of the advocates of order.

But if new historicist reductions of Shakespeare to an agent of royal power are hard to defend in the context of the Renaissance, they acquire a certain logic and justification in the context of the present. The social basis for this position is the United States government's mass murder of Indochinese peasants followed first by the failure of the American antiwar movement to achieve any of its radical goals and then by the rightist recovery of the 1980s. New historicism should accordingly be seen as a form of leftist disillusionment. From this perspective it is possible to account for the initial emphasis on New World imperialism, especially in Greenblatt's writings; for the abiding concern with state power; and for the strangely quietist feel of these radical critiques.

From this perspective too one can assess the opposition between English Marxist and American new historicist Shakespeareans. Recall that the British critics find everything about Shakespeare potentially progressive except the romances and especially *The Tempest*, whose connection with the origins of the empire seems to be more than they can stomach. By contrast the Americans discover only conservative integration. The differences between the two stances clearly have preinterpretive roots. The progressive appropriation in England attacks the central, elitist, and conservative function of Shakespeare in the national culture. The new historicist demystifying insistence on Shakespeare's conservatism challenges the more peripheral, aestheticist, and liberal oppositional use of the playwright in the United States, where he is routinely counterposed to the corporate/state hierarchy as well as to a universalizing, debased mass culture. Thus both the Marxist and the new historicist positions are potentially radical, although the stronger left tradition in England gives the British critics greater political clarity than the Americans, who have not fully accepted the consequences of their own work and settled accounts with Shakespeare in the fashion outlined by Bristol later in this volume.

A certain political confusion also informs new historicist treatments of gender, although no other group of male Shakespeareans has taken problems of gender as seriously or produced work with as great a potential utility for feminism. This confusion arises from new historicism's assumption of arbitrary connectedness and focus on the absolutist court. Montrose's fine discussion of *As You Like It* is the exception that almost proves the rule. Its marginalization of Rosalind in an account of social relations among men poses a challenge to standard criticism blind to her ultimate subordination but in so doing may inadvertently contribute to the erasure of the female (Montrose, 1981). In an even more impressive study of the contradictions in *A Midsummer Night's Dream*, Montrose argues, apparently in sympathy with Shakespeare: "When a female ruler is ostensibly the virgin mother of her subjects, then the themes of male procreative power, autogeny, and mastery of women acquire a seditious resonance" (Montrose, 1983, 82). But since this argument is confined to upper-class men, it provides only a limited critique of monarchy; more disturbingly, the critique depends on misogyny.

In a deconstructive rather than new historicist piece, Goldberg is openly dubious about the subordination of women: "Perhaps – just perhaps – the reason we cannot find Shakespeare reflecting his culture's supposed patriarchalism and sexism is that the culture represented on stage *is* the culture offstage" (Goldberg, 1985, 134). Patriarchy has disappeared. A further step in the argument is taken by Greenblatt: "Shakespearean women are in this sense the representation of Shakespearean men, the projected mirror images of masculine self-differentiation" (Greenblatt, 1986a, 51). And Tennenhouse agrees, in his focus on "the state as the body of an aristocratic female": "my point is to dissolve the sexual theme into those which, in my view, determined the components of Jacobean drama and the nature of their relationship"

(Tennenhouse, 1986, 106, 123). Women have disappeared.

How does this happen? First, the assumption of arbitrary connectedness seems to preclude a systematic survey of the available evidence, leading instead to a kind of synecdoche in which a single text or group of texts stands in for all texts and thus exhausts the discursive field. Original, fascinating material on gynecological treaties or on the aristocratic body (Greenblatt, 1986a; Tennenhouse, 1986) is taken without argument to represent adequately the massive, heterogeneous discourse on gender during the Renaissance. Note that the problem here precedes a potential Marxist concern with a hierarchy of causes and effects within a society. Second, partly influenced by Foucault's relative indifference to the gender of subjects, new historicists understand gender in relation to the body or to power more than in relation to women. The orientation toward the court only accentuates this tendency. Thus in the extreme case women cease to be historical actors or subjects. They can be victims or objects, but it is not, however complexly, their experience that matters.

4

With this return to the terrain of feminism the argument has apparently come full circle. But the polemical claim in the introduction for the centrality of political criticism is worth retrieving in conclusion, in order to consider what strategies might prove useful in consolidating and extending the gains that have already been made. The practice of anticipatory totalization adopted in this essay indicates one possible approach: a commitment to coalition politics marked by an ongoing effort to work out a synthetic position satisfactory to the various groups in the coalition. Whether or not this proposal wins support, proponents of political criticism will need to intervene institutionally at various levels. The atypical strength of such criticism in Shakespeare studies points to the work to be done in those periods and languages – medieval literature and Russian literature, for example – where there has traditionally been resistance to radical ideas. Its particular prominence in publications and at conferences suggests another kind of unevenness as well: a concentration at research universities to the relative neglect of colleges. The solution to the second problem and to a lesser degree to the first is for the political critics of today to train the political critics of tomorrow, a process that will also produce a broad enough chronological band of loosely sympathetic teachers and scholars in the field of literature to insure continuity and to prevent isolation. But since it is precisely the coherence and boundaries of that field which are called into question by the approaches reviewed above, leftist professors of literature will have to form far-reaching alliances across the faculty, alliances that include not only intellectual cooperation but also both collective resistance to ideological crackdowns by campus or governmental administrations and, in the best of circumstances, challenges to the structure and function of the academy.

With the exception of these last, crucial enterprises, such efforts are narrowly professional in their concern with the constitution of the faculty. That concern can have only limited significance unless it is connected with a broadly conceived pedagogical function. Presumably the political perspective that informs much current published criticism carries over into the classroom. But most innovative teaching continues to take place in traditional courses that form part of traditional curricula. The efficacy of political criticism depends on the ability of shifts in the conceptual organization of the discipline to generate comparable shifts in the institutional organization of the discipline within colleges and universities. One possible consequence might be the absorption of literary study into the more promising field of cultural criticism. Yet a successful political pedagogy must also address if not a logically then at least a chronologically prior concern: the literary education students receive before they enter college. This difficult undertaking entails not only the training of future teachers but also and more importantly the formation of lasting ties with current teachers already at work in primary and secondary education. Finally, pedagogy properly extends beyond the schools to other institutions – to the theater, film, and television in the particular instance of Shakespeare studies; to the apparatus of literary production, which encompasses composition, publication, promotion, distribution, and reviewing; and to the entire range of structures of ideological legitimation and contestation.

The purpose of these brief suggestions is to juxtapose the real but modest achievements of political criticism of Shakespeare with the far more formidable tasks that remain before that criticism can be carried to its logical conclusion. The same rhetorical effect can be obtained by recalling that although contemporary political criticism grew out of the radicalism of the 1960s, it also has quite different roots in the reaction of the 1980s. A politically serious criticism has no option but to connect concerns on the job with ongoing, larger movements for social change.

Note

1. Although the conversation and comments of many people have improved the arguments of this essay, I would particularly like to thank Jean E. Howard for her intellectual and logistical help. I am also grateful for permission to use here material that I developed more briefly in "Shakespeares Realität und Shakespeares Realismus: Neue politische Interpretationen," *Shakespeare Jahrbuch* (Weimar), 122 (1986), 59–64.

Bibliography 1: Works cited

Adelman, Janet (1980) " 'Anger's my meat': Feeding, Dependency, and Aggression in *Coriolanus*," in Schwartz, Murray M. and Kahn, Coppélia (eds) *Representing Shakespeare: New Psychoanalytic Essays*, Baltimore, Johns Hopkins University Press, 129–49.
Aers, David and Kress, Gunther (1981) "The Language of Social Order: Individual, Society and Historical Process in *King Lear*," in Aers, David, Hodge, Bob and Kress, Gunther, *Literature, Language and Society in England 1580–1680*, Dublin, Gill & Macmillan; Totowa, NJ, Barnes & Noble, 75–99.

Anderson, Perry (1984) *In the Tracks of Historical Materialism*, Chicago, University of Chicago Press.

Bamber, Linda (1982) *Comic Women, Tragic Men: A Study of Gender and Genre in Shakespeare*, Stanford, Ca., Stanford University Press.

Barber, C.L. (1980) "The Family in Shakespeare's Development: Tragedy and Sacredness," in Schwartz, Murray M. and Kahn, Coppélia (eds) *Representing Shakespeare: New Psychoanalytic Essays*, Baltimore, Johns Hopkins University Press, 188–202.

Barker, Francis (1984) *The Tremulous Private Body: Essays on Subjection*, London, Methuen.

Barker, Francis and Hulme, Peter (1985) "Nymphs and reapers heavily vanish: The Discursive Con-texts of *The Tempest*," in Drakakis, John (ed.) *Alternative Shakespeares*, London and New York, Methuen, 191–205.

Belsey, Catherine (1985a) "Disrupting Sexual Difference: Meaning and Gender in the Comedies," in Drakakis, John (ed.) *Alternative Shakespeares*, London and New York, Methuen, 166–90.

—— (1985b) *The Subject of Tragedy: Identity and Difference in Renaissance Drama*, London, Methuen.

Bristol, Michael D. (1985) *Carnival and Theatre: Plebeian Culture and the Structure of Authority in Renaissance England*, London and New York, Methuen.

Brown, Paul (1985) " 'This thing of darkness I acknowledge mine': *The Tempest* and the Discourse of Colonialism," in Dollimore, Jonathan and Sinfield, Alan (eds) *Political Shakespeare: New Essays in Cultural Materialism*, Manchester, Manchester University Press; Ithaca, NY, Cornell University Press, 48–71.

Cohen, Walter (1985a) *Drama of a Nation: Public Theater in Renaissance England and Spain*, Ithaca, NY, Cornell University Press.

—— (1985b) "*Heinrich IV*. und die Revolution," *Shakespeare Jahrbuch* (Weimar), 121, 57–63.

Dash, Irene G. (1981) *Wooing, Wedding, and Power: Women in Shakespeare's Plays*, New York, Columbia University Press.

Dollimore, Jonathan (1984) *Radical Tragedy: Religion, Ideology and Power in the Drama of Shakespeare and His Contemporaries*, Brighton, Harvester.

—— (1985a) "Introduction: Shakespeare, Cultural Materialism and the New Historicism," in Dollimore, Jonathan and Sinfield, Alan (eds) *Political Shakespeare: New Essays in Cultural Materialism*, Manchester, Manchester University Press; Ithaca, NY, Cornell University Press, 2–17.

—— (1985b) "Transgression and Surveillance in *Measure for Measure*," in Dollimore, Jonathan and Sinfield, Alan (eds) *Political Shakespeare: New Essays in Cultural Materialism*, Manchester, Manchester University Press; Ithaca, NY, Cornell University Press, 72–87.

Dollimore, Jonathan and Sinfield, Alan (1985a) "History and Ideology: The Instance of *Henry V*," in Drakakis, John (ed.) *Alternative Shakespeares*, London and New York, Methuen, 206–27.

—— (eds) (1985b) *Political Shakespeare: New Essays in Cultural Materialism*, Manchester, Manchester University Press; Ithaca, NY, Cornell University Press.

Drakakis, John (1985) Introduction, in Drakakis, John (ed.) *Alternative Shakespeares*, London and New York, Methuen, 1–25.

Dreher, Diane Elizabeth (1986) *Domination and Defiance: Fathers and Daughters in Shakespeare*, Lexington, University Press of Kentucky.

Eagleton, Terry (1986) *William Shakespeare*, Oxford, Basil Blackwell.

Erickson, Peter (1985) *Patriarchal Structures in Shakespeare's Drama*, Berkeley, University of California Press.

Evans, Malcolm (1986) *Signifying Nothing*, Brighton, Harvester.

Fineman, Joel (1985) "The Turn of the Shrew," in Parker, Patricia and Hartman,

Geoffrey (eds) *Shakespeare and the Question of Theory*, New York and London, Methuen, 138–59.

French, Marilyn (1981) *Shakespeare's Division of Experience*, New York, Ballantine Books.

Gohlke, Madelon (1980) "'I wooed thee with my sword': Shakespeare's Tragic Paradigms," in Lenz, Carolyn Ruth Swift, Greene, Gayle, and Neely, Carol Thomas (eds) *The Woman's Part: Feminist Criticism of Shakespeare*, Urbana, University of Illinois Press, 150–70.

Goldberg, Jonathan (1982) "The Politics of Renaissance Literature: A Review Essay," *English Literary History*, 49, 514–42.

—— (1983) *James I and the Politics of Literature: Jonson, Shakespeare, Donne, and Their Contemporaries*, Baltimore, Johns Hopkins University Press.

—— (1985) "Shakespearean Inscriptions: The Voicing of Power," in Parker, Patricia and Hartman, Geoffrey (eds) *Shakespeare and the Question of Theory*, New York and London, Methuen, 116–37.

Greenblatt, Stephen (1980) *Renaissance Self-Fashioning: From More to Shakespeare*, Chicago, University of Chicago Press.

—— (1982) Introduction, in Greenblatt, Stephen (ed.) *The Forms of Power and the Power of Forms in the Renaissance*, Norman, University of Oklahoma, 3–6.

—— (1983) "Murdering Peasants: Status, Genre, and the Representation of Rebellion," *Representations*, 1, 1–29.

—— (1985a) "Invisible Bullets: Renaissance Authority and its Subversion, *Henry IV* and *Henry V*," in Dollimore, Jonathan and Sinfield, Alan (eds) *Political Shakespeare: New Essays in Cultural Materialism*, Manchester, Manchester University Press, Ithaca, NY, Cornell University Press, 18–47; repr., revised and expanded, in Greenblatt, Stephen (1987) *Shakespearean Negotiations*, Berkeley, University of California Press.

—— (1985b) "Shakespeare and the Exorcists," in Parker, Patricia and Hartman, Geoffrey (eds) *Shakespeare and the Question of Theory*, New York, Methuen, 163–87; repr., revised and expanded, in Greenblatt, Stephen (1987) *Shakespearean Negotiations*, Berkeley, University of California Press.

—— (1986a) "Fiction and Friction," in Heller, Thomas C., Sosna, Morton, and Wellbery, David E., with Davidson, Arnold I., Swidler, Ann, and Watt, Ian (eds) *Reconstructing Individualism: Autonomy, Individuality, and the Self in Western Thought*, Stanford, Ca., Stanford University Press, 30–52; repr., revised and expanded, in Greenblatt, Stephen (1987) *Shakespearean Negotiations*, Berkeley, University of California Press.

—— (1986b) "Loudun and London," *Critical Inquiry*, 12 (2), 326–46.

Greene, Gayle (1981) "Feminist and Marxist Criticism: An Argument for Alliances," *Women's Studies*, 9 (1), 29–45.

Hawkes, Terence (1986) *That Shakespeherian Rag: Essays on a Critical Process*, London, Methuen.

Heinemann, Margot (1980) *Puritanism and Theatre: Thomas Middleton and Opposition Drama under the Early Stuarts*, Cambridge, Cambridge University Press.

—— (1985) "How Brecht Read Shakespeare," in Dollimore, Jonathan and Sinfield, Alan (eds) *Political Shakespeare: New Essays in Cultural Materialism*, Manchester, Manchester University Press; Ithaca, NY, Cornell University Press, 202–30.

Hill, Christopher (1985) *The Collected Essays of Christopher Hill*, vol. 1, *Writing and Revolution in Seventeenth-Century England*, Brighton, Harvester; Amherst, University of Massachusetts Press.

Hill, Errol (1984) *Shakespeare in Sable: A History of Black Shakespearean Actors*, Amherst, University of Massachusetts Press.

Holderness, Graham (1985a) "Radical Potentiality and Institutional Closure: Shakespeare in Film and Television," in Dollimore, Jonathan and Sinfield, Alan (eds)

Political Shakespeare: New Essays in Cultural Materialism, Manchester, Manchester University Press; Ithaca, NY, Cornell University Press, 182–201.

——— (1985b) *Shakespeare's History*, Dublin, Gill & Macmillan.

Howard, Jean E. (1986) "The New Historicism in Renaissance Studies," *English Literary Renaissance*, 16, 13–43.

Hulme, Peter (1981) "Hurricanes in the Caribbees: The Constitution of the Discourse of English Colonialism," in Barker, Francis, Bernstein, Jay, Coombes, John, Hulme, Peter, Stone, Jennifer, and Stratton, Jon (eds) *1642: Literature and Power in the Seventeenth Century*, Colchester, University of Essex, 55–83.

Jardine, Lisa (1983) *Still Harping on Daughters: Women and Drama in the Age of Shakespeare*, Brighton, Harvester.

Kahn, Coppélia (1981) *Man's Estate: Masculine Identity in Shakespeare*, Berkeley, University of California Press.

——— (1985) Introduction, in Erickson, Peter and Kahn, Coppélia (eds) *Shakespeare's "Rough Magic": Renaissance Essays in Honor of C.L. Barber*, Newark, University of Delaware Press, 15–18.

Kavanagh, James H. (1985) "Shakespeare in Ideology," in Drakakis, John (ed.) *Alternative Shakespeares*, London and New York, Methuen, 144–65.

Lenz, Carolyn Ruth Swift, Greene, Gayle, and Neely, Carol Thomas (1980a) Introduction, in Lenz, Carolyn Ruth Swift, Greene, Gayle, and Neely, Carol Thomas (eds) *The Woman's Part: Feminist Criticism of Shakespeare*, Urbana, University of Illinois Press, 3–16.

——— (eds) (1980b) *The Woman's Part: Feminist Criticism of Shakespeare*, Urbana, University of Illinois Press.

McLuskie, Kathleen (1985) "The Patriarchal Bard: Feminist Criticism and Shakespeare – *King Lear* and *Measure for Measure*," in Dollimore, Jonathan and Sinfield, Alan (eds) *Political Shakespeare: New Essays in Cultural Materialism*, Manchester, Manchester University Press; Ithaca, NY, Cornell University Press, 88–108.

Montrose, Louis Adrian (1980) "The Purpose of Playing: Reflections on a Shakespearean Anthropology," *Helios*, n.s. 7, 51–74.

——— (1981) "'The place of a brother' in *As You Like It*: Social Process and Comic Form," *Shakespeare Quarterly*, 32, 28–54.

——— (1983) "'Shaping fantasies': Figurations of Gender and Power in Elizabethan Culture," *Representations*, 2, 61–94; abridged repr. in Ferguson, Margaret W., Quilligan, Maureen, and Vickers, Nancy J. (eds) (1986) *Rewriting the Renaissance: The Discourses of Sexual Difference in Early Modern Europe*, Chicago, University of Chicago Press.

——— (1986) "Renaissance Literary Studies and the Subject of History," *English Literary Renaissance*, 16, 5–12.

Moretti, Franco (1982) "'A huge eclipse': Tragic Form and the Deconsecration of Sovereignty," in Greenblatt, Stephen (ed.) *The Forms of Power and the Power of Forms in the Renaissance*, Norman, University of Oklahoma, 7–40.

Mullaney, Steven (1980) "Lying Like Truth: Riddle, Representation and Treason in Renaissance England," *English Literary History*, 47, 32–47; repr. in Mullaney, Steven (1987) *The Place of the Stage: License, Play, and Power in Renaissance England*, Chicago, University of Chicago Press, ch. 5.

——— (1983) "Strange Things, Gross Terms, Curious Customs: The Rehearsal of Cultures in the Late Renaissance," *Representations*, 3, 40–67; repr. in Mullaney, Steven (1987) *The Place of the Stage: License, Play, and Power in Renaissance England*, Chicago, University of Chicago Press, ch. 3.

——— (1987) *The Place of the Stage: License, Play, and Power in Renaissance England*, Chicago, University of Chicago Press.

Neely, Carol Thomas (1985) *Broken Nuptials in Shakespeare's Plays*, New Haven, Yale University Press.

Newman, Karen (1986) "Renaissance Family Politics and *The Taming of the Shrew*," *English Literary Renaissance*, 16 (1), 86–100.

Novy, Marianne (1984) *Love's Argument: Gender Relations in Shakespeare*, Chapel Hill, University of North Carolina Press.

Orgel, Stephen (1982) "Making Greatness Familiar," in Greenblatt, Stephen (ed.) *The Forms of Power and the Power of Forms in the Renaissance*, Norman, University of Oklahoma, 41–8.

Patterson, Annabel (1984) *Censorship and Interpretation: The Conditions of Writing and Reading in Early Modern England*, Madison, University of Wisconsin Press.

Reiss, Timothy J. (1980) *Tragedy and Truth: Studies in the Development of a Renaissance and Neoclassical Discourse*, New Haven, Yale University Press.

Renaissance Drama (1982) n.s. 15, *Drama and Society*.

Serpieri, Alessandro (1985) "Reading the Signs: Towards a Semiotics of Shakespearean Drama," trans. Keir Elam, in Drakakis, John (ed.) *Alternative Shakespeares*, London and New York, Methuen, 119–43.

Shepherd, Simon (1981) *Amazons and Warrior Women: Varieties of Feminism in Seventeenth-Century Drama*, Brighton, Harvester; New York, St Martin's Press.

—————— (1986) *Marlowe and the Politics of Elizabethan Theatre*, Brighton, Harvester; New York, St Martin's Press.

Siegel, Paul N. (1986) *Shakespeare's English and Roman History Plays: A Marxist Approach*, Rutherford, NJ, Fairleigh Dickinson University Press.

Sinfield, Alan (1983) *Literature in Protestant England 1560–1660*, Beckenham, Croom Helm.

—————— (1985a) "Give an account of Shakespeare and education . . .," in Dollimore, Jonathan and Sinfield, Alan (eds) *Political Shakespeare: New Essays in Cultural Materialism*, Manchester, Manchester University Press; Ithaca, NY, Cornell University Press, 134–57.

—————— (1985b) "Royal Shakespeare: Theatre and the Making of Ideology," in Dollimore, Jonathan and Sinfield, Alan (eds) *Political Shakespeare: New Essays in Cultural Materialism*, Manchester, Manchester University Press; Ithaca, NY, Cornell University Press, 158–81.

Stallybrass, Peter (1982) "*Macbeth* and Witchcraft," in Brown, John Russell (ed.) *Focus on "Macbeth"*, London, Routledge & Kegan Paul, 189–209.

Sundelson, David (1983) *Shakespeare's Restorations of the Father*, New Brunswick, NJ, Rutgers University Press.

Tennenhouse, Leonard (1986) *Power on Display: The Politics of Shakespeare's Genres*, New York and London, Methuen.

Tokson, Elliot H. (1982) *The Popular Image of the Black Man in English Drama, 1550–1688*, Boston, G.K. Hall.

Weimann, Robert (1978) *Shakespeare and the Popular Tradition in the Theater: Studies in the Social Dimension of Dramatic Form and Function*, ed. Robert Schwartz, Baltimore, Johns Hopkins University Press.

—————— (1984) *Structure and Society in Literary History: Studies in the History and Theory of Historical Criticism*, 2nd edn, Baltimore, Johns Hopkins University Press.

—————— (1985) "Mimesis in *Hamlet*," in Parker, Patricia and Hartman, Geoffrey (eds) *Shakespeare and the Question of Theory*, New York and London, Methuen, 275–91.

—————— (1986) "History and the Issue of Authority in Representation: The Elizabethan Theater and the Reformation," *New Literary History*, 17, 449–76.

Wells, Susan (1985) *The Dialectics of Representation*, Baltimore, Johns Hopkins University Press.

Wheeler, Richard P. (1981) *Shakespeare's Development and the Problem Comedies: Turn and Counter-Turn*, Berkeley, University of California Press.

Woodbridge, Linda (1984) *Women and the English Renaissance*, Urbana, University of Illinois Press.

Bibliography 2: Political studies of Shakespeare in the 1980s

The following chronological list is inevitably arbitrary in its boundaries. It is limited to books written in English. Though it includes studies not entirely devoted to Shakespeare, it does so only if the remainder of the volume is concerned primarily with political analyses of Renaissance theater or literature. Finally, the records for 1986, the year in which this bibliography was compiled, and especially for 1987 are obviously more fragmentary than for 1980–5.

1980

Greenblatt, Stephen *Renaissance Self-Fashioning: From More to Shakespeare*, Chicago and London, University of Chicago Press.

Lenz, Carolyn Ruth Swift, Greene, Gayle, and Neely, Carol Thomas (eds) *The Woman's Part: Feminist Criticism of Shakespeare*, Urbana, University of Illinois Press.

Reiss, Timothy J. *Tragedy and Truth: Studies in the Development of a Renaissance and Neoclassical Discourse*, New Haven and London, Yale University Press.

Schwartz, Murray M., and Kahn, Coppélia (eds) *Representing Shakespeare: New Psychoanalytic Essays*, Baltimore and London, Johns Hopkins University Press.

1981

Aers, David, Hodge, Bob, and Kress, Gunther *Literature, Language, and Society in England 1580–1680*, Dublin, Gill & Macmillan; Totowa, NJ, Barnes & Noble.

Barker, Francis, Bernstein, Jay, Coombes, John, Hulme, Peter, Stone, Jennifer, and Stratton, Jon (eds) *1642: Literature and Power in the Seventeenth Century*, Proceedings of the Essex Conference on the Sociology of Literature, July 1980, Colchester, University of Essex.

Dash, Irene G. *Wooing, Wedding, and Power: Women in Shakespeare's Plays*, New York, Columbia University Press.

French, Marilyn *Shakespeare's Division of Experience*, New York, Ballantine Books.

Kahn, Coppélia *Man's Estate: Masculine Identity in Shakespeare*, Berkeley, University of California Press.

Shepherd, Simon *Amazons and Warrior Women: Varieties of Feminism in Seventeenth-Century Drama*, Brighton, Harvester; New York, St Martin's Press.

Wheeler, Richard P. *Shakespeare's Development and the Problem Comedies: Turn and Counter-Turn*, Berkeley, University of California Press.

1982

Bamber, Linda *Comic Women, Tragic Men: A Study of Gender and Genre in Shakespeare*, Stanford, Ca., Stanford University Press.

Coursen, H.R. *The Leasing Out of England: Shakespeare's Second Henriad*, Washington, DC, University Press of America.

Greenblatt, Stephen (ed.) *The Forms of Power and the Power of Forms in the Renaissance*, Norman, University of Oklahoma.

Tokson, Elliot H. *The Popular Image of the Black Man in English Drama, 1550–1688*, Boston, G.K. Hall.

Women's Studies, 9 (1–2) (1981–2), *Feminist Criticism of Shakespeare*.

1983

Goldberg, Jonathan *James I and the Politics of Literature: Jonson, Shakespeare, Donne, and Their Contemporaries*, Baltimore and London, Johns Hopkins University Press.
Jardine, Lisa *Still Harping on Daughters: Women and Drama in the Age of Shakespeare*, Brighton, Harvester.
Sinfield, Alan *Literature in Protestant England 1560–1660*, Beckenham, Croom Helm.
Sundelson, David *Shakespeare's Restorations of the Father*, New Brunswick, NJ, Rutgers University Press.

1984

Barker, Francis *The Tremulous Private Body: Essays on Subjection*, London and New York, Methuen.
Dollimore, Jonathan *Radical Tragedy: Religion, Ideology and Power in the Drama of Shakespeare and His Contemporaries*, Brighton, Harvester; Chicago, University of Chicago Press.
Hill, Errol *Shakespeare in Sable: A History of Black Shakespearean Actors*, Amherst, University of Massachusetts Press.
Novy, Marianne *Love's Argument: Gender Relations in Shakespeare*, Chapel Hill, University of North Carolina Press.
Patterson, Annabel *Censorship and Interpretation: The Conditions of Writing and Reading in Early Modern England*, Madison, University of Wisconsin Press.
Stevenson, Laura Caroline *Praise and Paradox: Merchants and Craftsmen in Elizabethan Popular Literature*, Cambridge, Cambridge University Press.
Woodbridge, Linda *Women and the English Renaissance*, Urbana, University of Illinois Press.

1985

Belsey, Catherine *The Subject of Tragedy: Identity and Difference in Renaissance Drama*, London and New York, Methuen.
Bergeron, David M. *Shakespeare's Romances and the Royal Family*, Lawrence, University Press of Kansas.
Bristol, Michael D. *Carnival and Theatre: Plebeian Culture and the Structure of Authority in Renaissance England*, London and New York, Methuen.
Cohen, Walter *Drama of a Nation: Public Theater in Renaissance England and Spain*, Ithaca, NY, and London, Cornell University Press.
Dollimore, Jonathan, and Sinfield, Alan (eds) *Political Shakespeare: New Essays in Cultural Materialism*, Manchester, Manchester University Press; Ithaca, NY, Cornell University Press.
Drakakis, John (ed.) *Alternative Shakespeares*, London and New York, Methuen.
Erickson, Peter *Patriarchal Structures in Shakespeare's Drama*, Berkeley, University of California Press.
Erickson, Peter and Kahn, Coppélia (eds) *Shakespeare's "Rough Magic": Renaissance Essays in Honor of C.L. Barber*, Newark, University of Delaware Press; London and Toronto, Associated University Presses.
Hill, Christopher *The Collected Essays of Christopher Hill*, vol. 1, *Writing and Revolution in Seventeenth-Century England*, Brighton, Harvester; Amherst, University of Massachusetts Press.
Holderness, Graham *Shakespeare's History*, Dublin, Gill & Macmillan; New York, St Martin's Press.

Neely, Carol Thomas *Broken Nuptials in Shakespeare's Plays*, New Haven and London, Yale University Press.

Parker, Patricia, and Hartman, Geoffrey (eds) *Shakespeare and the Question of Theory*, New York and London, Methuen.

Wells, Susan *Dialectics of Representation*, Baltimore and London, Johns Hopkins University Press.

1986

Dreher, Diane Elizabeth *Domination and Defiance: Fathers and Daughters in Shakespeare*, Lexington, University Press of Kentucky.

Eagleton, Terry *William Shakespeare*, Oxford and New York, Basil Blackwell.

Evans, Malcolm *Signifying Nothing*, Brighton, Harvester; Athens, University of Georgia Press.

Ferguson, Margaret W., Quilligan, Maureen and Vickers, Nancy J. (eds) *Rewriting the Renaissance: The Discourses of Sexual Difference in Early Modern Europe*, Chicago and London, University of Chicago Press.

Hawkes, Terence *That Shakespeherian Rag: Essays on a Critical Process*, London and New York, Methuen.

Siegel, Paul N. *Shakespeare's English and Roman History Plays: A Marxist Approach*, Rutherford, N.J., Fairleigh Dickinson University Press; London, Associated University Presses.

Tennenhouse, Leonard *Power on Display: The Politics of Shakespeare's Genres*, New York and London, Methuen.

1987

Greenblatt, Stephen *Shakespearean Negotiations*, Berkeley, University of California Press.

Howard, Jean E. and O'Connor, Marion F. (eds) *Shakespeare Reproduced: The Text in History and Ideology*, London and New York, Methuen.

Mullaney, Steven *The Place of the Stage: License, Play, and Power in Renaissance England*, Chicago and London, University of Chicago Press.

2

Power, politics, and the Shakespearean text: recent criticism in England and the United States[1]

Don E. Wayne

A recent *Time* magazine article quotes a well-known literary critic: "Shakespeare's work has ceased to be a literary consideration. It has become part of our culture, almost part of our ideology and religion" (Friedrich, 1985, 76). Such an assertion no longer sounds as controversial as it might have just a few years ago. It certainly will not seem out of place in the context of the present collection of essays. But the identity of the critic who made the statement may come as something of a surprise: it is Harvard Professor Emeritus Harry Levin. For a scholar of Professor Levin's generation to tie Shakespeare to ideology in such unmitigated terms is an indication of the degree to which the language of literary criticism in America has changed over the past few years. Presumably, words like "ideology" and "power" are now quite acceptable signifiers in authorized institutional discourse concerning Shakespeare and English literature generally.

In the past, many of us who employed such terminology encountered considerable opposition. Now that the terms are no longer held to be indecorous it strikes me as important to determine why there was once so much resistance

---

DON E. WAYNE teaches at the University of California, San Diego. His publications include *Penshurst: The Semiotics of Place and the Poetics of History* (Madison, University of Wisconsin Press; London, Methuen, 1984), and essays on Renaissance literature and cultural criticism and theory. He is currently at work on a book concerning the relationship between politics and aesthetics in the modernist version of the English literary canon, focusing on the unreadability of Ben Jonson as an exemplary instance.

to issues of power and ideology in Renaissance studies and why these issues are currently so prominent, even fashionable. I want to begin a line of inquiry here that may help to account for the recent reorientation of critical discourse on Shakespeare. A further and more elusive goal of this essay is to analyze the conjuncture in which we find ourselves as academic scholars and critics formed in the political crucible of the 1960s, now moving into positions of institutional authority and power in the 1980s. The procedure of this inquiry will be to look at the shift of focus, in recent Renaissance scholarship produced in the United Kingdom and in the United States, from ideas to relationships of power as the fundamental units of historical analysis and interpretation, and then to examine the cultural and historical factors that have distinguished the kind of work produced in the United States from that in Britain.

1

We seem to be on the way to establishing a new consensus, if not a new orthodoxy in Renaissance studies, especially with respect to the Shakespearean canon. To the extent that the old consensus included a historical component, its history was, we are now being told, unitary, idealist, and exclusionary. Most often taken to task in this connection is Tillyard's *Elizabethan World Picture* (1943). As Raymond Williams points out (1985, 233–4), Tillyard and his contemporaries were motivated in part by a desire to contain rash interpretations of Shakespeare's plays that confounded Elizabethan beliefs and actions with those of our own time. But the effect of their efforts to situate the plays against the background of a one-dimensional "world picture" was to contain the dynamic complexities of the dramatic works themselves, and of the social conditions that produced them. Williams's remarks occur in his afterword to the recently published volume *Political Shakespeare* (Dollimore and Sinfield, 1985). The essays collected there and in another recent volume, *Alternative Shakespeares* (Drakakis, 1985), are committed to demythologizing the modern Shakespearean aesthetic in which dramatic resolution is viewed as the expression of a unified poetic sensibility and of a coherent world picture.

These collections exemplify a movement in criticism that has already called forth something of a critical backlash. In a recent issue of *Shakespeare Quarterly*, a noted Shakespearean, M.M. Reese, insists that "the World Picture may indeed be discredited and dead. But we miss a great deal if we try to read Shakespeare without it." In justifying his claim that the Elizabethans could cling to the doctrine of fixed hierarchical order in spite of so much real evidence to the contrary, Reese draws a modern parallel with "the persistent affirmation of "democracy" as a sort of talisman in today's Western nations that in practice have become increasingly, and perhaps irrevocably, collectivist" (Reese, 1985, 256). One might want to argue over the legitimacy of pitting the terms "democracy" and "collectivist" against one another as though they were irreconcilable opposites; but what is most striking here is to find these terms popping up in a latter-day defense of the Elizabethan World Picture. It seems to me that in drawing this analogy Mr Reese has acknowledged, however indirectly, what is finally at stake in the current debate over our reading of the Shakespearean text.

Ironically, his use of this analogy with present-day European politics places him in closer proximity to some of the most radical critics writing in the UK today than to many here in the US who would share his anxiety and indignation at how these critics are treating the Shakespearean text. In reading through some of the most recent work on Shakespeare by British scholars, one is struck by the number of references to the present political scene. Essays on Shakespearean subjects by British contributors to the two above-mentioned collections are filled with allusions to the Thatcher government's domestic policies, to the 1984/5 coalminers' strike, to the Falklands campaign, to the persistence of colonialist and patriarchal ideologies, and to the role of Shakespeare as the central ideological figure in a national culture.

The last of these categories is broadly the subject of two exemplary pieces of sociocriticism that Sinfield has contributed to *Political Shakespeare*. One of his essays deals with the centrality of Shakespeare in Britain's national educational curriculum with its standardized examinations. Sinfield's title, "Give an account of Shakespeare and Education, showing why you think they are effective and what you have appreciated about them. Support your comments with precise references" (1985a, 134), parodies the sort of questions on Shakespeare asked in the O-level and A-level examinations which are usually required for university entrance. Sinfield shows convincingly that such examination questions are framed in a manner requiring the student to discover in her or himself a spontaneous response that has in fact been learned. The appropriate response will usually entail notions of human nature that reinforce culturally specific institutions and relationships of power.[2]

In another essay, "Royal Shakespeare: Theatre and the Making of Ideology" (1985b), Sinfield surveys the Royal Shakespeare Company's transformation after World War II from a local operation catering to the nostalgic and complacent expectations of tourist-pilgrims to Stratford into a major, innovative theatrical company of international renown. Under the direction of Peter Hall and, subsequently, Trevor Nunn, the RSC built its reputation on a programmatic commitment to producing Shakespeare from the vantage point of a modernist aesthetic and, at times, from an avowed concern with contemporary political and social issues. Without questioning the sincerity of Hall's and Nunn's claims that their theatre was more "radical," more "open," more "relevant," Sinfield discloses the paradoxical nature of their project for a "radical" theatre under the "royal" aegis. In his analysis the effect of the RSC has been to validate Shakespeare not only as a central figure but as a centralizing force in modern British culture. Shakespeare "is the cultural token which gives significance to the interpretations which are derived from him. Rival productions are, in effect, contests for the authority of Shakespeare, rival attempts to establish that he speaks this position rather than (or, at least, as well as) that" (Sinfield, 1985b, 174). The problem with *any* institutionalized interpretation – and presumably this is no less true of academic criticism than of theatrical production – is that what it affirms, more than anything else, is the authority and power of the institution:

> For even when the resistances set up by received notions of the plays are over-come and genuinely radical interpretation is rendered persuasive (and it is not clear that this has occurred), the idea of the real Shakespeare from which it all emanates nevertheless registers cultural authority, and implies that every innovation has been anticipated. The underlying pressure is towards deference and inertia. (p. 178)

Implied here is a critique of all interpretations. We are accustomed nowadays to reading attacks on older modes of interpretation that located the "real" Shakespeare through notions of formal and thematic unity (New Criticism), moral and psychological verity (F.R. Leavis and his associates), or by means of a one-dimensional conception of the text's historicity (Tillyard). But Sinfield's argument touches *any* interpretation. It would thus apply to the most innovative work on Shakespeare of the past ten years, work by feminists, by Marxists, by new historicists, and by the most recent generation of textual scholars who tend to view the Shakespearean text not as the creation of a unique, genial author but, in accordance with Elizabethan theatrical practice, as the product of a collaborative venture.[3] Finally, the argument would apply to the efforts of Sinfield himself and of his British colleagues in the attempt by "cultural materialists" to appropriate Shakespeare for an oppositional politics. Sinfield is well aware of this dilemma. His point is not, however, to invalidate interpretation. Rather, what distinguishes him and his colleagues from their opponents in the struggle for the appropriation of Shakespeare in Britain is that they attempt to go beyond traditional critics (of both the right and the left) to interrogate the motives that drive their own interpretations of Shakespearean texts and of Shakespeare's role in modern British culture.

Both Reese and Sinfield are indicative in their opposing ways of the degree to which scholarly discussion of Shakespeare in Britain today is directly linked up with political debate. There is, however, a major difference in the epistemological basis of arguments on either side of this opposition. Moralists of the right cite Shakespeare as a source of absolute and universal truths of the human condition, truths on which to base policy. While there is also such a tradition on the left – especially in England where the socialist political heritage is mixed with various strains of reformed religion and with the sentimental idealism of the English Romantics – the more recent current in British criticism on the left is toward a radical historicizing of the Shakespearean text.[4] In another essay published in *Political Shakespeare*, Margot Heinemann locates a source for such a critical historicism in portions of Brecht's theoretical writings on the drama. She begins her essay on Brecht and Shakespeare by citing a *Guardian* interview with Mrs Thatcher's chancellor of the exchequer, Nigel Lawson, who invokes Shakespeare in support of conservative fiscal policy and the dismantling of the welfare state. Lawson describes Shakespeare as a Tory whose pronouncements on the necessity of hierarchy in Ulysses' speech on degree in *Troilus and Cressida* and in the resolution of a play like *Coriolanus* are still relevant today because, in Lawson's words, "man's nature doesn't change" (Heinemann, 1985, 203). Heinemann also points to a BBC production of *Julius Caesar* which aimed for "relevance" by comparing the fickle and unruly Roman crowd to a modern trade-unionist demonstration. The effect was to "merely confirm the Lawson stereotype of trade unionists motivated by inferiority and envy, incapable of uniting for any constructive change" (p. 226). Against such interpretations which annihilate historical perspective and cultural difference, Heinemann opposes Brecht's conception of a theatre in which Shakespearean plays are staged in a way that emphasizes the distance and discontinuity between Shakespeare's society and our own. In such a production "our sense of [the characters'] social situation, the inescapable pressures on them, makes their actions and feelings credible and human to us without our having to pretend to react like Elizabethans, which of course we can't do" (p. 216).

This concept of distantiation is aesthetic, though not in the Kantian sense of being disinterested. The effect of historical distancing on the apprehending subject is held to be a sensuous delight in difference or dissimilarity, a quality that is seen as having an immediate political force in the present through its capacity to remind us of the possibilities for change. British advocates of such historicizing strategies are not aiming primarily to bring new vitality to the staging and teaching of Shakespearean drama (though that is, ironically, what they may accomplish in the short run). Their main concern is with the decanonization of Shakespeare as a cultural token and with the delegitimation of institutional strategies of containment that rely on Shakespeare as the keystone of an ideology according to which "man's nature doesn't change."

In Britain, then, there is no question of the relevance of the Shakespearean text to recent history, only a question of whether one uses the Shakespearean text to authorize or to interrogate the status quo. But the situation in America is significantly different, and it is surprising to find little effort to account for that difference in representations of the recent new approaches to the Shakespearean text. In his introduction to *Political Shakespeare*, Dollimore orders this new criticism under two rubrics: in Britain, cultural materialism; in the United States, new historicism.[5] But for reasons that are not entirely clear to me, these two movements are treated as something of a unity, and the volume presents a new, *political* Shakespeare as the product of a shared political project.

2

Yet when one reads through essays and books that have appeared in recent years on either side of the Atlantic, one is struck, I believe, by a fundamental discontinuity between the work of British and American scholars. We Americans tend to be meticulous readers and diligent historiographers.[6] We study texts of various kinds, aiming to restore or to retrieve a political, social,

and anthropological context for the original production of Shakespeare's plays
and to establish the specific historical forms of power that are reflected,
refracted, displayed, mediated, or even produced by these plays in concert with
other contemporaneous social practices. Many of us would acknowledge that our
rejection of an earlier critical tradition and our focus on the issue of *power* in
Renaissance society is politically motivated. But the reasons why we may be so
motivated in the present moment to produce this shift in critical focus on the past
remain largely unarticulated. By contrast, the British are relatively freewheeling
in the way they range from Shakespeare's time to our own and back again, and
in the polemical bite of the rhetoric by means of which they debunk their own
earlier critical tradition.

I would suggest that this difference is a further historical extension of a
divergence that has characterized British and American criticism through most
of this century. On the British side, there is a tradition that descends from
Matthew Arnold, through Leavis and his associates, to the more radical criticism
that began to appear in the work of Raymond Williams and has since been
developed by a whole new generation of scholars; a tradition which decrees that
culture, literature preeminently, is a legitimate and necessary vehicle of political
action and engagement. This may seem like a strange line of descent when one
thinks of the Arnoldian version of *disinterestedness* as specifically removing
criticism from the realm of practical politics. But in Arnold, as in Leavis after
him, there is a passionate sense of the political and social mission of literary
criticism as a civilizing force. Thus, in the British cultural context the field of
literary criticism periodically takes on the appearance of a battleground on which
a struggle is waged for control over the representational power of texts that are
understood to be the nation's cultural patrimony – for better or worse!

At the present moment in Britain it is difficult to locate oneself within the field
of Shakespeare studies without at the same time acknowledging the coordinates
of one's position, not only in the territory of academic politics but in the larger
political domain as well. Moreover, the affective intensity of the language in
which critics debate the Shakespearean text in Britain is an index of the degree
to which they are connected (and cathected) psychologically and existentially to
the culture which is their polemical object.

In America, on the other hand, ever since Eliot and the New Critics
established the principle of aesthetic distance (though, significantly, *not*
historical distance) as a *sine qua non* of literary study, we have tended to repress
the political nature of our activity as critics. This much has been noted frequently
in recent retrospective commentary on the New Criticism. But I would suggest,
too, that the most effective means by which this depoliticization was achieved
in American criticism was by the repression of an affective response that might
provide the energy for a politically engaged criticism. By this I mean not a
response to a given literary text or corpus but to our respective cultural
backgrounds which are more heterogeneous than in Britain, and which entail
mediations of a different kind between the Shakespearean text and ourselves.

It is not my aim to establish a hierarchy that would validate the politics of current British criticism over our own. I believe that the contrast has to be drawn with an eye to our different cultural histories, especially in the century during which the study of English became established as an academic discipline. In Britain Shakespeare has long been an unequivocal component of a national culture. The situation of Shakespeare and of English literature in America is somewhat different.

After World War II, we inherited a type of Shakespeare criticism in which American scholars largely identified with real or imagined English ancestors, whether of the Established or Nonconformist persuasions. For scholars of the immediate postwar period, many of whom were first-generation Americans of non-English ancestry, a fundamental political problem was to negotiate an entitlement to the role of critic with respect to English culture. The New Criticism, though originating in a southern regionalist oppositional politics, became more widely assimilated in part because it provided the objective grounds for claims to the universality of works of high culture regardless of their specific national derivation.[7] Indeed, the hegemony achieved by American formalism in that period can be understood as the result of a strategy of reification. Literature was finally established as an autonomous domain. Even those who insisted on the necessity of historicizing the literary text tended to argue in behalf of a purely *literary* historicism. This much Richard Ohmann demonstrated ten years ago in his book *English in America*. For Ohmann, the single most significant factor governing literary theory and practice in the period of McCarthyism and the cold war was the "flight from politics" (1976, 79).

But there is another side to the sociology of postwar literary studies in the United States. Granted that escape may have been a motive in the theoretical abstraction of Literature from the social conditions of its production. Granted, too, that the institutionalization of Literature as a privileged conduit of timeless, "human" values was an ideological response to an intensified collective experience of alienation in the emerging consumer society of the 1950s. There was, nonetheless, a political dimension to this apparently apolitical moment in the history of American literary studies which Ohmann's survey of the period overlooked. The strategy of reification successfully established English and American literature as a cultural object which poets and critics of incredibly diverse backgrounds could share in common. It also established literary criticism as work-discipline rather than genteel reflection by men of taste and proper breeding. For a generation of intellectuals many of whose parents did not speak English as their primary language, let alone read or write it, the appropriation of a notion of art as an autotelic activity and of the New Critical aesthetic as a measure of that activity was, I would argue, a political choice whether or not it was recognized as such.[8] I would also argue that it was not just a conservative political choice; that in the specific postwar historical and cultural situation the adoption of neo-Kantian aesthetic theory was a way of altering the norms of high culture in American society. Among other things, it was a way of opening the halls of academe – especially of English departments – to scholars who didn't happen to come to school equipped with English surnames. Of course, the other side of this development in American literary studies was the containment of difference, the effacement of historical and cultural specificity in an aesthetic that emphasized principles of unity, universality, and textual autonomy.

Concurrent with the project of the New Criticism was an effort among New York intellectuals to make the Arnoldian tradition work in an American context, where assimilation was a necessary condition of cultural authority beyond the narrow confines of the immigrant community. Arnold's *Culture and Anarchy* (1869) is, among other things, an important document in the history of modern notions of subjectivity. For Arnold, the institutionalizing of literary studies was a way to cultivate "delicacy of perception" and, thereby, to repress anarchic forces that lurked in the individual and threatened social order. Hierarchy and opposition among the Victorian social classes – the aristocracy, the middle class, the working class, which Arnold designated by the quainter terms *Barbarians, Philistines*, and *Populace* – were thus discounted by a psychological theory of sublimation, control exercised by the "best self" (culture) over the "ordinary self" (anarchy) (Arnold [1961], 101–6, 182–3). But the theory required modification if the idea of cultivating delicacy of perception through literary study were to take root in the United States.

The main standard-bearer of Arnoldian values in American criticism was Lionel Trilling. In order to transpose Arnold's defense of literary study into the more heterogeneous and democratic context of twentieth-century America, Trilling had to depsychologize Arnold's notion of literature as a civilizing agent, to make it rather a means of social and political emancipation.[9] But the price of such emancipation for those who, like Trilling, were first-generation Americans was assimilation. This entailed the reduction of cultural diversity to what appeared, from an intellectual standpoint, to be the highest common denominator, the English cultural tradition. Perhaps this was an inevitable price that intellectuals of Trilling's generation and some who came immediately after had to pay. If that is the case, then we are privileged today to use what they purchased in order to write the history of what they had to give up.

By 1965, in an essay entitled "The Two Environments," Trilling had come to recognize that the success of literary studies had changed the conditions under which Arnold's defense of the classics had applied. A century after the publication of *Culture and Anarchy*, literature had become an established institution. There were now two dominant cultures, one still philistine, the other defining itself in opposition to philistinism. Trilling worried that the Arnoldian project for a moral adversary culture might defeat itself through its extraordinary successes, that the field of literary studies was in danger of losing its critical function and of becoming instead a "trivializing force" (Trilling, 1965, 228–9; Ohmann, 1976, 67–9). Yet Trilling was forced by his own cultural formation to pull back from the implications of what he rather acutely observed. The limits of his capacity to doubt the efficacy of the traditional English curriculum are evident in an essay which he had published a few years earlier under the title "Reflections on a Lost Cause: English Literature and American Education." It startles one in 1987 to read that already in 1958 "the survey course in English literature, once universally believed to be a necessity in any curriculum, becomes increasingly rare," that "in the high schools English texts are scarcely used at all – even Shakespeare barely holds a place" (Trilling, 1958, 345). Trilling recognized that his subject was political as much as it was literary: "If we talk politically, we must talk brutally: we must say that a chief reason for the decline of the study of the literature of England is the decline of England. For certainly the bulking power of Engalnd was one of the chief reasons for the study of English literature in America" (p. 346). He had more difficulty, however, in understanding the political origins of his own defense of the study of English literature. Arguments then current held that American studies were more relevant than English literature to the American student's personal experience, and that to ignore that experience was an affront to democratic principles. Trilling mourned this trend away from English literature as "a form of anti-intellectualism" (p. 356). Ultimately for him the trend was also anti-democratic because it would deny future generations of students access to the chief monuments of enlightened, liberal morality and politics: England was "the land that licensed the wonderful multiplicity of Shakespeare, the land of Milton . . . and of Cromwell, the land that would not brook tyranny" (p. 356). The most telling portion of Trilling's argument is worth quoting at length:

> There is no doubt much to be charged against the old curriculum – in its conception and in its teaching there was probably a considerable infusion of mere gentility. And I suppose it has the political disadvantage, in a nation whose ethnic origins are so various, of seeming to suggest that one ethnic group, by reason of our special interest in the culture associated with it, is superior to all others. And of course the secondary school situation is far more complex and difficult than it used to be. Yet the New York high school I attended drew its students chiefly from the sons of immigrant families, and to these boys those genteel teachers of ours taught Burke's Speech on Conciliation, and Hazlitt, Lamb, De Quincey, and Macaulay, and *As You Like It*, *The Merchant of Venice*, *Macbeth*, *Hamlet*, *A Tale of Two Cities*, and a good deal more. They taught with authority – Mr Walter Johnson's lessons on Milton's minor poems are the basis of everything I may now know about poetry – and they would have said that exactly *because* the texts were beyond the experience of the boys it was necessary for the boys to master them. I look back at the experience as being of the very essence of democracy. (Trilling, 1958, 356–7)

One cannot help but wonder what interpretation of *The Merchant of Venice* Mr Walter Johnson would have taught "with authority" to the children of Jewish and Italian immigrants in a New York high school in 1920.[10] To me what is so extraordinary about the passage just quoted is that in its measured, reasonable way it describes a crucial moment in the history of an intellectual generation and manages to reveal most about that generation by what it conceals. The rhetorical mastery of tone and turn of phrase prompts trust in the judiciousness of the author's account. And yet suspended in the balance of judgement here are two attitudes, submission and defiance, attitudes that any immigrant son of a non-English father must have had to contain within himself if he wished to be recognized as a man of culture in the United States. The means of that containment was the mastery of the Arnoldian rhetoric.

The morality of the Arnoldian tradition and the metaphysics that regulated the New Critics' notions about language and method have been undermined from a variety of theoretical standpoints over the past twenty years. But we need to ask ourselves what changes in the society and in the political organization of the profession of English in the United States may have motivated this repudiation in theory. Ohmann recalls "that as I came to graduate school in 1952, those leaving Harvard with Ph.D's counted $3,000 a good salary. Professors were poor; I thought of entering the profession as tantamount to taking vows of poverty" (1976, 80). He goes on to discuss the demographic and political reasons for the improved fortunes of academics in the ensuing years: "universities, recall, became an instrument in the cold war – the battle for men's minds" (p. 81).

By the time I entered graduate school, toward the end of the boom period of the 1960s, those who contemplated a career in the profession of English could have greater expectations. We certainly did not think of ourselves as taking vows of poverty in order to pursue the life of the mind. Doubtless we might have made more money in some sector of the business world. But we were willing to sacrifice income for time, and for an environment that would stimulate our intellectual faculties – that is, as long as there was sufficient income to ensure a reasonably comfortable middle-class existence. We counted on eventually, if not immediately, having all that people of taste ought to have and what we saw our senior colleagues already possessing: a nice home, good food, good wine, the edifying benefits of travel to the world's cultural centers. The last of these "perqs" would be facilitated by the round of international conferences that became a staple of the academic profession in the 1960s and that is by now sufficiently institutionalized to warrant caricature in David Lodge's best-selling prose. Generationally we constituted a group of students and younger faculty of predominantly middle-class origin who assumed, albeit naively, that sharing power was our birthright. We had been brought up under a reigning individualist ideology which was no longer in pace with the developing corporate structure of the American economy and its social consequences. Undaunted by this discrepancy, we set out to determine our own destinies professionally. Moreover, although not all of us were political activists in the campus struggles of the 1960s, in many instances we also imagined ourselves to be setting the nation on a new social and political course. If such assumptions governed the behavior of many students at elite university campuses in the 1960s, we can perhaps understand why political protest was sometimes more militant at such institutions than at campuses which served mainly minority, working-class, or lower-middle class students.[11] But regardless of the political stances we may have taken as students, the presumption of an entitlement to share in institutional power touched most of us who moved on into the ranks of the academic profession.

One expression of this presumption is the confidence with which scholars of this generation have been engaged, since the early 1970s, in dismantling cultural axioms that remained relatively stable over more than a century. For the past ten years we have been in a professional environment characterized by ever more sophisticated debunking of an earlier cultural tradition. Feminists, neo-Marxists, neo-Freudians, Foucauldians contest the ontological, moral, and ideological basis of that tradition. Deconstructionists and pragmatists undermine its epistemological basis, to which they claim the other modes of radical critique are still hopelessly bound. But the content of much of this critical debate (by which I mean something more like its *motive*) often remains obscure. Theoretical models are, of course, partly at issue. Controversy appears to be an effect of competing theoretical orientations, each claiming to produce a more radical break with past convention than the others. There are also those who have taken it as their main objective to debunk theory itself. They include not only traditional scholars who wish to protect established spheres of influence, nor those who are merely intimidated by the discipline that most theoretical discourses demand, but also some critics who have a thorough grasp of the issues that have been central in the past decade of theoretical discussion and debate. Among the last one would count that strain in poststructuralist thought that views any hermeneutic as repressive because it must inevitably arrest the freeplay of the signifier. And there are those contributors to the current revival in American pragmatism who would demolish theory once and for all by exposing it as a self-contradictory attempt to separate knowledge from belief.[12] Yet I suspect that critics who are sophisticated enough to use theory against itself must also be aware that when discourse fails to account for its own authority, its power can rest only on privilege. Such privilege depends on institutional license which immediately renders problematic the claim that literary interpretation – regardless of whether the critic is a theorist, is naively unaware of his own theoretical premises, or is cleverly engaged in demolishing theory by exposing its internal contradictions – can ever be apolitical.

I have been arguing that an important determining factor of the theoretical controversy that has characterized recent literary critical discourse was the audacity of the politics of the 1960s. Elsewhere, I have argued that in the 1970s even the most conservative forms of poststructuralist theory in the US had their roots in an oppositional European politics (Wayne, 1980). For middle-class intellectuals confronted with the specter of institutional control through either corporate or state management of production, this audacity is the expression of a presumptive title to power in one form or another. Most traditional fields of scholarship have been indelibly marked by the assertiveness of the generation of the 1960s. In the case of Renaissance studies in the US, the major impact, in addition to feminist criticism, has come from the diverse corpus of scholarship and criticism alluded to by the phrase ''new historicism.'' Shakespeare's plays and other canonical literary works of the period are no longer being treated as unique and privileged artifacts that fit the vision of literary history as a pageant of timeless monuments to an indomitable human spirit. These texts are now being studied in relation to a broader range of representational strategies of legitimation or contestation in Elizabethan and Jacobean culture. In such criticism the figure of *Power* has displaced that of the *Idea* which was the essential constituent of Renaissance scholarship in Tillyard's generation.

But to what degree is this encroachment the forecast of an ideological shift within our own culture? There has been a noticeable lag between our ability to recognize the role of power in the plays and poems of Shakespeare and his contemporaries, and our ability to articulate the forms that power takes in our own historical moment. However distant we may imagine ourselves to be from the humanist doctrines of those who interpreted and taught Shakespeare in the 1950s, we still tend to efface the factors in our respective genealogies and in our immediate social life that motivate the representations we construct of Shakespeare's time. From this perspective, the condition of the male academic literary critic in the United States is dismaying in its continuity, characterized as it has been for more than thirty years by an institutionally enforced alienation from the actual conditions that lead him to produce scholarship in one or another mode of critical discourse. This is one reason why the peevishness of critical debate in literary studies today can sometimes seem absurdly out of proportion to what is finally at stake.

3

In Britain, a new *political* Shakespeare is the product of oppositional practices that involve a sense of subjectivity construed primarily in terms of class and gender, though certainly cultural and ethnic differences have begun to play an increasing role.[13] Here in the States, however, the sheer complexity of cultural differentiation and the fact that in terms of ancestry many of us have, at most, an indirect connection with English culture, complicate further the matter of how we appropriate or are appropriated by the Shakespearean text. On this side of the Atlantic, recent efforts to reconstruct that text have included a politics of gender and sexuality. But, for the most part, issues of class and the history of successive waves of immigrant culture have not yet been factored into the way in which we theorize our own current readings of the Shakespearean text.

The project of the new historicism is, it seems to me, an important first stage in identifying our particular, historically and culturally specific relation to the Shakespearean text. It may be precisely because our cultural links to that text are not so direct as the UK critics' are that we are able to maintain a certain distance from it, to objectify it and the historical conditions of its production. But it is one thing to say that we are in a better position than British critics to distantiate ourselves from the national mythology for which Shakespeare is the central figure, and quite another to believe and behave as though we stand at a distance from our own culture, its politics and its myths. In America up to now we have maintained a certain decorum in our reconstruction of the Shakespearean text and its context. Our polemics are exceedingly polite – and perhaps this essay is no exception. By means of this decorum that is rooted in the American critical tradition of dispassionate "close reading," power is displaced; so that while we are becoming expert at analyzing the mechanisms of power in Tudor and Stuart England, we have been either unable or reluctant to focus on the manner and degree to which power operates in the political and social order within which our present critical discourse is institutionalized. If we think that our concern with power in the Renaissance constitutes in itself a disruption of a dominant ideology in our culture, then I suggest we consider what is happening concurrently in the nation's business schools. A recent Associated Press report on this subject quotes a professor at the oldest and one of the most prestigious of these schools. He says: "Power is like sex 15 years ago – it *was* a dirty word. It wasn't nice to think of power. You were better off to talk of motivation." At this professor's institution today, the most popular course in the business curriculum and the most popular course in the school's history is entitled "Executive Power and Negotiation" (Associated Press, 1985). A question we may wish to ask ourselves as new historicists is what may be the relationship between this revision in the business and marketing curriculum and the changes we have managed to produce thus far in the reading and the teaching of the Shakespearean text. It would be naive of us to imagine that the unmasking of power in the public sphere would not touch the more traditional disciplines in the nation's universities. So rather than applaud ourselves for being superior to earlier generations of Shakespeare scholars in our ability to elucidate the play of power in Elizabethan and Jacobean society, perhaps we ought to examine the conditions in our own discipline that may be part of the general unmasking of power in our time.

In the field of English, as in the academic world generally, there appear to be two facets to what I've been calling the unmasking of power. First, there is the critical, demythologizing, or demystifying activity which began in the late 1960s and which, however excessive and self-indulgent at times, produced irrevocable changes that made the culture and the society in certain respects more open than in the past (these benefits accrued mainly in the form of a cautious opening of professional ranks to women and minorities). Second, there is the outright display of power that is so oppressive in an era of expanding corporate control over the quality of people's lives, the era of the Reagan/Rambo styles of adventurism in American foreign policy, of programmatic efforts by some elected officials and fundamentalist preachers to reverse the gains of the civil-rights and feminist movements, and of the reliance by conservative ideologues in the field of education on a blatant theme of containment and repression in their calls for curricular "reform."

These may appear to be antithetical tendencies, the one aimed primarily at disclosing power, the other at displaying it. But I suspect they are related as antinomies of the same general phenomenon in American society at the present time. If, in our work as scholars, we fail to examine how our focus on power in history is related to power (including our own, however limited, institutional power) in the present, then we run the risk of seeing the opposition between these two kinds of unmasking collapse into what will be merely two aspects of a fascination with the same imposing spectacle. As intellectuals our subjectivity will be constituted through an identification with what that spectacle displays; and our respective, individual forms of narcissism will then merely reflect and be reflected by the imperturbable façade of the dominant culture and its powerful institutions.

4

Implicit in what I have said above is the assumption that as new historicists we must be held more accountable to the demand that we reflect on our own ideology than adherents to earlier movements, whether formalist or historicist, in the history of Renaissance studies. I want to conclude by explaining my rationale for this imperative. Because we place the issues of ideology and power in the forefront of our descriptive and narrative accounts of Renaissance culture, those of us who are identified as new historicists have a special responsibility to articulate the relationship between our constructions of the past and our present situation. To put it another way, questions concerning the relationship between power in the past and power in the present are necessary rather than incidental to the task of theorizing the critical practice that we call the new historicism.

The responsibility here is a logical, if not ethical, consequence of our discourse. I am aware of the fact that within the new historicism there are strains of the poststructuralist critique of notions of the subject on which a term like "responsibility" conventionally rests. What distinguishes the "new" historicism from the "old" is not so much a difference in how the object of historical investigation is approached as a difference in the way these critics construe the nature of the cultural object itself. This entails a different conception as well of the subject in history, exemplified most emphatically in a tendency to undermine the privileged status of the author and of the canonical literary text in the study of culture. New historicists stress the intertextuality of various types of discourse and of ritualized practices in a given social and cultural context. Thus, in varying degrees the new historicists diverge from the assumptions of an earlier humanist tradition regarding the role of consciousness and intention in the production of such cultural artifacts as plays and poems. Sources for this divergence vary. Some rely on the work of symbolic anthropologists, most notably Clifford Geertz. Others depend primarily on the writing of French theorists such as Lacan, Althusser, Bourdieu, Derrida, and Foucault. For the most part, such theory is used to place in the foreground of historical study the categories of desire, power, or ideology. From an epistemological standpoint, it is perhaps true that the most radical forms of poststructuralist theory can be employed to deny the very notion of a subject and therefore the possibility of either self-reflexivity or agency. But even for such skeptics, metacommentary remains a privileged activity. And so long as one continues to engage in this metadiscursive practice, regardless of whether one imagines oneself to do so as a "self-conscious subject," it seems to me that the demand for internal consistency holds. Especially in instances where discourse is studied primarily in terms of power relations, an adequate metatheory will have to include an account of the theorist's own relationship to the production of discourse, hence to the production or reproduction of power.

If we fail to acknowledge this logic inherent in our shift of focus from ideas to figures of power and authority as the constituents of cultural history, then we run the risk of aestheticizing power in a new formalism that traces relationships among historical documents of various kinds. Such intertextual relations in a given historical moment will then operate in our criticism in the way that generic categories, narrative functions, and stylistic devices did formerly. Another danger is that we will misconstrue the manner and degree to which by making power the province of our historical investigations we have gained access to power in our own society. The new historicism may not yet constitute the main force in American Renaissance studies; but it has gained a sufficient foothold in Shakespeare criticism to render its chief practitioners authorities on an international scale. The fact that there may be less demand for preprofessional study in English literature than in more technical fields should not blind us to the potential impact that scholars in the humanities – especially in the central field of Shakespearean studies – continue to have on American culture. In the era of corporate capitalism that culture has become steadily more technocratic. But those who administer it have yet formally to renounce their nostalgic attachment to the Arnoldian ideals. As long as this remains the case, academics who work in the humanities can hardly claim to be powerless or even marginal with respect to the dominant culture. There will continue to be a social space and an ideological function for an elite interpretive community that debates and adjudicates the cultures of the past. New historicists must recognize that as our influence increases within that interpretive community any claims to being powerless or marginal will be proportionally more disingenuous.

The aestheticizing of power in the past and the disavowal of our power in the present are potential obstacles to the new historicism's effort to define itself as engaged in a revisionary, if not a radical, critique of traditional Renaissance scholarship. If these dangers are imminent or, perhaps, already evident, in our work, then they are to some degree inevitable, given the social organization of our discipline. Certainly there are facets to the disciplinary structure of academic life today that bear comparison with the system of clientage that obtained at court and even touched the theatrical companies in Elizabethan and Jacobean England.[14] It may be that our fascination with power in Shakespeare's society is a specular means by which we negotiate power relations in our own specific social context. The field of Renaissance studies, perhaps the field of English literature generally, has long been infused with a residual form of that "aristocratic romanticism" which Norbert Elias identifies "in particular elevated classes, especially in their elites, whose own claims to power are essentially unfulfilled despite their high position, and cannot be fulfilled without destroying the regime which guarantees their high position'' (Elias, 1983, 222). Beginning with the courticized nobility of seventeenth-century France, Elias cites several historical instances of this type of romanticism. Among such elites, ambivalence toward the existing social order can take the form of an idealization of declining or already defunct social formations; or, "it may find expression in a discontent that is not clearly localized, in the form of a romantic pessimism" (223). Let us hope that the new historicism, as it joins with other forms of theoretical practice in a critique of longstanding humanist doctrines, represents something more than just a shift in Renaissance studies from an idealizing to a pessimistic romanticism.

With the language of power now fashionable in business and government in the US, it is likely that we are moving into an era when literature, to the extent that it survives as an important component of our culture and of our school curriculum, will be a field of more open ideological conflict and debate. Those who defend the status quo will no longer be able to do so in the area of culture by appealing to an uncontested set of moral ideals and formal values. The interpretive power of recent critical practices such as the new historicism will not be overcome by a stolid adherence to older intellectual traditions. But in order to accomplish more than just the disestablishment of an existing critical orthodoxy, new historicists will have to provide a positive alternative to the tired rhetoric of liberal humanism. Such a positive appropriation of the Shakespearean text and its contexts will occur only when the historicizing project is committed to a politics that is not just restricted to the field of Renaissance studies, or, for that matter, of American academia as a whole. Such an appropriation of the past – in a sense of the German *Aneignung*, or "making things one's own" (Weimann, 1983, 466–9) – as part of a conscientious engagement in the present, will help to produce a new culture at the horizon of what we currently term the "post"-modern. That culture cannot be prescribed by any authority, individual or institutional. But at the risk of sounding naive and scandalously optimistic, I shall claim that it will emerge out of a broad range of social practices with which our work as scholars, critics, and teachers intersects. On our part, the task will involve study and criticism not only of Shakespeare and his time, but of our own recent past and, above all, of the conflicts and differences that characterize our own moment in history.[15]

Notes

1. Some preliminary qualifications relating to the rhetoric of this essay:
    (i) Women scholars have been concerned for more than a decade with the task of analyzing and criticizing patriarchal power relationships within cultural institutions past and present. In this essay I touch on the matter of how the current revisionary history of Renaissance culture under the category of power is related to the structuration of power within academia and American society at large. Clearly, I cannot speak for women on this matter, but I would hope that what I have to say is linked to their concerns.
    (ii) What I have to say about ethnicity in connection with the history of Shakespeare

scholarship and criticism in this country is directed to those of my own and earlier generations. I don't presume to speak for ethnic minorities who are currently entering the dominant cultural institutions of American society. But perhaps what follows will be relevant for an understanding of protocols of containment and resistance in cultural and historical contexts other than those specifically addressed here.

(iii) Canadian and Latin American colleagues who read earlier drafts of this paper have called my attention to a problem of nomenclature. I have retained the term ''American'' in places where an adjective was required, but wish to make it clear that in discussing the ideology of recent Shakespeare criticism on this side of the Atlantic I refer to work produced in the United States.

2. It would be difficult to establish a data base from which to attempt a comparable study in the United States, given the fact that we do not have national or regional boards that regulate syllabuses and examinations. This notwithstanding, there is historical evidence of a national educational policy of cultural discipline with Shakespeare at its center. For a brief but useful account see S.J. Brown (1978).

3. Research on the history of subjectivity – provoked in part by Foucauldian and Derridean critiques of the notion of the sovereign author – is leading some textual scholars to problematize received notions of how the works of Shakespeare were composed. See Orgel (1981) and two papers from the 1985 MLA Shakespeare Division meeting on ''New Views of the Shakespearean Text'': Goldberg (1986) and Trousdale (1986).

4. An early call for a criticism that would measure the distance between the social conditions that produced the Shakespearean plays and the conditions in which those plays are performed and studied today was the volume *Shakespeare in a Changing World* (Kettle, 1964). The collection represents an interesting transitional moment in modern Shakespeare scholarship. While Kettle's introduction and some of the essays persist in idealizing Shakespeare and in sentimentalizing popular audiences, there is already evident here a commitment to a more critical historicism than that of Tillyard, most notably in Robert Weimann's ''The Soul of the Age: Towards a Historical Approach to Shakespeare'' (Weimann, 1964).

5. For background and bibliography on both movements, see Dollimore (1985) and Howard (1986). If I appear to address my more critical remarks primarily to the Americans, it is only because I believe I have a better grasp of the history and the politics of literary studies in the US than in Britain. My own work has been identified in several places with the new historicism. Since I see no reason to eschew the tag, I have adopted the first-person-plural pronoun and a rhetoric of autocritique in pointing to discernible limits in the movement's capacity, as yet, to historicize and to criticize its own discourse.

6. *Political Shakespeare* includes two exemplary instances of the kind of historical criticism being produced in the United States today: Greenblatt (1985) and Tennenhouse (1985).

7. In defending the poetics of the New Criticism, Murray Krieger distinguished his ''objectivist'' position from historical and cultural relativism, on the one hand, and from an aesthetic absolutism based on purely intuited value, on the other (1956, 156–7). Retrospectively, it is possible to identify an ideological motive for this refutation, in 1956, of both relativism and absolutism by means of an objectivist theory of the structural unity of the object and the integrity of the poetic experience in the subject. The objectivist could thereby preempt exclusionary aesthetics based either on the principle that English literature is comprehensible only in terms of the culture by and for which it was produced (historical relativism), or on the more overtly elitist principles of taste and breeding (absolutism).

8. From this historical vantage point it is possible to comprehend why groups as far apart ideologically as the New Critics and the New York intellectuals connected with

Partisan Review could share a common cultural mission. In his autobiography, Irving Howe acknowledges this relationship: "I came to feel that, clashes of opinion aside, there was something symmetrical in the situations of the writers from Nashville and the writers from New York – both groups semi-outsiders starting to break into the central space of American culture, yet unwilling to succumb to its slackness, its small optimisms" (1982, 181).

9. Thus, in a 1934 book review for *The Nation*, Trilling wrote critically of "the essentially religious culture of unorthodox mysticism which was so strong in England, and America, in the nineteenth century . . . the culture which Matthew Arnold well exemplifies with his 'disinterestedness', his 'best self', his turning from economic reality" (1934, 90).

10. We can, perhaps, get some idea of how *The Merchant of Venice* would have been presented in the classroom in the early 1920s by considering how it was then being played in the theater. During the first two decades of this century several major productions reacted against the Victorian idealization of Shylock which had culminated in Henry Irving's celebrated portrayal of the role. Toby Lelyveld (1961) surveys this shift in interpretation in which Shylock developed from Irving's sentimentalized victim into a more and more repulsive and malevolent stage figure. By the early 1920s, when Trilling would have been in high school, stereotypes of the perverse yet pathetic Jew and the callous, Jew-baiting Venetians dominated the stage. Lelyveld offers a brief sociohistorical explanation for this revision of the portrayal of Shylock in England. Irving had played the role for twenty-five years beginning in 1879, a period during which the Jewish population of London grew from 50,000 to 160,000. In 1905 the Aliens Immigration Act was passed in Britain to limit immigration of East European Jews who sought refuge from Czarist repression: "The Jewish question was about to become acute, and what had been inspiring in 1879 was no longer adequate in 1905" (Lelyveld, 1961, 95).

Lelyveld does not mention the even more staggering immigration figures for New York City where, by 1910, the foreign born constituted 40 per cent of the population, with 341,000 from Italy and 484,000, mostly Jews, from Russia (Taylor, 1972, 194–5). During Trilling's high-school years economic and political factors contributed to increasing antiimmigrant sentiment in the US heartland. Taylor concludes that given "the wave of rural and small-town puritanism which brought about Prohibition, it is safe to say that, in millions of minds, fear and hatred of the city, the foreigner, the Catholic, the Jew, the infidel, the radical, became linked" (p. 251). In this atmosphere, during the 1922–3 theatre season, David Belasco presented New York audiences with a production of *The Merchant of Venice* featuring David Warfield as a Shylock who "had a slight, drooping figure, emaciated hands, a scrawny beard and a long pinched nose" (Lelyveld, 1961, 108). The actors were drenched in an atmosphere of Oriental opulence created by lavish sets which situated the Rialto in the Jewish ghetto. Wanton interpolations in the text exaggerated both the pettiness of Shylock and the cruelty of his Italian tormenters: "When last seen, Shylock is restrained by Gratiano, while a monk raises a crucifix before him. The on-lookers in the courtroom jeered and hooted as he made his exit" (p. 109). In the following year the Immigration Act (1924) established quotas on the basis of national origin and effectively cut back the flow to the US of immigrants from Southern and Eastern Europe.

The other side of Trilling's faith in Shakespeare and English literature as the "essence of democracy" was articulated by Joseph Quincy Adams in an address at the opening of the Folger Library in 1932:

"Fortunately, about the time the forces of immigration became a menace to the preservation of our long-established English civilization, there was initiated throughout the country a system of free and compulsory education for youth. In a spirit of efficiency, that education was made stereotyped in form; and in a spirit of democracy, every child was forced by law to submit to its discipline . . . . In our fixed plan of elementary schooling, [Shakespeare] was made the cornerstone of cultural discipline . . . . Not Homer, nor Dante, nor Goethe, nor Chaucer, nor Spenser, nor even Milton, but Shakespeare was made the chief object of their study and veneration." (Quoted in S.J. Brown, 1978, 231)

The history of what Adams termed a "cultural discipline" continues to unfold. Witness the recent passage of a California ballot measure declaring English the official language of the state – a state in which nearly 20 per cent of the current population has Spanish as its primary language, and in which demographic projections suggest a steady increase in the proportion of Hispanic and Asian immigrants over the next two decades.

11. I am not suggesting that political activism was confined solely to the most elite institutions. The news media tended to give more play to events at Harvard, Columbia, and Berkeley, than at other colleges and universities. It took the killing of students at Jackson State and at Kent State before most of the nation was aware of political protests at those campuses. At the same time, one would expect that those working-class young adults who were not pressed into service in Vietnam and who attended college had as their primary objective the acquisition of technical training that would give them a foothold in the middle class.

12. See Stephen Knapp and Walter Benn Michaels, "Against Theory," and the lively set of responses collected in Mitchell (1985).

13. In addition to the essays from *Political Shakespeare* (Dollimore, 1985) already cited, see P. Brown (1985), McLuskie (1985), and Holderness (1985), as well as the essays collected in Drakakis (1985).

14. It has not been all that long since Renaissance scholars could describe themselves in courtly figures without the slightest embarrassment. In the introduction to a *festschrift* for A.S.P. Woodhouse (MacLure and Watt, 1964), the editors write: "if we could assemble his letters of recommendation . . . we who have been his proteges would appear as heroic figures prepared to dare the provincial philistines, if not in 'the armour of a Christian man' (though that too in some cases, we suspect), at least in the humanist equipment which he and his trusted colleagues had done their best to provide" (p. vii). The phallocentric and patrilineal nature of academic patron–client relations is the subtext of Page duBois's powerful study of *Coriolanus* (DuBois, 1985).

15. Thanks are due to the following: to Stephen Orgel for inviting me to present the first version of this essay in the Shakespeare Division meeting over which he presided at the 1985 MLA Convention in Chicago; to Nancy Armstrong, Carlos Blanco, Michael Davidson, George Mariscal, and William Tay who read and commented on the manuscript at various stages of research and writing; to Richard Helgerson for permitting me to read the manuscript of his review of *Political Shakespeare*; and to the members of the seminar organized by Jean E. Howard and Marion F. O'Connor on "Shakespeare and Ideology" at the 1986 World Shakespeare Congress in Berlin for a stimulating week of discussion that provoked me to revise certain points and to elaborate on others.

Works cited

Arnold, Matthew (1869) *Culture and Anarchy*, ed. J. Dover Wilson (1961), Cambridge, Cambridge University Press.

Associated Press (1985) "'Power' is no longer a four-letter word," *San Diego Union*, 15 September, AA-1.

Brown, Paul (1985) " 'This thing of darkness I acknowledge mine': *The Tempest* and the Discourse of Colonialism," in Dollimore, Jonathan and Sinfield, Alan (eds) *Political Shakespeare: New Essays in Cultural Materialism*, Manchester, Manchester University Press; Ithaca, NY, Cornell University Press, 48–71.

Brown, Stephen J. (1978) "The Uses of Shakespeare in America: A Study in Class Domination," in Bevington, David and Halio, Jay L. (eds) *Shakespeare: Pattern of Excelling Nature*, papers from the World Shakespeare Congress, Washington, DC, 1976, Newark, University of Delaware Press; London, Associated University Presses, 230–8.

Dollimore, Jonathan (1985) "Introduction: Shakespeare, Cultural Materialism and the New Historicism," in Dollimore, Jonathan and Sinfield, Alan (eds) *Political Shakespeare: New Essays in Cultural Materialism*, Manchester, Manchester University Press; Ithaca, NY, Cornell University Press, 2–17.

Dollimore, Jonathan and Sinfield, Alan (eds) (1985) *Political Shakespeare: New Essays in Cultural Materialism*, Manchester, Manchester University Press; Ithaca, NY, Cornell University Press.

Drakakis, John (ed.) (1985) *Alternative Shakespeares*, London and New York, Methuen.

DuBois, Page (1985) "A Disturbance of Syntax at the Gates of Rome," *Stanford Literature Review*, Fall, 185–208.

Elias, Norbert (1983) *The Court Society*, trans. Edmund Jephcott, Oxford, Basil Blackwell.

Friedrich, Otto (1985) " 'Shall I die? Shall I fly . . .'," *Time*, 9 December, p. 76.

Goldberg, Jonathan (1986) "Textual Properties," *Shakespeare Quarterly*, 37 (2), 213–17.

Greenblatt, Stephen (1985) "Invisible Bullets: Renaissance Authority and its Subversion, *Henry IV* and *Henry V*," in Dollimore, Jonathan and Sinfield, Alan (eds) *Political Shakespeare: New Essays in Cultural Materialism*, Manchester, Manchester University Press; Ithaca, NY, Cornell University Press, 18–47.

Heinemann, Margot (1985) "How Brecht Read Shakespeare," in Dollimore, Jonathan and Sinfield, Alan (eds) *Political Shakespeare: New Essays in Cultural Materialism*, Manchester, Manchester University Press; Ithaca, NY, Cornell University Press, 202–30.

Holderness, Graham (1985) "Radical Potentiality and Institutional Closure: Shakespeare in Film and Television," in Dollimore, Jonathan and Sinfield, Alan (eds) *Political Shakespeare: New Essays in Cultural Materialism*, Manchester, Manchester University Press; Ithaca, NY, Cornell University Press, 182–201.

Howard, Jean E. (1986) "The New Historicism in Renaissance Studies," *English Literary Renaissance*, 16 (1), 13–43.

Howe, Irving (1982) *A Margin of Hope: An Intellectual Autobiography*, San Diego and New York, Harcourt Brace Jovanovich.

Kettle, Arnold (ed.) (1964) *Shakespeare in a Changing World*, London, Lawrence & Wishart.

Krieger, Murray (1956) *The New Apologists for Poetry*, Minneapolis, University of Minnesota Press.

Lelyveld, Toby (1961) *Shylock on the Stage*, London, Routledge & Kegan Paul.

MacLure, Millar and Watt, F.W. (eds) (1964) *Essays in English Literature from the Renaissance to the Victorian Age, Presented to A.S.P. Woodhouse*, Toronto, University of Toronto Press.

McLuskie, Kathleen (1985) "The Patriarchal Bard: Feminist Criticism and Shakespeare: *King Lear* and *Measure for Measure*," in Dollimore, Jonathan and Sinfield, Alan (eds) *Political Shakespeare: New Essays in Cultural Materialism*, Manchester, Manchester University Press; Ithaca, NY, Cornell University Press, 88–108.

Mitchell, W.J.T. (ed.) (1985) *Against Theory: Literary Studies and the New Pragmatism* (a collection of essays which originally appeared in *Critical Inquiry* from 1982 to

1985), Chicago, University of Chicago Press.

Ohmann, Richard (1976) *English in America: A Radical View of the Profession*, New York, Oxford University Press.

Orgel, Stephen (1981) "What is a Text?" *Research Opportunities in Renaissance Drama*, 24, 3–6.

Reese, M.M. (1985) " 'Tis My Picture; Refuse It Not'," *Shakespeare Quarterly*, 36 (2), 254–6.

Sinfield, Alan (1985a) "Give an account of Shakespeare and Education, showing why you think they are effective and what you have appreciated about them. Support your comments with precise references," in Dollimore, Jonathan and Sinfield, Alan (eds) *Political Shakespeare: New Essays in Cultural Materialism*, Manchester, Manchester University Press; Ithaca, NY, Cornell University Press, 134–57.

—— (1985b) "Royal Shakespeare: Theatre and the Making of Ideology," in Dollimore, Jonathan and Sinfield, Alan (eds) *Political Shakespeare: New Essays in Cultural Materialism*, Manchester, Manchester University Press; Ithaca, NY, Cornell University Press, 158–81.

Taylor, Philip (1972) *The Distant Magnet: European Emigration to the U.S.A.*, New York, Harper Torchbooks.

Tennenhouse, Leonard (1985) "Strategies of State and Political Plays: *A Midsummer Night's Dream, Henry IV, Henry V, Henry VIII*," in Dollimore, Jonathan and Sinfield, Alan (eds) *Political Shakespeare: New Essays in Cultural Materialism*, Manchester, Manchester University Press; Ithaca, NY, Cornell University Press.

Trilling, Lionel (1934) "Politics and the Liberal," review of *Goldsworthy Lowes Dickinson* by E.M. Forster, *The Nation*, 4 July, repr. in Trilling, Lionel, *Speaking of Literature and Society*, ed. Diana Trilling (1980), New York, Harcourt Brace Jovanovich, 89–91.

—— (1958) "Reflections on a Lost Cause: English Literature and American Education," *Encounter*, September, repr. in Trilling, Lionel, *Speaking of Literature and Society*, ed. Diana Trilling (1980), New York, Harcourt Brace Jovanovich, 343–60.

—— (1965) "The Two Environments: Reflections on the Study of English," in Trilling, Lionel, *Beyond Culture: Essays on Literature and Learning*, New York, Viking Press, 209–33.

Trousdale, Marion (1986) "A Trip Through the Divided Kingdoms," *Shakespeare Quarterly*, 37 (2), 218–23.

Wayne, Don E. (1980) "*Gnosis* without *Praxis*: On the Dissemination of European Criticism and Theory in the United States," *Helios*, n.s. 7 (2), 1–26.

Weimann, Robert (1964) "The Soul of the Age: Towards a Historical Approach to Shakespeare," in Kettle, A. (ed.) *Shakespeare in a Changing World*, London, Lawrence & Wishart, 17–42.

—— (1983) " 'Appropriation' and Modern History in Renaissance Prose Narrative," *New Literary History*, 14 (3), 459–95.

Williams, Raymond (1985) "Afterword," in Dollimore, Jonathan and Sinfield, Alan (eds) *Political Shakespeare: New Essays in Cultural Materialism*, Manchester, Manchester University Press; Ithaca, NY, Cornell University Press, 231–9.

3

Theatre of the Empire: "Shakespeare's England" at Earl's Court, 1912

Marion F. O'Connor

The year 1897 marked Queen Victoria's Diamond Jubilee. On Monday 21 June, the eve of the state procession and public thanksgiving to mark sixty years of her reign, a banquet was held at Buckingham Palace. For the first time since the death of the Prince Consort in 1861, the Queen set aside her widow's weeds and wore, by her own description, 'a dress of which the whole front was embroidered in gold, which had been especially worked in India' (quoted in Lytton, 1961, 110). Ten days later, the Duchess and the Duke of Devonshire, who was Lord President of Victoria's Council, gave a ball at Devonshire House, which surveyed Green Park from a site north of Piccadilly, between Stratton and Berkeley Streets. The guests who arrived at this eminently aristocratic address on the evening of 2 July 1987 were, like the Queen at her Jubilee banquet, very unusually attired: the invitations to the ball had given notice that guests were expected to wear 'allegorical or historical costume before 1815' (Murphy, 1984, 47). While invitations to the ball were sent out only on 31 May (Murphy, 1984, 55), four and a half weeks before the occasion, members of high society had been getting their acts together for a rather longer time. According to one recipient of an invitation,

MARION F. O'CONNOR is Lecturer in English and American Literature at the University of Kent at Canterbury, England, where she also teaches drama and film. She is the author of *William Poel and the Elizabethan Stage Society* (Cambridge, Chadwyck-Healey, 1987).

rarely had the London social world been so stirred as by the fancy-dress ball given at Devonshire House on the 2nd of July, 1897. For weeks, not to say months, before hand it seemed the principal topic of conversation. The absorbing question was what characters our friends and ourselves were going to represent. Everyone of note and interest was there, representing the intellect, beauty, and fashion of the day.

(J.J.S. Churchill, 1908, 301–2)

The writer of the above reminiscence was Lady Randolph Churchill: a representative of the beauty and fashion of the day, she represented the Empress Theodora at the ball. Her teenaged son Jack, dressed up as a Louis-Quinze courtier and seconded by his elder brother, Winston, got his pink silk stockings bloodstained in a duel – impromptu but in earnest – out in the garden with a guest who was dressed as a Crusader knight and armed with a double-edged sword (Martin, 1971 [1972, 91]). Lady Randolph Churchill's sister went to the ball as Brünnhilde, and her future sister-in-law went as the Queen of Sheba, 'surrounded by a retinue in Oriental garb some of whom so far sacrificed their appearance as to darken their faces' (J.J.S. Churchill, 1908, 303). Her host and hostess appeared as the Emperor Charles V (his costume copied from Titian's portrait) and Queen Zenobia (her costume devised by M. Worth of Paris). The 'real' royalty, the Prince and Princess of Wales, dressed down, the one as the Grand Prior of the order of St John of Jerusalem and the other as Marguerite de Valois. There were at least two Napoleons and two Mazarins; and a duchess appeared as Charlotte Corday. There was some division of the guests into courts around five impersonated monarchs (Elizabeth I, Maria Theresa, Guinevere, Marie Antoinette, and Catherine the Great) and into three national/generic groups (orientals, Italians, and allegoricals) (Murphy, 1984, 47–8); but the real power relations among the guests were masked, temporarily fragmented by fictions. For one evening 'polite society' was transformed into an assembly of individual disguises, the wearers 'bowing, curtseying or salaaming, according to the characters they represented' (J.J.S. Churchill, 1908, 302), the power relations frozen into picturesque postures:

A charming Hebe, with an enormous eagle poised on her shoulder and a gold cup in her hand, made a perfect picture, but alas! in one attitude only, which she vainly tried to preserve throughout the entire evening; while the late Hereditary Prince of Saxe-Coburg as the Duke of Normandy . . . in casque and chain armour, kept his visor down until heat and hunger forced him to sacrifice his martial appearance.

(303)

Not surprisingly, the guests experienced and remembered the evening more as fancydress than as ball: the programme of fifteen dances was 'not undertaken with much enthusiasm except by the very young and energetic, for many of the guests were not suitably dressed, especially those in armour and those with long heavy trains' (Murphy, 1984, 160). It was not just that the guests found dancing physically difficult but also that they presented distracting spectacles to each other: 'Few danced, as in a raree-show of that kind people are too much occupied in gazing at each other or in struggling to play up to their assumed parts' (J.J.S. Churchill, 1908, 304). Photographed for a volume which was presented to the Duchess of Devonshire, the costumes were not easily set aside. The following weekend Lady Randolph Churchill was among the guests at the home of the Duchess of Manchester. The Duchess (née Consuelo Iznaga) was, like Lady Randolph Churchill (née Jenny Jerome), an American society beauty whose aristocratic English husband had predeceased her. At her friend's home, Lady Randolph Churchill recalled, 'most of the company were persuaded to don their fancy dress once more, and of course the ball was discussed ad nauseam' (J.J.S. Churchill, 1908, 304).

Both spectators and spectacle in the fancy dress of the Duchess of Devonshire's ball in the summer of 1897, participants in London high society had earlier in the Jubilee Year attended another dress-up occasion more as observers than as the observed. Perhaps their relegation to the sidelines explains why the earlier occasion, graced through it was by the presence of both the Prince of Wales and the Lord Chief Justice, received far less glittering publicity than would the ball. The earlier event was the first of three performances of Shakespeare's *Twelfth Night* which William Poel's Elizabethan Stage Society gave in the hall of the Middle Temple on 10, 11 and 12 February 1897. The Elizabethan Stage Society was a play-producing society, a club that sponsored productions of non-commercial drama. This particular play-producing society had been founded to serve an end which programmes for its earliest productions variously defined as 'the principle that Shakespeare should be accorded the build of stage for which he designed his plays' and 'the principle that Shakespeare's plays should be accorded the conditions of playing for which they were designed'.[1] Staging *Twelfth Night* in Middle Temple Hall, the Elizabethan Stage Society had such a build of stage and such conditions of playing immediately at hand, built into the very fabric of their venue. Like the halls of other inns of court, Middle Temple Hall, which dates from the 1560s, exhibits the standard architectural features of a Tudor great hall. At one end, a narrow dais is raised some 6 feet above the floor. Across the other end, a carved wooden screen block draughts from the passage into the kitchens: the screen contains two doors of entrance for servants' access to and from the kitchens, while a gallery above it accommodates musicians. The doors of entrance in the screen and the gallery above have been persuasively shown to have left their marks on early Tudor drama (Southern, 1973, especially 45–55); and a staging plot proves them to have been sufficient unto a performance of *Twelfth Night* (King, 1971, 97–115). It has even been argued that the text of IV. ii, the scene of Malvolio's imprisonment, alludes to the architecture of Middle Temple Hall and that consequently it must have been written for performance there (Akrigg, 1958). It is at least virtually certain that *Twelfth Night* was, very early in its stage history, performed in Middle Temple Hall. A famous passage in the diary ascribed to the Elizabethan law student John Manningham records how in that hall on

Feb[ruar]y 2nd [1602]. At our feast we had a play called Twelfth Night or What You Will, much like the Commedy of Errors or Menechmi in Plautus, but most like and neere to that in Italian called Inganni. A good practise in it to make the Steward beleeve his Lady Widdowe was in love with him by counterfeyting a letter from his Lady in generall terms, telling him what shee liked best in him and prescribing his gesture in smiling his apparaile etc., and then when he came to practise making him beleeve they tooke him to be mad. (Quoted, from J. Bruce Williamson, *The History of the Middle Temple, London* [1924], in King, 1971, 97)

The programme for the 1897 Elizabethan Stage Society performances of *Twelfth Night* in Middle Temple Hall reprinted the diary passage twice over, in manuscript facsimile and in printed transcript. In effect an invocation of the Ghost of Candlemas Past, the programme invited the audience to pretend that time had been reversed and to savour some imaginary aura of place. Having thus conjured up the *genius loci*, the production paid no regard to the physical place itself. Setting aside the principle(s) for which he had founded the Elizabethan Stage Society and ignoring the incomparably appropriate set which was the architecture of Middle Temple Hall, Poel brought into that hall the flagrantly fake Elizabethan stage which he regularly erected on the stages of proscenium theatres for Elizabethan Stage Society productions. This fake Elizabethan stage was known as the 'Fortune fit-up' – the substantive designating the kind of collapsible and adaptable stage used by small Victorian touring companies playing one-night stands in the covered markets, parish halls, etc., of provincial towns and villages too small to have regular theatre buildings. The adjective by which Poel's fit-up was known is so misleading as to invite prosecution under the Trades Descriptions Act: only minor details of its decoration were derived from the 1600 builder's contract for the rectangular Fortune Theatre. Poel's fit-up was a compromise between the amphitheatrical structure shown in the so called DeWitt drawing of the Swan Theatre in 1596 (a document which had resurfaced only in the 1880s) and the dimensions of the Victorian theatre building (the no longer extant Royalty, in Soho's Dean Street) in which the fit-up was first used in 1893 (O'Connor, 1987, 26–32). The Fortune fit-up required a space some 30 feet wide by 24 feet deep by 23 feet high for its assembly; and when knocked down, it was easily stored.[2] It was made of pieces of wood, imitation-tapestry hangings and painted canvas. The conjunction of this tawdry specimen of low-budget late Victorian stagecraft with the mid-Tudor carpentry and joinery of Middle Temple Hall must have been startling. Visual aesthetics aside, a Victorian image of Shakespeare's theatre was superimposed on the Elizabethan architecture which had accommodated Shakespeare's company playing Shakespeare's text; an ersatz Elizabethan structure was erected in a genuine Elizabethan space; and history was at once remade and revisited.

Queen Victoria's Jubilee Year is a useful point of entry into yet another superimposition of extant and manufactured cultural images at the turn of this century. Friday 8 January 1897 brought the first issue of *Country Life*

Illustrated, published in London by Edward Hudson. From that day to this, ninety years later, *Country Life Illustrated* has endured as the principal purveyor of cultural self-images to the British landed gentry — and as the distributor of these same images to the middle classes. *Country Life Illustrated* subtitled itself '*The* Journal for all interested in Country Life and Country pursuits': as represented in its pages, country life and pursuits consist of the sports (especially equestrian ones) associated with the upper classes and the houses owned by those same upper classes. (The people who *worked* the rural land, as distinct from those who managed it and disported themselves on it, are only occasionally to be glimpsed in the pages of *Country Life Illustrated*. Now and then they are reproached for their cooking or romanticized for their courting: of their labour on the land nothing is said or shown, except in times of a shortage of agricultural labour.)[3] Of interest here are the images which *Country Life Illustrated* gave currency through its publication of photographs of country houses – at first, mainly of their exteriors and gardens, but later, soon after the turn of the century, of their interiors. There was at the time some vogue for trying to make photographs look as if they were paintings (Arts Council, 1978). Not so arty as that, Charles Latham, who established the house photographic style of *Country Life Illustrated*, did record the interior fall of light very much in the manner of seventeenth-century Dutch genre painting.[4] The effect of Latham's photographs of the interiors of English country houses is of visual closure – complete and perfect images, out of historical time and in mythical space, of Englishness and domesticity.

From 1900 the buildings on which Latham and his colleagues regularly turned their cameras were often wholly or partly the work of Edwin Landseer Lutyens (1869–1944), whose decade as the leading architect of the English country house begins in Victoria's Jubilee Year. Lutyens's practice of domestic architecture was so strongly associated with *Country Life Illustrated* that he has been called 'house architect to *Country Life*' (Gradidge, 1981, 39). Among the links between architect and periodical are: (1) the house which Lutyens built in 1899 for Edward Hudson at Sonning-on-Thames, near Reading, and his subsequent conversion of Lindisfarne Castle for the publisher; (2) the *Country Life* office building in Tavistock Street, Covent Garden, one of only three London office buildings for which Lutyens was sole architect and entirely responsible (Butler, 1950, 25); and (3) Lutyens's alterations to Hudson's London house in 1906 and Lutyens's removal of himself, his practice, and his household to the building next door in 1910. Meanwhile, *Country Life* publicized Lutyens: some fourteen of his houses were featured in the magazine during the first decade of this century, and it is thanks to the photographers of *Country Life* that many of Lutyens's houses were photographed inside and out soon after their completion.

Lutyens's architectural language was an often playful polyglot, an Esperanto in which visual puns abounded. While this architectural accent is usually distinctive, and recognizable, for its exaggeration of line (especially rooflines) and its baffling of an observer's assumptions and expectations, he did not develop a new architectural idiom. Rather, he reverted to archaic usages, notably Tudor and

then Queen Anne. From the beginning he showed considerable skill at faking
— more politely, at 'the falsification of history to give houses a sense of age that
they did not really possess' (Colin Amery, in Arts Council, 1981, 80). An
excellent example of such falsification is Munstead Wood, built for Gertrude
Jekyll, horticulturalist and heroine of the turn-of-the-century Arts and Crafts
movement, whose subsequent patronage of Lutyens would make this building
a key project in his early career. Jekyll's published account of Munstead Wood
devotes four lyrical paragraphs to the structural oak-timberwork of her house.
She rhapsodized both over the craftsmanship of 'the old country builder', using
'grand old tools' and 'working according to local tradition', and also over

> the actual living interest of knowing where the trees one's house is built of
> really grew. The three great beams, ten inches square, that stretch across the
> ceiling of the sitting-room . . . and bear up a good part of the bedroom space
> above (they are twenty-eight feet long) were growing fifteen years ago a mile
> and a half away, on the outer edge of a fir wood just above a hazel-fringed
> hollow lane. . . . Often driving up the lane from early childhood I used to see
> these great grey trees, in twilight looking almost ghostly against the darkly
> mysterious background of the sombre firs. . . . I am glad to know that my
> beams are these same old friends, and that the pleasure that I had in watching
> them green and growing is not destroyed but only changed as I see them
> stretching above me as grand beams of solid English oak.
> (Gertrude Jekyll, *Home and Garden*, 1901, 3–5, quoted by Gradidge, 1980,
> 117–18)

Where the owner's sight of the hall beams was overlaid with memories of the
trees standing fifteen years earlier, outsiders beheld on them the forged patina
of centuries. A fifteen-minute chemical treatment had served to make the hall
beams appear far older than they were (Margaret Richardson, in Arts Council,
1981, 73)! This was but a detail, albeit a conspicuous and telling one, in an ensemble of 'age effects' at Munstead Wood. Another architect wrote of the place:

> It looks so reasonable, so kindly, so perfectly beautiful, that you feel that
> people might have been making love, and living and dying there and dear little
> children running about for – the last – I was going to say 1000 years – anyway
> 600. They've used *old* tiles which of course helps – but the proportion, the
> way the thing's built – (very low coursed rubble with thick joints, and no
> corners) – in fact it has been built 'by the old people of the old materials in
> the old unhurrying way' but at the same time 'sweet to all modern uses' . . .
> and who do you think did this for her – a young chap called Lutyens, 27 he
> is – and I've always heard him derided . . . as a 'society' architect . . . what
> a Gods mercy that for once in a way these people have got hold of the right
> man and what a thing for England.
> (Robert Lorimer to R.S. Dods, 22 November 1897, quoted, from Peter
> Savage, *Lorimer and the Edinburgh Craft Designers*, 1980, by Margaret
> Richardson, in Arts Council, 1981, 74)

Not surprisingly, some of Lutyens's most characteristic works were homogeneous alterations and appendages to centuries-old buildings. At Great Dixter in Sussex, for example, he pieced together two fifteenth-century buildings (one already on site and the other transported cross-country to it) and added a new wing.

Lutyens is now recognized for his attention to the flow of domestic traffic and hailed as 'a master of spatial planning' (Colin Amery, in Arts Council, 1981, 80). In his professional prime he was in high reputation for craftsmanship, for consideration of locally available building materials, and for use of local motifs. His attention to parochial particulars was publicized as something like a patriotic practice, an exemplar of Englishness. Referring to the designs for inlaid panels in the hall of Marshcourt, for example, the author of a feature article in *Country Life* noted 'that Mr Lutyens had taken a particular interest in working into his designs the plants and flowers of the neighbourhood', and cited this interest as evidence of 'the entirely national character of his work' (Phillips, 1906, 314). As for the part, so – in the opinion of the *Country Life* feature writer – for the whole of Marshcourt.

> The spirit of the whole is the spirit of English sixteenth-century work, of Tudor, that is to say, and Elizabethan. . . . Architecture is essentially a national art; and though a certain refinement may be learnt by independent thought and foreign study, yet the main structural forms and features must, if the art is to retain, or regain, strength and simplicity, be of native growth and origins. Hence I lay stress on the thoroughly English character of Mr. Lutyens' work. . . . It looks a genuine bit of England, and as I left it I could easily imagine its walls hallowed already by associates of romance and senti-ment such as cling to old English houses.
>
> (Phillips, 1906, 310–12, 317)

Marshcourt was built, near Stockbridge in Hampshire, for a man who has been described as an 'adventurer, stockjobber and sportsman' (Christopher Hussey, quoted by Amery, in Arts Council, 1981, 106). Having bought himself what 'look[ed] a genuine bit of England' in which to live, the client made himself look a genuine bit of English landed gentry. The falsification of history executed in Lutyens's domestic architecture was not simply a falsification of the quantifiable age of the buildings he built. It was also a falsification of the rela-tionship of his clients to the land on which they built and of their hereditary status in English society. The clients for whom Lutyens built houses, mansions, even castles (Castle Drogo in Devonshire, for a successful grocer) were, in the phrase of a practising architect turned architectural historian, 'second generation *nouveau riche*' (Gradidge, 1980, 114). Romantic and sentimental associations of place did not just cling to the walls which Lutyens erected but also accrued to the owners of those walls.

It was not only by designing and altering private residences for wealthy individuals that Lutyens cast the image of the well-appointed English household. He was also directly and personally responsible for the image of English domesticity which the 390 million visitors to the Paris Exhibition of 1900 took away from the British pavilion in the rue des Nations. This pavilion was a full-scale replica of an early-seventeenth-century manor house, Kingston House in Bradford-on-Avon. Praising both the Royal Commission's selection of this building to represent British architecture and also Lutyens's construction, the reporter for *Country Life* pronounced: 'It would have been difficult to find any type more appropriate . . . in the whole of the exhibition there is nothing to surpass it, for there is nothing more charming. . . . It is . . . as remarkable for its solidity, as for the wealth, the richness and the artistic merit' (Spielmann, 1900, 488). It would also, of course, have been difficult to find any type less representative of the real buildings and actual conditions which the majority of the British population called 'home' in the penultimate year of Queen Victoria's reign. Moreover, the visitor to the 1900 Paris reconstruction of Kingston House passed from the fake Cotswold stone of its exterior face into an exhibit of architectural bricolage, every bit of it forged:

> The interiors were reproductions of various historical examples. The drawing-room, for instance, had a ceiling taken from the famous example at Broughton Castle, and the moulds for it were provided by the Victoria and Albert Museum. The chimney-piece was reproduced from the Cartoon Gallery at Knole Park.
>
> (Weaver, 1913, 308)

Of the same imaginary order as the reconstruction of Kingston House in Paris was the scenery which Lutyens designed for the première productions, both in London's West End, of two plays by his friend J.M. Barrie – *Quality Street* at the Vaudeville Theatre in 1902 and *Peter Pan* at the Duke of York's Theatre in 1904. Barrie's requirements for the principal set in *Quality Street* would have made it an interesting first exercise in stage design. Of greater interest to the observer of cultural images, however, is Lutyens's interior set for *Peter Pan*. According to the youngest of Lutyens's five children, 'It was through our night-nursery window at Bloomsbury Square that the Darling children flew to the Never Land' (Lutyens, 1980, 66). In 1904 the Lutyens children, like the Darling children, numbered three. Their night nursery and their day nursery were at the front of the top floor of the house. Lutyens's stage design for the Darling children's night nursery reproduced from the Lutyens children's night nursery even such a detail as the pair of painted wooden soldiers that stood by the fireguard (Mary Lutyens, in Arts Council, 1981, 137). The stage design, however, gave no hint that on the same floor as the two nurseries for three children and their nanny there was a single small room for three maids – nor even of the existence of those maids, one of whom was the nurserymaid. Erased from the *Peter Pan* image, the three maids and the Lutyens children's nanny were replaced by the dog Nana, a Lutyens invention.

* *

Ruling-class dress-ups; antiquarian adjustments to modern and physical facts;

charming images comprised of forgeries and erasures: these are the antecedents and elements of 'Shakespeare's England' – an exhibition, largely designed by Lutyens, which was held in London from May to October, 1912. By then, fifteen years after Victoria's Jubilee, Lutyens was transforming himself from architect of English country life to architect of the British Empire. His professional mainstay had been cut by Lloyd George's 1909 budget: the introduction of death duties, the steep increase in income tax, and the proposal of a land tax meant a sharp falling off in orders for country houses (Hussey, 1950, 185), and Lutyens turned to public projects (notably, Hampstead Garden Suburb). One of the public buildings which he planned for an imperial capital city, the new Dublin Municipal Art Gallery which was to have been built on a bridge over the River Liffey, is best known because the municipal authorities turned it down. In so doing they provoked W.B. Yeats to a poem which secured greater fame for the art gallery which Lutyens did not build in Dublin than for the one which he did build in Johannesburg. In 1912, when these two imperial public projects were in progress, Lutyens made his first voyage to India, going there as the architect in the triumvirate which was the New Delhi Planning Commission. In India Lutyens would jockey for architectural dominance and lobby for an emphatically European and aggressively imperial style of architecture, unalloyed by Indian elements such as British architects had used for imperial buildings elsewhere in the subcontinent, notably Bombay. He dismissed these as 'half-caste' ('Sir E. Lutyens's Plans for the New Delhi', *Indian Daily News*, Calcutta, 5 December 1920, quoted in Irving, 1981, 42); and his objection to architectural miscegenation was grounded in no more than the contempt of the master race for the culture it had conquered. 'Personally,' he wrote, 'I do not believe there is *any* real Indian architecture or any great tradition. There are just spurts by various mushroom dynasties with as much intellect as there is in any other *art nouveau*' (quoted by Stamp, in Arts Council, 1981, 37). Securing the commission for the Viceroy's palace, the greatest jewel in the crown, Lutyens did achieve dominance in the building of New Delhi, a project which would occupy him over the next two decades. On the architectural idioms to be used there, however, he had to compromise. While some of Lutyens's professional colleagues shared his determination that the purpose-built capital of India should be made to speak the idiom of western, specifically English, architecture, others argued for an adoption of the local vernacular, or at least some admission of its accents. On this latter side stood the Secretary of State for India, the Marquess of Crewe (see *The Times*, 5 August 1912, 9); the Viceroy, Lord Hardinge of Penshurst, a building deeply implicated in architectural politics (Wayne, 1984); and also Lutyens's wife, née Emily Lytton, who was both the daughter of a previous viceroy and also, in her own right, a theosophist with strong sympathies for Indian nationalism.

In one of the many letters which Lutyens wrote to his wife on his first visit to India, he enquired rather anxiously about the reception of a London project which was also an imperial monument, albeit a less enduring one:

Earl's Court news was so interesting. What did Vic & Pam think. I am afraid that it was full of critisms [sic] holes. Was it?? Was it in any way convincing? . . . Did Vic & Pam like it? I pray goodness for Mrs W's sake that it is a success financially.

(Edwin Lutyens, autograph letter signed to Emily Lutyens, Simla, 26 May 1912)[5]

The 'it's abounding in this quotation refer to the 'Shakespeare's England' exhibition, which had opened in London on 9 May 1912; 'Mrs W' is the organizer of the exhibition, the former Lady Randolph Churchill, renamed Mrs George Cornwallis-West by virtue of her second marriage, in the summer of 1900; and the 'Vic & Pam' whose opinion weighed so heavily with the writer are Lutyens's brother-in-law, Victor, Earl of Lytton, and his Countess, née Pamela Plowden.

The site of 'Shakespeare's England' in 1912 was the Earl's Court exhibition grounds, a triangle bounded on one side by the extension of the West London Railway (which ran from Willesden through Kensington down to Clapham) and on the other sides by the Metropolitan and District underground-railway lines. The exhibitions held on this site, and on its extension, the Western Garden on the far side of the West London Railway, between 1887 and 1914 were part of the cultural legacy of the Great Exhibition. Unlike that occasion at Crystal Palace and Hyde Park in 1851, and unlike its immediate offspring on a succession of sites in South Kensington in 1862, 1871–4, and 1883–6, the exhibitions at Earl's Court were all privately sponsored (Altick, 1978, 507–8). Initially, the Earl's Court exhibition had had national themes. The first, in 1887, was an American exhibition; and for it the organizer, J.R. Whitley, built a large arena, the Empress Theatre, in the Western Gardens as a venue for Colonel Buffalo Bill Cody and his Cowboys and Indians show. Whitley's American exhibition at Earl's Court had four sequels in as many years, again defined on national themes and again centered on shows in the Empress Theatre. The shows enacted myths of alien beings:

Next year [1888], for the Italian exhibition the arena became the Colosseum (its dimensions incidentally happening to be identical with those of the original in Rome) in which the gladiators were butchered to make a London Holiday; for the French exhibition [1890] it was transformed into the 'Wild East', with an Algerian village as its setting; and for the German exhibition [1891] it became 'Germania', in which was displayed the story of German militarism from the days of the Romans.

(Luckhurst, 1951, 170, supplemented by Ardagh, 1935)

Prominent among Whitley's successors was Imre Kiralfy, author and entrepreneur, who was responsible both for at least fifteen exhibitions between 1896 and 1914, and for the building of the White City exhibition grounds, further west in suburban London, in 1908:

Thus Whitley's . . . national exhibitions set a new fashion, and many other popular and unofficial exhibitions, organized on a purely commercial basis, were held during the next twenty years. . . . Some of them were national in type, like Whitley's, and others dealt with special subjects . . . but all of them made a strong point of spectacles and pageants.

(Luckhurst, 1951, 170)

Like its predecessors on the Earl's Court site, then, the 'Shakespeare's England' exhibition was a private, commercial venture. Mrs Cornwallis-West formed a limited company and secured guarantees amounting, according to her husband, to £35,000 from the bankers Cox & Co., and £15,000 from a wealthy American widow who was a friend of his (Cornwallis-West, 1930, 163–4). In the up-market press especially, the 1912 exhibition at Earl's Court was publicized as having been organized by Mrs Cornwallis-West for the benefit of the Shakespeare Memorial National Theatre Fund, like the 'Shakespeare Ball' which she had organized, and Lutyens had decorated, in the Albert Hall the summer before, on 20 June 1911.[6] A letter which Lutyens wrote to his wife during that long hot Coronation summer of 1911, when 'Shakespeare's England' was still on the drawing board, raises some questions as to whose benefit Mrs Cornwallis-West had in mind for the 1912 exhibition:

Emmie –
O its hot.
This morning I woke at 6, having been awake till 4. . . . 10.30 I went to Mrs West and found Victor there. This magnificent scheme of hers – but don't repeat it, is for her own profit, which makes her a sort of Imre Kiralfi and quite different to a bona fide charity – or good object – scheme. I feel rotten sorry that I have anything to do with it, as under the banner of good intentions and names of bona fide Endeavours she means to whip up the public & her society smarts – to her own benefit! We went off to Earl's Court to look at the site.

(Edwin Lutyens, autograph letter signed to Emily Lutyens, London,
9 August 1911)

It has not been possible to investigate this accusation,[7] to which Lutyens would seem to have been alluding in a later letter to his wife. Writing a few weeks after the Marquess of Crewe, Secretary of State for India, had announced Lutyens's appointment as architect to the New Delhi Planning Commission, Lutyens reported: 'O! such a busy day. Committee on School of Rome Lord Esher in Chair – lunched with Ld Crewe – Earls Court Finance Committee at Earls Court – !! – dined with Mrs. West' (Edwin Lutyens, autograph letter signed to Emily Lutyens, London, 21 March 1912). However, since reports published after the fact have it that 'Shakespeare's England' made a heavy loss (Cornwallis-West, 1930, 119, 163–4; Cochran, 1925, 180–3), the question of the destination intended for its profits would seem to entail a contrary-to-fact hypothesis. And in any case, the concern of this article is rather with the images constructed, and the interests thereby served, at 'Shakespeare's England'.

Spectacle and pageantry surrounded the visitor to Earl's Court in the summer of 1912: 'Thanks to Mrs. Cornwallis-West . . . Londoners are now able to walk straight into the sixteenth century and visualise the environment and atmosphere of Shakespeare's day' (*The Graphic*, 11 May 1912, 674–5). The official publicity for 'Shakespeare's England' claimed that it was 'not an exhibition in the ordinary sense of the word . . . but . . . an accurate representation of the life of England three hundred years ago' (quoted in *The Sketch*, 15 May 1912, 188). What this entailed was the reconstruction of a Tudor village, wherein shops were let to modern firms at rents of up to £500 for the six-month duration of the exhibition (*Pall Mall Gazette*, 11 May 1912, 9). For Mrs Cornwallis-West, Lutyens designed what one of the building-trade papers described as an

> historic grouping of old typical buildings illustrative of the period of Shakespeare . . . laid out . . . with due regard to the Old English ideas of street formation, and fittingly contrived also to meet the exigencies of a modern display in a series of modern shops to be visited by thousands of people by night and by day.
>
> (*Building News*, 26 April 1912, 596)

Lutyens's acknowledged sources for 'old typical buildings' included the compendious works of some late Victorian and Edwardian architectural antiquarians – J. Alfred Gotch's *Architecture of the Renaissance in England* (published in 1894 and known to have been in Lutyens's office library: Arts Council, 1981, 198) and Thomas Garner and Arthur Stratton's newly published *The Domestic Architecture of England during the Tudor Period*, an extensively and exactly illustrated celebration of what its preface designates 'the essentially national type of fifteenth and sixteenth-century domestic architecture' (Garner and Stratton, 1911, I, v). A third acknowledged source of Lutyens's plans for the buildings at 'Shakespeare's England' was a series of sketchbooks published by the Architectural Association (*The Times*, 1 April 1912, 11). How much Lutyens actually derived from these sources has not been established: in Garner and Stratton he would have found, at least, the plans for Ford's Hospital, Coventry (Garner and Stratton, 1911, I, 96–7, plates XLIX-LII; II, plate CLXXVI). However, a comparison of a list of the buildings at 'Shakespeare's England' with a list of Lutyens's projects to 1911/12 suggests that the purported typicality of some of the replicas must have been, to at least some degree, a matter of Lutyens's direct professional knowledge of their originals. Notably, both Great Dixter, on which Lutyens had worked in 1910, and Ashby St Ledgers, on which he worked early in 1912, were represented at 'Shakespeare's England'.

Great Dixter is in Sussex and Ashby St Ledgers is over 100 miles away in Northamptonshire. Their replicas in this 'accurate representation' were placed to either side of a square which also gave place to replicas of Windsor Cloisters (Berkshire), of Shakespeare's house, Stratford-on-Avon (Warwickshire), and of St Mary's Church, Coventry (also in Warwickshire). At the centre of the same square was a replica of Ledbury Market Hall (Herefordshire); the firm to whom this shop space was let was the Chiswick Polish Company, who advertised their exhibition as 'the centre of attraction daily to admiring crowds. The work of lidding and packing the tins of the famous Cherry Blossom Boot Polish is seen in actual operation at the stand' (*Illustrated London News*, 15 June 1912, 952). Elsewhere in 'Shakespeare's England', a replica of Ford's Hospital, Coventry, was lined up with a replica of the fountain of Trinity College, Cambridge, while a replica of St John's College, Oxford, was linked to a replica of Queen's College, Cambridge, a replica of the Guildhall, Exeter, standing as an intermediate term. These space-erasing and time-cancelling conjunctions made nonsense, or but very restricted sense, of the claim that 'Shakespeare's England' was 'an accurate representation of the life of England 300 years ago'; but they also meant that the exhibition was congruent with Lutyens's architectural practices. As with housing the makers and the inheritors of fortunes in Victoria's and her son Edward's England, so with re-presenting Shakespeare's England: architectural bricolage secured both vistas pleasing to the eye and spaces conducive to circulation. The end served was less accuracy than charm, and commerce: 'The picturesque lay-out . . . shows great ingenuity, not only in the ample footways left for public use, affording delightful vistas in all directions, but in the arranging, spacing, and scale of the buildings represented and in adapting them for the use of exhibitors' (Collard, 1912, 349). Rather less ingenuity, however, seems to have been devoted to anticipating the needs of employees at the exhibition. Some weeks into the Earl's Court season, the National Organisation of Girls' Clubs found it necessary to make public protest at the lack of ' "restroom or refreshment accommodation, apart from the public restaurants, for the women and girls employed at Shakespeare's England and Earl's Court Exhibition" ' (*The Times*, 7 July 1912, 7).

In securing his visually charming and commercially useful effects, Lutyens was constrained by the dimensions and shapes of the Earl's Court exhibition grounds and of the permanent buildings which stood there and had to be masked (see the site plan, reproduced as Figure 3.1). 'Shakespeare's England' was built to a slightly reduced scale, imperceptible because uniformly maintained throughout the exhibition.[8] The permanent Earl's Court buildings – the rectangular Queen's Palace, the T-shaped Ducal Hall (and, over the railway tracks in the Western Gardens, the amphitheatrical Empress Theatre) — were covered inside and out with the façades of temporary 'Shakespeare's England' buildings. The façades were made of plaster, which was reinforced by fibre, carried by wood, and painted. The substance could either be deployed in slabs for flat surfaces or be moulded and then tooled to look like tiles, timbering, brickwork, or stonework – 'the effect being, at first glance, absolutely illusive', at least to the eyes of a reporter from the theatrical press (*The Era*, 11 May 1912, 18). The illusion could be made to falsify time as well as material; but the use made of 'age effects' – 'mortar chipped here and there from the red brick walls of some of the smaller houses and . . . bits of green moss growing on the red-tiled roofs' (*Pall Mall Gazette*, 9 May 1912, 9) – was judicious. For the age simulated in the replicas was not that of the original buildings as they stood in 1912 but rather as they were then imagined

Figure 3.1 Plan of the 'Elizabethan' village at the 'Shakespeare's England' Exhibition, Earl's Court, London, 1912. Façades and buildings designed by Edwin Lutyens are indicated by diagonal shading. (Reproduced by permission of the British Architectural Library, RIBA, London, from *The Builder*, 27 September 1912, facing p. 355.)

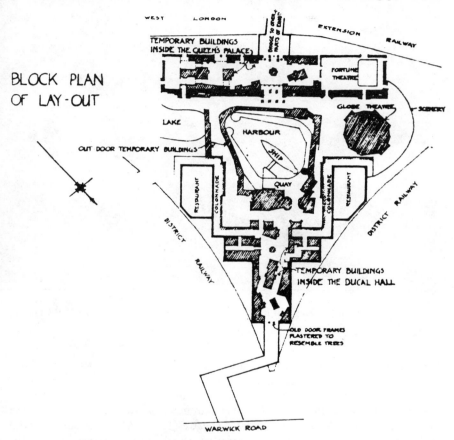

to have looked some 300 years earlier – 'a point which appeals to antiquaries but does not strike superficial observers, who have been heard to remark on the new appearance of some of the Elizabethan counterfeits, forgetting that at the time represented they actually were new' (Collard, 1912, 350). The counterfeiting in Lutyens's 'Shakespeare's England' buildings, moreover, was continued in the backgrounds of flat scenery painted for some of them by John Bull. Bull had painted Poel's Fortune fit-up almost twenty years earlier, in 1893. At Earl's Court in 1912, Bull was kept very busy:

Fifteen miles of blue sky . . . will be found at Earl's Court this year in the corridors and palaces, and the ugliness of the old bridge [over the railway] into the Western Gardens and the passageway at the Warwick Road entrance

Figure 3.2 Replica of the *Revenge* in a facsimile of Plymouth harbour
(Reproduced by permission of the University of London Library

has been turned into English lanes and pasture lands by the brush of the scenic
artist.

(*The Stage*, 9 May 1912, 21)

The re-presentation of 'Shakespeare's England' at Earl's Court in 1912 was
not merely a matter of masking the permanent features of the site but also entailed
the building of free-standing temporary structures. Two of these stood out on
the skyline of the exhibition and still stand out in journalistic accounts of it: these
were reconstructions of the first Globe Theatre (1599–1613), the building with
which Shakespeare's playwriting career is principally associated, and of the
Revenge, the ship commanded by Sir Francis Drake against the Armada in 1588
and then lost three years later by Sir Richard Grenville in a suicidal battle off
the Azores, an encounter of which Grenville's cousin Sir Walter Ralegh wrote
a justification and Alfred Lord Tennyson wrote a celebration.

The replica of the *Revenge* stood at the geographical centre of the 'Shakespeare's
England' exhibition. No hollow shell but a full reconstruction inside and out,
the replica had an iron skeleton – but plaster artillery (*The Times*, 1 April 1912,
11)! – and was 28 feet broad across the beam and 127 feet high from waterline
to top of mainmast (*Illustrated London News*, 11 May 1912, 723–4).[9] The
replica and part of the lake on which it appeared to be floating were enclosed
by a cobblestoned quay and beyond that by a panorama of Plymouth harbour,
a circle of scenery (painted by Bull), itself enclosed by a circle of Tudor façades
(designed by Lutyens) through which a city gate gave passage. The reconstruction

c. 1588. Disembarkation of the royal party, Armada Day, 20 July 1912.
from the *Illustrated London News*, 27 July 1912, p. 129.)

of the galleon itself had been supervised by Sir John Seymour Lucas, a Royal
Academician who specialized in historical costume and had advised such disparate
theatrical producers as William Poel and Henry Irving. The replica was actually

> manned by old naval reserve men in the dress of the period. It was . . . Mr.
> Lutyens' idea to have the ship moving up and down, motioned by the waves,
> but this part of the programme was abandoned, for the leverage would be very
> considerable, owing, for one thing, to the great height of the masts and rigging.
> (*Building News*, 26 April 1912, 596)

The costumed sailors are visible in Figure 3.2, reproducing a photograph of the
visit which King George V and Queen Mary made to the *Revenge* on the morning of Saturday, 20 July 1912. That day various London Devonian societies
celebrated the 324th anniversary of the sighting of the Armada. In the hours after
the royal visitation, the pretended Plymouth harbour at Earl's Court was the scene
of a re-enactment of Drake's legendary game of bowls and its interruption by
a messenger reporting the approach of the Armada, a reception for London Devon-
ians on board the *Revenge* replica, and then a speech from Winston Churchill,
who had been appointed First Lord of the Admiralty the preceding October.
Churchill reminded his audience of their hereditary association with 'the greatest
traditions of the British Fleet' and praised the replica as a model of 'one of the
most historic vessels on which the glories of the British Navy had depended' (*The
Times*, 22 July 1912, 10). The subtext was Churchill's determination to secure

Figures 3.3 and 3.4 Reconstruction of the first Globe Theatre, exterior views. (Reproduced by permission of the Reference Library, Languages and Literature Department (Shakespeare Library), Birmingham Public Libraries)

Figure 3.5 Reconstruction of the first Globe Theatre, stage, pit, and galleries. (Reproduced by permission of the Reference Library, Languages and Literature Department (Shakespeare Library), Birmingham Public Libraries)

a massive expansion of the British navy in the North Sea: the Armada that imagination saw approaching offshore of 'Shakespeare's England' in 1912 was not the Spanish but the German navy, over which the First Lord of the Admiralty wanted the British to maintain a superiority of at least 60 per cent. This was the principle which Churchill laid down in March 1912, when he presented Parliament with his first naval budget, a 10 per cent rise on the preceding year's (R.S.

Churchill, 1967, 565–6; cf. 561). He presented a supplementary budget, representing an increase of another 11 per cent on the Spring figures, on Monday, 22 July 1912 – two days after his appeal both to the ancestors of his Devonian listeners and to the original of the *Revenge* replica at 'Shakespeare's England', Earl's Court.

As an instance of a (re-)construction of the past serving the interests of the present, the 1912 commemoration of Armada Day at 'Shakespeare's England' is egregious, but not isolated. Churchill would later write that his 'three programmes of 1912, 1913 and 1914 comprised the greatest additions in power and cost ever made to the Royal Navy' (quoted in R.S. Churchill, 1967, 607–8); and the discourse which determined and directed these programmes was riddled with appeals to Elizabethan antecedents. Proposals of names for new battleships, for example, were thus justified, even in opposition to the wishes of the King (R.S. Churchill, 1967, 646–54; R.S. Churchill, 1969, 1760–4). And the Earl's Court replica of the *Revenge* was not the only Elizabethan naval reconstruction to be found in London in the summer of 1912. At the Royal Naval and Military Tournament in the Olympia stadium in Kensington, 'The Call to Arms, 1588' was re-enacted and the arena disguised as Tilbury Field, onto which Queen Elizabeth rode 'on a white horse amidst a retinue of 518 mounted and unmounted men-at-arms, heralds and others' (*The Graphic*, 25 May 1912, 763). The leading theatre in the West End, Herbert Beerbohm Tree's His Majesty's Theatre, saw the production of *Drake*, a pageant play which one journalist categorized as 'to all intents and purposes a big-navy play' (*Illustrated London News*, 7 September 1912, 339).

Less obvious then, and perhaps now, were the intentions and purposes informing the other replica which dominated 'Shakespeare's England' at Earl's Court in 1912. This full, working reconstruction of the Globe Theatre was evidently the first of its kind to be built in post-Restoration England (see the previously unpublished photographs reproduced as Figures 3.3–3.5). The kind and manner of theatrical production in this building suggest that its intended audience catchment was a popular one. The regularly scheduled performances in the Globe Theatre as reconstructed at 'Shakespeare's England' were the work of Patrick Kirwan, an Irish-born actor-manager. Kirwan's company, the Idyllic Players, specialized in staging pastoral plays alfresco. From 1904 the Idyllic Players had given what Kirwan's obituary would term 'pretty shows on and about the knoll and the neighbouring lake in Regent Park' (*The Times*, 15 February 1929, 9), and in 1910 Kirwan had given a seven-week season of open-air performances at the Crystal Place exhibition grounds. At Earl's Court in the summer of 1912, Kirwan's players included the 23-year-old Walter Bridges-Adams. Later head of the Shakespeare Memorial Theatre, Stratford-on-Avon, Bridges-Adams would there be nicknamed 'Unabridges-Adams' on account of his insistence upon playing complete texts of Shakespearean plays. This habit of his maturity may have been a reaction to his youthful experiences at Earl's Court: the performances which Kirwan's company gave three times a day – at 3.30, 5.30, and 9.00 p.m. – in the replica of the Globe Theatre at 'Shakespeare's Engand' were half-hour-long stagings of excerpts from Elizabethan and Jacobean dramatic texts. The repertoire was mostly, but not solely, Shakespearean. On the programme announced for the first fortnight, for example, were scenes from Marlowe's *Doctor Faustus* and Fletcher's *A Wild Goose Chase*, as well as scenes from Shakespeare's *A Midsummer Night's Dream, The Merchant of Venice, The Merry Wives of Windsor, Twelfth Night*, and *As You Like It* (*Pall Mall Gazette*, 11 May 1912, 7).[10]

The textual analogues of architectural bricolage, Shakespearean excerpts were, in the years immediately prior to World War I, popular as music-hall and variety entertainments. This was particularly the case at the London Coliseum, where Basil Gill gave the tent scene from *Julius Caesar*, Fred Storey appeared in a 'tableau version' of *The Merchant of Venice*, Seymour Hicks reduced *King Richard III* to two tableaux followed by six scenes, and Violet Vanbrugh repeated the sleepwalking scene (and borrowed the scenery) from the production of *Macbeth* in which she had been playing opposite Tree at His Majesty's Theatre. Such importations were part of an ongoing effort to bridge the gulf – imposed by law in 1843 and subsequently encoded with class significance – between music hall and variety theatre on the one hand and 'legitimate' theatre on the other hand. The other, and upper, hand fought back to hold on to its audiences, the Theatre Managers Association initiating prosecutions for trespasses on their legally demarcated territory. The potted version of *Richard III*, for example, brought the Coliseum manager a fine of £50 because its playing time averaged 44 minutes: a dramatic performance of more than 30 minutes (conventionally, the maximum length of a music-hall 'turn') was held to be the exclusive prerogative of the legitimate theatre (Barker, 1957, 95–7). Late in 1911, however, music halls began to be issued licenses for the performance of drama as well as of variety (Sanderson, 1984, 122). Matching this change in the interpretation of the law governing theatrical production, an indication of change in the class catchment of the consumers of the product came in the following year, with the first Royal Command Performance of variety theatre. But the affixing of a royal seal of approval did not strip the product of its original class associations, associations which obtain for the staging of Shakespeare in the replica Globe at 'Shakespeare's England'.

What was being offered for popular audience consumption in the replica Globe of 1912 was an enactment of something more than extended passages from Elizabethan and Jacobean dramatic texts. The visitor to the replica Globe received both a spectacular, 'environmental' entertainment such as earlier exhibitions had offered – and at the same time, a image of himself [*sic*] as virile, patriotic Englishman. In the variety theatre, the performance of Shakespearean excerpts was subsumed within an evening's programme of entertainments. Variety theatre lived up to its name: Seymour Hicks's potted *Richard III* at the Coliseum shared a 'bill with comics like Gus Elen and Harry Weldon, a zither virtuoso, and George Garstow singing "Captain Ginjah, O.T."' (Barker, 1957, 100); at the 'most tragic moment' of her music-hall performance of a scene from *King John* Constance Benson 'suddenly caught sight of an elephant, standing in the wings, with a pierrot's hat on one ear, nodding' (Benson, 1926, 273); and Violet Vanbrugh changed her Coliseum turn after a week when her performance of Lady Macbeth's sleepwalking scene proved to be in 'too violent a contrast to turns which proceded it' (Vanbrugh, 1948, 105). Somewhat similarly, the performances of playlets like 'The Enchantment of Titania' and 'The Tricking of Malvolio' in the replica of the Globe at 'Shakespeare's England' were only part of the show, for the show also went on in the sanded pit, where performers impersonated an Elizabethan audience. There they seem to have diverted attention from their on-stage colleagues, of whose efforts there is very little journalistic trace outside the theatrical trade papers. What non-specialist reviewers noted, rather, was the surrounding performance:

> In the unroofed pit of the Globe Theatre, 'prentices in quaint flat 'prentice caps and vari-coloured fustian suits settle themselves on three-legged stools, or lounge on the ground smoking old white pipes, which somewhat resemble modern cigarette holders. They . . . while away the waiting time by playing leap-frog, etc., and listening to the thin sweet strains of the viola de gamba, the viola d'amore, the oboe, and the lute, etc.
>
> (*Pall Mall Gazette*, 17 May 1912, 3)

Nearly forty years later a viewer still recalled

> the excitement of sitting on a wooden bench in one of the shallow galleries, fascinated not only by the play itself but by the orange-girls and brawling hangers-on who lounged about the pit of the theatre, doing comic turns from time to time, all in contemporary costume.
>
> (Whitworth, 1951, 95)

The Shakespearean excerpts enacted on the replica Globe stage were thus not so much plays, or even playlets, as plays-within-plays, or rather plays-within-performances. The encompassing performance was a representation of an Elizabethan theatrical event. In effect, although probably not in intention, that representation was a realization – in the sense which is so impressively worked through by Meisel (1983) – of Edgar Bundy's representation of *The First Performance of 'The Merry Wives of Windsor' 1599*. One of half a dozen Shakespearean-subject paintings exhibited at the Royal Academy that summer season of 1912, Bundy's oil painting is reproduced here, via a printed reproduction (*Illustrated London News*, 11 May 1912, supplement, p. vii), as Figure 3.6. The intermediate reproduction being monochromatic, it is necessary to take the word of a journalist that this is a 'highly coloured scene'; but it is at least obvious that in Bundy's representation 'the pit is crowded, and the stage . . . a mad medley of nobles and players . . . the Bard himself in the midst of the throng, complacently surveying the production' (*The Era*, 11 May 1912, 15).

It was at Kirwan's theatrical enactment of such an Elizabethan audience that William Poel took antiquarian offence in a contemptuous review of the Earl's Court reconstruction of the Globe. The object of his 'not amusement' is at first glance a little surprising. On the one hand, there was much else in the reconstruction to which an antiquarian might have objected; and indeed, Poel's review did tick off 'several errors, notably, on the stage, in the position of the

Figure 3.6 The First Performance of The Merry Wives of Windsor, 1599: painting by Edgar Bundy exhibited at the Royal Academy, Summer 1912. (Reproduced by permission of the University of London Library from the Illustrated London News, 11 May 1912, supplement p. vii.)

traverse, in that of the staircases, and in the use made of the side boxes as approaches to the stage', and then dismissed these as 'details which are not of interest to the general public' (Poel, 1912, 208).[11] On the other hand, Poel himself had deployed an 'Elizabethan' audience in costume on stage when he first used the Fortune fit-up, nineteen years earlier. Those 'Elizabethans' of 1893, however, had done nothing more rollicking than to puff on clay pipes: one formidable critic had thought them to be too implausibly well-behaved.[12] The Elizabethans of 1912 were too indecorously active to suit Poel:

> exception might be taken to the movement of the costumed figures who are supposed to impersonate the 'groundlings'. . . . The handling of these incidents in the auditorium at Earl's Court have [sic] the appearance of being planned by one who is only superficially acquainted with the period and not in sympathy with the conditions of theatrical representation then in vogue – a circumstance to be regretted at an exhibition which was ostensibly organized to raise funds for a memorial to Shakespeare. Apparently it is forgotten that between 1590 and 1610 the finest dramatic literature which the world perhaps ever has known was being written in London, a coincidence which is inconceivable were the staging so crude and unintelligent as that which is shown at Earl's Court. Everything there appears to have been done on the assumption that three hundred years ago there was a less amount of brain power existing among dramatists, actors and audience than there is found among them to-day, while the reverse argument is nearer to the truth.
>
> (Poel, 1912, 209)

Poel's differential equation is impossible because the two sides of it were at once incomparable and yet also identical. The Earl's Court 'Elizabethans' were exhibited as exotic beings from a mythically distant past. As such they had to compete with another Earl's Court display, over in the Western Gardens, of exotic beings, these rivals being from a mythically distant place:

> A most interesting feature in the Western Gardens is the Igorrote Village, inhabited by a number of barbarians from the mountainous districts of the Philippine Islands. These natives are to give exhibitions of war and peace dances to the music of the inevitable tom-tom, as well as of their more industrial pursuits, and the whole show affords an interesting insight into their life. The extreme scantiness of their attire, however, gives one cause to wonder how they will fare under the attentions of a typical London east wind!
>
> (*The Stage*, 9 May 1912, 21)

> An attraction to which all should repair is the village of Philippine islanders, wherein natives execute war dances, sing weird songs, and go through mimic combats with assegai and shield. The practice of the natives in carrying on their warfare is particularly interesting, and great is the evident pride of the scarred and tattooed warrior who has the distinction of having cut off most heads. The way in which the natives climb imitation coconut trees is astounding.
>
> (*The Era*, 18 May 1912, 15)

Arguably, any astonishment at the habiliments and habits of the inhabitants of the Philippino village in the Western Gardens went some way to secure an impression of accuracy and accessibility in the Olde English village on the other side of the tracks. For the Earl's Court Elizabethans – the sailors climbing up the riggings of the *Revenge*, the groundlings rollicking around the pit of the Globe – were not solely exotic spectacles. They were also on display as objects of popular-audience identification. The mythical past which they re-presented was, after all, English national history – or rather, one version of English national history. Visitors to 'Shakespeare's England' were implicated in a cultural fiction, just as surely and almost as literally as the reconstruction of the *Revenge* was wholly, and the reconstruction of the Globe was partly, surrounded by painted scenery. The advertising campaign for the exhibition promised access – priced at a shilling for adults, sixpence for children – to 'Merrie England as it was in Shakespeare's Day' (advertisement in the *Daily Mirror*, 15 May 1912, 15; *Lloyd's Weekly News*, 12 May 1912, 14; *Pall Mall Gazette*, 15 May 1912, 9). The press obligingly saw in the exhibition just that which it was supposed to be selling:

> The Elizabethan atmosphere grows apace at the Shakespeare's England exhibition, Earl's Court, and as the days go by those who participate in the work seek to catch more of the spirit that was England's – that keen joy in living – in the days of Shakespeare and Spenser, Drake and Frobisher.
>
> (*Pall Mall Gazette*, 17 May 1912, 3)

The reporter's pairing of Shakespeare and Spenser with Drake and Frobisher is a verbal reminder of the pair that dominated the visual display of 'Shakespeare's England' at Earl's Court – the Globe and the *Revenge*. The same association was being made in the latest instalment of a monthly magazine series retelling 'England's Story in Portrait and Picture'. The merriment of the Elizabethan chapter in the national story was, to the unidentified author of that series, a matter of machismo, imperialism, and – Shakespeare.

> In every walk of life it was an age of bourgeoning and renaissance, an age of virility and ability. Maritime enterprise and exploration . . . not only brought new commercial prosperity to England, but laid the foundations of her colonial empire; and the literature of the period, with which the name of Shakespeare is for ever associated, forms an imperishable memorial of an extraordinarily brilliant epoch in the history of the world.
>
> (*Windsor Magazine*, 35, December 1911–May 1912, 156).

In the second clause of the second sentence quoted above, the work of Shakespeare is construed as a monument to the Elizabethan epoch. But the first clause of the sentence, ostensibly in praise of the Elizabethan age, has presented Elizabethan enterprise and exploration as the cause of post-Victorian conditions: commercial prosperity and a colonial empire. The celebration of the past turns out to be a justification of the present. Shakespeare thus memorializes an 'extraordinarily brilliant epoch in the history of the world' which is now as much as then. Transfer such logic to the interior of the Globe – as represented either by Bundy or by Lutyens and Kirwan – and it is not difficult to discern 'the Bard himself in the midst of the throng, *complacently* surveying the production'.

In the reconstruction of the Globe, the 1912 audience was free to mingle with the *c*. 1599 audience (*The Times*, 14 August 1912, 8). Given such obvious incongruities of costume as are recorded in Figure 3.2, the 'real' 1912 audience could never have so merged with the impersonated 1599 audience as to become indistinguishable from it. On one spectacular occasion in the 'Shakespeare's England' season, however, the 'real' and the 'impersonated' did collapse into each other. The occasion was not one of the regularly scheduled performances in the reconstruction of the Globe nor any of the other entertainments – such as the programmes of Morris dancing in a reconstruction of the Fortune Theatre within the Queen's Palace – which were available to all comers to 'Shakespeare's England'. Rather, it was one of the events and amenities which Mrs Cornwallis-West, who was said to be 'catering for Mayfair equally with Clapham and Camden Town' (*Daily Express*, 20 May 1912, quoted in *The Literary Digest*, 6 July 1912, p. 19), arranged for her social peers. Her base at the exhibition was a (genuine) Tudor building which had been brought from Ipswich and re-erected in the Western Gardens. The permanent Earl's Court building next to it was transformed into the Mermaid Tavern and run, directly under the control of the organizing committee, as a private club for 'all her friends and her friends' friends . . . it contained a very good restaurant and a room where one could read the papers and write' (Cornwallis-West, 1930, 164). And at at least two points in the summer, the Empress Hall in the Western Gardens was given over to fancy-dress occasions for the upper classes. Thursday, 27 June saw a Venetian masked ball. The designer Fortuny was brought over from Venice to clothe some of the 2000 guests, as was Maxime de Thomas from Paris (*The Times*, 16 February 1912, 9). The Empress Hall had already been transformed, for the duration of the exhibition, into the courtyard of Warwick Castle: to the castle gateway already erected for 'Shakespeare's England' were added pine groves, golden standards, and, on the sidelines, an Italian villa (*The Times*, 28 June 1912, 11). Two weeks later, having recovered its faked identity as Warwick Castle, the Empress Hall was the scene of a rather more bizarre masquerade. This was, to quote the title of the thirty-six-page programme for the occasion, 'THE TRIUMPH HOLDEN AT SHAKESPEARE'S ENGLAND ON THE ELEVENTH DAY OF JULY IN THE THIRD YEAR OF THE REIGN OF KING GEORGE THE FIFTH' (Cripps-Day, 1912). This reconstruction of a *c*. 1580 triumph was devised by Mrs Cornwallis-West and Seymour Lucas. Stage-management was entrusted to Frank Benson, the Oxford graduate whose Shakespearean touring company played at Cheltenham Ladies' College in morning dress, secured the social respectability of the acting profession, and 'put poetry right with the middle classes' (Brown and Fareon, 1939, 267). To the results of the collective efforts of Cornwallis-West, Seymour Lucas, and Benson, *The Times* devoted an entire full-column report, beginning:

When the great bell struck six, the merry Elizabethan populace, morris-dancing, footballing, and singing, poured into the tilt-yard and made it their playground until the scarlet halberdiers came and drove them away. Then the trumpets sounded and the Knight Martiall of the Lists (Lord Lonsdale), splendidly mounted and attired, rode in. Before him went his four gorgeous pursuivants on foot, and the Herald (Mr F.R. Benson) rode in his train. The four judges (Lord Shrewsbury and Talbot, Lord Essex, Lord Dudley, and Major-General Brocklehurst), all in sober black, came with him and his Esquire (Mr Guy Laking) bore his staff. The trumpets sounded again, and the great concourse on the green scaffolding within the frowning walls was blessed with the sight of the Queen of Beauty (Lady Curzon) and her train. With the pen, and the freedom, of an Elizabethan writer we might hope to do justice to the Queen of Beauty, as, robed in white with a diamond crown on her golden hair, and a great jewelled collar to frame her face, she came in her purple-plumed litter, borne by eight henchmen; and to her 'wayting ladies' (Miss Lucia White, Mrs Rupert Beckett, Miss Muriel Wilson, Lady Acheson, Mrs Wilfred Sheridan, Miss de Trafford, Lady Diana Manners, Mrs Ralph Peto, Miss Sackville-West, Countess Zia Terby, Mrs Raymond Asquith, and Miss Violet Keppel), on their rose-wreathed palfreys.

(*The Times*, 12 July 1912, 8)

The audience paid dearly – £200 for a box, 15 guineas (£15.75) for a ticket – for such visions as the entrance of Mrs Cornwallis-West's sister-in-law, the 1897 Queen of Sheba turned Princess Errant of 1912, 'on an enormous piebald horse, heavily caparisoned and draped in ropes of roses, that belonged (without the roses) to the Drum-Major of the First Life Guards' (Trewin, 1960, 192). (Sounds were provided by the band of the Second Life Guards.) Six titled aristocrats in armour jousted at the tilt and then, their ranks augmented by another six knights in armour, broke papier-mâché lances on each other in a general mêlée. Of the several exertions of the tilting knights it was judged

that the Duke of Marlborough had well jousted, but that Lord Ashby St. Ledgers had jousted best. Then the victorious knight dismounted, climbed the steps to the Queen of Beauty's throne, and there, kneeling, kissed her hand and received from it the prize – a gold cup of the price of £600.

(*The Times*, 12 July 1912, 8)

The victorious knight was not Lord Ashby St Ledgers but his younger brother, Freddie Guest, MP for East Dorset. Noting that 'tilting by proxy . . . is not permitted by the rules', *The Times* (20 July 1912, 11) solemnly announced the discovery of the substitution and the consequent transfer of the prize to the runner-up. What seems to have escaped attention, or at least announcement, was a fraternal substitution in the second group of knights, among whom Harold Smith passed himself off as his brother F.E. (Martin, 1971, [1972, 363]).

But if the shining armour disguised some individual identities, still, there was no mistaking the ruling class of 1912, as a group, in the display of expenditure and equestrian abilities which was the 'Triumph Holden at "Shakespeare's England"'. The Triumph aped an earlier extravaganza of antiquarian recon- struction and aristocratic exhibition, the ill-fated Eglinton Tournament of 1839 (on which, see Ansruther, 1963; Girouard, 1981, 87–110). The antecedent occasion, the active involvement therein of several ancestors of the 1912 combatants, even the use at Earl's Court of a suit of armour made for Eglinton, did not escape notice (see Girouard, 1981, 8, and references cited there; *The Times*, 11 July 1912, 8; *Illustrated London News*, 13 July 1912, 58). Less widely remarked was the image of an even longer continuity that was embodied by occupants of seats in the scaffolded galleries which had been erected for the triumph. Wearing fancy dress, these spectators were assimilated to the spectacle (*The Times*, 10 July 1912, 11).

> Each one of them was part of the living picture. . . . Here indeed, so unbroken are the traditions of our history, were men and women bearing the same names and titles, children of the same blood, as those who did homage to Elizabeth and to sovereigns further back in the roll call as knights or judges.
>
> (Gibbs, 1912, 50)

Both words in the phrase 'our history' invite challenge. The *tableau vivant* presented at the Earl's Court triumph that evening of 11 July 1912 was, like the realization of Shakespeare's (Merrie) England, enacted every day of that summer in and around the reconstructions of the Globe Theatre and the *Revenge*, a re-presentation of but one version of English history. It was a version that so emphasized one class as to exclude most of the nation and so emphasized continuity as to occlude change.

Reality, however, had its revenges on 'Shakespeare's England'. Shortly before the triumph was 'holden' there, plans were announced for the exhibition to go to Germany the following summer (*Literary Digest*, 6 July 1912, 18). It is not yet clear whether these plans were carried out: if so, the ironies of the afterlife of the 1912 exhibition would be rendered almost absurd. For the 1913 exhibition at Earl's Court was devoted to 'The Imperial Services' (see *Pall Mall Gazette*, 13 May 1913, 4). And some of the 'Shakespeare's England' buildings were re-erected at the Bristol Exhibition in the summer of 1914. That autumn, after the long-awaited war had finally begun, they were 'used as officers' quarters for Bristol's Own, a special battalion recruited among young profes- sional and business men' (*London Shakespeare League Journal*, November 1914, 8).

Notes

1. The former quotation is from the programme for the Elizabethan Stage Society's first production, *Twelfth Night*, in Burlington Hall, 21 and 22 June 1895; and the latter is from the programme for the society's second production, *The Comedy of Errors*, in Gray's Inn Hall, 7 December 1895.
2. The principal sources for the specifications of Poel's Fortune fit-up are: first, the entry for lot no. 1 in the printed catalogue of the sale by auction, on 5 July 1905,

of the property of the Elizabethan Stage Society; and second, an unpublished letter which Poel wrote on 3 June 1905 to William Salt Brassington, Librarian and Chief Curator of the Shakespeare Memorial Theatre, Stratford-upon-Avon, where Poel hoped to lodge the model stage after the dissolution of his play-producing society.

3. See, for instance, the issues of *Country Life* for 7 October 1911 (leading article on 'Economy in Living'); 3 February 1912 (article by Mrs Keyser on 'How the *French* Peasant Cooks' [emphasis added]); 4 May 1912 (article on 'Cookery for the Cottage'); and 18 May 1912 ('Country Notes'). The last of these is a quotably succinct instantiation of the superior tones which all adopt on their common culinary theme: 'The English housewife . . . does not know the value of soup or broth, and in consequence there is more waste in the cottage than there is in the hall.'

4. In an article entitled 'Lutyens and Country Life: 81 Not Out' for the catalogue of the 1981/2 Lutyens exhibition at the Hayward Gallery, London, John Cornforth draws attention to Latham's careful (re-)arrangement of the rooms he photographed, to 'the way in which Latham pulled the furniture about and placed flowers and objects to create the composition he wanted, so recreating in photographic terms the mood of the interiors of de Hooch and Vermeer' (Arts Council, 1981, 26). What is also striking about the domestic-interior photographs published in *Country Life* during its first fifteen or so years is the way in which they, like the paintings of de Hooch and Vermeer, are traversed by a strong directional light which seems to have originated just outside frame. An especially good instance of this is a photograph, published in *Country Life* for 8 December 1900, of the Oak Gallery at Munstead Wood.

5. I am grateful to Dr Jane Ridley, owner and copyright holder of the Lutyens correspondence in the British Architectural Library, Royal Institute of British Architects, for her permission to quote from this letter and from those of 9 August, 1911 and 26 March, 1912.

6. An illustrated *Shakespeare Memorial Souvenir of the Shakespeare Ball, 20 June 1911*, edited by Mrs Cornwallis-West and including contributions from G.B. Shaw and G.K. Chesterton, was published by Frederick Warne in 1912, presumably to coincide with the opening of the 'Shakespeare's England' exhibition that summer. Among its illustrations is a reproduction of the portrait which John Lavery painted of Mrs Cornwallis-West as Olivia. A portrait by Sigismund Goetze entitled *Souvenir of the Shakespeare Ball* was in the 1912 summer exhibition at the Royal Academy. More accessibly, William Seymour Leslie's *The Jerome Connexion* reproduces a photograph from Mrs Cornwallis-West's Elizabethan Pageant in 1911 (W.S. Leslie, 1964, facing p. 55): among the costumed group posed for this shot are Mrs Cornwallis-West, her sisters Leonie Jerome Leslie and Clara Jerome Frewen, and her son's secretary, Eddie Marsh. Behind the group is scenery, obviously painted, and not quite completely concealing the wall it covers.

7. A biography co-authored by Mrs Cornwallis-West's grandson offers some tantalizing terse confirmation of Lutyens's claim: 'Jenny wasn't entirely altruistic about it [i.e. 'Shakespeare's England']. She was to receive a percentage of the profits. . . . There were no profits . . . from the Exhibition' (P. Churchill and Mitchell, 1974, 236).

8. The collection of Lutyens's architectural drawings in the Royal Institute of British Architects includes drawings of only one of his 'Shakespeare's England' replicas. These are nos. 137.1 and 137.2 in the published catalogue of the collection (Richardson, 1973, 29). Half-elevations of what is recognisably St John's College, Oxford (or something very like it), the sketches seem to record two stages in the plans. On the rougher of the two are some dimensions and calculations, but I have not been able to work out the exact scale of the building from these.

9. The picture story from which these specifications are taken includes a cut-away working drawing of the *Revenge* construction. The following week's issue of *The Illustrated London News* (18 May 1912, 784) printed a photograph of the reconstructed Plymouth quayside with its panoramic background, and a photograph of the replicated city gate.

The former photograph was printed in that same day's issue of *The Graphic* (18 May 1912, 704), together with a photograph of the *Revenge* model under construction.

10. According to Mazer (1981, 75), 'Kirwan's repertoire at Earls Court included seven plays by Shakespeare and *The Chaste Maid of Cheapside*, presumably pieces already in the repertoire of the Idyllic Players'. Mazer, whose account of Kirwan deals primarily with his direction of the 1914 season at the Shakespeare Memorial Theatre, Stratford-upon-Avon, does not give his source for this statement, which I have been unable to verify. Editorial imagination boggles at how Middleton's play might have been excised and expurgated by Kirwan, who was active in the newly formed Catholic Stage Guild (Sanderson, 1984, 151–2).

11. Writing to *The Times* fifteen years later, Poel made objection to further points in the reconstruction: 'Although the building erected in 1912 at Earl's Court . . . was advertised on the programme as being a copy of the Globe Theatre, yet the dimensions and proportions of the building were not the same. Moreover, it lacked the essential feature of an Elizabethan playhouse – that is, the projection of the platform into the middle of the arena. At Earl's Court these differences were due to economic reasons – namely, want of space together with a desire to add to the seating capacity within the playhouse' (*The Times*, 7 November 1927, 10). Later still, Philip Carr (1951, 6) would cite the exhibition for its 'reproduction of the Globe Theatre and the plays as Shakespeare staged them – more or less'.

12. William Archer's review in *The World* for 15 November 1893 praised Poel's reconstruction but added: 'The gallants, smoking their Elizabethan clay pipes on their sixpenny stools on the stage, certainly contributed to the illusion; but I fear it was very seldom that the ruffling blades of the Court and the Inns of Court conducted themselves with such propriety. To make the realism perfect they should have called for and consumed burnt sack in the midst of the performance, exchanged banter with the citizens in the "yard," and between-whiles quarrelled among themselves. It would not have been amiss if one of them had casually run another through the body' (Archer, 1894, 268).

Works cited

Unpublished

Album of Photographs of the Elizabethan Buildings reconstructed at the 'Shakespeare's England' Exhibition at Earl's Court, London, 1912, in the Shakespeare Library, Department of Languages and Literature, Central Reference Library, Birmingham Public Libraries.

Elizabethan Stage Society programme for *The Comedy of Errors*, Grays Inn Hall, 7 December 1895, in Poel Collection, Theatre Museum, Victoria & Albert Museum, London.

Elizabethan Stage Society programme for *Twelfth Night*, Burlington Hall, 21 and 22 June 1895, in Shakespeare Centre Library, Shakespeare Birthplace Trust, Stratford-on-Avon.

Lutyens, Edwin, autograph letters signed to Emily Lutyens, 9 August 1911 (LUE/12/3/6), 21 March 1912 (LUE/12/6/7), 26 May 1912 (LUE/12/10/3), in Lutyens Correspondence, British Architectural Library, Royal Institute of British Architects, Portland Place, London.

—— 'Preliminary study & design for a Tudor mansion [St John's College, Oxford], 1912', in Drawings Collection, Royal Institute of British Architects, Portman Square, London.

Poel, William, autograph letter signed to W.S. Brassington, 3 June 1905, in Poel Collection, Theatre Museum, Victoria & Albert Museum, London.

Published

Akrigg, G.P.V. (1958) '*Twelfth Night* at the Middle Temple', *Shakespeare Quarterly*, 9, 422–4.

Altick, Richard D. (1978) *The Shows of London*, Cambridge, Mass., and London, Harvard University Press.

Anstruther, Ian (1963) *The Knight and the Umbrella: An Account of the Eglinton Tournament, 1839*, London, Geoffrey Bles.

Archer, William (1894) *The Theatrical 'World' for 1893*, London, Walter Scott.

Ardagh, J. (1935) 'London Exhibitions in the 'Eighties', *Notes & Queries*, 168, 233.

Arts Council (1978) *Pictorial Photography in Britain 1900–1920*, exhibition catalogue, London, Arts Council of Great Britain, in association with Royal Photographic Society.

Arts Council (1981) *Lutyens: The Work of the English Architect Sir Edwin Lutyens, 1869–1944*, exhibition catalogue, London, Arts Council of Great Britain.

Barker, Felix (1957) *The House that Stoll Built: The Story of the Coliseum Theatre*, London, Frederick Muller.

Benson, Constance (1926) *Mainly Players: Bensonian Memoirs*, London, Thornton Butterworth.

Brown, Ivor, and Fareon, George (1939) *Amazing Monument: A Short History of the Shakespeare Industry*, London, Heinemann.

Butler, Arthur Stanley George (1950) *The Architecture of Sir Edwin Lutyens*, III, London, Country Life; New York, Scribner's.

Carr, Philip (1951) 'The National Theatre Plan: Memories of the Early Struggle', *Manchester Guardian*, 13 July 1951, 4, 6.

Churchill, Jenny Jerome Spencer (1908) *The Reminiscences of Lady Randolph Churchill*, London, Edward Arnold.

Churchill, Peregrine, and Mitchell, Julian (1974) *Jenny: Lady Randolph Churchill – A Portrait with Letters*, London, William Collins.

Churchill, Randolph S. (1967) *Winston S. Churchill*, II: *Young Statesman 1901–1914*, London, Heinemann.

———— (1969) *Winston S. Churchill*, II: *Young Statesman 1901–1914, Companion*, part 3, London, Heinemann.

Cochran, Charles B. (1925) *The Secrets of a Showman*, London, Heinemann.

Collard, A.O. (1912) 'Exhibition Buildings at "Shakespeare's England"', *The Builder*, 53, 348–50, 355.

Cornwallis-West, George (1930) *Edwardian Heydays or A Little About a Lot of Things*, New York, Putnam.

Cripps-Day, Francis Henry (1912) *The Triumph Holden at Shakespeare's England on the Eleventh Day of July in the Third Year of the Reign of King George the Fifth*, London, W.H. Smith.

Garner, Thomas, and Stratton, Arthur (1911) *The Domestic Architecture of England during the Tudor Period*, London, Batsford.

Gaudet, Claire (1912) 'Shakespeare's England – At Earl's Court', *The Graphic*, 85, 672.

Gibbs, Philip (1912) 'The Elizabethan Tourney in Shakespeare's England', *The Graphic*, 86, 50.

Girouard, Mark (1981) *The Return to Camelot: Chivalry and the English Gentleman*, New Haven and London, Yale University Press.

Gradidge, Roderick (1980) *Dream Houses: The Edwardian Ideal*, London, Constable.

———— (1981) *Edwin Lutyens: Architect Laureate*, London, George Allen & Unwin.

Hussey, Christopher (1950) *The Life of Sir Edwin Lutyens*, London, Country Life; New York, Scribner's.

Irving, Robert Grant (1981) *Indian Summer: Lutyens, Baker and Imperial Delhi*, New Haven and London, Yale University Press.

King, T.V. (1971) *Shakespearean Staging 1599–1642*, Cambridge, Mass., Harvard University Press.

Leslie, Anita (1969) *Jennie: The Life of Lady Randolph Churchill*, London, Hutchinson.

Leslie, William Seymour (1964) *The Jerome Connexion*, London, John Murray.

Luckhurst, Kenneth W. (1951) *The Story of Exhibitions*, New York and London, Studio Publications.

Lutyens, Mary (1980) *Edwin Lutyens*, London, John Murray.

Lytton, Edith (1961) *Lady Lytton's Court Diary 1895–1899*, ed. Mary Lutyens, London, Rupert Hart-Davis.

Martin, Ralph G. (1971) *Lady Randolph Churchill: A Biography*, II, New York; (1972) London, Cassell.

Mazer, Cary (1981) *Shakespeare Refashioned: Elizabethan Plays on Edwardian Stages*, Ann Arbor, UMI Research Press.

Meisel, Martin (1983) *Realizations: Narrative, Pictorial, and Theatrical Arts in Nineteenth-Century England*, Princeton, Princeton University Press.

Murphy, Sophia (1984) *The Duchess of Devonshire's Ball*, London, Sidgwick & Jackson.

O'Connor, Marion (1987) *William Poel and the Elizabethan Stage Society*, Cambridge, Chadwyck-Healey.

Phillips, L. March (1906) 'Country Homes: Marshcourt, Hampshire, the Residence of Mr. Herbert Johnson', *Country Life Illustrated*, 1 September 1906, 306–17.

Poel, William (1912) 'Shakespeare at Earl's Court', *New Age*, 22 September 1912, reprinted in Poel's *Shakespeare in the Theatre*, London, Sidgwick & Jackson, 208–12.

Richardson, Margaret (1973) *Catalogue of the Drawings Collection of the Royal Institute of British Architects: Lutyens*, Farnborough, Gregg International.

Sanderson, Michael (1984) *From Irving to Olivier: A Social History of the Acting Profession*, London, Athlone Press.

'Shakespeare's England' at Earl's Court May to October 1912: Loan Collection Catalogue (1912) London, W.H. Smith.

Southern, Richard (1973) *The Staging of Plays Before Shakespeare*, New York, Theatre Arts Books.

Spielmann, Isidore (1900) 'At the Paris Exhibition', *Country Life Illustrated*, 20 October 1900, 488–94.

Trewin, John Courtney (1960) *Benson and the Bensonians*, London, Barrie & Rockcliff.

Vanbrugh, Irene (1948) *To Tell My Story*, London, Hutchinson.

Wayne, Don E. (1984) *Penshurst: The Semiotics of Place and the Poetics of History*, London, Methuen.

Weaver, Laurence (1913) *Houses and Gardens by Sir Edwin Lutyens*, London, Country Life.

Whitworth, Geoffrey (1951) *The Making of a National Theatre*, London, Faber & Faber.

4

Prospero in Africa: *The Tempest* as colonialist text and pretext

Thomas Cartelli

> No part of the house was stamped more clearly with his
> individual taste than was his library.
> (Lockhart and Woodhouse, 1963, on Cecil Rhodes)

Most literate arts graduates are likely to understand what Secretary of State
Shultz means when he asserts, in respect to America's policy towards
Nicaragua, that America will not become "the Hamlet of nations," since most
presumably share his well-worn reading of Hamlet as a character who (with fatal
consequences) "could not make up his mind."[1] Remembrance of the ruined
bodies scattered across the stage at play's end feeds into familiarity with present-
day Latin American political events to suggest that if a more aggressive Fortinbras is required to put Denmark back together, America is well-qualified to play
that role. Shakespeare functions in such political transactions as an unassailable
source of moral wisdom and common sense, as a touchstone not only of what
is right and just but also of what is necessary and practical. His name lends both
respectability and moral probity to the positions his appropriators wish to
advance.

I digress at such length at the beginning of a paper on *The Tempest* because

THOMAS CARTELLI is Associate Professor of English and Chair of the Humanities
Division at Muhlenberg College. He has published widely in the field of Renaissance
drama, and is in the early stages of a book on Marlowe, Shakespeare, and the psychology
of theatrical experience. The present essay is the product of a deepening involvement in
the study of postcolonial literature and its clarifying impact on our understanding of
western cultural practices.

I will in the following be concerned with other, less conspicuous "rewritings" of Shakespeare and the consequences of such practices, and because I wish to emphasize from the start the ideological ramifications of producing readings and misreadings of Shakespearean texts. I borrow my working definition of ideology from Louis Althusser who writes that "it is not their real conditions of existence, their real world, that men 'represent to themselves' in ideology, but above all it is their relation to those conditions of existence which is represented to them there" (1971, 164). Viewed from such a perspective, Secretary Shultz's statement about *Hamlet* can be construed as a representation of what he has brought to his reading of the play; as the product of what he associates (or thinks Shakespeare associates) with its title character, e.g. cowardice, indecisiveness. The political success of his reading depends upon its consonance with the way in which the play is generally read, which, in turn, can be traced to the way in which it has been taught or transmitted to its readers. And it depends as well on the compatibility of the literary prescriptions of British and American educational institutions with prevailing political views regarding American intervention in the internal affairs of Third World countries. His reading is not, in short, exclusively identifiable with the text of *Hamlet* itself, much less with Shakespeare's own disputable intentions regarding his play. It is, instead, symptomatic of the ideological assumptions which produce it.

Clearly, a Hamlet who cannot make up his mind is very different from a Hamlet who has, for very good reasons, decided not to do what his ghostly father urges him to do and what, presumably, the less introspective Fortinbras would do were he in Hamlet's position. Approached from this direction, *Hamlet* may be said to be about an understandably alienated individual's attempt at self-determination in the face of a paternal imposition that presents revenge as a "natural" response to his dilemma and delay as an "unnatural" deviation from a social obligation which has taken on the force of a moral imperative. This latter Hamlet swims against an ideological tide that, oddly enough, appears not to have changed greatly in the 386 years since his play's making. Were *he* the Hamlet authoritatively transmitted to a younger George Shultz and his far-flung interpretive community, it is at least imaginable that today's Secretary of State might be affirming America's ties to a Hamlet who chooses *not* to play the protagonist in a bloody vendetta, in the name of an America that chooses *not* to intervene in the internal affairs of another nation.

The scenario I have concocted clearly overstates the effect of art on those in high places. But it is not fanciful to contend that the reading and transmission of culturally privileged texts (and there are no western texts that are as privileged as Shakespeare's) play influential roles in the development of those imaginary representations of the real world Althusser identifies as ideologies. This is not to suggest that texts like *Hamlet* are themselves free of ideology and, hence, bear no responsibility for the uses to which they are put. Indeed, Hamlet protests far too much against his own indecisiveness for one to deny the dramatic significance of so salient a characteristic. In a similar vein, I shall argue in the following that *The Tempest* is a responsible party to its successive readings and rewritings insofar as it has made seminal contributions to the development of the colonialist ideology through which it is read.

There are, of course, many who would quarrel with the notion of a *Tempest* that speaks the predatory language of colonialism on behalf of the governing structures of western power and ideals. But there is another, nonwestern interpretive community for whom *The Tempest* has long served as the embodiment of colonial presumption. The development of "new literatures," both critical and creative, in the newly independent nations of Africa and the West Indies has witnessed the repeated use of *The Tempest* as a site on which the age-old conflicts between colonizer and colonized continue to be played out and rehearsed.[2] In most of these works, recent British and American attempts to problematize the traditionally stereotyped critical estimate of the relationship of Prospero and Caliban are resisted in favor of recuperating the starkness of the master / slave configuration, thus making it appear to function as a foundational paradigm in the history of European colonialism.[3] In this process, writers such as the Kenyan Ngugi Wa Thiong'o and the West Indian George Lamming regenerate out of their own first-hand experience of colonization a conception of Shakespeare as a formative producer and purveyor of a paternalistic ideology that is basic to the material aims of western imperialism. Thus Ngugi, in *A Grain of Wheat* (1967), has a brutal but (in his own eyes) "well-meaning" British colonial functionary plan to write a book on his experiences in Kenya entitled "Prospero in Africa." The character's movement towards this resolve is worth following in detail:

After the war he returned to his interrupted studies in Oxford. It was there . . . that he found himself interested in the development of the British Empire. At first this was a historian's interest without personal involvement. But, drifting into the poems of Rudyard Kipling, he experienced a swift flicker, a flame awakened. He saw himself as a man with destiny, a man poised for great things in the future. He studied the work and life of Lord Lugard. And then a casual meeting with two African students crystallized his longings into a concrete conviction. They talked literature, history, and the war; they were all enthusiastic about the British Mission in the World. The two Africans, they came from a family of Chiefs in what was then Gold Coast, showed a real grasp of history and literature. This filled Thompson with wonder and admiration. . . . Here were two Africans who in dress, in speech and in intellectual power were no different from the British. Where was the irrationality, inconsistency and superstition so characteristic of the African and Oriental races? They had been replaced by the three principles basic to the Western mind: i.e. the principle of Reason, of Order and of Measure.

(Ngugi, 1967 [1968, 47])

What must first strike a critical reader of this passage is the seemingly caricatured nature of Ngugi's portrayal of John Thompson. Thompson's movement from professional detachment to "personal involvement" through the presumably old-fashioned medium of Kipling seems rather unrealistic, as does his equally bookish adoption of a more practical estimate of the white man's burden as taught by Lugard, under whom the British first secured Nigeria. Our credulity is stretched further when his refresher-course approach to British imperialism culminates in the "wonder and admiration" with which he responds to its success in transforming Africans into veritable Englishmen. Thompson's virtually classic adjustment of his initial view of Africans as different and therefore unequal to the more "enlightened" position that transforms equality into identity – hence denying Africans the integrity of an otherness that balances the English claim to selfhood – also reads like a textbook version of inverse racial stereotyping.[4] But Ngugi opposes here what may be termed aesthetic realism with a historical realism which he deftly employs to raise and resolve the charge of caricature. What the sophisticated reader might consider a naivety stretched beyond the bounds of belief is, in actuality, strongly grounded in western fact and fiction. Indeed, Thompson's attitudes are symptomatic representations of beliefs that have characterized western encounters with the "Other" throughout the course of colonial history.

Thompson's initial conception of Africans as both different and unequal, for instance, has an influential literary precedent in Prospero's insistence on Caliban's incapacity to master civil behavior. And it has a purportedly literal source in the stories of African intractability brought home by such Victorian explorers as Richard F. Burton: "[The African] is inferior to the active-minded and objective . . . European, and to the . . . subjective and reflective Asiatic. He partakes largely of the worst characteristics of the lower Oriental types – stagnation of mind, indolence of body, moral deficiency, superstition, and childish passion" (*The Lake Regions of Central Africa*, vol. 2, 1876, quoted in Brantlinger, 1985, 179). If one requires a more modern example of a "Victorian" attitude toward racial difference, one need look no further than the colonial writings of the otherwise progressive George Orwell (see, especially, his depiction of Burmans in "Shooting an Elephant" and *Burmese Days*). In short, Thompson's naivety is as much a culturally conditioned and historically reinforced habit of mind as is the two Africans' notion that to be civilized is to be British. That it seems so caricatured testifies to the absurd persistence of the colonialist stereotypes from which it derives. And there is more than a little irony in this being brought home to us by a latter-day Caliban with a far better "grasp of history and literature" than John Thompson can claim. Ngugi continues:

> Thompson was excited, conscious of walking on the precipice of a great discovery: what, precisely, was the nature of that heritage? . . .
>
> "My heart was filled with joy," he wrote later. "In a flash I was convinced that the growth of the British Empire was the development of a great moral idea: it means, it must surely lead to the creation of one British nation, embracing people of all colours and creeds, based on the just proposition that all men were created equal. . . ."
>
> Transform the British Empire into one nation: didn't this explain so many

things, why, for instance, so many Africans had offered themselves up to die
in the war against Hitler?

From the first, as soon as he set his hands on a pen to write down his
thoughts, the title of the manuscript floated before him. He would call it:
PROSPERO IN AFRICA.

(Ngugi, 1967 [1968, 47–8]).

As Ngugi reconstructs Thompson's enthusiastic development of his "great
moral idea" of fraternity and equality, he again moves into the realm of
caricature. In this instance, however, it is colonialist idealism, not racism, that
is the object of his critical scrutiny. What makes Thompson's otherwise laudable
sentiments deserving of censure is, of course, the fact that they are just as
ethnocentric as his racist attitudes. While the latter are premised on a belief in
African difference and inequality consistent with an assumed sense of British
superiority, the former start from an "improved" notion of African equality
only to become "corrupted" by an assimilationist ethic which also operates in
concert with an ethnic chauvinism (see Todorov, 1984, 42–3, 146). Caricature
thus again yields to an incisive statement of the truth behind colonialist
appearance, or, more correctly, of truth as the colonized other perceives it,
independent of whatever unresolved mix of intentions may preoccupy the
colonizer.

Although it may be objected that Thompson's association of *The Tempest* with
the "great moral idea" that is the British Empire is critically mistaken and
historically inaccurate, what makes his apparent misappropriation of Shakespeare's text both possible and plausible is his identification of the same with a
series of other texts and events which it variously resembles, rehearses, and
anticipates. In the complicated interplay of texts and observations that goes into
the forging of Thompson's project, Britain's alleged success in the voluntary
enlistment of Africans into military service recuperates Prospero's failed attempt
to civilize Caliban (that is, to have Caliban *willingly* do his bidding) in the form
of a moral idea. Success on this front promotes the possibility of a second chance
for Prospero in Africa. It promotes as well a second chance for the actual literary
proponents of the great moral idea Thompson mistakenly (or presciently?)
associates with Prospero. For it is Marlow and, to a greater extent, Kurtz from
Conrad's *Heart of Darkness* – perhaps the most influential colonial text in
postcolonial Africa's literary circles (see Hamner, 1984; Brantlinger, 1985b) –
who fill in the outline first sketched by Prospero's treatment of Caliban in *The
Tempest*. However, Thompson never explicitly refers to Conrad, much less
Kurtz who, if we allow literary history to supply chronology, had already tried
and failed to apply his moral idea to Africa, and had revealed his own moral
and cultural impoverishment in the process. Nor does he exhibit any awareness
that the Africans who "had offered themselves up to die in the war against
Hitler" had, in fact, like modern Calibans, been involuntarily conscripted. By
means of such lapses in the logic of fact and fiction, Ngugi challenges the
informed western reader to bring his "superior" grasp of history and literature

to bear on the gaps in Thompson's argument but complicates the challenge by revealing related gaps in the reader's own interpretive strategies. We know, for example, that it is Kurtz, not Prospero, Conrad, not Shakespeare, who employ the language of missionary idealism which occupies so prominent a position in nineteenth-century colonialist discourse. Such knowledge compels us to "correct" Thompson's obvious misreading of Shakespeare by dissociating Prospero from his implied connection with Kurtz. But Ngugi is actually insisting on the validity of the connection we attempt to resist. He opposes our intervention by again making strictly literary history blend with colonial fact, rehearsing both on the level of plot by having John Thompson reenact Prospero's failure to make a willing slave of Caliban in the colonial present, and by linking that failure to Thompson's subsequently brutal treatment of intractable Africans in the manner of Kurtz.

A full appreciation of the intertextual complexity of *A Grain of Wheat* requires a broader knowledge of the novel than I can depend on here. But it should be sufficient to note that as a result of the Mau Mau rebellion, Thompson experiences a profound disillusionment with Africa and Africans. His disillusionment leads ultimately not to a book, but to an official investigation of his role in the deaths of eleven prisoners in the concentration camp over which he comes to preside. One of his notebook entries, made prior to his taking command of this camp, reveals the gradual emergence of the Kurtz latent from the start in Thompson's conception of Prospero:

> Colonel Robson, a Senior District Officer in Rung'ei, Kiambu, was savagely murdered. I am replacing him at Rung'ei. One must use a stick. No government can tolerate anarchy, no civilization can be built on this violence and savagery. Mau Mau is evil; a movement which if not checked will mean complete destruction of all the values on which our civilization has thriven.
> (Ngugi, 1967 [1968, 49])

And a last echo of Kurtz before the eleven prisoners are killed should make plain Ngugi's point of view: "Thompson was on the edge of madness. Eliminate the vermin, he would grind his teeth at night. He set the white officers and warders on the men. Yes – eliminate the vermin" (p. 117). It is clear from Ngugi's close paraphrase of Kurtz's desperately scrawled message, "Exterminate all the brutes," that he cannot avoid the charge of caricature in this instance. But I am committed less to evaluating his style on this occasion than to determining the validity of his placement of Shakespeare at the center of this intertextual transaction. Can we simply say that Thompson's identification with Prospero is the product of misreading, and that his ultimate reproduction of Kurtz's rhetoric and violence is symptomatic of Ngugi's ill-considered attempt to reveal the arbitrariness of colonialist distinctions? Or should we ask to what extent Kurtz *can* be considered a latent, potential, or actualized version of Prospero? Might Ngugi be telling us something about the ideological function of *The Tempest* we would do well to heed, something that could contribute to a fuller understanding of Prospero's contribution to the development of colonialist discourse and behavior?

As Ngugi presents it, Thompson's identification with Prospero is motivated by an ideological single-mindedness that is not and cannot be careful about distinctions. Thompson's inability to discern a break or juncture between the "moral idea" he associates with "Prospero in Africa" and his actions in Rung'ei is meant to serve as a representative instance of his culture's limitations. "Civilization" is the privileged commodity in each instance, and what stands in civilization's way is simply an obstacle to be surmounted or destroyed. It is in direct opposition to Thompson's designation of European civilization as "the centre of the universe and man's history" that Ngugi's own ideological position takes shape: a position that reads into Prospero's dispossession of Caliban the entire history of the destruction of African culture (Ngugi, 1972, 14, 7–11). That he advances, through Thompson, a reading of Shakespeare in which Prospero – the character who is critically identified with his playwright-creator more often than any other Shakespearean figure – is associated with Kurtz suggests an aggressive attempt to bring European assumptions of cultural superiority into unflattering contact with the history those assumptions have imposed on the culturally dispossessed. And, in choosing Shakespeare to represent those assumptions, Ngugi takes strategic aim at the one aspect of colonialism that continues to resist unconditional censure, namely, its purportedly high-minded intentions. In this respect, it may be said that if Thompson and Ngugi misread Shakespeare at all, they do so in consistency with the way colonial history has inscribed itself on colonizer and colonized alike.

One can attempt to free Shakespeare from these competing ideological appropriations by employing a developmental model to explain Thompson's implicit association of Prospero with Kurtz. From this perspective, it may appear that Thompson's initial identification with Prospero actually represents his identification with an early, idealist phase in western imperialism, and that his subsequent embrace of Kurtz's "unsound methods" is representative of what becomes of such idealism in the course of colonial history. Working through this model would allow us to recuperate *The Tempest* as a historically "innocent" text that is corrupted by later historical developments. It would also allow us to construct an innocent moment in colonial history to which we could refer with the same nostalgia some historians bring to bear on their representations of early European explorations of Africa and the New World.[5] But colonial history is no longer exclusively written in ethnocentric isolation by and for western eyes in a manner that privileges the glory of discovery at the expense of the people discovered. Nor does Ngugi present Thompson's development in evolutionary terms; Kurtz is latent in this would-be Prospero from the start. For Ngugi, a Kurtz whose crimes are premised on an unquestioned claim to superiority is culturally and psychologically coextensive with a Prospero whose "high-minded" treatment of Caliban is premised on the same. And, by extension, a Prospero who can meditate "rarer actions" but actually executes rougher justice against his designated inferiors is coextensive with a Kurtz who would suppress savage customs in the name of his own definitions of what is human or humane.

What Prospero contributes to the possibilities of a Kurtz (or a Thompson, or a Rhodes or Stanley, for that matter) is a culturally privileged rationale for objectifying what are really always subjective representations of the Other, for presenting as facts what are really only fictions. Although no precise equation can be drawn between Kurtz's unsound methods and Thompson's murder of his prisoners, on the one hand, and Prospero's "stying" of Caliban "in this hard rock," on the other, each character's actions derive from and focus on a representation of the colonized Other as "A devil, a born devil, on whose nature / Nurture can never stick" (*The Tempest*, IV. i. 188–9).[6] Roughly schematized, a psychological profile of the three characters reveals a movement from an ethnocentric idealism that founders on difference and defiance to an equally ethnocentric pragmatism that rationalizes violence as a suitable response to frustration. Each, moreover, rehearses a movement that may be considered characteristic of the European response to the colonial encounter. As Ngugi writes elsewhere, "In the story of Prospero and Caliban, Shakespeare had dramatized the practice and psychology of colonization years before it became a global phenomenon" (Ngugi, 1972, 7–11).

The Tempest, then, would appear to operate in concert with enduring colonialist assumptions from both Thompson's and Ngugi's respective points of view. For character and author alike, *The Tempest* supplies a pedigreed precedent for a politics of imperial domination premised on the objectified intractability of the native element. It provides a pretext for a paternalistic approach to colonial administration that sanctions a variety of enlightened procedures, ranging from the soft word to the closed fist. The play's ability to fix the shared parameters of two otherwise opposed ideological positions should not, of course, obscure the extent to which *The Tempest* resists oversimplification and subordination to the ideological functions it has been made to serve. To clarify a point I have made above, in considering himself a Prospero in Africa, Thompson may be accurately reading his own colonialist condescension into a character but also misreading Shakespeare's attitudes toward that character. The position which *The Tempest* occupied at its moment of production may not, for example, have been as decidedly colonialist as Thompson and Ngugi consider it to be at its point of reception. Paul Brown, in his recent demonstration that *The Tempest* "is not simply a reflection of colonialist practices but an intervention in an ambivalent and even contradictory discourse" (1985, 48), provides a comprehensive reexamination of the play's position in its historic moment that is especially persuasive given the oft-noted lengths to which Shakespeare goes in endowing the play's colonized voices with an undeniable grace and authority. And Francis Barker and Peter Hulme's equally recent observation that "Prospero's play and *The Tempest* are not necessarily the same thing," and hence that Prospero is himself often the object of Shakespeare's critical scrutiny, would appear to offer a crucial corrective to those who "identify Prospero's voice as direct and reliable authorial statement" (1985, 199).[7]

For his part, Ngugi presents Thompson's identification with Prospero as a predictable choice, given the available possibilities in a colonialist canon within which *The Tempest* maintains a prominent position, along with such other seminal texts as *Heart of Darkness*. Shakespeare's attitude toward Prospero is no more to his point than is Conrad's similarly complex attitude towards Kurtz. Given Ngugi's position as a politically committed African writer, *The Tempest*'s historical distance from *Heart of Darkness* is insignificant, Prospero's difference from Kurtz negligible, insofar as each participates in a common colonialist enterprise that has seldom been known to make distinctions between its colonized subjects.[8] Ngugi thus creates a character whose apparent contradictions are presented as symptomatic traits of a colonialist temperament that habitually represents its own inhumanity in the form of virtuous activity.[9] Since contradiction is, for Ngugi, the characteristic state of Prospero in Africa, he sees nothing contradictory in the ensemble of texts to which John Thompson alludes and from which he derives. With respect to the problem of Shakespeare's attitude toward Prospero, Ngugi would, then, appear to endorse Tony Bennett's observation that "The position which a text occupies . . . at its originating moment of production is . . . no necessary indicator of the positions which it may subsequently come to occupy in different historical and political contexts;" and that it is "not a question of what texts mean but of what they might be *made to mean* politically" (1982, 229). For Ngugi, a historically or critically "correct" reading of *The Tempest* that isolates the play "at its originating moment of production" would serve merely an antiquarian's interest, documenting an alleged "intervention" in colonialist discourse that made no discernibly positive impact on the subsequent development of colonial practices. His own variety of historicity would, on the other hand, focus on all that has intervened between the text's originating moment and the present moment of reception; it would thus focus less on the text's status as a historically determined literary artifact, now open to a variety of interpretations, than on its subordination to what history has made of it.

Since history, as he perceives it, has made *The Tempest* a celebrated early example of white paternalism exercising its prerogatives on and against its colonial subjects, Ngugi employs Prospero as a figure who would "naturally" appeal to an idealistic Englishman seeking a high-minded rationale for his own and his nation's imperial designs in the repository of his cultural heritage. In so doing, he offers an implied commentary on a seldom acknowledged contributor to history's productions, that is, a scholarly tradition which has long prided itself on its professed objectivity and disdain for ideologies and ideologues alike, but which is responsible for the dissemination of the ideologically charged reading of Shakespeare that makes Thompson's identification with Prospero inevitable. It is only reasonable to assume that Prospero's appeal would be felt most strongly by someone whose estimate of his dramatic status in *The Tempest* was uncomplicated by critical considerations of the kind we have reviewed above: considerations which are, for the most part, products of the past twenty years of Shakespeare criticism during which time Shakespeare's assigned status as "national poet" and as spokesman for British political and social ideals has been in the process of radical revision. Were we to review slightly earlier examples of the critical literature on the play – not necessarily drawn from Britain's high imperial past – we would find that Prospero's dramatic status has, for the most part, been unclouded. The admittedly extreme example of G. Wilson Knight's identification of Prospero with "Plato's philosopher-king" and of *The Tempest* as "a myth of the national soul" (1947, 254–5) cannot be considered representative. But Knight's ability to celebrate within the same pages of a book originally published by Oxford University Press (and reprinted at least six times thereafter) *The Tempest*'s "alignment with Shakespeare's massed statements elsewhere in definition of true sovereignty and . . . of British destiny" and, in respect to that destiny, British colonization – "especially [Britain's] will to raise savage peoples from superstition and blood-sacrifice, taboos and witchcraft and the attendant fears and slaveries, to a more enlightened existence" – strongly suggests the availability and staying power of such ideas. Were we to look further afield, into the domain of American Shakespeare criticism, we would find equally conspicuous examples of the ways in which Prospero's dramatic burdens – vis à vis his usurping brother, Antonio; the "foul conspiracy" of Caliban and friends, etc. – have been traditionally privileged at the expense of the burdens actually carried in the play by Ariel, Caliban, and Ferdinand.[10] We observe here, as in the previous example, that an ethnocentric scholarly community has generally discerned in an ethnocentric Prospero the mirror image of its own self-involvement and obliviousness to the claims of an Other who does not really seem to inhabit the same dimension of existence as itself.

Academic scholarship is not, of course, the sole mediator between *The Tempest*'s moment of production and the modern moment of its reception. As should be obvious from the example of Wilson Knight, the ideological position of the scholarly community itself, with respect to works like *The Tempest*, has been largely shaped by its understandably one-sided acquaintance with colonial history. For many members of that community, colonial history has presented itself (as in the case of the young Joseph Conrad) in the form of a succession of romantic exploration narratives that celebrate the courage and daring of adventurers in the wilds of Africa and the south Pacific, while only superficially portraying the lives of indigenous peoples (which are frequently presented with less regard than the authors lavish on the local landscapes; see Pratt, 1985). That such a mode of transmission should eventuate in the racial chauvinism of a Thompson or the nationalism of Wilson Knight is not surprising. But it is one of the many ironies of colonial history that the reading of *The Tempest* I have attributed to Ngugi also appears to draw heavily from the same literary and historical matrix that compels Thompson to effect the imaginative transfer of Prospero from Shakespeare's fictionally cross-referenced island to Africa.[11]

The Tempest's capacity to make a significant intervention in the formation of colonialist discourse and in the development of colonialist practices was, I believe, inhibited from the start by the play's generic resemblances to and rehearsals of contemporary reports of colonial encounters.[12] Indeed, the play's very participation in this formative moment through the medium of Prospero's appropriation of Caliban's island, and his act's perceived consistency with the colonial ventures of a Raleigh and the partisan writings of the Hakluyts, can be said to have condemned the play to participate also in that discourse's evolution and eventual rigidification in the imperial moment of Britain's colonization of Africa. It is, of course, in the nature of colonial encounters that stereotypes are privileged at the expense of distinctions. Prospero's unqualified assertion that Caliban is a devil "on whose nature / Nurture can never stick" resonates more strongly in a mind bent on self-justification and an escape from uncertainty than does his ambiguous and, finally, puzzling acknowledgement of Caliban as his own. But this is also the case because the assertion finds so many echoes in the literature and history of colonization, and the acknowledgement so few echoes that are problematic. In a similar vein, it will ultimately be the "unsound methods" of a Stanley that will prove more influential than the efforts of a milder-mannered Livingstone among practical colonialist considerations. An example of the kind of intervention such a figure could make in Ngugi's reading of Prospero into Africa is provided in the following excerpt from Stanley's exploration diaries:

> We tried to make a camp at Kiunyu. . . . As we spoke they mocked us. When we asked them if they would sell some grain, they asked us if they were our slaves that they should till their land and sow grain for us. Meanwhile, canoes were launched and criers sent ahead to proclaim we were coming. The beach was crowded by infuriates and mockers. Perceiving that a camp was hopeless in this vicinity, we pulled off, but [quickly] perceived we were followed by several canoes in some of which we saw spears shaken at us. We halted and made ready, and as they approached still in this fashion I opened on them with the Winchester Repeating Rifle. Six shots and four deaths were sufficient to quiet the mocking . . . and to establish a different character for ourselves – somewhat more respectable, if not more desirable. We captured three canoes, some fish and nets etc. as spoil.
>
> (Stanley and Neame, 1961, 125)

From its reminder that magic in *The Tempest* occupies "the space inhabited in colonial history by gunpowder" (Hulme, 1981, 74), to the comparison it suggests between Stanley's "respectable" transformation of stolen goods into "spoils" and Prospero's self-righteous transformation of Caliban's bid for freedom into a "foul conspiracy," there is much here that could negatively color any latter-day Caliban's reading of Prospero into Africa. Yet Stanley can also invoke the idealist strain of colonialist discourse, and does so in a disturbingly apposite manner in concluding the preceding anecdote:

> I had an opportunity also to prove that although able to resent affronts and meet hostility we were not inhuman nor revengeful, for a wounded man struggling to escape from dread decapitation – the common fate of the wounded in battle – cried out for mercy and the rifle was lowered and he was permitted to go.
>
> (Stanley and Neame, 1961, 125–6)

In its own context, Stanley's choice of the "rarer action" is clearly six shots too late for those who have just been taught a different lesson; it is a largely gratuitous gesture that hardly offers proof of the humanity he claims to anyone apart from himself and his companions. But placed within the broader framework of colonial history, Stanley's lesson of mercy exemplifies that curious convergence of a mind convinced of the virtuousness of its intentions with a will focused on demonstrating its mastery through force, which characterizes the colonialist temperament from Prospero on down to John Thompson. This convergence of assumed high-mindedness with brutality is exactly what dissolves the differences between Prospero and Stanley from the perspective of the colonized Other, whose claim to self-determination ("they asked us if they were our slaves") is summarily denied in each instance and made the basis for his exclusion from humane consideration. In *The Tempest*, what appears to disturb Prospero even more than Caliban's foiled attempt to violate Miranda's honor is Caliban's insistence on recalling his former sovereignty, his repeated effort to lay claim to a history and inheritance which imply a state of equality at odds with his assigned status as slave. It is in the face of Caliban's assertion that "I am all the subjects that you have, / Which first was my own King" (and not to any denial of his attempt to rape Miranda) that Prospero responds, "Thou most lying slave, / Whom stripes may move, not kindness" (I. ii. 343–4, 346–7). And, similarly, in Stanley's anecdote it is more the mockery of the African "infuriates" than their show of hostility that incites him to a show of the same.

It will, perhaps, be objected that in comparison to Stanley's methods, Prospero's punishment of Caliban is negligible in intensity and consequence, and eventuates in a pardon that is prelude to Caliban's liberation. But in terms of *The Tempest*'s status as a privileged text in the history of colonialist discourse, it is difficult to recuperate this apparent exercise in enlightened paternalism as a historically insignificant action. Because Prospero's brutality – like Stanley's – operates out of an assumption of high-mindedness that differentiates itself from the brutality of an Other who does not make the same assumption or cannot claim the same relationship to "civil behavior," it will remain privileged in the eyes of actor and civil beholder alike.[13] Caliban's unregenerate response to Prospero's accusation regarding his attempted rape of Miranda – "O ho, O ho! would't had been done" (I. ii, 351) – and Stanley's unqualified remark about the "common fate" of "dread decapitation" both serve to disqualify the Other from the consideration we would otherwise grant him were he to subscribe to our own standards of civil behavior. They both confirm the Other's ineradicable difference from us and sanction the measures taken to assure his containment (recall Wilson Knight's remarks about blood sacrifice). We should, moreover, notice that an ultimately chastened Caliban's acceptance of the pardon that succeeds punishment – 'I'll be wise hereafter, / And seek for grace" (V. i. 294–5) – actually serves to validate Prospero's procedures from the victim's perspective, thus making the duly conditioned slave a willing accomplice in a system of domination that has come to seem natural. Wisdom, for Caliban, has now become synonymous with complete acquiescence to Prospero's early claim to cultural superiority (cf. Cohen, 1985, 400). In this respect, Shakespeare's staged fantasy establishes the parameters of a colonialist procedure Stanley will rehearse with a rougher magic in Africa; and it produces exactly that effect on the Other Stanley aims at in his lesson.[14]

I am not suggesting here that Stanley needed *The Tempest* as a pretext either for his brutality or for the lesson in moral superiority that succeeds it, anymore than I suggest in my epigraph that Cecil Rhodes's attachment to his library was modeled on Prospero's attachment to his books. My point is that the well-advertised colonialist methods of men like Stanley and Rhodes – to the extent that they resemble and rehearse the actions and rhetoric of Prospero – have the effect of valorizing what they resemble and rehearse, and of dissolving distinction into identification. And these effects will be felt more strongly in those readings of *The Tempest* which are motivated and informed by the culturally divisive history of colonization than in those which maintain a critical distance from ideological polarization. As the West Indian George Lamming writes:

> I cannot read *The Tempest* without recalling the adventure of those voyages reported by Hakluyt; and when I remember the voyages and the particular period in African history, I see *The Tempest* against the background of England's experiment in colonisation. . . . *The Tempest* was also prophetic of a political future which is our present. Moreover, the circumstances of my life, both as a colonial and exiled descendant of Caliban in the twentieth century, is an example of that prophecy.
>
> (Lamming, 1960, 13)

In a more incisive vein, Derek Walcott has a character in his play, *Pantomime*, demonstrate that the specific form colonialism takes in different places makes no real difference from the perspective of the colonized Other. Prospero is always master, Caliban is always slave:

> For three hundred years I served you. Three hundred years I served you breakfast . . . in my white jacket on a white veranda, boss, bwana, effendi, bacra, sahib . . . in that sun that never set on your empire I was your shadow, I did what you did, boss, bwana, effendi, bacra, sahib . . . that was my pantomime.
>
> (Walcott, 1980, 112)

What plays no role in Ngugi's depiction of Thompson – and emerges only at the end of Walcott's play as a result of his Caliban's overpowering insistence – is the possibility of Prospero's acknowledgement of responsibility for making a "thing of darkness" out of someone who never really was his own. This is, of course, no more than a possibility in the text of *The Tempest* itself, one that has, moreover, occasioned all manner of critical dispute regarding its precise implications.[15] On this account, we would do well to recall that the way in which *The Tempest* serves the competing ideologies of colonizer and colonized has, finally, as little to do with ambiguity as it does with whatever intervention in the formation of colonialist discourse Shakespeare may have attempted to contribute. But it is also worth recalling that similarly promising examples of Shakespeare's possible departures from the colonialist rule have not been generally acknowledged by representatives of the colonized Other who have, in different circumstances, been willing to accept dissenting colonial voices as genuine interventions in a characteristically one-sided conversation.[16] In attempting to extricate Shakespeare from the politically divisive functions he has been made to serve, we should not, then, be blind to the possibility that the apparent marginality of Shakespeare's interventions may also be predicated on their actual marginality in Shakespeare's text where departures from the colonialist rule – "You taught me language, and my profit on't / Is, I know how to curse" (I. ii. 365–6) – always lead back to the same colonialist destination: "I'll be wise hereafter."

It is no doubt true that *The Tempest* has long functioned in the service of ideologies that repress what they cannot accommodate and exploit what they can. One consequence of this subordination of text to ideological transaction is that it is still a generally uneducable, bestial Caliban who survives the adjustments that have been made in western racial prejudices; mainly a blindly self-righteous, authoritarian Prospero who presides in Third World inversions of the same.[17] Yet the text of *The Tempest* continues to allow Prospero the privilege of the grand closing gesture; continues to privilege that gesture's ambiguity at the expense of Caliban's dispossession; continues, in short, to support and substantiate the very reading of itself transacted by the ideologies in question. It is in this respect, among others, that *The Tempest* is not only complicit in the history of its successive misreadings, but responsible in some measure for the development of the ways in which it is read.

Notes

1. For the Shultz quotation and for provocative remarks about political uses of Shakespeare, I am indebted to Donald K. Hedrick, whose paper, "How to Find Authors," was presented at the ideology seminar of the World Shakespeare Congress (West Berlin, 1986), which gave rise to this volume.
2. Some examples are: Lamming (1960, 1970) and Césaire (1969).
3. Two new essays which involve attempts of this kind actually move in two directions at once insofar as they consider the play's complexity symptomatic of its inescapable participation in the discourse of colonialism. See Brown (1985) and Barker and Hulme (1985).
4. In *The Conquest of America* (1984), Tzvetan Todorov distinguishes "two component parts" in Columbus's attitude toward the Amerindians which, he contends, "we shall find again in the following century and, in practice, down to our own day in every colonist in his relations to the colonized." The colonist either "conceives the Indians . . . as human beings altogether, having the same rights as himself; but then he sees them not only as equals but also as identical, and this behavior leads to assimilationism, the projection of his own values on the others. Or else he starts from the difference, but the latter is immediately translated into terms of superiority and inferiority. . . . What is denied is the existence of a human substance truly other, something capable of being not merely an imperfect state of oneself" (p. 42).

5. A good recent example of such an approach is Hibbert (1982).

6. All quotations from *The Tempest* are taken from Frank Kermode's Arden edition (1958).

7. Each of these critics writes in the unacknowledged shadow of Harry Berger, Jr, who has convincingly exposed the flaws in an uncritical identification of Prospero with Shakespeare, but whose portrayal of Prospero's motivations bears a remarkable resemblance to O. Mannoni's classic depiction of Prospero as the prototypical embodiment of colonialist psychology. Where Berger observes that "Shakespeare presents in Prospero the signs of an ancient and familiar psychological perplex connected with excessive idealism and the longing for the golden age; a state of mind based on unrealistic expectations; a mind therefore hesitant to look too closely at the world as it is" and capable of exercising "violent repressiveness" in the face of "the pressure of actual life" (1968, 258), Mannoni contends that "the colonial in common with Prospero lacks [an] awareness of the world of Others, a world in which Others have to be respected." And, he concludes, this lack of awareness of the other is often "combined with an urge to dominate" (1964, 108). The difference between these seemingly overlapping points of view is that Berger makes Shakespeare an active partner in his critical distinction, implicitly assigning priority to Shakespeare's critical acuity, whereas Mannoni appears to implicate Shakespeare in the psychology of his dramatic surrogate.

8. Ngugi's thinking here is clearly indebted to Franz Fanon who, in *Black Skin, White Masks* (1952), eloquently argues against relative positions in respect to racism or colonialism. See, especially, pp. 85–91.

9. I choose the term "virtuous activity" because it was favored by another, more successful Prospero in Africa, namely, Cecil Rhodes, who, according to his biographers, "would often quote from Aristotle: 'The utmost good of man is the virtuous activity of the soul and pursuit of the highest virtue throughout life'" (Lockhart and Woodhouse, 1963, 203–4).

10. A good inventory of examples is supplied by Hallett Smith (1969), who provides an example of his own making in his introduction where he remarks that "[Caliban's] yearning for freedom is in no way respectable, since if he had it he would use it for devilish purposes" (p. 5). Another instance worth recording can be found in Norman Rabkin (1967). In the course of a seven-page commentary on *The Tempest*, Rabkin reiterates the oft-cited designation of Prospero as "a symbolic representation of Shakespeare himself" (p. 224); likens Prospero's maturation to that of Odysseus when he decides to leave Phaeacia; and mentions Caliban only twice, once as the alleged embodiment of the "brutal, earthy, fleshbound, treacherous" aspects of nature (p. 227), and later as a character whose "irremediable bestiality" exemplifies "certain facts [that] are absolute and finally beyond the distorting vision of a single mind" (pp. 227–8). Apart from the revealing wording which he employs to objectify Caliban's intractability in the face of an admirably flexible Prospero, susceptible both to change and growth (and which may also be employed to exemplify the critic's ideological bias), Rabkin's reading of *The Tempest* may be considered representative.

11. See Hulme (1981) for a detailed discussion of *The Tempest's* joint participation in Mediterranean and Caribbean discourse.

12. It is worth noting here that Shakespeare may have modeled his treatment of the colonial encounter on William Strachey's historically prior account of Sir Thomas Gates's successive encounters with the Virginia Indians which, as Harry Berger observes, "supplies a close analogue to Prospero's experience with Caliban" (1968, 261–2). In this account, Gates's initial resistance to any "violent proceeding" against the Indians ultimately cedes, after a particularly troubling example of the Indians' alleged intractability, to a resolve "to be revenged" against them, Gates having now "well perceived, how little a faire and noble intreatie workes upon a barbarous disposition" (quoted in Kermode, 1958, 140).

13. On the idea of "civility" with specific reference to Stanley, see Spurr (1985).
14. See Barker and Hulme (1985) who throughout their essay try "to show how much of *The Tempest's* complexity comes from its *staging* of the distinctive moves and figures of colonialist discourse" (p. 204).
15. See, e.g., Greenblatt (1970) who, after entertaining several possible interpretations, concludes that "Shakespeare leaves Caliban's fate naggingly unclear. Prospero has acknowledged a bond; that is all" (pp. 570–1).
16. For example, Abdul JanMohamed (1983) makes a persuasive case for the "characteristic openness" of Isak Dinesen's colonial encounters in Kenya (p. 53). He considers Dinesen "a major exception to the . . . pattern of conquest and irresponsible exploitation" (p. 57), not least because "she does not distance herself [from the native cultures surrounding her] through the notion of racial superiority" (p. 60). However, one should note that Ngugi, a native Kenyan, does not share JanMohamed's high opinion of Dinesen, as he makes abundantly clear in *Homecoming* (1972, 9) where he directly associates her with Prospero.
17. In *The Stranger in Shakespeare* (1972), Leslie Fiedler notes that some "exponents of *negritude*" actually make Caliban "the hero, not the villain of the piece," thus inverting "the racist mythology of their former masters" (p. 248).

Works cited

Althusser, Louis (1971) "Ideology and Ideological State Apparatuses," in *Lenin and Philosophy and Other Essays*, trans. Ben Brewster, New York, Monthly Review Press; London, New Left Books.
Barker, Francis and Hulme, Peter (1985) "Nymphs and reapers heavily vanish: The Discursive Con-texts of *The Tempest*," in Drakakis, John (ed.) *Alternative Shakespeares*, London and New York, Methuen, 191–205.
Bennett, Tony (1982) "Text and History," in Widdowson, Peter (ed.) *Re-Reading English*, London, Methuen, 223–36.
Berger, Jr, Harry (1968) "Miraculous Harp: A Reading of Shakespeare's *Tempest*," *Shakespeare Survey*, 5, 253–83.
Brantlinger, Patrick (1985a) "Victorians and Africans: The Genealogy of the Myth of the Dark Continent," *Critical Inquiry*, 12 (1), 166–203.
—— (1985b) "*Heart of Darkness*: Anti-Imperialism, Racism, or Impressionism?" *Criticism*, 27 (4), 363–85.
Brown, Paul (1985) "'This thing of darkness I acknowledge mine': *The Tempest* and the Discourse of Colonialism," in Dollimore, Jonathan and Sinfield, Alan (eds) *Political Shakespeare: New Essays in Cultural Materialism*, Manchester, Manchester University Press; Ithaca, NY, Cornell University Press, 48–71.
Césaire, Aimé (1969) *Une Tempête*, Paris, Seuil.
Cohen, Walter (1985) *Drama of a Nation: Public Theater in Renaissance England and Spain*, Ithaca, NY, Cornell University Press.
Fanon, Franz (1952) *Black Skin, White Masks*, repr. 1967, New York, Grove.
Fiedler, Leslie (1972) *The Stranger in Shakespeare*, New York, Stein & Day.
Greenblatt, Stephen J. (1970) "Learning to Curse: Aspects of Linguistic Colonialism in the 16th Century," in Chiapelli, Fredi (ed.) *First Images of America: The Impact of the New World on the Old*, Berkeley, University of California Press, 561–80.
Hamner, Robert (1984) "Colony, Nationhood and Beyond: Third World Writers and Critics Contend with Joseph Conrad," *World Literature Written in English*, 23 (1), 108–16.
Hibbert, Christopher (1982) *Africa Explored: Europeans in the Dark Continent, 1769–1889*, repr. 1984, London, Penguin.
Hulme, Peter (1981) "Hurricanes in the Caribbees: The Constitution of the Discourse of

English Colonialism,'' in Barker, Francis, Bernstein, Jay, Coombes, John, Hulme, Peter, Stone, Jennifer, and Stratton, Jon (eds) *1642: Literature and Power in the Seventeenth century*, Proceedings of the Essex Conference on the Sociology of Literature, July 1980, Colchester, University of Essex, 55–83.

JanMohamed, Abdul (1983) *Manichean Aesthetics: The Politics of Literature in Colonial Africa*, Amherst, University of Massachusetts Press.

Kermode, Frank (ed.) (1958) *The Tempest* by William Shakespeare, Arden edn, London, Methuen.

Knight, G. Wilson (1947) *The Crown of Life: Essays in Interpretation of Shakespeare's Final Plays*, repr. 1966, New York, Barnes & Noble.

Lamming, George (1960) *The Pleasures of Exile*, repr. 1984, London, Allison & Busby.

—— (1970) *Water with Berries*, London, Longman.

Lockhart, J.G. and Woodhouse, C.M. (1963) *Cecil Rhodes: The Colossus of Southern Africa*, New York, Macmillan.

Mannoni, [Dominique] O. (1964) *Prospero and Caliban: The Psychology of Colonization*, New York, Praeger.

Ngugi Wa Thiong'o (1968) *A Grain of Wheat*, London, Heinemann. First published 1967.

—— (1972) *Homecoming: Essays on African and Caribbean Literature, Culture and Politics*, repr. 1983, Westport, Conn., Lawrence Hill.

Pratt, Mary Louise (1985) "Scratches on the Face of the Country; or, What Mr. Barrow Saw in the Land of the Bushmen,'' *Critical Inquiry*, 12 (1), 119–43.

Rabkin, Norman (1967) *Shakespeare and the Common Understanding*, New York, Free Press.

Smith, Hallett (ed.) (1969) *Twentieth Century Interpretations of "The Tempest"*, Englewood Cliffs, NJ, Prentice-Hall.

Spurr, David (1985) "Colonialist Journalism: Stanley to Didion,'' *Raritan*, 5 (2), 35–50.

Stanley, Richard and Neame, Alan (eds) (1961) *The Exploration Diaries of H.M. Stanley*, London, William Kimber.

Todorov, Tzvetan (1984) *The Conquest of America: The Question of the Other*, trans. Richard Howard, New York, Harper & Row.

Walcott, Derek (1980) *Remembrance and Pantomime*, New York, Farrar, Straus & Giroux.

5

The Order of the Garter, the cult of Elizabeth, and class–gender tension in *The Merry Wives of Windsor*

Peter Erickson

The study of patriarchal ideology in Shakespeare's plays is a matter not chiefly of explicating fixed doctrine but of identifying stress points.[1] Patriarchal conventions that promote male power are significant because they cannot, in Shakespeare's work, be taken for granted as an automatic, settled norm. Instead, patriarchal control has to be negotiated each time, and the outcome is variable and uncertain. This uncertainty has two aspects. First, patriarchy is not monolithic but multivalent. Even within a historical period it has multiple versions rather than one version – versions that range from the simplistic and stereotypical to the complex and subtle. For example, one might see *The Taming of the Shrew* as an early play in which Shakespeare discovers a rudimentary distinction he later refines between two modes of patriarchy: a crude, violent form based on force and a benevolent form based on persuasion, the latter reflected not only in the need for Kate's consent but also in the concern for her welfare, even her happiness. The line between these two models is here surely too thin for comfort; and, when subsequently refined, the mode of persuasion still involves an element of psychological coercion that rules out any simple notion of male–female equality. Nevertheless, there is a significant difference between these two patriarchal approaches.

PETER ERICKSON is the author of *Patriarchal Structures in Shakespeare's Drama* (Berkeley, University of California Press, 1985) and coeditor, with Coppélia Kahn, of *Shakespeare's "Rough Magic": Renaissance Essays in Honor of C.L. Barber* (Newark, University of Delaware Press; London and Toronto, Associated University Presses, 1985).

Second, in some plays male control cannot be achieved at all, in either mode. These exceptions offer vivid evidence that the conclusion is not guaranteed in advance and that we are witnesses to genuine exploration and struggle rather than to the unfolding of doctrinal formula. *The Merry Wives of Windsor* is a case in point of female dominance. As the title acknowledges, the most striking thing about the play is the role of the wives, whom Muriel Bradbrook sees as "the women's league."[2] Their power is consciously presented as a direct challenge to orthodox sexual politics: "Why, I'll exhibit a bill in the parliament for the putting down of men" (II. i. 28–9).[3]

The prevention of an orthodox patriarchal ending by pervasive female dominance in this play should not, however, be construed as protofeminist insight or sympathy. As Madelon Sprengnether (1980, 180) has pointed out, strong women are ultimately figured as maternal, and "matriarchal" is not equivalent to "feminist." The wives by and large retain the dominant power position, but this does not make Shakespeare a feminist before his time or the play a liberated, protected cultural space. Rather, we confront the paradox that the women's superior power is granted, yet the play's spirit is not progressive.

Stuart Hall (1986) defines ideologies in part as "frameworks of interpretation" that are neither completely conscious nor self-consistent:

> Nowadays the term ideology includes the whole range of concepts, ideas and images which provide the frameworks of interpretation and meaning for social and political thought in society, whether they exist at the high, systematic, philosophical level or at the level of casual, everyday, contradictory, common-sense explanation. . . . this way of defining ideology helps us to underline the point that *no* ideology is ever wholly logical or consistent. . . . There are always loose ends, breaks in the logic, gaps between theory and practice, and internal contradictions in *any* current of thought.
>
> (Hall, 1986, 36)

I can clarify my use of the concept ideology by distinguishing it from the dismissive connotations of the term "ideologue."[4] The latter implies adherence to a systematic set of ideas and beliefs, narrow in scope and dogmatically held; it further suggests a contrast between the doctrinaire and the eclectic, the simplified and the complex, that can then be used to underwrite the division of types of people, parts of the self, or realms of experience into the ideological and the nonideological. This binary opposition leads to the erroneous view that the complexities of actual living transcend mere ideology, which is, by contrast, confined to the level of theory or ideas. My definition of ideology rejects this nonideological preserve and extends ideology to everyone and to the most complicated aspects of experience. Ideologies have relative degrees of sophistication, but all are ideologies. Attainment of a sufficient degree of complexity does not mean that one then escapes from ideology into the nonideological.

In order to counter the notion that ideology is exclusively relegated to ideas, theories, abstractions, I find it useful to emphasize the emotional dimension of ideology by linking it to Raymond Williams's term "structure of feeling."[5] An adequate formulation requires that we understand the operation and pull of ideology at the deeper levels of individual and institutional psyches. It is in the emotional charge and psychological investment involved in the engagement with a set of issues that we may locate an ideological stance in its full, particularized complexity. With regard to Shakespeare's representation of class and gender relations, ideology marks an area of emotional stressfulness and psychological turbulence in which values and expectations are placed under intense dramatic pressure; ideology is thus lived out, not merely thought out.

However, my linkage of ideology with "structure of feeling" goes against the grain of Williams's own usage.[6] In thus bringing together two terms that Williams holds apart, I am responding to a development in cultural studies that Stuart Hall cogently summarizes as a contrast between two distinct lines, one represented by Williams and E.P. Thompson, the other by Lévi-Strauss and Althusser. Crucial to Hall's distinction is the reopening of the question of ideology: "whereas the 'culturalist' paradigm can be defined without requiring a conceptual reference to the term 'ideology' (the *word*, of course, does appear: but it is not a key concept), the 'structuralist' interventions have been largely articulated around the concept of 'ideology'" (Hall, 1980, 64). In particular, Hall favourably notes the "strength which structuralism exhibits . . . in its decentering of 'experience' and its seminal work in elaborating the neglected category of 'ideology'" (1980, 69); the result is to remove the barrier between the two.[7]

Finally, an account of ideology in the English Renaissance period must allow not only for a diversity of ideological options, but also for conflict between ideologies and hence for the possibility of subversion and change.[8] This allowance does not, however, suggest a privileged, radicalized nonideological space. Criticism of an ideology is possible, but it is made not from a standpoint outside ideology but from the perspective of another ideology. By the same token, the twentieth-century critic of whatever persuasion (myself included) is also in ideology.

The present study of *The Merry Wives of Windsor* focuses on class and gender as the two crucial ideological elements in the play. If one believes that Shakespeare gives a progressive valuation to both elements, then the play becomes a positive celebration of female, middle-class power. This is a reading I oppose. I shall argue on the contrary that both class and gender are strongly marked by a conservative valence: neither supports an enlightened egalitarian image of the play. What gives *The Merry Wives of Windsor* its special edge is that the two terms, class and gender, are in conflict rather than in alignment with each other. As dramatized in the play, the Order of the Garter reinforces class hierarchy, while the cult of Elizabeth, of which the Order is a part, reverses traditional gender hierarchy by affirming female authority. This asymmetry prevents the fulfillment of a unified scheme of class and gender hierarchy, and the desire for both thus produces unresolvable tension. Ultimately my thesis involves making a connection between the wives and Queen Elizabeth: the female-controlled plotting within the play parallels the Queen-dominated court politics and arouses a similar male uneasiness. The opening section of the essay, however, focuses on the play's representation of the Windsor community. This starting point is essential because the concept of community and especially the wives' role are so frequently idealized.

1

The standard view, while conceding that the society of *The Merry Wives of Windsor* is not perfect, nonetheless finds it fundamentally sound:

> Must successful productions of the play within recent years have been comparatively realistic in style, stressing the particularity and completeness of the play's picture of contemporary, small-town life. This seems right. Windsor itself, a corporate entity, is the true protagonist of the comedy, not Falstaff, the shadowy young lovers, or even the merry wives themselves, who uphold its values so well . . .
>
> The community at Windsor has its flaws and delusions . . . but at heart it is sound, stable, and remarkably well defined.
>
> (Barton, 1985, 142)[9]

Though appealing, this sanguine view encourages a sentimentality that obviates the need for detailed close examination of how the society operates. In actuality, the play communicates disparity between the characters' activity and the over-worked stock vocabulary they use to describe it. The constant offhand recourse to "sport" and "jest" as catch-all terms to describe the handling of such sensitive topics as money, courtship, violence, and deception puts on display a terminology so thin that it becomes conspicuously inadequate. The tension between verbal self-justification and potentially unsavory action is manifested, for example, in Evans's avid plotting: "it is admirable pleasures and fery honest knaveries" (IV. iv. 79–80). The blunt word "knaveries" pulls uneasily against the profession of honesty, retroactively qualifying the assertion about the admirableness of the pleasures.

The society of the play exhibits a pervasive pattern for dealing with conflict: characters promote an imbalance between conflict and reconciliation by stimulating conflict as much as possible, while making rhetorical exhortations to peace after things have gone too far. I begin, as the play does, with minor characters and then proceed to Ford and the wives, who do not emerge until act II (except for the wives' brief, wordless appearance at I. i. 170–8). My goal is to show that the entire Windsor group, from the miscellany of minor characters to the wives at the apex, shares a common mode of social interchange which cannot be ascribed to harmless, inconsequential farce because Shakespeare's characterization of their collective social action cuts too deeply.

The play immediately introduces the motif of conflict by opening in the midst of Shallow's angry outburst: "Sir Hugh, persuade me not: I will make a Star Chamber matter of it" (I. i. 1–2). Not until well into the first scene, at lines

104–5, is the referent of "it" specified by Shallow's clear-cut accusation in direct confrontation with Falstaff. In the meantime, since unclarified bones of contention allow one to bark louder and longer, we are made to feel that the theme is generalized contention for its own sake and to notice that prolonged conflict invites mediation. For it is Evans, in his role as mediator, who is highlighted here: "If Sir John Falstaff have committed disparagements unto you, I am of the church and will be glad to do my benevolence, to make atonements and compromises between you" (28–31). The nature of the reconciliation Evans effects is subsequently shown to be permanent postponement of a resolution. In a verbose announcement of his intervention whose spirit is compressed into the single word "discreetly," Evans indicates that the conflict will be avoided by tabling it:

> *Evans.* Peace, I pray you. Now let us understand: there is three umpires in this matter, as I understand; that is, Master Page (fidelicet Master Page); and there is myself (fidelicet myself); and the three party is (lastly and finally) mine host of the Garter.
> *Page.*   We three to hear it and end it between them.
> *Evans.* Fery goot; I will make a prief of it in my notebook, and we will afterwards 'ork upon the cause with as great discreetly as we can.
>
> (124–32)

The grammatically incorrect use of an adverb in place of a noun calls our attention to Evans's finesse word, giving it a more active inflection and intimating the crucial role discretion plays in urging the acceptance of this nonresolution. Page's pseudofestive gesture – "I hope we shall drink down all unkindness" (178) – ratifies the policy of avoidance signaled by Evans's arbitration.

Evans's approach allows Shallow to overlook the conflict with Falstaff because his discretion includes a proposed new plot that deflects attention away from the initial problem: "It is petter that friends is the sword, and end it; and there is also another device in my prain, which peradventure prings good discretions with it. There is Anne Page, which is daughter to Master Thomas Page, which is pretty virginity" (39–43). Shallow needs laughably little persuasion to take up the suggestion that he turn to the more profitable business of advancing his nephew's courtship of Page's well-dowried daughter. The pattern of problem solving established here in relatively transparent form involves the substitution of a diversionary plot for the original difficulty; but since the new plot leads to a new contention this pattern becomes an endless, potentially vicious cycle with a tendency to escalate.

As creator and director of the plot to marry Slender to Anne Page, Evans soon finds himself deprived of the role of mediator and forced into that of victim. The diversionary plot generates a new source of conflict by arousing Caius, who himself desires Anne Page, to rhetoric whose violence surpasses the earlier aggressive rant of Falstaff's men: "I will cut his troat in de Park, and I will teach a scurvy jack-a-nape priest to meddle or make. . . . By gar, I will cut all his two stones" (I. iv. 103–6). Now cast in the role of mediator, the host of the

Garter Inn employs his own version of bully rhetoric to "meddle" and the viciousness of his interference more than matches the viciousness of Caius' ire. Of course by sending Evans and Caius to different places, the host prevents their literal combat, but violence is nonetheless expressed through the sport of provoking anger while simultaneously "throw[ing] cold water on thy choler" (II. iii. 79–80). The host needles and taunts the two opponents and, playing on the word "amends" (retribution vs. reparation), makes a mockery of the very notion of reconciliation:

> *Host.* He will clapper-claw thee tightly, bully.
> *Caius.* Clapper-de-claw? Vat is dat?
> *Host.* That is, he will make thee amends.
> *Caius.* By gar, me do look he shall clapper-de-claw me, for, by gar, me vill
> have it.
>
> (61–5)

Only after pushing enmity nearly to the point of no return, does the host relent and invoke amity: "Peace, I say. . . . Am I politic? Am I subtle? Am I Machiavel? . . . Boys of art, I have deceived you both . . .; your hearts are mighty, your skins are whole, and let burnt sack be the issue" (III. i. 92–3, 98–101).

Again, the manner of dealing with overheated conflict is avoidance – the sudden pretense that there is no problem. The disproportion between the difficulty and its proposed resolution is so great that we cannot regard this sport as wholesome purging of aggression. Rather, the result is further conflict since the host's nonresolution cannot be expected to satisfy Caius and Evans, who redirect their enmity by collaborating on a new plot against the host (108–12). Their revenge successfully carried out, the host is momentarily disconsolate, but is soon caught up in the exciting distraction of yet another new plot:

> *Host.* Master Fenton, talk not to me, my mind is heavy.
> I will give over all.
> *Fenton.* Yet hear me speak. Assist me in my purpose
> And, as I am a gentleman, I'll give thee
> A hundred pound in gold more than your loss.
>
> (IV. vi. 1–5)

This trend of bypassing problems in favor of involvement in further plotting becomes more serious when it extends to a major character such as Ford. The trivial, freefloating violence that hovers around the minor characters is, in the character of Ford, brought to frightening psychological concentration.[10] Though he does not have Othello's capacity to destroy because the balance of power here favors the women, Ford's compressurized vulnerability to suspicion – "Well, I hope it be not so" (II. i. 106) – suggests Othello's simmering jealousy, as does Ford's need to "torture my wife" (III. ii. 36). This context makes it impossible to respond to the climactic moment of violence, when Ford releases his frustration through beating a woman, as mere slapstick. The old woman of Brainford occasions the uninhibited expression of Ford's anxiety about women in general: "We are simple men . . . we know nothing" (IV. ii. 160, 164). The symbolic woman he attacks is actually the disguised Falstaff, yet this fact does not undercut the seriousnes of Ford's genuine distress but rather doubles male exposure and humiliation since Ford's and Falstaff's delusions about women are simultaneously punished.

The crucial question is whether this scene serves as the exorcism that enables Ford's change of heart, as the negative precondition of his positive conversion:

> Pardon me, wife. Henceforth do what thou wilt;
> I rather will suspect the sun with cold
> Than thee with wantonness; now doth thy honour stand,
> In him that was of late an heretic,
> As firm as faith.
>
>   (IV. iv. 6–10)

This passage is less of a resolution than it may appear, as Page's immediately following response to Ford's religiosity signals: " 'Tis well, 'tis well; no more. / Be not as extreme in submission / As in offence. / But let our plot go forward" (10–13). The play's standard paradigm of reconciliation – eager participation in a fresh plot as a means of avoiding difficult issues – is enacted by Page's hasty change of subject. In shifting to the ongoing sport, he deflects attention from his telling glance at Ford's problematic "submission" and the unresolved tension between inequality and mutuality in gender relations. What particularly gives Ford's confession of faith the aspect of premature closure is his subsequent compulsive taunting of Falstaff throughout the play's final scene. Though others participate in the strenuous scapegoating of Falstaff, Ford is conspicuous in his need to rub it in:

> Now, sir, who's a cuckold now? Master Brook, Falstaff's a knave, a cuckoldly knave; here are his horns, Master Brook; and, Master Brook, he hath enjoyed nothing of Ford's but his buck-basket, his cudgel, and twenty pounds of his money, which must be paid to Master Brook; his horses are arrested for it, Master Brook.
>
>   (V. v. 110–16)

Ford's gloating effort to deny his own disgrace in the Master Brook role rings false, but, when Evans reminds him, Ford cannot gracefully accept the point:

> *Evans*. And leave your jealousies too, I pray you.
> *Ford*. I will never mistrust my wife again, till thou art able to woo her in good English.
>
>   (133–5)

Ford's revenge against Falstaff conforms to the general social pattern of evasion through plotting; his particular evasiveness calls into question the new-found harmony with his wife, suggesting that bad feeling remains which finds indirect release in this unbecoming fashion.

Despite their assertions of moral impunity, the wives too participate in the shared ethic of manipulative plotting: they are not above it but rather its most successful and sophisticated embodiment. Their strategy with Falstaff of "leading him on with a fine-baited delay" (II. i. 92) corresponds to the host's method of egging on Evans and Caius while stopping just short of consummation. From the outset, the wives are concerned to absolve their behavior from association with the nasty side of plotting, as though aware their actions needed defending: "Nay, I will consent to any villainy against him that may not sully the chariness of our honesty" (II. i. 95–6). In the formulation that echoes the play's title, the wives boldly insist on the compatibility of villainy and honesty:

> We'll leave a proof, by that which we will do,
> Wives may be merry and yet honest too.
> We do not act that often jest and laugh;
> 'Tis old, but true: 'Still swine eats all the draff'.
> (IV. ii. 95–8)

The weight in this patly aphoristic, rhyming format falls on "merry," which, like Evans's elliptical and flexible use of "discretion," functions as an all-purpose euphemism for attractions of plotting that can be neither candidly acknowledged nor clearly defined.

As the wives seek a plot to bring the plotting to an end – "there would be no period to the jest" (IV. ii. 208–9) – their self-justification becomes both more pressing – 'What think you: may we, with the warrant of womanhood and the witness of a good conscience, pursue him with any further revenge?" (193–5) – and more gnomic – "Against such lewdsters and their lechery / Those that betray them do no treachery" (V. iii. 21–2). Like other characters, the wives evade difficult questions by rushing on to new action: "Come, to the forge with it, then; shape it: I would not have things cool" (IV. ii. 210–11).

Ultimately the women's power is qualified when Fenton, in secretly marrying Anne Page against her parents' wishes, beats Mrs Page at her own game: "Th' offence is holy that she [Anne] hath committed, / And this deceit loses the name of craft" (V. v. 222–3). In my view, Fenton's sanctimonious tone should not be taken at face value because his use of moral position to deny craft mirrors the wives' own rhetorical method. Neither the wives nor Fenton are shown to be superior moral beings; both sides are implicated in the social system of plotting in which all the characters are engaged. Central to this system is tension stemming from class and gender differences – a tension that can be related to fundamental conflict in the society at large, outside the play. Shakespeare's comedies perform cultural work in their period, and in the case of *The Merry Wives of Windsor* the figure of Fenton is a crucial indicator of the nature of this work because of both his class and his gender. The next section focuses on the former, while section 3 turns to the latter and to the cross-cut relationship between class and gender.

2

The play's class dynamic can be represented in three principal ways: as the victory of a bourgeois solidarity over the artistocratic court, as the reconciliation of the best of both bourgeois and aristocratic worlds, or as the consolidation of aristocratic power through a populist approach. The first version is suggested by the wives' repeated triumph over Falstaff, in which rural bourgeois values defeat the corrupted court, symbolized by Falstaff's ill-earned knighthood. Prominent as the Falstaff episodes are, however, the play's overall design depends on the pairing and counterpointing of Falstaff with Fenton. The latter's climactic success checks and even reverses the straightforward reading of simple middle-class victory. What Falstaff loses, Fenton recuperates. By providing a clear contrast with Falstaff's aristocratic imposture, Fenton enacts the rehabilitation and vindication of true aristocracy. Since Fenton reinstates aristocratic integrity, Falstaff becomes a parodic scapegoat who carries the burden of court corruption and who is easily sacrificed to dispel resentment towards it.

The play is surprisingly explicit in its expression of the potential for class antagonism. Fenton, like Prince Hal, is in need of reformation because of "My riots past, my wild societies" (III. iv. 8), while the class-conscious Page adamantly rejects him as his daughter's suitor: "He is of too high a region; he knows too much. He shall not knit a knot in his fortunes with the finger of my substance" (III. ii. 67–9). This class conflict is averted by the correction both of Fenton's profligacy and of Page's provincialism and economic tightness. In particular, the sensitive issue of money is mediated through the medium of love. Fenton's sincerity in transmuting his financial interest into authentic feeling must be articulated:

> Albeit I will confess thy father's wealth
> Was the first motive that I woo'd thee, Anne,
> Yet, wooing thee, I found thee of more value
> Than stamps in gold or sums in sealed bags;
> And 'tis the very riches of thyself
> That I now aim at.
>
> (III. iv. 13–18)

Thus an idealized vision of love underwrites an idealized view of class reconciliation and national unity.

This reading of class as class harmony does not yield an accurate account, however. The marriage between Fenton and Anne Page symbolizes the synthesis of aristocratic status and bourgeois wealth, but the strength of this cultural system is that it allows the redistribution of wealth upwards and hence the revitalization of the aristocratic class. This result implies a third reading of class: the play resolves class tension in a way that favors aristocratic interests. This is not cynically to discredit Fenton's profession of love nor to disallow the emotional content of the love; Fenton's personal sincerity is not at issue. Rather, it is a question of showing that larger social forces operate through their love, of explaining the obvious paradox that Fenton's need for money – his "first motive" – is satisfied through the ideal of love that requires him to eschew it. Fenton's final declaration of the sacredness of love, for example, by no means excludes financial considerations. He reckons with and protects against the possibility of Anne's disinheritance by denying that her elopement constitutes "unduteous title" (V. v. 224). Ford's blunt follow-up keeps the economic dimension of love to the fore: "Money buys lands, and wives are sold by fate" (230).

The marriage works not only to transfer financial resources from the bourgeoisie to the aristocracy but also to transfer control out of female and into male hands. Unlike her mother, Anne succeeds in "alter[ing] the article of [her] gentry" (II. i. 50–1). But, also unlike her mother, she defers to her husband (if not to her father). Anne is no Portia to Fenton's Bassanio. Class synthesis is purchased at the price of diminution of female power in the next generation.

The argument that the play supports aristocratic power does not rest on the single character of Fenton, for the force of aristocratic culture is represented in ways that escape character analysis. One reason the assessment of community in this play has been so difficult is a particular stress on the uniqueness of its location in Windsor. One can make Windsor emblematic of a rural bourgeois enclave and stronghold in opposition to the urban court, and one can enlist the resemblances of Windsor to Stratford and thus to the whole ethos of Shakespeare's native Warwickshire to prove his sympathy for this interpretation.[11] Yet Windsor has a double class meaning because of the location there of St George's Chapel. As Quickly's allusion – "When the court lay at Windsor" (II. ii. 258–9) – reminds us, and as the later invocation of the Order of the Garter dramatizes, the court is literally present in Windsor because the chapel is a focal point for Garter ritual.[12] This fact needs to be treated not only as a realistic detail of local colour but also as a cultural force.

Elaboration of the play's reference to the actual topography of Elizabethan Windsor has led to overemphasis on the town as a real rather than fictional place. As antidote, it is important to insist that, just as much as the Duke's wood in *A Midsummer Night's Dream* and the Forest of Arden in *As You Like It*, Windsor with its fields, park, and forest is a pastoral place. The Garter chapel evokes the institution of royal progresses that brought the London-based court out into the country and, as a pastoral environment, Windsor provides a green world for the masque celebrating the Garter ideal of aristocratic chivalry. The play's pastoral mode involves not only the external setting, but also a state of mind. The mood of literary pastoral is exemplified by Evans's attempted recitation of Marlowe's poem, "Come live with me and be my love" (III. i. 16–28).[13] The effect of Evans's halting, garbled rendition is mockery of the lyric's confident male voice of invitation and seduction, but the overall pastoral consciousness is nonetheless established.

As deployed in this play, both general pastoral convention and the specific Garter masque are courtly forms that convey and reinforce courtly stances and values. Through these forms a strong court presence pervades the play, deeply shaping the actions of its middle-class characters. The class transformations made possible by Renaissance pastoral negotiate class difference by circumventing the lower-class perspective it purportedly evokes. The motif of the courtier as shepherd, for example, allows the upper class to play at lower-class roles while making the lower class express aristocratic preoccupations, thus deflecting and neutralizing the potential disruptiveness of a genuinely different point of view. The bourgeois country folk who perform the Garter masque in *The Merry Wives of Windsor* are, like shepherds, made to speak and identify with courtly values. The final scene becomes the occasion for the convergence of classes in the sense that all classes are subsumed in a celebration of national identity that is aristocratic rather than egalitarian in orientation.

The extended passage (V. v. 57–74) rehearsing themes and rituals of the Order of the Garter is often held to be extraneous to the main action of the play and assumed to be interpolated solely for a specific Garter occasion.[14] I contend that the Garter reference is not incidental and anomalous but directly relevant and integral to the play as a whole since the play's concern with courtly forms is part of its overall ambience. To show how the allusion of the Garter contributes to the play, I shall sketch the cultural significance of the Order of the Garter.

The primary function of chivalric orders was political; their ritual provided an organizing device whereby a sovereign could ensure the loyalty and subordination of various aristocratic factions.[15] Frances Yates notes that Elizabeth's "position as head of the Order, which, with its Arthurian associations, had been made a vehicle for the glorification of the national monarchy established by the Tudors, was a very important aspect of her legend" (1957, 109). Roy Strong (1977) devotes an entire chapter to the Order of the Garter as one specific element in the whole cult of Elizabeth by which the Queen induced and enforced political allegiance.[16] Strong's *Portraits of Queen Elizabeth I* (1963) lists five portraits explicitly celebrating the Garter motif, the most prominent of these perhaps being the portrait at Windsor of the Queen holding the Garter badge, which is reproduced both by Yates and Strong.[17]

Membership in the Order was limited to twenty-five. Though member knights took part in the process of nominating new members and voted on candidates, the Queen herself made the final decision (Green, 1962, 31; Strong, 1977, 173), and she did not always fill vacancies: "This proceeding was, however, part of Elizabeth's favourite system of government. Every vacant Honour or Office, secured the fidelity and zeal of numerous candidates; and she preferred relying on the hopes of many expectants, than upon the gratitude of the few who could be appointed" (quotation from Green, 1962, 33, footnote 23). The importance attached by the Queen to this honor is suggested by the insistence on her personal involvement: "The Earl of Cumberland was at Plymouth, but the Queen would not allow the Garter to be conveyed to him, for she wished to confer it upon him herself" (Strong, 1977, 173). This action is consistent with the Queen's general policy of making visible her authority to confer prestige, as is her attention to popular display. One of Elizabeth's contributions to the development of the Garter as an institution was to extend its visibility to a larger public.

> As the reign progressed, however, the ceremonies, like the tilts, became more of a public spectacle and the procession, which was the part seen by onlookers, was deliberately developed. . . . The Chapel Royal was packed with visitors, and the magnificent procession made its way not once but three times around the courtyard so that all might see the Queen, who spoke graciously to everyone, even to the common people who fell upon their knees in homage.
>
> (Strong, 1977, 172–3)

The double appeal of the Garter ceremony to both elite and public is particularly pertinent to the theme of class reconciliation in *The Merry Wives of Windsor*, for it counters the notion that a popular audience could have no interest in Garter lore pertaining exclusively to aristocratic need and suggests instead a convergence of classes around an all-purpose symbol.

This double appeal is reflected in the play's conditions of performance – its dual existence as court entertainment for a special Garter occasion and as sure-fire popular theater. Elizabeth's populist use of royal mythology helps to explain the play's successful double life as a cross-over play that worked in both contexts for two differently composed audiences. In using the Garter, Shakespeare is drawing not on intrinsically esoteric, arcane matter but rather on popular material that the Queen had already turned into public drama.

Literary representations of the Order of the Garter prior to *The Merry Wives of Windsor* include George Peele's *The Honour of the Garter* (1593) and Edmund Spenser's use of the Garter in *The Faerie Queene*.[18] Especially important here is Shakespeare's own earlier use of the Order in *1 Henry VI* (IV. i. 9–47), in which Talbot unmasks Falstaff as a false knight whose ritual degradation reveals his true class status as "a hedge-born swain / That doth presume to boast of gentle blood" (43–4). The positive force of the negative example is soon enacted in the battle cry "God and Saint George, Talbot and England's right" (IV. ii. 55). Compressed into this single line are not only the military and nationalistic meanings of St George as patron of soldiers and of England, but also, more specifically, his significance as patron of the Order of the Garter, the institution designed to foster the other two meanings.

The motif is reiterated in *Henry V* in the King's call "God for Harry, England and Saint George!" (III. i. 34). The repeated invocations of his great-grandfather Edward III and of the English victory at Crécy, which inspire in Henry V a conviction of entitlement to France, give the play a Garter dimension since the Order of the Garter originates with Edward III, who founded it precisely in this military context: "Participation at Crécy is the most immediately striking common factor among the first knights of the Garter" (J. Vale, 1982, 87). In addition, Henry V's military brotherhood – "For he to-day that sheds his blood with me / Shall be my brother; be he ne'er so vile / This day shall gentle his condition" (IV. iii. 61–3) – corresponds to his predecessor's practice: "Edward III actually took pains to ensure that membership of the

Garter should not be confined to the high and mighty. . . . Thus we encounter once more a theme that is familiar, especially from the literary sources, the bond of equal standing in chivalry that draws together high and low among the aristocracy'' (Keen, 1984, 196–7). Like Elizabeth's, Henry V's popular ''touch'' goes further, reaching out to comfort ''mean and gentle all'' (IV. Chorus. 47, 45).[19] However exaggerated or spurious, this sense of class mobility, class reconciliation, and even suspension of class hierarchy connects with the similar treatment of class I have already noted in *The Merry Wives of Windsor*, and this connection helps to account for Fredson Bowers' surprising remark that, like *Henry V, The Merry Wives of Windsor* is ''a patriotic play'' (1963, 25).[20]

This construct of essential Englishness which *Henry V* and *The Merry Wives of Windsor* have in common provides a richer basis for connecting them than the elaborate effort to track the individual characters they share. We must compare the plays at the level of ideological and dramatic structure rather than particular characters. Both plays can be seen as one-dimensional public art that affirms official values. Both center on a similar social action – the expulsion of Falstaff. In the *Henriad*, Falstaff is eventually eliminated as an illegitimate martial hero; in *The Merry Wives of Windsor*, he is rejected as a fraudulent courtly lover. The inclusion of ''Sir John and all'' (V. v. 240) in the latter's festive finale is nominal because what Falstaff stands for has been thoroughly repudiated.

Both Hal/Henry V and the wives pursue and maintain power through moral posturing; both manipulate for the larger good of the community. In both cases, political order and unity is finessed by giving short shift to discordant elements.[21] As an endearing comic butt, Evans, the Welsh priest in *The Merry Wives of Windsor*, is given parallel treatment to Fluellen, Macmorris, and Jamy in *Henry V*. Caius, the French doctor, is equivalent to the comic Dauphin in the history play. No non-English nationalist aspiration is allowed to obtrude upon the image of England's capacity to assimilate and unify. The patriotism of *The Merry Wives of Windsor* consists in two mutually reinforcing elements: the dramatization of ordinary citizens in small-town Windsor dovetails with the national affirmation symbolized by the Garter institution. As the link with *Henry V* shows, this patriotic motif cuts across genres and can be every bit as potent in an apparently slight comedy as in an epic history play.

3

Fenton's triumph in the final scene sets a limit to the wives' power, a limit that specifically signals the reimposition of an aristocratic framework. However, Fenton's successful completion of his quest for Anne Page does not have the conclusive, definitive impact that might be expected. In particular, there is no clear-cut restoration of male control. Fenton is, in his turn, implicitly outflanked and counterbalanced because ultimate authority is vested in a woman, the ''radiant Queen'' (V. v. 47) upon whose position as head of the Order of the

Garter the play conspicuously remarks.

The Queen has two distinct and irreconcilable functions. On one hand, Elizabeth epitomizes class hierarchy. Her popular touch was cultivated for conservative political ends, and *The Merry Wives of Windsor* replicates this process. The harmony represented by the bourgeois townsfolk's participation and assimilation in the aristocratic rites of the Order of the Garter promotes royal power and thus ratifies, while palliating, the existing class structure. To the Queen's class function, the play raises no objection; the injustice of class divisions is not a serious concern for the play. On the other hand, Elizabeth symbolizes female ascendancy and this gender function becomes a source of misogynist discomfort.

The affirmation of aristocracy that puts the rural bourgeois wives in their place leads to the female power at a higher level, at the apex of the political system. This raises the possibility of a latent cross-class link between the wives and Elizabeth. Elizabethan culture hedged the Queen's power by defining her as an exception to normal definitions of gender. But Shakespeare's jocularity in *The Merry Wives of Windsor* plays out and defends against an anxious suspicion that Elizabeth may not be exceptional at all if her power extends to ordinary women. The Queen's presence doubles the effect of female domination in the play, and the impression of the Queen and the wives as strong women is further amplified because their power comes from a similar source – the culture-specific Elizabethan ideology of "political Petrarchism."

Leonard Forster (1969) uses this term to describe the way Queen Elizabeth, who "is known to have read Machiavelli and Petrarch (the combination is suggestive)" (p. 129), turned poetic love convention into a mode of political control. She transformed "a ruling class composed of energetic, violent and ruthless men" (p. 128) by presenting herself as the ideal beloved and making them her suitors. This posture extends and elicits intimacy, yet also preserves Elizabeth's distance since, as virgin, she is ultimately unattainable and since, as Queen, she has the power to withstand the pressure to marry and to enforce her virginity. In his study of Ralegh's relationship with Elizabeth, for example, Stephen Greenblatt demonstrates that the logic of courtship assigned the two poetic speakers sharply different roles and degrees of commitment: "Elizabeth manages both to play the game of poetic love and to remain aloof from it, to indulge herself without commitment and to participate without danger. Ralegh, however, must assert his total involvement" (1973, 59).

The Queen's combination of participation and aloofness is put in mythological terms by Elkin Calhoun Wilson (1939, 213): "Elizabeth wrought her spell over the loyalties of her Renaissance knights because she played at serving Venus all the while that she abode in fealty to Diana."[22] Wilson uses this specific repertoire of images to explain Elizabeth's potency as a national symbol, for her paradoxical embodiment of sexuality and virginity serves as a patriotic force that evokes, channels, and converts erotic energy into nationalistic fervor:

Remaining aloof from all entangling alliances, yet never ceasing to sport with
love, she came to embody the conquest of desire. . . . She came to stand for
patriotic restraint of passion. . . . She demanded that affection be given first
to England as she personified it. She directed a maximum of amorous energy
into action for the greater glory of that England.

(Wilson, 1939, 214)

Once established, Elizabeth's virgin status makes her use of courtship for
political control a permanent institution because marital closure is indefinitely,
perpetually, postponed. Her contemporary Francis Bacon makes clear how
essential her rejection of marriage was to the maintenance of her absolute
authority and independence: "the reigns of women are commonly obscured by
marriage; their praises and actions passing to the credit of their husbands;
whereas those that continue unmarried have their glory entire and proper to
themselves" (c. 1608, 310). Elizabeth's refusal to marry enabled her to avoid
the conventional subordination implied by the role of wife; hence even in
England, "a nation particularly fierce and warlike, all things could be swayed
and controlled at the beck of a woman" (p. 307). Bacon concludes, "she was
herself ever her own mistress" (p. 310). The same thing might be said of the
women in *The Merry Wives of Windsor*, however.

The issue of marriage, which seems to be one of the points of greatest contrast
between Elizabeth and the wives, is far less so because the wives' marriages
have not consigned them to subordinate roles; like Elizabeth, they have made
themselves exceptions to the orthodox conception of genders. Though the wives
are not an exact analogue of the Queen, there are strong connections between
the wives' marital chastity, which is figured in the penultimate scene as Diana's
attack on Actaeon, and the Queen's mythologized virginity. Emphasizing the
power of female purity and integrity, the Diana image is apt for Elizabeth, but,
in spite of their married status, the wives are also cast in this role through their
punishment of Falstaff.[23] Moreover, Queen Elizabeth's use of poetic love
conventions to enhance her political power resonates with the position of the
wives in the play. Bacon's language for Elizabeth – she "allows of amorous
admiration but prohibits desire" (c. 1608, 317) – can be applied to the wives'
practice since they present a similar spirit of allowance within strict limits. The
power of the wives and Elizabeth coincides in a political Petrarchism whose
logic of control requires that amorous invitation – Falstaff's "leer of invitation"
(I. iii. 42) and "tempest of provocation" (V. v. 21) – first be set in motion in
order that desire can then be prohibited. English warriors may not know the
meaning of the word – "Submission, Dauphin! 'Tis a mere French word: / We
English warriors wot not what it means" (*1 Henry VI*, IV. vii. 54–5) – but Page
applies it to Ford's hard-won declaration of faith in his wife (IV. iv. 11). Like
Elizabeth, the wives use love as a political device to shape, contain, and deny
male desire; like the ageing queen in the 1590s, they engage in this activity as
older women past "the holiday time of my beauty" (II. i. 1–2). The play
reproduces and magnifies the pattern of provocation, deferral, prohibition, and

frustration found in the cult of Elizabeth and the styles of courtship it activated.

The motif of courtship, as developed in *The Merry Wives of Windsor*, plays up the feeling that the woman is unapproachable. Despite coaching, Slender remains ineffectual through two painfully comic wooing scenes, while Falstaff, who as a well-versed courtier is fully prepared to devote himself not only to "the simple office of love" but also to "all the accoutrement, complement, and ceremony of it" (IV. ii. 4–5), fares no better. Like an extravagant Petrarchan lover, Falstaff undergoes the "suffering" inflicted by the tyrannical beloved. With his irrepressible body and his inexhaustible inflated lyricism, Falstaff keeps going back for more but never gets further than "the prologue" (III. v. 68). The cultural idiom of Petrarchism is brought explicitly into the play through Falstaff's exuberant quotation from Sidney's *Astrophel and Stella* – "Have I caught thee, my heavenly jewel?" (III. iii. 38). The Second Song, of which this is the opening line, portrays a classic Petrarchan moment, with the lover caught between his mistress's cruel rejection and the pressure of his desire, whose partial fulfillment is momentarily possible only because she is asleep and can be accomplished only by her violation. In the vivid phrase of the poem, Falstaff's attempt to legitimize male sexual prowess by appealing to Jove's abduction of Europa and his rape of Leda (V. v. 3–7) meets with the women's "frankly niggard NO."

But the play's most convincing image of lack of fulfillment is Ford's. His long speech as the disguised Brook is not simply a clever fiction designed for Falstaff. It carries a deeper ring of actual fantasy suggested by his confessional pose that "I shall discover a thing to you, wherein I must very much lay open mine own imperfection" (II. ii. 177–9):

> I have long loved her and, I protest to you, bestowed much on her; followed her with a doting observance; engrossed opportunities to meet her; fee'd every slight occasion that could but niggardly give me sight of her. . . . But whatsoever I have merited, either in my mind or in my means, meed I am sure I have received none, unless experience be a jewel, that I have purchased at an infinite rate.
>
> (188–99)

This passage gives full expression to the disappointment men may feel when they experience love as a Petrarchan game controlled by women. Ford's delusion about his wife suggests a male pathology induced in part by a court culture in which a Queen does rely on deferred sexuality to maintain power. Given the problem that the inaccessible lady "is too bright to be looked against" (235–6), the only recourse Ford can imagine is her degradation (236–42), a plot which the wives handily transform into his self-degradation, followed eventually by an idealized submission. This sequence releases a sexual discomfort that the play's conclusion does not entirely annul.

So great is Ford's alienation that he casts doubt on the wives' heterosexual desire – "I think, if your husbands were dead, you two would marry" (III. ii. 12–3). As though in reaction against his sense of a powerful female bond that excludes him, he fashions a male counterbond by entering into a series of secret rendezvous with Falstaff. His physical contact with the transvestized Falstaff provides a literal image of Ford's equivocal sexuality, an image reinforced by the pairing of Evans and Caius with transvestite boys in the last scene. The play's final words are given to Ford, whose triumphant declaration – "Sir John, / To Master Brook you yet shall hold your word, / For he to-night shall lie with Mistress Ford" (V. v. 240–2) – presents heterosexual satisfaction as a shaky male boast that retains the triangle with its male bond; Falstaff, it appears, is necessary to Ford's imagined sexual happiness. Ford's off-key tone continues to convey consternation even when he wins. The spirit of Ford's concluding remark prevents the adoption of the view that the dramatic action is simply the operation of a basically healthy society that restores anxiety-free marital love.

The critic who finds defects in characters' responses at the end of a comedy is likely to be accused of a deficient sense of humour, but the deficiency lies in the concept of humor as free-spirited pure fun. In reminding us that humor invovles an element of anxiety, Keith Thomas (1977) suggests how ideological analysis is relevant to the genre of comedy in the Elizabethan period: "For when we laugh we betray our innermost assumptions. Moreover, laughter has a social dimension. Jokes are a pointer to joking situations, areas of structural ambiguity in society itself; and their subject-matter can be a revealing guide to past tensions and anxieties" (p. 77). The pressures on Ford's character that make us laugh are symptomatic of a larger discomfort that goes beyond individual character analysis to structural ambiguity in the culture, an ambiguity that here specifically involves the tension between class and gender and the paradox that the play cannot reaffirm class hierarchy without also affirming female power in the Queen. The two elements of class and gender form an unstable mix that gives the play's ending its unresolved, ambivalent quality.

4

In conclusion, I should like to ask what this investigation of *The Merry Wives of Windsor* suggests about possible relationships between theatrical and royal power in the Elizabethan period. I would argue the play neither simply reproduces nor simply subverts the authority of the state. Rather, it enacts a complex third alternative which allows us to differentiate between the purposes of Elizabeth's and Shakespeare's theatricality.

Valuable as the chapters on "Court and Culture" and "Securing Compliance" in Penry Williams's *The Tudor Regime* (1979) are in showing the range and comprehensiveness of government controls, his account is inadequate. Williams cites *The Faerie Queene* to make his point that "intellectual chains" were voluntarily adopted and genuinely believed, that "high devotion to the monarchy had become an essential part of the consciousness of the articulate classes" (p. 402). Stephen Orgel's view of *The Faerie Queene* contrasts sharply with Williams's:

Recent criticism has tried to see in Elizabethan chivalry an effective cultural mediator, a social trope that allowed for the channeling and sublimation of potentially dangerous energies. Ceremonials and their attendant fictions certainly *can* function in this way . . .; but it is also clear that, by the last two decades of the reign at least, a strong sense of impatience and disillusion with the royal mythology was being felt.

(Orgel, 1985, 20)

In order to do justice to a poem like *The Faerie Queene*, we need a model of Elizabethan culture that recognizes the room for artistic manoeuver between the two extremes of total affirmation of royal mythology and all-out, open subversion. With regard to drama, we need a conception of the power of theater that allows for its potential ability to withstand royal cooption, despite government regulation, and to speak in its own way.[24] George Peele's *The Honour of the Garter* (1593) provides a point of reference for *The Merry Wives of Windsor* that compels such acknowledgement.[25] By comparison with Peele's straightforward homage, Shakespeare's evocation of orthodox values falls short of ringing endorsement.

A straightforward patriotic reading of *The Merry Wives of Windsor* has led to the theory that the Falstaff material comprises an antimasque that only confirms royal authority as instanced by Garter ideals.[26] H.J. Oliver's description of how the masque operates in context provides a point of departure for an alternate response to the play's ending:

Not only has the previous realistic play been turned in Act V into a kind of courtly masque, in which characters can step out of their main roles to play other parts, particularly for the purpose of compliment, in true masque style; but also now the masque has, as it were, been allowed to fade out, that the characters of the main play may step forward again and *all* be seen in their true colours.

(Oliver, 1971, lxix–lxx)

Thus the masque's putative effect of exaltation is counteracted by the return to "realistic" drama. This counterpointing of masque and drama highlights the rhetoric of the masquers – rhetoric equivalent to Pistol's earlier overstimulated language:

> And I to Page shall eke unfold
> How Falstaff, varlet vile,
> His dove will prove, his gold will hold,
> And his soft couch defile.
>
> (I. iii. 91–4)

The moral posture is compromised because the melodramatic rhetoric calls attention to itself. Similarly, the language used in the final defeat of Falstaff overdoes it. For example, the culminating song – "Fie on sinful fantasy, / Fie on lust and luxury!" (V. v. 94–103) – sounds shrill and excessive. The corrosive

effect of drama overexposes the masque's language and the characters who
speak it, and this quality unsettles and complicates the reconciliation abruptly
imposed by proverb: "What cannot be eschew'd must be embrac'd" (V. v. 234).

Paradoxically, it is female sexuality that is under intensive review in the
masque of Herne the Hunter: the treatment of male sexuality, the management
of Falstaff, has become routine and predictable. The final scene is a fitting
culmination and intensification of the power that the women have wielded all
along because it makes the wives "ministers" (IV. ii. 206) of the Order of the
Garter and thus implies a convergence with the Queen's chastity. The wives'
"honest" (IV. ii. 96) actions validate the Garter motto, which, in turn,
legitimizes their probity. However, though the wives' chastity gives them a
police power that is never in doubt, their style of enforcement is. The tension
between their rectitude and the license they derive from it is brought close to
breaking point. The restraint implied by chastity is contradicted by the hyped-up
rhetoric applied without restraint to the hapless Falstaff. The result is a
paroxysm of chastity that momentarily leaves the representation of chastity
tinged with mockery but that stops short of outright satire. Escalation of the
force of chastity to a point that verges on loss of control helps to account both
for the chastened mood and for the sheepish, evasive quality of the play's final
moments – the characters seem on the one hand to relent and on the other to
fall back on pseudosententious proverbs that deflect stocktaking. This elliptical
style has to do with qualms about strong women that cannot be more fully
articulated.

In *The Merry Wives of Windsor*, consequently, female power is duly
acknowledged but subject to residual male discontent. In the culture at large,
Leicester's relations with the Queen and, more strikingly, Essex's open revolt
provide evidence of male frustration with female rule.[27] Male protest in *The
Merry Wives of Windsor* is, by contrast, muted and covert, but Shakespeare
nonetheless gainsays the official line of the cult of Elizabeth. His subversiveness
in this case is not progressive, however, since he distances himself from state
power for patriarchal reasons.

In the absence of a firm, unequivocal gesture of female subordination (such
as that dramatized by Oberon's humiliation of Titania), *The Merry Wives of
Windsor* exerts male control indirectly through the culture's terms of discourse
for gender. Both for the culture and for this play, chastity is the central term
through which male leverage over women is effected. It designates the one
condition on which women are allowed to exercise power. Chastity provides the
conceptual and emotional basis for the cult of Elizabeth, and the wives are made
compulsively to stress their honesty as the source of their license. Carole Levin
(1986) shows how rebellious attempts to destabilize Elizabeth's power took the
specific form of accusations that she had betrayed her chastity. Nonetheless,
even when the image of chastity prevails, as it does in the cases of Elizabeth and
the wives, female power is still defined in terms of sexual standing and hence
confined by the same basic chaste/unchaste paradigm.[28] Since male power is
not similarly linked to an exclusive focus on sexuality, these built-in constraints

apply to women only. Queen Elizabeth manoeuvered masterfully within the strict limits granted by patriarchal conventions, but she also accepted and cooperated with these conventions. She was thus manipulated by their terms as much as she manipulated them. The Queen used the concept of chastity to insure that she would not become subordinate to any individual man, but the concept itself originated in and remained beholden to male cultural discourse.

Parody would be too strong a term to describe Shakespeare's exposure of the rhetorical denunciation of lust in the Garter language that celebrates the Queen and enhances the wives' mastery; nonetheless, by overextending this language to the point of strident propaganda, he dissociates himself from the royal mythology of virginity which depends on it and registers uneasiness with the male powerlessness to which it leads. In so doing, Shakespeare brings women's power back within reach of a patriarchally inflected framework, albeit as an expression of patriarchal anxiety rather than of decisive male control.

Notes

1. Essays by Newton and Rosenfelt (1985) and by Kuhn (1978) provide valuable critical discussion of the term patriarchy.
2. Bradbrook notes: "The women's league in one form or another is an ancient source of comic dread" (1969, 81). Neely (1986) finds a far more immediate and specific source of female power in her study of the women of Stratford and the women in Shakespeare's family.
3. All quotations are from H.J. Oliver's New Arden edition of the play (1971). Oliver and G.R. Hibbard (1973) support the textual authority of the Folio version of *The Merry Wives of Windsor*. Roberts (1979, ch. 1) surveys the textual history of the play and makes the case for this current consensus.
4. For a full-scale discussion of ideology, I refer the reader to Stuart Hall's work, to which I am greatly indebted.
5. Williams uses the term "structure of feeling" in *The Long Revolution* (1961, 48); "Literature and Sociology" (1971, 22–7); and *Marxism and Literature* (1977, 128–35); see also his survey of the word "structural" in *Keywords* (1985, 301–8). Despite the rigorous questioning of the concept in *Politics and Letters* (1979, 156–74), I still find the term helpful and necessary.
6. In *Marxism and Literature* (1977) Williams discusses ideology (pp. 55–71) and structure of feeling (pp. 128–35) in separate places and with sharply contrasting sympathies. The final sentence in the section on ideology makes clear that Williams sees little promise in the term, while the chapter on hegemony gives a negative cast to ideology in order to present hegemony as a conceptual improvement. The senses of ideology in *Keywords* (1985, 153–7) continue this generally negative evaluation. As defined by Williams, ideology is seen as too formal and narrow to encompass the experiential subtleties he intends by structures of feeling: "'feeling' is chosen to emphasize a distinction from more formal concepts of 'world-view' or 'ideology'" (1977, 132). But I do not agree that ideology need be thus restrictively defined and applied. Following Stuart Hall, I believe the concept can be revised, made more supple, and thus attuned to the levels of experience Williams thinks must necessarily elude it. For example, what Williams sees as novel emergent structures of feeling I would see as the development of new ideologies.
7. In a related discussion, Johnson (1979) comments similarly on the status of "experience" in the work of Williams and E.P. Thompson. Williams defends the

concept of experience, using it as a virtual synonym for structure of feeling in the conversation in *Politics and Letters* (1979, 158–74).

8. In this connection, see the discussion of the "containment/subversion debate" in my review of *Political Shakespeare* (Erickson, 1986). Stuart Hall's critique of Althusser's equation of ideology with the dominant ideology is crucial here.

9. Barton also expresses this view in "Harking Back to Elizabeth" (1981) when she connects the "affectionate re-creation of a long-ago world of rustic innocence" and "the picture of a fresh, simple, essentially uncorrupted country world" of Jonson's *A Tale of a Tub* with *The Merry Wives of Windsor*: "Although it had its jealous lunatics like Ford, Shakespeare's Windsor was essentially a good and cheering place" (Barton, 1981, 726).

10. The psychological depth of Ford's character and the complexity of his "curious relation to Falstaff" are attested by Carroll (1985) in his chapter on the play. The presentation of Ford, however rudimentary as an anticipation of Othello, is far more substantial and inward than that offered by Claudio in *Much Ado About Nothing*.

11. See Greer (1986) and my review (Erickson, 1988).

12. Green (1962) presents the internal and external evidence that links the play to the Order of the Garter.

13. As Richard Cody (1969) observes: "In this kind, the paragon for the 1590s is Marlowe's *Passionate Shepherd to His Love*, its primacy being acknowledged by Ralegh, Donne, and Milton" (p. 98; also pp. 155–9). Pertinent here is the series of brilliant essays by Montrose on Queen Elizabeth, courtship, pastoral form, and political power.

14. Hibbard, who accepts the textual validity of this passage, nonetheless claims that it has "no relevance at all to the rest of the scene": "Strangest of all is the introduction here into this play of action of matter which has no bearing whatever on the action" (1973, 47).

15. M. Vale (1981, ch. 2) and Keen (1984, ch. 10) both emphasize the political function of chivalric orders.

16. The chapter, "Saint George for England: The Order of the Garter," was written in 1964 and comprises pp. 164–85 of Strong's *The Cult of Elizabeth* (1977). Important though it is, work by Frances Yates and Roy Strong has been justly criticized because its sympathetic involvement in Elizabethan iconography has resulted in insufficient political analysis of royal mythology. The criticism is exemplified by Stephen Greenblatt's review (1978) of *The Cult of Elizabeth* and by David Norbrook's discussion of the Warburg Institute (1984, 2–4). Christopher Haigh (1985) demonstrates the tendency of scholars to participate in, rather than to analyze, the Queen's mythology.

17. Paintings 28–30, 39–40; also engraving 10, Marcus Gheeraerts's *Procession of Knights of the Order of the Garter*, which includes the Queen in her Garter robes. For the Garter portrait at Windsor, see Yates (1975), plate 14a, and Strong (1977) plate 79. Strong gives *c.* 1575 as the date for this portrait.

18. Leslie (1983) discusses the relation of *The Faerie Queene* to the Order of the Garter in chapters 5–7.

19. The closest analogue to the Chorus's depiction of Henry V in act IV is Elizabeth's prebattle scene at Tilbury, as described by Schleiner (1978).

20. In view of the play's patriotic aspect, I think it is entirely appropriate that David Cannadine's incisive review article (1986) on twentieth-century British royal mythology be entitled "The Merry Wives of Windsor." Nor are Americans necessarily immune to appeals to the mystique of royalty; Harbage (1971, 24) records that "The late John Kennedy was neither English nor recognizably kin to Macmorris, but when Shakespeare entered the White House in the brave new days of 1961, Henry's speech at Agincourt was the Shakespearean passage which this young leader was most eager once more to hear."

21. Dollimore and Sinfield (1985, 217) show how in *Henry V* national identity is

achieved through the transformation and incorporation of counternational trends: "systematically, antagonism is reworked as subordination and supportive alignment. It is not so much that these antagonisms are openly defeated but rather that they are represented as inherently submissive. Thus the Irish, Welsh and Scottish soldiers manifest not their countries' centrifugal relationship to England but an ideal subservience of margin to centre.''

22. Like Leonard Forster and Stephen Greenblatt, Wilson (1939) sees Elizabeth's cultivation of courtly love as a matter of political policy – see, for example, pp. 208–15. The detailed historical development and changing politics of Elizabeth's image as Diana are available in Marie Axton's work (1977a, 1977b).

23. Studies of the Actaeon myth with reference to *The Merry Wives of Windsor* include Steadman (1963) and Barkan (1980). Barkan shows that Elizabeth's adoption of the Diana image extends to the Actaeon story, with Actaeon's punishment by Diana serving as an emblem of the Queen's political power (pp. 332–3).

24. Walter Cohen (1985), for example, locates the theater's inimitable effect in the material conditions of theatrical performance: "However aristocratic the explicit message of a play, the conditions of its production introduced alternative effects. The total theatrical process meant more than, and something different from, what the dramatic text itself meant.'' Hence, for Cohen, "the subversion of aristocratic and clerical superstructure by artisanal substructure" constitutes "the inherent subversiveness of the institution" (pp. 183–4). This kind of subversion cannot be dissolved by monitoring since it is built into the very structure of theater.

25. In A.R. Braunmuller's account (1983, 6), "Peele offers us a chance to observe a working Elizabethan writer whose literary product owes less to the artist's own individual nature than it does to the corporate natures of the audiences he sought to entertain.'' While Shakespeare is certainly attuned to this corporate dimension, he does not simply reproduce and reflect it as Peele does, but more actively engages it. On Peele's Garter poem, see Braunmuller (1983), 26–8.

26. In her introduction to the play in *The Riverside Shakespeare*, Anne Barton (1974, 286) comments: "One might also argue that a comedy concerned, as this one is, with the punishment of a knight whose principles and behavior contravene all the ideals of his rank would be appropriate, almost as a kind of antimasque, at a Garter feast.'' William Green, in the Signet edition, says "Shakespeare's aim in *The Merry Wives* was to entertain, to counterpoint the serious ceremonials of the 1597 Feast of St. George with mirth. This he does by writing a farce. Thus he tries to make everyone happy'' (Green, 1965, xxxvii).

27. The pair of essays by Richard McCoy (1983, 1984) nicely points up the contrast between Leicester and Essex. Steven Mullaney (1987, 96) shows how the Lopez incident illustrates Essex's ability to manipulate Elizabeth rather than the reverse: "as far as Elizabeth was concerned what was displayed on the scaffold was not the restoration of her own authority, but rather its manipulation and even usurpation.'' Akrigg's important study (1968) of the relations between Essex and Southampton, Shakespeare's patron, brings the cultural phenomenon of explosive masculinity closer to Shakespeare.

28. Lisa Jardine (1986) shows how this paradigm dictates women's preoccupation with defending their reputation for chastity: "The woman is defined by sexuality, she has no other occupation, her conduct stands or falls in terms of men's reading of her" (p. 12). Also relevant is Jardine's commentary on Elizabeth in the final chapter of *Still Harping on Daughters* (1983).

Works cited

Akrigg, G.P.V. (1968) *Shakespeare and the Earl of Southampton*, Cambridge, Mass.,

Harvard University Press.

Axton, Marie (1977a) *The Queen's Two Bodies: Drama and the Elizabethan Succession*, London, Royal Historical Society.

—— (1977b) "The Tudor Mask and Elizabethan Court Drama," in Axton, Marie and Williams, Raymond (eds) *English Drama: Forms and Developments: Essays in Honour of Muriel Clara Bradbrook*, 24–47.

Bacon, Francis (*c.* 1608) "On the Fortunate Memory of Elizabeth Queen of England," in *The Works of Francis Bacon*, ed. James Spedding, Robert Leslie Ellis, and Douglas Denun Heath (1878), London, Longmans, 305–18.

Barkan, Leonard (1980) "Diana and Actaeon: The Myth as Synthesis," *English Literary Renaissance*, 10, 317–59.

Barton, Anne (1974) Introduction to *The Merry Wives of Windsor*, in *The Riverside Shakespeare*, ed. G. Blakemore Evans, Boston, Houghton Mifflin, 286–9.

—— (1981) "Harking Back to Elizabeth: Ben Jonson and Caroline Nostalgia," *English Literary History*, 48, 706–31.

—— (1985) "Falstaff and the Comic Community," in Erickson, Peter and Kahn, Coppélia (eds) *Shakespeare's "Rough Magic": Renaissance Essays in Honor of C.L. Barber*, Newark, University of Delaware Press, 131–48.

Bowers, Fredson (1963) Introduction to *The Merry Wives of Windsor*, Baltimore, Penguin, 15–25.

Bradbrook, Muriel (1969) "Royal Command: The Merry Wives of Windsor," repr. in Bradbrook, Muriel (1979) *Shakespeare the Craftsman*, Cambridge, Cambridge University Press, 75–96.

Braunmuller, A.R. (1983) *George Peele*, Boston, Twayne.

Cairncross, Andrew S. (ed.) (1962) *King Henry VI, Part 1*, by William Shakespeare, Arden edn, London, Methuen.

Cannadine, David (1986) "The Merry Wives of Windsor," *New York Review of Books*, 33, (June 12), 15–17.

Carroll, William C. (1985) *The Metamorphoses of Shakespearean Comedy*, Princeton, NJ, Princeton University Press.

Cody, Richard (1969) *The Landscape of the Mind: Pastoralism and Platonic Theory in Tasso's Aminta and Shakespeare's Early Comedies*, Oxford, Oxford University Press.

Cohen, Walter (1985) *Drama of a Nation: Public Theater in Renaissance England and Spain*, Ithaca, NY, Cornell University Press.

Dollimore, Jonathan and Sinfield, Alan (1985) "History and Ideology: The Instance of *Henry V*," in Drakakis, John (ed.) *Alternative Shakespeares*, London, Methuen, 206–27.

Erickson, Peter (1986) Review of *Political Shakespeare: New Essays in Cultural Materialism*, ed. Jonathan Dollimore and Alan Sinfield, *Shakespeare Quarterly*, 37 (2), 251–5.

—— (1988) Review of *Shakespeare* by Germaine Greer, *Women's Studies*, 14.

Forster, Leonard (1969) *The Icy Fire: Five Studies in European Petrarchism*, Cambridge, Cambridge University Press.

Green, William (1962) *Shakespeare's Merry Wives of Windsor*, Princeton, NJ, Princeton University Press.

—— (1965) Introduction to *The Merry Wives of Windsor*, Signet edn, New York, New American Library.

Greenblatt, Stephen (1973) *Sir Walter Ralegh: The Renaissance Man and His Roles*, New Haven, Yale University Press.

—— (1978) Review of *The Cult of Elizabeth: Elizabethan Portraiture and Pageantry* by Roy Strong, *Renaissance Quarterly*, 31, 642–4.

Greer, Germaine (1986) *Shakespeare*, New York, Oxford University Press.

Haigh, Christopher (1985) Introduction to Haigh, Christopher (ed.) *The Reign of Elizabeth I*, Athens, University of Georgia Press.

Hall, Stuart (1978a) "The Hinterland of Science: Ideology and the 'Sociology of Knowledge,'" in Centre for Contemporary Cultural Studies, *On Ideology*, London, Hutchinson.

―――― (1978b) "Some Problems with the Ideology/Subject Couplet," *Ideology and Consciousness*, 3, 113–21.

―――― (1980) "Cultural Studies: Two Paradigms," *Media, Culture and Society*, 2, 57–72.

―――― (1982) "The Rediscovery of 'Ideology': Return of the Repressed in Media Studies," in Gurevitch, Michael, Bennett, Tony, Curran, James, Woollacott, Janet (eds) *Culture, Society and the Media*, London, Methuen, 56–90.

―――― (1983) *Ideology in the Modern World*, La Trobe Working Papers in Sociology, Melbourne, La Trobe University.

―――― (with Donald, James) (1986) *Politics and Ideology: A Reader*, Milton Keynes, Open University Press.

Harbage, Alfred (1971) Introduction to *Henry V*, Baltimore, Penguin.

Hibbard, G.R. (1973) Introduction to *The Merry Wives of Windsor* by William Shakespeare, New Penguin Shakespeare edn, Baltimore, Penguin.

Jardine, Lisa (1983) *Still Harping on Daughters: Women and Drama in the Age of Shakespeare*, Brighton, Harvester Press.

―――― (1986) "'The Moor, I know his trumpet': Problems with Some New Historicist Readings of Shakespearean Female Figures," paper presented at the World Shakespeare Congress, West Berlin.

Johnson, Richard (1979) "Histories of Culture/Theories of Ideology: Notes on an Impasse," in Barrett, Michèle, Corrigan, Philip, Kuhn, Annette, and Wolff, Janet (eds) *Ideology and Cultural Production*, New York, St Martin's Press, 49–77.

Keen, Maurice (1984) *Chivalry*, New Haven, Yale University Press.

Kuhn, Annette (1978) "Structures of Patriarchy and Capital in the Family," in Kuhn, Annette and Wolpe, AnneMarie (eds) *Feminism and Materialism: Women and Modes of Production*, London, Routledge & Kegan Paul, 42–67.

Leslie, Michael (1983) *Spenser's "Fierce Warres and Faithfull Loves": Martial and Chivalric Symbolism in* The Faerie Queene, Cambridge, D.S. Brewer.

Levin, Carole (1986) "Queens and Claimants: Political Insecurity in Sixteenth Century England," in Sharistanian, Janet (ed.) *Gender, Ideology, and Action: Historical Perspectives on Women's Public Lives*, Westport, Conn., Greenwood Press.

McCoy, Richard C. (1983) "'A dangerous image': the Earl of Essex and Elizabethan Chivalry," *Journal of Medieval and Renaisssance Studies*, 13, 313–29.

―――― (1984) "From the Tower to the Tiltyard: Robert Dudley's Return to Glory," *Historical Journal*, 27, 425–35.

Montrose, Louis Adrian (1977) "Celebration and Insinuation: Sir Philip Sydney and the Motives of Elizabethan Courtship," *Renaissance Drama*, n.s. 8, 3–35.

―――― (1979) "'The perfecte paterne of a Poete': The Poetics of Courtship in *The Shepheardes Calendar*," *Texas Studies in Language and Literature*, 21, 34–67.

―――― (1980a) "'Eliza, Queene of Shepheardes,' and the Pastoral of Power," *English Literary Renaissance*, 10, 153–82.

―――― (1980b) "Gifts and Reasons: The Contexts of Peele's *Araygnement of Paris*," *English Literary History*, 47, 433–61.

―――― (1983a) "'Shaping Fantasies': Figurations of Gender and Power in Elizabethan Culture," *Representations*, 2, 61–94.

―――― (1983b) "Of Gentlemen and Shepherds: The Politics of Elizabethan Pastoral Form," *English Literary History*, 50, 415–59.

―――― (1986) "The Elizabethan Subject and the Spenserian Text," in Parker, Patricia and Quint, David (eds) *Literary Theory/Renaissance Texts*, Baltimore, Johns Hopkins University Press.

Mullaney, Steven (1987) "Brothers and Others, or the Art of Alienation," in Garber,

Marjorie (ed.) *Cannibals, Witches, and Divorce: Estranging the Renaissance: Selected Papers from the English Institute, 1985*, Baltimore, Johns Hopkins University Press, 67–89.

Neely, Carol Thomas (1986) "Shakespeare's Women: Historical Facts and Dramatic Representations," paper presented at the World Shakespeare Congress, West Berlin.

Newton, Judith and Rosenfelt, Deborah (1985) "Introduction: Toward a Materialist-Feminist Criticism," in Newton, Judith and Rosenfelt, Deborah (eds) *Feminist Criticism and Social Change: Sex, Class and Race in Literature and Culture*, New York and London, Methuen, xv–xxxix.

Norbrook, David (1984) *Poetry and Politics in the English Renaissance*, London, Routledge & Kegan Paul.

Oliver, H.J. (ed.) (1971) *The Merry Wives of Windsor* by William Shakespeare, Arden edn, London, Methuen.

Orgel, Stephen (1985) "Making Greatness Familiar," in Bergeron, David M. (ed.) *Pageantry in the Shakespeare Theater*, Athens, University of Georgia Press, 19–25.

Peele, George (1593) *The Honour of the Garter*, in Horne, David H. (1952) *The Life and Minor Works of George Peele*, New Haven, Yale University Press, 245–59.

Roberts, Jeanne Addison (1979) *Shakespeare's English Play: The Merry Wives of Windsor in Context*, Lincoln, University of Nebraska Press.

Schleiner, Winfried (1978) "*Divina virago*: Queen Elizabeth as an Amazon," *Studies in Philology*, 75, 163–80.

Sprengnether (Gohlke), Madelon (1980) "'I wooed thee with my sword': Shakespeare's Tragic Paradigms," in Schwartz, Murray M. and Kahn, Coppélia (eds) *Representing Shakespeare: New Psychoanalytic Essays*, Baltimore, Johns Hopkins University Press, 170–87.

Steadman, John M. (1963) "Falstaff as Actaeon: A Dramatic Emblem," *Shakespeare Quarterly*, 14, 230–44.

Strong, Roy (1963) *Portraits of Queen Elizabeth I*, Oxford, Oxford University Press.

—— (1977) *The Cult of Elizabeth: Elizabethan Portraiture and Pageantry*, London, Thomas & Hudson.

Thomas, Keith (1977) "The Place of Laughter in Tudor and Stuart England," *Times Literary Supplement*, 3906 (January 21), 77–81.

Vale, Juliet (1982) *Edward III and Chivalry: Chivalric Society and its Context, 1270–1350*, Woodbridge, Suffolk, Boydell Press.

Vale, Malcolm (1981) *War and Chivalry: Warfare and Aristocratic Culture in England, France and Burgundy at the End of the Middle Ages*, London, Duckworth.

Walter, John H. (ed.) (1954) *King Henry V* by William Shakespeare, Arden edn, London, Methuen.

Williams, Penry (1979) *The Tudor Regime*, Oxford, Oxford University Press.

Williams, Raymond (1961) *The Long Revolution*, London, Chatto & Windus.

—— (1971) "Literature and Sociology: In Memory of Lucien Goldman," repr. in Williams, Raymond (1980) *Problems in Materialism and Culture*, London, Verso, 11–30.

—— (1977) *Marxism and Literature*, Oxford, Oxford University Press.

—— (1979) *Politics and Letters: Interviews with New Left Review*, London, Verso.

—— (1985) *Keywords: A Vocabulary of Culture and Society*, New York, Oxford University Press; (1983) London, Fontana.

Wilson, Elkin Calhoun (1938) *England's Eliza*, Cambridge, Mass., Harvard University Press.

Yates, Frances (1957) "Elizabethan Chivalry: The Romance of the Accession Day Tilts," in Yates, Frances (1975) *Astraea: The Imperial Theme in the Sixteenth Century*, London, Routledge & Kegan Paul, 88–111.

—— (1975) *Astraea: The Imperial Theme in the Sixteenth Century*, London, Routledge & Kegan Paul.

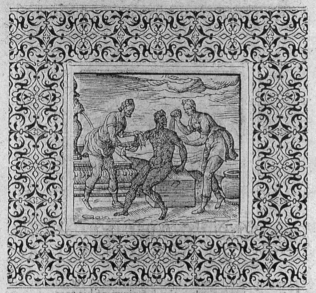

L EAVE of with paine, the blackamore to skowre,
  With washinge ofte, and wipinge more then due :
For thou shalt finde, that Nature is of powre,
  Doe what thou canste, to keepe his former hue:
Thoughe with a forke, wee Nature thruste awaie,
Shee turnes againe, if wee withdrawe our hande:
And thoughe, wee ofte to conquer her assaie,
Yet all in vaine, shee turnes if still wee stande:
    Then euermore, in what thou doest assaie,
    Let reason rule, and doe the thinges thou maie.

Erasmus ex Luciano.
Abluis Æthiopem fru-
stra: quin desinis arte?
Haud vnquâ efficies
nox sit vt atra, dies.
Horat. 1. Epist. 10.
Naturam expellas fur-
ca tamen vsque re-
surret.

——— equusq́;
Nunquam ex degeneri fiet generosus asello,
Et nunquam ex stolido cordatus fiet ab arte.

Anulus in pict.
poësi.

        H   *Non*

"I have found PEARS' SOAP matchless for the Hands and Complexion."

BY SPECIAL APPOINTMENT TO   H.R.H. THE PRINCE OF WALES.

FOR THE   ESTABLISHED   PURE,
1789
COMPLEXION.   FRAGRANT,
SOLD EVERYWHERE.   AND DURABLE.

"To wash an Ethiop white" is an ancient proverb used to express impossibility and bootless labor. Scholars speculate that it originated with Aesop, where the image of scrubbing an Aethiopian is used to demonstrate the power and permanence of nature. The proverb was common in Greek, and in Latin took the form "abluis Aethiopem: quid frustra" (you wash an Aethiopian: why the labor in vain). The emblem reproduced overleaf, from Geoffrey Whitney's widely circulated emblem book, *A Choice of Emblemes* (Leyden, 1586), moralizes the proverb in the poem printed beneath the wood-cut.[1] The expression was proverbial in early modern England and commonplace on the English and Jacobean stage; in *The White Devil*, for example, the Moorish waiting woman Zanche promises Francisco coin and jewels, a dowry "should make that sun-burnt proverbe false, / And wash the Ethiop white."[2] By the nineteenth century, the proverb is so familiar that it works as the underlying presupposition of the popular adver-tisement reproduced above, which paradoxically inverts its meaning. Unlike the sixteenth-century emblem in which the Aethiop remains black despite the ministrations of the washerwomen, in the Pears soap poster the black baby has been scrubbed almost white. In the burgeoning consumer culture of the nineteenth century, the man-made promises to reveal beneath black skin a hidden whiteness unimaginable to early modern man. In the modern period, difference is effaced and whiteness is the neutral term. So on a sign posted outside a Sussex inn called "The Labour in Vain," two men are represented "hard at work scrubbing a nigger [sic] till the white should gleam through" (Lucas, 1904, 311).[3] (The Whitney emblem is reproduced with permission from the Folger Shakespeare Library. I am grateful to William McLaughlin for sharing his collec-tion of nineteenth century advertisements.)

6

"And wash the Ethiop white": femininity and the monstrous in *Othello*

Karen Newman

Shakespear, who is accountable both to the *Eyes* and to the *Ears*, And to convince the very heart of an Audience, shews that *Desdemona* was won by hearing *Othello* talk. . . . This was the Charm, this was the philtre, the love-powder, that took the Daughter of this Noble Venetian. This was sufficient to make the Black-amoor White, and reconcile all, tho' there had been a Cloven-foot into the bargain.

(Rymer, 1693, 221–2)

It would be something monstrous to conceive this beautiful Venetian girl falling in love with a veritable negro.

(Coleridge [1960], I, 42)

To a great many people the word "negro" suggests at once the picture of what they would call a "nigger", the woolly hair, thick lips, round skull, blunt features, and burnt-cork blackness of the traditional nigger minstrel. Their subconscious generalization is as silly as that implied in Miss Preston's "the African race" or Coleridge's "veritable negro". There are more races than one in Africa, and that a man is black in colour is no reason why he should, even to European eyes, look sub-human. One of the finest heads I have ever seen on any human being was that of a negro conductor on an American Pullman car. He had lips slightly thicker than an ordinary European's, and he had somewhat curly hair; for the rest he had a long head, a magnificent forehead, a keenly chiselled nose, rather sunken cheeks, and his expression was grave, dignified, and a trifle melancholy. He was coal-black, but he might have sat to a sculptor for a statue of Caesar.

(Ridley, 1958, li)

KAREN NEWMAN, Associate Professor of Comparative Literature and English at Brown University, has published articles on a variety of topics including psychoanalysis, Shakespeare, Ovid, and Italian Renaissance comedy. She is the author of *Shakespeare's Rhetoric of Comic Character* (New York and London, Methuen, 1985) and is currently working on the problem of female subjectivity in the drama of early modern England.

M.R. Ridley's "they" is troublesome. As scholars and teachers, we use his Arden edition of *Othello* (1958, repr. 1977) and find ourselves implicated in his comfortable assumptions about "a great many people."[4] In answer to the long critical history which sought to refute Othello's blackness, Ridley affirms that Othello was black, but he hastens to add the adversative "but." Othello was not a "veritable negro," he assures us, a type from vaudeville and the minstrel show, a figure of ridicule unworthy of tragedy who would evidently appear "sub-human" to European eyes, but a black who looks white and might have represented the most renowned general of the western tradition, Caesar.[5] What are we to make of a widely used scholarly edition of Shakespeare which, in the very act of debunking, canonizes the prejudices of Rymer and Coleridge? Can we shrug our shoulders, certain that Ridley's viewpoint represents a long ago past of American Pullman cars and dignified black conductors? Are such prejudices dismantled by the most recent reprint which represents on its cover a "veritable negro" of exactly the physiognomy Ridley assures us "a great many people" are wrong in imagining?

Much of the disgust Rymer, Coleridge, and other critics betray comes not from the fact of Othello's individual blackness, but from the *relation* of that blackness to Desdemona's fair purity. Coleridge calls it "monstrous." Embedded in commentaries on the play which seek to ward off Othello's blackness is the fear of miscegenation, and particularly the white man's fear of the union of black man with white woman. Such commentators occupy the rhetorical position of Roderigo, Brabantio, and Iago who view the marriage of Othello and Desdemona as against all sense and nature: "I'll refer me to all things of sense, / . . . Whether a maid, so tender, fair, and happy, / . . . Would ever have (to incur a general mock) / Run from her guardage to the sooty bosom / Of such a thing as thou?" (I. ii. 64, 66, 69–71).

In *Othello*, the black Moor and the fair Desdemona are united in a marriage which all the other characters view as unthinkable. Shakespeare uses their assumption to generate the plot itself – Iago's ploy to string Roderigo along is his assurance that Desdemona could not, contrary to nature, long love a black man. Even his manipulation of Othello depends on the Moor's own prejudices against his blackness and belief that the fair Desdemona would prefer the white Cassio.

Miscegenation is an issue not only on the level of plot, but also of language, for linked oppositions, especially of black and white and their cultural associations, characterize the play's discourse.[6] "Black ram" tups "white ewe;" "fair" Desdemona runs to Othello's "sooty bosom." The Duke mollifies Brabantio with "Your son-in-law is far more fair than black." Desdemona is described, in what for the Renaissance would have been an oxymoron, as a "fair devil," and as "fair paper" and a "goodly book" across the white pages of which Othello fears is written "whore." In the final scene Emilia exclaims in response to Othello's confession that he has killed Desdemona, "O, the more angel she, / And you the blacker devil!" Like the proverb "to wash an Ethiop white," Emilia's lines exemplify what I will term rhetorical miscegenation, for despite the semantics of antithesis, the chiasmus allies the opposing terms rhetorically.

In the Renaissance no other colors so clearly implied opposition or were so frequently used to denote polarization. As Winthrop Jordan points out in his monumental study, *White over Black*, the meaning of *black* even before the sixteenth century, according to the *OED*, included "deeply stained with dirt, soiled, dirty, foul. . . . Having dark or deadly purposes, malignant; pertaining to or involving death, deadly, baneful, disastrous . . . iniquitous, atrocious, horrible, wicked . . . indicating disgrace, censure, liability to punishment, etc." (Jordan, 1968, 7). Of Jonson's *Masque of Blacknesse*, a preeminent example of the black/white opposition in the period, Stephen Orgel observes that it is "only necessary that the 'twelve *Nymphs*, *Negro's*' be revealed – that we *see* them – for the 'antimasque' to have taken place" (1967, 120). *White* represented the opposite. The emphasis in *Othello* on Desdemona's fairness and purity, "that whiter skin of hers than snow / And smooth as monumental alabaster" (V. ii. 4–5), and the idealization of fair female beauty it implies – the entire apparatus of Petrarchanism – is usually said to point up the contrast between Desdemona and Othello. But I want to argue to the contrary that femininity is not opposed to blackness and monstrosity, as white is to black, but identified with the monstrous, an identification that makes miscegenation doubly fearful. The play is structured around a cultural aporia, miscegenation.

Femininity interrupts not only the characterological, but also the critical discourse of the play. In his commentary, Ridley continues after the passage quoted above:

> to give an insult any point and barb it must have some relation to the facts. A woman may call a pale-complexioned rival "pasty" or "whey-faced", but it would be silly to call her swarthy . . . in the same way, "thick lips" would lose all its venom if it could not be recognizably applicable to Othello's mouth.

> (1958, lii)

Ridley's justification of Othello's blackness and his reading of "thick lips" betray a woefully inadequate sense of irony: literary discourse often works by means of negative example, as in Shakespeare's vaunt "My mistress' eyes are nothing like the sun." But more important than Ridley's limitations as a reader of texts is how he illustrates his point about Othello's blackness: he evokes a cultural prejudice against women, their supposed cattiness in response to a rival. Femininity interrupts Ridley's commentary on Othello's blackness; pitting women against women, the critic displaces the struggle of white against black man onto a cultural femininity.

Miscegenation: blacks and the monstrous

Until the late sixteenth century, speculation about the cause of blackness depended on classical sources rather than experience or observation.[7] In the myth of Phaëton, for example, and Ptolemy's *Tetrabiblos*, Africans' blackness was explained by their proximity to the sun. With the publication in 1589 of the many travel accounts and geographies in Hakluyt's *Principal Navigations*, however, the rehearsal of this ancient topos, though often quoted, was usually countered by the observation that many peoples living equally close to the sun in the Indies and other parts of the New World were of olive complexion and thus disproved the ancients' latitudinal etiology. Myth and empirical observation collided.

In his *Discourse* (1578, repr. in Hakluyt, 1600), George Best, an English traveler, gives an early account of miscegenation and the causes of blackness:

> I my selfe have seene an Ethiopian as blacke as a cole brought into England, who taking a faire English woman to wife, begat a sonne in all respects as blacke as the father was, although England were his native countrey, and an English woman his mother: whereby it seemeth this blacknes proceedeth rather of some natural infection of that man, which was so strong, that neither the nature of the Clime, neither the good complexion of the mother concurring, coulde any thing alter.
>
> (Hakluyt, 1600 [ed. Raleigh, 1904, VII, 262])[8]

Best's account of miscegnation is designed to refute the conventional latitudinal explanation, but it does much more. Not only does it emphasize the contrariety of black and white, "blacke as a cole" and "faire English woman;"[9] his repetitions also betray the Englishman's ethnocentric preoccupation with his native isle.[10]

Best also proffers an alternative explanation of blackness which he substitutes for the ancients' geographical theory: "this blacknes proceedeth rather of some natural infection of that man." Best's claim is more radical than his metaphor of disease implies because to assert that black and white were "naturally" different also posed a theological problem. If the union of black and white always results in black offspring, "in all respects as blacke as the father," then how can we account for the origin of blacks from our first parents? And so Best goes on to explain his claim by referring to Scripture and the story in Genesis of Noah and his three sons,

> who all three being white, and their wives also, by course of nature should have begotten and brought foorth white children. But the envie of our great and continuall enemie the wicked Spirite is such, that as hee coulde not suffer our olde father Adam to live in the felicitie and Angelike state wherein hee was first created, but tempting him, sought and procured his ruine and fall: so againe, finding at this flood none but a father and three sonnes living, hee so caused one of them to transgresse and disobey his father's commaundement, that after him all his posteritie shoulde bee accursed. The fact of disobedience was this: When Noe at the commandement of God had made the Arke and entered therein . . . hee straitely commaunded his sonnes and their wives, that they . . . should use continencie, and abstaine from carnall

copulation with their wives. . . . Which good instructions and exhortations notwithstanding his wicked sonne Cham disobeyed, and being perswaded that the first childe borne after the flood (by right and Lawe of nature) should inherite and possesse all the dominions of the earth, hee contrary to his fathers commandement while they were yet in the Arke, used company with his wife, and craftily went about thereby to dis-inherite the off-spring of his other two brethren: for the which wicked and detestable fact, as an example for contempt of Almightie God, and disobedience of parents, God would a sonne should bee borne whose name was Chus, who not onely it selfe, but all his posteritie after him should bee so blacke and lothsome, that it might remaine a spectacle of disobedience to all the worlde. And of this blacke and cursed Chus came all these blacke Moores which are in Africa.[11]

(Best, 1578 [repr. in Hakluyt, 1600, 263–4])

Best's myth of a second fall is an extraodinarily rich rehearsal of early English social attitudes. In it are revealed the stock prejudices against blacks in Elizabethan and Jacobean culture: the link between blackness and the devil, the myth of black sexuality, the problem of black subjection to authority, here displaced onto obedience owed to the father and to God. Best's story passes "segregation off as natural – and as the very law of the origin." Derrida's words about apartheid are suggestive for understanding not only Best's *Discourse*, but travel writing more generally:

there's no racism without a language. The point is not that acts of racial violence are only words but rather that they have to have a word. Even though it offers the excuse of blood, color, birth – or, rather, because it uses this naturalist and sometimes creationist discourse – racism always betrays the perversion of man, the "talking animal."

(Derrida, 1985, 292)

But Best's account also represents the specifically Elizabethan economic and social crisis historians such as Lawrence Stone have described. Noe's son Cham disobeys his father's will because he is ambitious; he seeks to displace his older brothers in the hierarchy of inheritance. Best's account textualizes the problem of social mobility during the period and ironically, given Best's conservatism, challenges definitions of social identity based on birth. Best betrays fear of the social changes taking place in Elizabethan England, of "masterless men" and of challenges to traditional notions of order and degree. At a time when "elite identity gradually came to depend not on inherited or god-given absolute attributes, but on characteristics which could be acquired by human efforts" (Whigham, forthcoming), Best's account stands in an interesting transitional relation to such changes in the social formation. Cham recognizes the authority of birthright, as does Best's own anxious parenthesis "(by righte and Lawe of nature)" but he seeks to enact the "Lawe of nature" through human effort, an effort duly punished by the ultimate authority, God.

Similarly Best's nationalism and fear of difference demarcate attitudes characteristic of the period. Even by 1578 the English had a considerable material investment in Africa: English explorers had begun to compete with Portuguese traders; John Hawkins had organized the first successful slave-trading venture between Africa and the West Indies in 1563. Best's is not just a fantasy about Africa and blackness, but an enabling discourse which sustains a series of material and economic practices and interests. In England itself, by 1596, blacks were numerous enough to generate alarm. Elizabeth wrote to the Lord Mayor of London and to other towns and observed "there are of late divers blackmoores brought into this realme, of which kinde of people there are allready to manie, consideringe howe God hath blessed this land with great increase of people of our own nation;" a week later she observed that "those kinde of people may be well spared in this realme, being so populous," and licensed a certain Casper van Senden, a merchant of Lübeck who had freed eighty-nine Englishmen imprisoned in Spain and Portugal, "to take up so much blackamoores here in this realme and to transport them into Spain and Portugal" for his expenses.[12] Five years later, in January 1601, van Senden was again licensed, this time to deport "the said kind of people . . . with all speed . . . out of this her majesty's realms" (Hughes and Larkin, 1969, III, 221).

Other travel accounts of the period display the intersection of ancient legends and myths about black Africa with contemporary experience, observation, and prejudice. Interspersed with descriptions of African tribal customs, language, and landscape were the legendary stories from Pliny and other classical sources, probably via Mandeville (whose popular *Travels* were included in the first [1589] edition of Hakluyt's *Principal Navigations*), of the Anthropophagi who wore skins and ate human flesh, of people without heads or speech, of satyrs and Troglodytes who lived in caves and dens.[13] The African landscape was presented descriptively in terms of safe harbors, intense heat, and gigantic waterfalls, but also mythically, as traversed by flames and fire which reached as high as the moon, and as ringing with the sound of pipes, trumpets, and drums.[14] Always we find the link between blackness and the monstrous, and particularly a monstrous sexuality. Early travelers describe women held in common and men "furnisht with such members as are after a sort burthensome unto them."[15] These accounts often bore no relation to African sexual habits, but they did confirm earlier discourses and representations of African sexuality found in Herodotus, Diodorus, and other classical authors.

The prejudices of the ancients were preserved into the fifteenth and sixteenth centuries: early cartographers ornamented maps with representations of naked black men bearing enormous sexual organs; Leo Africanus' *Historie of Africa* (1526), widely available in Latin in England, and translated in 1600 by John Pory, claimed "negros" were "prone to Venery." Jean Bodin, in his widely read work of political philosophy, *The Six Bookes of a Commonweale*, argues against slavery, but nevertheless betrays the conventional prejudice about black sexuality when he claims:

there be in mans bodie some members, I may not call them filthie (for that nothing can so be which is naturall) but yet so shamefull, as that no man except he be past all shame, can without blushing reveale or discover the same: and doe they [blacks] for that cease to be members of the whole bodie?[16]

Because of his organic conception of the state, Bodin's political theory does not permit a dualism, slavery for some, freedom for others. But he is so shamed by those members, and the Africans' custom of exposing them, that he dresses his prose in a series of parentheses and clauses which effectively obscure its meaning.

Such attitudes, both inherited from the past and reconstructed by contemporary historiographers, humanists, and travelers, were quickly assimilated into the drama and culture of early modern England.[17] In *Titus Andronicus*, for example, the lustful union of Aaron and Tamor resulted in a black baby called "a devil" in the play.[18] In *Tamar Cam* (1592) there is an entry of "Tartars, Geates, Amozins, Negars, ollive cullord moores, Canniballs, Hermaphrodites, Pigmes . . . ," company which testifies to the contemporary link between blackness and the monstrous. Similarly, Volpone's copulations resulting in his monstrous offspring, the fool, dwarf, and hermaphrodite, are accomplished with "beggars, gipseys and Jewes, and black moores." In Bacon's *New Atlantis* (1624), a holy hermit "desired to see the Spirit of Fornication; and there appeared to him a foul little Aethiop." Treatises on witchcraft and trials of the period often reported that the devil appeared to the possessed as a black man (Thomas, 1971, 475). Finally, contemporary ballads and broadsides, the Renaissance equivalent of the news story, popularized monstrous births such as one recorded by the Stationers' Register (1580): a child, born at Fenstanton in Huntingdonshire, was described as "a monster with a black face, the Mouth and Eyes like a Lyon which was both Male and Female."[19]

Monstrous desire in *Othello*

In *Renaissance Self-Fashioning* (1980), Stephen Greenblatt has argued persuasively that Othello submits to narrative self-fashioning, his own and Iago's. He demonstrates the congruence between their narratives and the ideological narratives of Renaissance culture, most powerfully the orthodox Christian attitude toward sexuality, and he shows how Iago and Othello are linked by shared, if dialectically opposed, cultural values about women and sexuality. Greenblatt quotes Kenneth Burke's claim that they are "consubstantial":

> Iago, to arouse Othello, must talk a language that Othello knows as well as he, a language implicit in the nature of Othello's love as the idealization of his private property in Desdemona. This language is the dialectical opposite of Othello's; but it so thoroughly shares a common ground with Othello's language that its insinuations are never for one moment irrelevant to Othello's

thinking. Iago must be cautious in leading Othello to believe them as true: but Othello never for a moment doubts them as *values*.[20]

For Greenblatt, Othello's "identity depends upon a constant performance, as we have seen, of his story, a loss of his own origins, an embrace and perpetual reiteration of the norms of another culture" (1980, 245).

What are Othello's lost origins? Greenblatt implies as somehow anterior to identity-as-performance an essential self, an ontological subjectivity, an Edenic moment of black identity prior to discourse, outside, in Derrida's phrase quoted earlier, "the perversion of man, the 'talking animal.'" Derrida's words about racism are also pertinent to a discussion of origins and permit the substitution of ontology for race: "there are no origins without a language." "Othello" doesn't lose "his own origins;" his only access to those origins are the exotic ascriptions of European colonial discourse. Othello's stories of slavery and adventure are *precisely* a rehearsal of his origins, from his exotic tales of monstrous races to the story of the handkerchief's genealogy in witchcraft and Sibylline prophecy. Othello charms by reiterating his origins even as he submits and embraces the dominant values of Venetian culture. His successful courtship of Desdemona suggests that those origins are not simply repressive, but also enabling. Greenblatt is moving in his representation of Othello's submission to such cultural plots, but by focusing on Othello's ideological complicity, he effectively erases the other which is constituted discursively in the play as both woman and black. Othello is both a speaking subject, a kind of George Best recounting his tales of conquest, and at the same time the object of his "Travellours historie" by virtue of his blackness which originates with the very monstrous races he describes.[21]

Similarly he is both the representative and upholder of a rigorous sexual code which prohibits desire and defines it even within marriage as adulterous, as Greenblatt claims, and yet also the sign of a different, unbridled sexuality. Greenblatt effaces the profound paradox of the black Othello's embrace of Christian sexual mores: Othello is both monster and hero, and his own sexuality is appropriately indecipherable.[22] As the champion of Christian cultural codes he assures the senators his wish to take his bride with him to Cyprus is not "to please the palate of my appetite, / Nor to comply with heat, the young affects / In my defunct, and proper satisfaction" (I. iii. 262–4). He loves Desdemona "but to be free and bounteous of her mind" (265). Like Brabantio, Iago, and Roderigo, Othello perceives of his love and indeed his human, as opposed to bestial, identity as depending on property rights, on absolute ownership:

> O curse of marriage,
> That we can call these delicate creatures ours,
> And not their appetites! I had rather be a toad,
> And live upon the vapour in a dungeon,
> Than keep a corner in a thing I love,
> For others' uses:
>
> (III. iii. 271–6)

But opposed to the representation of Othello's participation in the play's dominant sex/gender system is a conventional representation of black sexuality evoked by other characters and by Othello himself in his traveler's tales and through his passionate action. The textual allusions to bestiality, lubriciousness, and the demonic have been often noted. Iago rouses Brabantio with "an old black ram / Is tupping your white ewe . . . / . . . the devil will make a grandsire of you" (I. i. 88–9, 91), and "you'll have your daughter cover'd with a Barbary horse; you'll have your nephews neigh to you; you'll have coursers for cousins, and gennets for germans" (110–13). "Your daughter and the Moor, are now making the beast with two backs" (115–16) and Desdemona is transported, according to Roderigo, "to the gross clasps of a lascivious Moor" (126). Not until the third scene is the Moor named, and the delay undoubtedly dramatizes Othello's blackness and the audience's shared prejudices which are vividly conjured up by Iago's pictorial visions of carnal knowledge. To read Othello as congruent with the attitudes toward sexuality and femininity expressed in the play by the Venetians – Iago, Brabantio, Roderigo and Cassio – and opposed to Desdemona's desire is to ignore the threatening sexuality of the other which divides the representation of Othello's character.[23] Othello internalizes alien cultural values, but the otherness which divides him from that culture and links him to the play's other marginality, femininity, remains in visual and verbal allusion.

For the white male characters of the play, the black man's power resides in his sexual difference from a white male norm. Their preoccupation with black sexuality is not an eruption of a normally repressed animal sexuality in the "civilized" white male, but of the feared power and potency of a different and monstrous sexuality which threatens the white male sexual norm represented in the play most emphatically by Iago. For however evil Iago reveals himself to be, as Spivak pointed out (1958, 415 ff.), like the Vice in the medieval morality, or, we could add, the trickster/slave of Latin comedy, Iago enjoys a privileged relation with the audience. He possesses what can be termed the discourse of knowledge in *Othello* and annexes not only the other characters, but the resisting spectator as well, into his world and its perspective. By virtue of his manipulative power and his superior knowledge and control over the action, which we share, we are implicated in his machinations and the cultural values they imply.[24] Iago is a cultural hyperbole; he does not oppose cultural norms so much as hyperbolize them.[25]

Before the English had wide experience of miscegenation, they seem to have believed, as George Best recounts, that the black man had the power to subjugate his partner's whiteness, to make both his "victim" and her offspring resemble him, to make them both black, a literal blackness in the case of a child, a metaphorical blackness in the case of a sexual partner. So in *Othello*, Desdemona becomes "thou black weed" (IV. iii. 69) and the white pages of her "goodly book" are blackened by writing when Othello imagines "whore" inscribed across them. At IV. iii, she explicitly identifies herself with her mother's maid Barbary whose name connotes blackness. The union of Desdemona and Othello represents a sympathetic identification between femininity and the monstrous which offers a potentially subversive recognition of sexual and racial difference.

Both the male-dominated Venetian world of *Othello* and the criticism the play has generated have been dominated by a scopic economy which privileges sight, from the spectacular opposition of black and white to Othello's demands for ocular proof of Desdemona's infidelity. But Desdemona *hears* Othello and loves him, awed by his traveler's tales of the dangers he had passed, dangers which emphasize his link with monsters and marvels. Her responses to his tales are perceived as voracious – she "devours" his discourses with a "greedy ear," conflating the oral and aural, and his language betrays a masculine fear of a cultural femininity which is envisioned as a greedy mouth, never satisfied, always seeking increase, a point of view which Desdemona's response to their reunion at Cyprus reinforces.[26] Desdemona is presented in the play as a sexual subject who hears and desires, and that desire is punished because the non-specular, or non-phallic sexuality it displays is frightening and dangerous.[27] Instead of a specular imaginary, Desdemona's desire is represented in terms of an aural/oral libidinal economy which generates anxiety in Othello, as his account to the Senate of his courtship via fiction betrays.[28] Othello fears Desdemona's desire because it invokes his monstrous difference from the sex/race code he has adopted, or, alternatively, allies her imagined monstrous sexual appetite with his own.

Thomas Rymer, a kind of critical Iago, claims the moral of *Othello* is first, "a caution to all Maidens of Quality how, without their parents' consent, they run away with Blackamoors," an instruction which he follows with the version of his Italian source, Cinthio: "Di non si accompagnare con huomo cui la natura & il cielo & il modo della vita disgiunge da noi" (1693 [ed. Springarn, 1957, 221]).[29] Both Rymer and Cinthio reveal how Desdemona is punished for her desire: she *hears* Othello and desires him, and her desire is punished because it threatens a white male hegemony in which women cannot be desiring subjects. When Desdemona comes to tell her version of their wooing, she says: "I saw Othello's visage in his mind." The allusion here is certainly to her audience's prejudice against the black "visage" that both the Senators and Shakespeare's audience see in Othello, but Desdemona "saw" his visage through hearing the tales he tells of his past, tales which, far from washing the Moor white as her line seems to imply, emphatically affirm Othello's link with Africa and its legendary monstrous creatures. Rymer's moral points up the patriarchal and scopic assumptions of his culture which are assumed as well in the play and most pointedly summed up by Brabantio's often quoted lines: "Look to her, Moor, have a quick eye to see: / She has deceiv'd her father, may do thee" (I. iii. 292–3). Fathers have the right to dispose of their daughters as they see fit, to whom they see fit, and disobedience against the father's law is merely a prelude to the descent into hell and blackness the play enacts, a fall, we might recall, Best's tale uncannily predicts. Desdemona's desire threatens the patriarchal privilege of disposing daughters and in the play world signals sexual duplicity and lust.

The irony, of course, is that Othello himself is the instrument of punishment; he enacts the moral Rymer and Cinthio point, both confirming cultural prejudice by his monstrous murder of Desdemona and punishing her desire which transgresses the norms of the Elizabethan sex/race system. Both Othello and Desdemona deviate from the norms of the sex/race system in which they participate from the margins. Othello is not, in Cinthio's words, "da noi," one of "us," nor is Desdemona. Women depend for their class status on their affiliation with men – fathers, husbands, sons – and Desdemona forfeits that status and the protection it affords when she marries outside the categories her culture allows.[30] For her transgression, her desire of difference, she is punished not only in a loss of status, but even of life. The woman's desire is punished, and ultimately its monstrous inspiration as well. As the object of Desdemona's illegitimate passion, Othello both figures monstrosity *and* at the same time represents the white male norms the play encodes through Iago, Roderigo, Brabantio.[31] Not surprisingly, Othello reveals at last a complicitous self-loathing, for blackness is as loathsome to him as to George Best, or any male character in the play, or ostensibly the audience.

At IV. i., Iago constructs a drama which Othello is instructed to interpret, a scene rich in its figurations of desire and the monstrous. Cast by Iago as eavesdropper and voyeur, Othello imagines and thus constitutes a sexual encounter and pleasure that excludes him, and a Desdemona as whore instead of fair angel. Cassio's mocking rehearsal of Bianca's love is not the sight/site of Desdemona's transgression, as Othello believes, but its representation; ironically this theatrical representation directed by Iago functions as effectively as would the real. Representation for Othello is transparent. The male gaze is privileged; it constructs a world which the drama plays out. The aptly and ironically named Bianca is a cypher for Desdemona whose "blackened whiteness" she embodies. Plots of desire conventionally figure woman as the erotic object, but in *Othello* the iconic center of the spectacle is shifted from the woman to the monstrous Othello whose blackness charms *and* threatens, but ultimately fulfills the cultural prejudices it represents. Othello is both hero and outsider because he embodies not only the norms of male power and privilege represented by the white male hegemony which rules Venice, a world of prejudice, ambition, jealousy, and the denial of difference, but also the threatening power of the alien: Othello is a monster in the Renaissance sense of the word, a deformed ceature like the hermaphrodites and other strange spectacles which so fascinated the early modern period. And *monstrum*, the word itself, figures both the creature and its movement into representation, for it meant as well a showing or demonstration, a *representation*.

Historical contingency: rereading *Othello*

The position which a text occupies within the relations of ideological class struggle at its originating moment of production is . . . no necessary indication of the positions which it may

subsequently come to occupy in different historical and
political contexts.

(Bennett, 1982, 229)

His nose was rising and Roman, instead of African and flat:
His Mouth the finest shaped that could be seen; far from
those great turn'd Lips, which are so natural to the rest of the
Negroes. The whole Proportion and air of his face was so
nobly and exactly form'd, that bating his colour, there could
be nothing in Nature more beautiful, agreeable and
handsome.

(Aphra Behn, *Oroonoko*, 1688)[32]

Behn's description of her black protagonist Oroonoko is startling in its
congruence with Ridley's portrait of the black Othello with which we began. A
black tragic hero of Othello's proportions, or Behn's noble Oroonoko, is only
possible if black is really white, if features are "classical," that is European,
and color is merely an unfortunate accident. By the late seventeenth century,
the role and status of blacks in English society had changed, and the discourse
of racism was fully established. No longer "spectacles of strangeness" and
monstrosity who occupied unstable, exotic, and mythic ideological roles, they
were slaves, situated in a growing capitalist economy which their exploited
labor sustained. In the sixteenth and early seventeenth centuries, the slave trade
in England was desultory and the status of blacks liminal rather than fixed. As
Best's *Discourse* and the accounts of early voyagers illustrate, blacks occupied
mythic roles rather than positions as mere chattel or economic linchpin. In
Elizabethan and Jacobean England, blacks were not only servants; they owned
property, paid taxes, went to church.[33] But with the establishment of the sugar
industry in the Caribbean, and the tobacco and cotton industries in America,
the position of blacks changed and their value as slave labour was fully
recognized and exploited. The Royal African Company, chartered in 1672,
monopolized the African trade until 1698 when the rapid expansion of the
colonies dependent on slave labour was so great that it was deprived of its
exclusive rights and the market opened to competition. Newspapers of the late
seventeenth century testify to a changed view of blacks – advertisements of
slaves for sale, and more importantly, hue-and-cry notices seeking runaways
who were often described as wearing collars emblazoned with their owners'
arms, or with inscriptions such as one reported in the *London Gazette* (1688):
"The Lady Bromfield's black, in Lincoln's Inn Fields."

By the late seventeenth century, Englishmen had come to realize the
significance of the slave trade to the British economy. In 1746, M. Postlewayt
put that realization forcefully into words: "the most approved Judges of the
commercial Interests of these Kingdoms have ever been of Opinion, that our
West-India and African trades are the most nationally beneficial of any we
carry on . . . the daily Bread of the most considerable Part of our British

Manufacturers, [is] owing primarily to the Labour of Negroes.''[34] By the mid-
eighteenth century, the *Gentleman's Magazine* claimed there were some 20,000
blacks in London. Their increasing numbers led to growing prejudice and fear
that they threatened the position of white working people. In pamphlets and the
popular press, blacks were represented increasingly as caricatures, bestial,
apelike, inhuman, stripped of the exotic or mythic discourses of the sixteenth
and early seventeenth centuries. By the time of Rymer's attack on *Othello*,
Shakespeare's heroic and tragic representation of a black man seemed unthinkable. In his "Short View of Tragedy" (1693), Rymer found Shakespeare's
choice reprehensible, a transgression of both tragic and social decorum.[35]
Rymer's attitude toward the "blackamoor" is historically predictable; more
surprising, perhaps, is his critical slippage, like Ridley's some 250 years later,
from blackness to femininity.[36]

Rymer notoriously claimed that the moral of *Othello* was "a warning to all
good Wives that they look well to their Linnen" (1693, [1957, 221]). He
devotes the last pages of his attack to the "Tragedy of the Handkerchief,"
claiming that "had it been *Desdemona's* Garter, the Sagacious Moor might
have smelt a Rat; but the handkerchief is so remote a trifle, no Booby on this
side of *Mauritania* cou'd make any consequence from it. . . . Yet we find it
entered into our Poets head to make a Tragedy of this *Trifle*" (1693 [1957,
251, 254]). Rymer takes issue with Shakespeare's presentation of the handkerchief because he finds it too trifling a detail to sustain tragedy. His comment
here reflects not only the changing generic expectations of neoclassicism, but
also Rymer's cultural prejudices against women, their supposed materiality and
preoccupation with the trivial.[37]

In the early modern period, the handkerchief was in fact a sign of wealth and
status; by the early eighteenth century, however, it had become commonplace
(Elias, 1978, 143–52). In *cinquecento* Venice, possession of a lady's handkerchief was considered proof of adultery and led to stringent punishments. In
1416, a certain Tomaso Querini received a stiff sentence of eighteen months in
jail and a fine of 500 *lire di piccoli* for carrying out "many dishonesties" with
Maria, wife of Roberto Bono. Records from the case describe Tomaso's crime
as having

> presumed to follow the said lady and on this public street took from her
> hands a handkerchief, carrying it off with him. As a result of this deed the
> said Tomaso entered the home of Roberto many times during the day and
> night and committed many dishonesties with this lady with the highest
> dishonor for ser Roberto.
>
> (Ruggiero, 1985, 61–2)[38]

Many critics and readers of the play have sought to save Shakespeare's
handkerchief from Rymer's harsh judgement by demonstrating not its historical
significance as a sign of adultery, but its symbolic significance and meaning.
Their efforts have been limited by their own historical boundaries and by reigning critical preoccupations and practices which too often seek to work out

equations which restrict the richness of *handkerchief* as signifier. The handkerchief in *Othello* is what we might term a snowballing signifier, for as it passes from hand to hand, both literal and critical, it accumulates myriad associations and meanings.[39] It first appears simply as a love token given by Othello to Desdemona and therefore treasured by her; only later do we learn the details of its provenance and design. In the Renaissance, strawberries signified virtue or goodness, but also hypocritical virtue as symbolized by the frequently occurring design and emblem of a strawberry plant with an adder hiding beneath its leaves (Ross, 1960, 225–40). This doubleness is, of course, appropriate for Othello's perception of Desdemona, for when the handkerchief is first given it represents her virtue and their chaste love, but it later becomes a sign, indeed a proof, of her unfaithfulness. Iago's description of the napkin as "spotted" constitutes for Othello a new meaning to the handkerchief – the strawberries become signs of Desdemona's deceit.[40]

In psychoanalytic terms, the handkerchief which Othello inherits from his mother and then gives to Desdemona has been read symptomatically as the fetishist's substitution for the mother's missing phallus. Like the shoe Freud's young boy substitutes "for the woman's (mother's) phallus which the little boy once believed in and does not wish to forego," the handkerchief is the fetish which endows "women with the attribute which makes them acceptable as sexual objects" – that is, makes them like men (Freud, 1927 [1963, 215, 216]). For Othello, it both conceals and reveals Desdemona's imperfection, her lack. But the psychoanalytic scenario is problematic because it privileges a male scopic drama, casting the woman as other, as a failed man, thereby effacing her difference and concealing her sexual specificity behind the fetish. The handkerchief in *Othello* does indeed figure a lack, but ironically it figures not simply the missing penis, but the lack around which the play's dramatic action is structured, a desiring femininity which is described in the play as aberrant and "monstrous" or a "monster."[41] The handkerchief, with its associations with the mother, witchcraft, and the marvelous, represents the link between femininity and the monstrous which Othello and Desdemona's union figures in the play. It figures a female sexual topography that is more than a sign of male possession, violated virginity, even deceit, and more than the fetishist's beloved object. It figures not only Desdemona's lack, as in the traditional psychoanalytic reading, but also her own sexual parts – the nipples, which incidentally are sometimes represented in the courtly love blason as strawberries, lips, and even perhaps the clitoris, the berry of sexual pleasure nestled beneath phalanged leaves.[42]

The handkerchief, therefore, is significant not only historically as an indicator of class or transgression, or psychologically, because it signifies male fears of duplicity, consummation, and castration, but also politically precisely because it has become a *feminine* trifle. *Othello's* tragic action is structured not around a heroic act or even object – a battle, as in *Antony and Cleopatra*, or kingship as in *Macbeth* and *King Lear* – but around a trifle, a feminine toy. Instead of relegating *Othello* to the critical category domestic tragedy, always implicitly or explicitly pejorative because of its focus on woman, jealousy and a triangle, we can reread *Othello* from another perspective, also admittedly historically bound, that seeks to displace conventional interpretations by exposing the extraordinary fascination with and fear of racial and sexual difference which characterizes Elizabethan and Jacobean culture. Desdemona and Othello, woman and black man, are represented by discourses about femininity and blackness which managed and produced difference in early modern England.

Colonialism and sexual difference

Was Shakespeare a racist who condoned the negative image of blacks in his culture? Is Desdemona somehow guilty in her stubborn defense of Cassio and her admiring remark "Ludovico is a proper man?"[43] Or in a new critical vocabulary, in her "erotic submission, [which] conjoined with Iago's murderous cunning, far more effectively, if unintentionally, subverts her husband's carefully fashioned identity" (Greenblatt, 1980, 244)? Readers preoccupied with formal dramatic features claim such questions are moot, that the questions themselves expose the limits of moral or political readings of texts because they raise the specters of intention or ignore the touted transcendence of history by art. But as much recent poststructuralist and/or political criticism has demonstrated, even highly formalist readings are political, inscribed in the discourses both of the period in which the work was produced and of those in which it is consumed.

The task of a political criticism is not merely to expose or demystify the ideological discourses which organize literary texts, but to *reconstitute* those texts, to reread canonical texts in noncanonical ways which reveal the contingency of so-called canonical readings, which disturb conventional interpretations and discover them as partisan, constructed, made rather than given, natural, and inevitable. Such strategies of reading are particularly necessary in drama because the dramatic immediacy of theatrical representation obscures the fact that the audience is watching a highly artificial enactment of what, in the case of *Othello*, a non-African and a man has made into a vision of blackness and femininity, of passion and desire in the other, those marginal groups which stand outside culture and simultaneously within it.

Shakespeare was certainly subject to the racist, sexist, and colonialist discourses of his time, but by making the black Othello a hero, and by making Desdemona's love for Othello, and her transgression of her society's norms for women in choosing him, sympathetic, Shakespeare's play stands in a contestatory relation to the hegemonic ideologies of race and gender in early modern England. Othello is, of course, the play's hero only within the terms of a white, elitist male ethos, and he suffers the generic "punishment" of tragedy, but he is nevertheless represented as heroic and tragic at a historical moment when the only role blacks played on stage was that of a villain of low status. The case of Desdemona is more complex because the fate she suffers is the conventional fate assigned to the desiring woman. Nevertheless, Shakespeare's representation of her as at once virtuous and desiring, and of her choice in love as heroic rather than demonic, dislocates the conventional ideology of gender the play also enacts.

We need to read Shakespeare in ways which produce resistant readings, ways which contest the hegemonic forces the plays at the same time affirm. Our critical task is not merely to describe the formal parameters of a play, nor is it to make claims about Shakespeare's politics, conservative or subversive, but to reveal the discursive and dramatic evidence for such representations, and their counterparts in criticism, as representations.[44]

Notes

1. Whitney chose the woodcuts from a collection of Christopher Plantyn, the well-known printer whose shop published *A Choice of Emblemes*. See Lyons (1975), iv–v.
2. For references to this proverb in Elizabethan and Jacobean drama, see Cawley (1938), 85 ff.
3. I am grateful to Peter Stallybrass for this reference.
4. All references are to this edition.
5. Orkin (1987, 184) notes the telling preference in South Africa for Ridley's edition. Though aware of the political dimensions of *Othello* criticism, Orkin recuperates Shakespeare's play by claiming its universality in expressing the limitations of "human" judgements. His article appeared after this essay was in press.
6. For a useful general discussion of black and white and their cultural associations, see the opening chapter of Levin (1958).
7. For a general account of the classical materials, see Snowden (1983).
8. All the passages quoted appear in the 1600 edition of Hakluyt in which Best's *Discourse* was reprinted in a substantially cut version. The story of the origins of blackness in Noah's son Chus is also found in Leo Africanus' popular *Historie of Africa* (1526).
9. Jordan (1968, 6) observes that "English experience was markedly different from that of the Spanish and Portuguese who for centuries had been in close contact with North Africa and had actually been invaded and subjected by people both darker and more highly civilized than themselves. . . . One of the fairest-skinned nations suddenly came face to face with one of the darkest peoples on earth."
10. Hakluyt's book is said to have been a prime motivator of English colonial expansion and to have increased the profits of the East India Company by some £20,000; see Walter Raleigh's essay in Hakluyt (1904, I, 92).
11. Talmudic and Midrashic commentaries, which inspired interest in the humanist sixteenth century, seem to have been the source for the link between blackness and the curse on Cham (Jordan, 1968, 17–20, 35–9).
12. July 11 and 18, 1596 (Dasent, 1902, n.s. 26, 16, 20). These proclamations must be read in light of the similar dislike and resentment, based on economic distinctions, between the English and the Fleming and Hugenot clothworkers who fled religious persecution and emigrated to England. The clothworkers, however, not only brought needed skills; they were also European, more like the English than an African could ever be, and though they generated hostility, there is no evidence of similar legislation to oust them from England. See Chitty (1966); Barker (1978), 30.
13. Wittkower (1942) provides a thorough review, particularly of the visual material. Mary Louise Pratt's (1985) analysis of two modes of travel writing, the scientific-informational and the subject-centered, experiential, is suggestive not only for reading her nineteenth-century texts, but also for earlier examples which already manifest signs

of the distinctions she draws.

14. These accounts are strikingly similar to discourses about the New World, but comparison of the two would require another study.

15. See among others, John Lok's *Second Voyage to Guinea* (1554), in Hakluyt, VI, 154–77; William Towerson's voyage (1556-7), in Hakluyt, VI, 177–212; George Fenner's voyage (1556), in Hakluyt, VI, 266–84; and finally Jobson (1623), 1968 repr., 65–7. Lok's long and interesting account also appeared in the 1589 edition of Hakluyt as Robert Gainsh's voyage.

16. This passage did not appear in the French but in the Latin *De Republica* (Bodin, 1601, LI, 8ᵛ·); the English translation is that of Richard Knolles (London, 1606), available in a facsimile edition (Bodin, 1606, III, viii). Knolles is quoted in Davis (1966), 112.

17. For a review of Portuguese and Spanish sources, see George (1958). For a general view of Elizabethans and foreigners, see Hunter (1964). On the representation of blacks on the English stage, see Jones (1965); Hunter (1967); and more recently, Tokson (1982).

18. Indians and other New World peoples are similarly represented, as in *The Tempest*, in which Caliban is called a devil.

19. Quoted from R. Burton, *Admirable Curiosities* (1703), in Rollins (1924), 53. Teratological treatises often attributed monstrous births to the material imagination and desire, linking femininity to the production of monsters. As Marie Hélène Huet (1983, 74) observes, the "monster publicly signals all aberrant desire, reproves all excessive passion and all illegitimate fantasy." A contemporary English source specifically for the link between the maternal imagination and blackness is Sir Thomas Browne's *Pseudodoxia Epidemica* (1646). Martin (1880, 266–94) traces the theory of monstrosity and the maternal imagination.

20. See Burke (1969), quoted in Greenblatt (1980), 306. Recently Eve Sedgwick (1985) has deconstructed such versions of "consubstantiality" by showing how the female body, at once desired object and subject of discourse, becomes the territory across which male bonds, which she terms homosocial, are forged.

21. The Folio reading "Travellours historie," with, as Greenblatt notes, its generic implications, seems to me more convincing than "travel's history," since the tale Othello tells is drawn from accounts such as Mandeville's and repeated by the early Elizabethan travelers recorded in Hakluyt.

22. Williams' essay (1984) motivates part of the following discussion of *Othello*.

23. Homi Bhabha's notion of hybridity, which he defines as "the revaluation of the assumption of colonial identity through the repetition of discriminatory identity effects" (1985, 154), is suggestive for my reading of *Othello*.

24. Casual assumptions about the Shakespearean audience are problematic, and the "we" of my own critical discourse is equally so. Shakespeare's audience was not a classless, genderless monolith. The female spectators at a Globe performance, both the whores in the pit and the good English wives Stephen Gosson chastises for their attendance at the theater in *The Schoole of Abuse*, view the play from different perspectives from those of the white male audience of whatever social and economic station. As women, if we are implicated in Iago's perspective and Othello's tragedy, we are unsexed, positioned as men; however, if we identify with Desdemona, we are punished. See the interesting work on female spectatorship in film theory by Laura Mulvey (1975) and Mary Ann Doane (1983) in *Screen*.

25. In Leo Africanus' *Historie of Africa*, the "Portugals" are most often singled out as the destroyers of Africa and her peoples. From this perspective, the Iberian origins of Iago's name suggest that his destruction of Othello/Africa can be read as an allegory of colonialism. For detailed if occasionally dubious parallels between Leo's *Historie* and *Othello*, see Johnson (1985).

26. Compare Thomas Becon's lively description of a whore in his *Catechisme* (1564,

XX, ii$^{v.}$), typical of such representations in the period: "the whore is never satisfied, but is like as one that goeth by the way and is thirsty; even so does she open her mouth and drink of everye next water, that she may get. By every hedge she sits down, & opes her quiver against every arow." Becon makes explicit what is only implied in *Othello*: the link between female orifices – ear, mouth, genitals – and the perceived voraciousness of females.

27. This alternative sexual economy suggests another trajectory of desire in *Othello* which cannot be explored further here. Iago's seduction is also cast in terms of the aural/oral, as for example when he claims to pour "pestilence into his [Othello's] ear" (II. iii. 347). For an interesting discussion of *Othello* and the "pathological male animus toward sexuality," particularly Desdemona's, see Snow (1980), 388.

28. I am grateful to Rey Chow and the other members of the Brown University seminar "Cultural Constructions of Gender" (1987) at the Pembroke Center for Teaching and Research on Women for valuable discussion of the play's sexual economies.

29. For the status of blacks and moors in Renaissance Venice, see Fedalto (1976).

30. For an excellent discussion of gender and class in *Othello*, see Stallybrass (1986).

31. For a psychoanalytic reading of Othello's relation to "the voice of the father," see Snow (1980), 409–10.

32. Quoted in Jordan (1968), 28.

33. See Walvin (1972), 13, and Shyllon (1977). It is worth noting that slavery between Europe and Africa was reciprocal. W.E.B. DuBois (1947, 52) points out that during the sixteenth century "the [black] Mohammedan rulers of Egypt were buying white slaves by the tens of thousands in Europe and Asia." Blonde women were apparently in special demand: quoted in Chandler (1985), who points out that the "moors" were black, and that historians' efforts to claim their tawniness represent racial prejudice.

34. Postlewayt writes in order to justify the Royal African Company's attempts to regain its monopoly; his pamphlet is exemplary, but many others could also be cited. Quoted in Walvin (1972), 51–2.

35. Rymer's attack on Shakespeare in the age of growing Shakespeare idolatry prompted other critics to a different tack – to dispute Othello's blackness altogether rather than reprehend it.

36. This same slippage from blackness to femininity is implicit in the commonly believed notion that apes and negroes copulated, and especially that "apes were inclined wantonly to attack Negro women." For contemporary references, see Jordan (1968), 31.

37. Rymer's characterization of Emilia as "the meanest woman in the Play" (1693, 254) requires comment. The moralism of his "Short View" might lead most readers to award Bianca that superlative, but predictably Rymer cannot forgive Emilia her spunky cynicism toward men and her defense of women.

38. I am grateful to Jonathan Goldberg for this reference.

39. My argument about the handkerchief has much in common with Stallybrass (1986).

40. Boose (1975) argues that the handkerchief represents the lovers' consummated marriage and wedding sheets stained with blood, a sign of Desdemona's sexual innocence. She links the handkerchief to the folk custom of displaying the spotted wedding sheets as a proof of the bride's virginity.

41. See, for example, I. iii. 402; III. iii. 111, 433.

42. Snow associates the spotted "napkin" not only with Desdemona's stained wedding sheets, but also with menstrual blood. He argues that the handkerchief is therefore "a nexus for three aspects of woman – chaste bride, sexual object, and maternal threat" (1980, 392).

43. For a discussion of critical attitudes toward Desdemona, and particularly this line, see Garner (1976).

44. For a discussion of the problem of representation and colonialist discourse, see Said (1978).

Works cited

Africanus, Leo (1526, repr. 1556) *Historie of Africa*, Antwerp.

Barker, Anthony (1978) *The African Link*, London, Frank Cass.

Becon, Thomas (1564) "Catechisme," in *Workes*, London.

Bennett, Tony (1982) "Text and History," in Widdowson, Peter (ed.) *Re-reading English*, London and New York, Methuen, 223–36.

Bhabha, Homi (1985) "Signs Taken for Wonders: Questions of Ambivalence and Authority under a Tree Outside Delhi, May 1817," *Critical Inquiry*, 12, 144–65.

Bodin, J. (1606) *The Six Bookes of a Commonweale*, trans. Richard Knolles, ed. Kenneth Douglas McRae (1962), Cambridge, Mass., Harvard University Press.

Bodin, Ioan. (1601) *De republica*.

Boose, Lynda (1975) "Othello's Handkerchief: The Recognizance and Pledge of Love," *English Literary Renaissance*, 5, 360–74.

Burke, Kenneth (1969) *A Grammar of Motives*, Berkeley, University of California Press.

Cawley, Robert R. (1938) *The Voyages and Elizabethan Drama*, Boston, D.C. Heath.

Chandler, Wayne B. (1985) "The Moor: Light of Europe's Dark Age," in *African Presence in Early Europe*, special issue of *Journal of African Civilizations*, 7, 144–75.

Chitty, C.W. (1966) "Aliens in England in the Sixteenth Century," *Race*, 8, 129–45.

Coleridge, S.T., *Shakespearean Criticism*, ed. Thomas M. Raysor (1960) London, J.M. Dent. First published in 1930.

Davis, David B. (1966) *The Problem of Slavery in Western Culture*, Ithaca, NY, Cornell University Press.

Dasent, John Roche (ed.) (1902) *Acts of the Privy Council*, new series, London, Mackie.

Derrida, Jacques (1985) "Racism's Last Word," trans. Peggy Kamuf, *Critical Inquiry*, 12, 290–9.

Doane, Mary Ann (1983) "Film and the Masquerade: Theorizing the Female Spectator," *Screen*, 23, 74–87.

DuBois, W.E.B. (1947) *The World and Africa*, New York, Viking.

Elias, Norbert (1978) *The Civilizing Process: The History of Manners*, trans. Edmund Jephcott, New York, Urizen.

Fedalto, Giorgio (1976) "Stranieri a Venezia e a Padova," in Arnaldi, Girolamo and Stocchi, M.P. (eds) *Storia della cultura veneta dal primo quattrocento al concilio di Trento*, Vicenza, N. Pozza, III, 499–535.

Freud, Sigmund (1927) "Fetishism," in *Sexuality and the Psychology of Love*, ed. Phillip Rieff (1963, repr. 1978), New York, Collier.

Garner, S.N. (1976) "Shakespeare's Desdemona," *Shakespeare Studies*, 9, 232–52.

George, Katherine (1958) "The Civilized West Looks at Primitive Africa: 1400–1800," *Isis*, 49, 62–72.

Greenblatt, Stephen (1980) *Renaissance Self-Fashioning From More to Shakespeare*, Chicago, University of Chicago Press.

Hakluyt, R. (1600) *The Principal Navigations, Voyages, Traffiques & Discoveries of the English Nation*, ed. Walter Raleigh (1903–5), Glasgow, J. MacLehose.

Huet, Marie Hélène (1983) "Living Images: Monstrosity and Representation," *Representations*, 4, 73–87.

Hughes, Paul L. and Larkin, James F. (eds) (1969) *Tudor Royal Proclamations, III*, New Haven, Yale University Press.

Hunter, G.K. (1964) "Elizabethans and Foreigners," *Shakespeare Survey*, 17, 37–52.

—— (1967) "*Othello* and Colour Prejudice," *Proceedings of the British Academy*, 53, 139–63.

Jobson, Richard (1623) *The Golden Trade*, ed. Walter Rodney (repr. 1968), London, Dawsons.

Johnson, Rosalind (1985) "African Presence in Shakespearean Drama: *Othello* and Leo

Africanus' *Historie of Africa*,'' *African Presence in Early Europe*, special issue of *Journal of African Civilizations*, 7, 267–87.

Jones, Eldred (1965) *Othello's Countrymen: The African in English Renaissance Drama*, Oxford, Oxford University Press.

Jordan, Winthrop (1968) *White Over Black*, Chapel Hill, University of North Carolina Press.

Levin, Harry (1958) *The Power of Blackness*, New York, Alfred Knopf.

Lucas, E.V. (1904) *Highways and Byways in Sussex*, London, Macmillan.

Lyons, Charles H. (1975) *To Wash an Aethiop White: British Ideas About African Educability 1530–1960*, New York, Columbia Teachers' College Press.

Martin, Ernest (1880) *Histoires des monstres*, Paris.

Mulvey, Laura (1975) ''Visual Pleasure and the Narrative Cinema,'' *Screen*, 16, 6–18.

Orgel, Stephen (1967) *The Jonsonian Masque*, Cambridge, Mass., Harvard University Press, repr. New York, Columbia University Press, 1981.

Orkin, Martin (1987) ''Othello and the Plain Face of Racism,'' *Shakespeare Quarterly*, 38, 166–88.

Pratt, Mary Louise (1985) ''Scratches on the Face of the Country; or, What Mr Barrow Saw in the Land of the Bushmen,'' *Critical Inquiry*, 12, 119–43.

Ridley, M.R. (ed.) (1958) *Othello* by William Shakespeare, Arden edn (repr. 1977), London, Methuen.

Rollins, Hyder (1924) ''An analytical Index of the Ballad Entries in the Registers of the Stationers of London,'' *Studies in Philology*, 21, 1–124.

Ross, Lawrence (1960) ''The Meaning of Strawberries in Shakespeare,'' *Studies in the Renaissance*, 7, 225–40.

Ruggiero, Guido (1985) *The Boundaries of Eros, Sex Crimes in Renaissance Venice*, New York, Oxford University Press.

Rymer, Thomas (1693) ''A Short View of Tragedy,'' in Spingarn, J.E. (ed.) (1957) *Critical Essays of the Seventeenth Century*, Bloomington, Indiana University Press, II.

Said, Edward (1978) *Orientalism*, New York, Pantheon.

Sedgwick, Eve (1985) *Between Men: English Literature and Homosocial Desire*, New York, Columbia University Press.

Shyllon, Folarin (1977) *Black People in Britain 1555–1833*, Oxford, Oxford University Press.

Snow, Edward A. (1980) ''Sexual Anxiety and the Male Order of Things in *Othello*,'' *English Literary Renaissance*, 10, 384–412.

Snowden, Frank M., Jr (1983) *Before Color Prejudice*, Cambridge, Mass., Harvard University Press.

Spivak, Bernard (1958) *The Allegory of Evil*, New York, Columbia University Press.

Stallybrass, Peter (1986) ''Patriarchal Territories: The Body Enclosed,'' in Ferguson, Margaret, Quilligan, Maureen and Vickers, Nancy (eds), *Rewriting the Renaissance*, Chicago, University of Chicago Press.

Thomas, Keith (1971) *Religion and the Decline of Magic: Studies in Popular Beliefs in Sixteenth- and Seventeenth-Century England*, London, Weidenfeld & Nicolson.

Tokson, Elliot H. (1982) *The Popular Image of the Black Man in English Drama 1550–1688*, Boston, G.K. Hall.

Walvin, James (1972) *The Black Presence*, New York, Schocken Books.

Whigham, Frank (1984) *Ambition and Privilege*, Berkeley, University of California Press.

—— (forthcoming) in the *Spenser Encyclopedia*.

Williams, Linda (1984) ''When the Woman Looks,'' in Doane, Mary Ann, Mellencamp, Patricia and Williams, L. (eds) *Revision: Essays in Feminist Film Criticism*, Frederick, Md., American Film Institute.

Wittkower, Rudolf (1942) ''Marvels of the East: A Study in the History of Monsters,'' *Journal of the Warburg and Courtauld Institutes*, 5, 159–97.

7

Renaissance antitheatricality and the politics of gender and rank in *Much Ado About Nothing*

Jean E. Howard

Much Ado is filled with playlets, staged shows, actors, and interior dramatists. Don Pedro and Don John both devise pageants designed to deceive specific audiences; most of Messina pretends to be someone else at a masked ball at the outset of the play; and the work ends with two shows involving Claudio: in one he plays the role of mourner before an empty tomb he believes contains his betrothed; in the other he plays the groom to a woman – really Hero – whom he believes to be Hero's cousin. Consequently, critics have often thematized the play as being "about" truth, illusion, and how to live in a world of deceptive appearances.[1] Viewed metadramatically, the play has yielded readings which have seen in its assorted dramatists and dramatic projects Shakespeare's self-reflexive meditations on his own theatrical craft.[2] Much of this criticism aspires to articulate an unchanging or universal meaning for the play – a task both impossible and impossibly idealist. Instead, I am interested in the historical contingency of meaning and want to explore *Much Ado*'s preoccupation with theatrical practices in relationship to a body of Elizabethan texts overtly concerned with the nature, control, and "morality" of theatrical power: namely, the antitheatrical tracts. I will argue that these tracts – through their discussions of theater – were a site where anxieties about a changing social order were discursively produced and managed. The presentation of theatrical practices

JEAN E. HOWARD teaches literature and critical theory at Syracuse University. She is the author of *Shakespeare's Art of Orchestration: Stage Technique and Audience Response* (Urbana, University of Illinois Press, 1984) and is working on a book-length study of the politics of antitheatrical discourse in Renaissance culture.

in Shakespeare's *Much Ado*, far from being "above ideology," also participates in the process by which a historically specific understanding of a patriarchal and hierarchical social order is both secured against threats to itself and also laid open to their demystifying power. In contradistinction to a criticism committed to the drama's place "above ideology" and to its aesthetic and thematic unity, a political criticism of Renaissance drama will focus precisely on the silences and contradictions which reveal the constructed – and interested – nature of dramatic representations and on the ideological functions served by the plays as produced and read at specific historical junctures and through the mediation of specific theatrical and critical practices.

I start from the assumption that the public theater constituted one of the chief ideological apparatuses of Elizabethan society, that is, it provided a popular institutional site for the dissemination of images and narratives through which imaginary relations to the real were represented and playgoers positioned within ideology.[3] Just how completely this theater – at least during Shakespeare's working career – served the hegemonic interests of the state and dominant classes is a key issue now confronting those exploring the political function of Elizabethan drama.[4] That the major companies played at court, enjoyed the patronage of noblemen and monarch, and operated under conditions of censorship and public regulation implies that the theater must to some extent have served, or been made to serve, the interests of the powerful. But the very fact that censorship and regulation were necessary, that dramatists were occasionally imprisoned for sedition, that actors and dramatists often came from nonaristocratic social strata and drew on popular as well as elite traditions, and that the theaters geographically occupied a liminal cultural space in the city's suburbs – all of these factors suggest the volatility of the stage's production and dissemination of dominant ideologies and the susceptibility of plays to subversive appropriation. To say, however, that the state and the theater were not coextensive and that the material circumstances of theatrical writing and theatrical production created conditions for ideological contest and contradiction, does not mean that Elizabethan drama was inherently subversive, simply that its implication in the mediation of social conflict and in the reproduction of dominant ideologies was often strongly marked by contradictions and fissures, and the outcome of its recuperative strategies always uncertain.

In approaching the question of *Much Ado*'s ideological function within Elizabethan culture by way of contemporary antitheatrical tracts, I am seeking, not a "source" for *Much Ado*, but a point of reference in examining how the play's representations of theatrical practice naturalize and/or contest particular Elizabethan understandings of the social order. While the upstart public theater is the main object of attack in these tracts, they construct a picture of a besieged society threatened by an array of groups and practices perceived as disturbing the established order. Consequently, attacks on theater often become attacks on marginal or unruly social groups discursively constructed as demonic, illegitimate, or duplicitously "theatrical." Writing the antitheatrical tracts becomes, in effect, a conservative writing/righting of the entire social order. I am interested in the extent to which the same can be said for Shakespeare's play.

Moreover, since ideological effects are not fixed and immutable, but are affected by a play's reproduction in differing discourses and material stage practices, I want briefly to examine *Much Ado*'s use in certain critical discourses of our own day. In particular, I will attend to that brand of moral criticism which, preoccupied with distinguishing good from evil theatricality in the play, has displaced a political analysis of why particular social groups "naturally" play the opprobrious part in this moral drama and of how representations of theatricality function to reproduce class and gender difference within a social order dependent on these differences to justify inequalities of power and privilege.

The antitheatrical literature

Antitheatrical tracts appeared with great frequency between the opening of the commercial theaters in 1576 and their closing in 1642. While these tracts bear enough resemblances to one another to form a distinct polemical genre, there are also considerable variations among them, reflecting, in part, the changing social circumstances of this sixty-year period and changing perceptions of what constituted the source of social disorder.[5] By a brief look at some of the tracts written before 1600 I hope to show several things: that the tracts repeatedly connect the theater and theatrical practices with threats to established gender and class categories and hierarchies; that they demonize social groups presented as embodying these threats; and that they are highly selective in their condemnation of theatrical practices. Repeatedly, debates about the inherent morality of the theater reveal themselves as political debates about *who* will control the theater and *whose* theatrical practices will be considered legitimate.

The link between the theater and the fear of unruly social groups occurs as early as 1577 in John Northbrooke's *A Treatise wherein Dicing, Dauncing, Vaine Playes or Enterluds . . . are reproved*. In it Northbrooke decries the emergence of the commercial theater as one of many evils threatening the social stability of England. Specifically, Northbrooke fears idleness (of which the theater is presented as both symptom and cause) and the idle (among whom he includes actors who were, by law, ranked with vagabonds and "masterless men" unless officially in the service of the nobility or court). Northbrooke's fear about the potential for disorder posed by the idle or the "illegitimately" employed, like actors, dominates the tract. His solution is clear: everyone, especially the lower orders, must work. His tract is peppered with enjoinders for all the idle, including actors, to engage in productive labor and works of charity. For pastime, people are directed to attend sermons and to avoid plays.[6] What we see here is Northbrooke's participation in the construction of a distinctively Reformation ideology emphasizing hard work and the proper husbanding of time, a doctrine suited to the emergence of protocapitalist economic practices and to the regulation of the lives of a swelling urban populace and work force (Fraser, 1970, 52–76; Hill, 1964, 124–218).[7]

Northbrooke's fear of the idle, and of the theater as a magnet for those who will neither work nor assent to the authority of their masters, provides only a mild anticipation of the anxiety about uncontrolled social change discernible in the antitheatrical tracts written from the late 1570s up to about 1600. Philip Stubbes, whose *Anatomie of Abuses* was published in 1583, provides a fuller idea of the nostalgic tone of many antitheatrical writings and of the specific nature of the pernicious changes associated with the rise of the theater. Stubbes's attack on the theater, like Northbrooke's, is embedded in a more general attack on a host of social abuses. What he most fears are those who transgress class and gender boundaries and in doing so destabilize a social order that in the past held everyone in his or her proper and productive place. Interestingly, Stubbes begins his treatise by castigating excesses in apparel, supposedly because they signify the sin of pride. Like many Puritan writers, Stubbes takes a perverse delight in cataloguing the absurdities of his contemporaries' costume: cork shoes, French hose, double stacks of starched ruffs, false hair, oversized doublets, etc. But while the impracticality and exorbitant cost of these fashions outrage him, they signify a more fundamental evil: namely, these clothes are "more gorgeous, sumptuous and precious than our State, calling or condition of lyfe requireth" (sig. B7). In short, they conceal the real conditions of a man's or a woman's existence and make them mere players who cannot be located in terms of rank or social station. As Stubbes says:

> there is such a confuse mingle mangle of apparell in Ailgna (England), and such preposterous excesse therof, as every one is permitted to flaunt it out, in what apparell he lust himselfe, or can get by anie kind of meanes. So that it is verie hard to knowe, who is noble, who is worshipfull, who is a gentleman, who is not.
>
> (sig. C2^{v})

In short, fixed hierarchies within the social order are no longer stable and no longer reliably marked, visually. The resulting confusion seems ontologically intolerable. Moreover, while lamenting the general "mingle mangle" of apparel on the streets of London, Stubbes finds such transgressions literally institutionalized on the public stage where men of mean rank wore the clothes of noblemen – or, worse, of women. In denigrating the stage and its actors, as well as social upstarts of all kinds, Stubbes seems intent on denying the actual fluidity of the social order and possibilities for mobility within it, and on demonizing those who "play" with their identities and social positions. To counter such dramatistic play, Stubbes evokes an essentially feudal notion of identity as determined by the estate or social position to which one had been born. People may be seen as actors, certainly, but as actors in a play scripted by God in which individual parts are preordained and fixed.

In attempting to impose upon the present a mythicized and highly idealized conception of a past social order, Stubbes ignores the fact that the public, commercial theater in England came into being as feudal social structures were disintegrating and as new social practices were putting pressure on the official ideology of a static social order. David Underdown writes: "In the century before 1640 the country had undergone a social and economic transformation while retaining a static theory of society to which the changes could not be accommodated" (1985, 9). These changes included the rapid expansion of London into a major urban center; the depopulation of certain rural areas; the expansion of the ranks of the gentry, in some cases at the expense of the traditional aristocracy; and major economic changes occasioned by the enclosure movement, by the transition to a protocapitalist mercantile society, and by a steady rise in prices, coupled with stasis in wages. While the practices, social arrangements, and modes of consciousness associated with England's feudal past did not disappear overnight, by this time they coexisted, sometimes tensely, with emerging practices and social structures of quite a different sort.[8]

An example is the emergence of a rhetoric of self-fashioning in which the ancient trope of man as actor bears a new emphasis (Greenblatt, 1980, 1–3). No longer an actor in a God-given script, man is presented as writing the script in which, through studious self-cultivation and artful self-presentation, he will perform.[9] The courtesy literature which became one site for authorizing this view of identity may well have been *intended* to stem social mobility by defining the traits by which a true gentleman was known. Ironically, what these tracts revealed was that the characteristics of a gentleman were not inherent in any particular class, but were learnable. Consequently, upstarts appropriated the lessons of this literature and used it to increase the very mobility it was intended to suppress (Whigham, 1984, 5). Stephen Greenblatt is undoubtedly correct in arguing that the notion of infinite possibility such rhetoric promised was an illusion (1980, 256). Renaissance men and women were constructed by discursive and material forces over which they could have little control. But this does not mean that the language of self-fashioning and the notion of man as self-motivating actor were not culturally important, particularly as counters to the official ideology of social stasis.

Stubbes, however, was committed to the older paradigm. He idealizes a mythic past in which individual self-assertion and entrepreneurship had not opened a gap between God-given identity and satanic transgressions of it. He despises "shape-shifters," of whom actors (wearing the cast-off clothes of noblemen or the dresses of women) are the epitome; just as he despises the flouting on the London streets of Elizabeth's sumptuary proclamations, those directives by which, in setting forth what kinds of textiles, ornaments, furs, and even colors of clothing could be worn by men and women of various ranks, the Queen attempted to arrest the appropriation by the unworthy of social roles deemed above their proper station in life (Hooper, 1915, 436–7). In obvious ways, flouting of the sumptuary laws was often associated with the theater. In the 1579 treatise, *The Schoole of Abuse*, Stephen Gosson writes: "How often hath her Majestie with the grave advice of her honorable Councell, sette downe the limits of apparell to every degree, and how soone againe hath the pride of our harts overflowed the chanel? How many times hath accesse to Theaters been restrayned, and how boldly againe have we reentered'' (sig. C6). He goes on to talk about how actors attire themselves in the borrowed or cast-off outfits of aristocrats and, thus attired, thumb their noses at their betters. His tract thus both produces anxiety about those seen as having aspirations beyond their proper social station and describes practices which implicitly contest the essentialist ideology that sees identity as God-given and unchanging, rather than as forged through participation in social processes.

There is another group, however, which also figures prominently in the antitheatrical narrative of social disruption, and that group is women, who are constructed in these texts as the duplicitous, inherently theatrical sex. They, like the idle and the aspiring, are said to cause social disruption, partly because they have natures prone to change and inconstancy. Under special attack in these treatises is women's apparel which, whether described as too mannish, too sumptuous, or too exotic, becomes the sign of woman's changeability.[10] Stubbes is typical in his disgust at women's excesses in dress. He writes: ''Proteus that Monster could never chaunge him self into so many fourmes and shapes as these women do, belike they have made an obligation with hel and are at agreement with the devil, els they would never outrage thus'' (sig. F5). His rhetoric stresses distortion and adulteration. Women who wear men's clothes are characterized as ''hermaphroditii; that is, monsters of bothe kindes, half women, half men'' (sig. F5ᵛ·). Women who wear great hoops and petticoats are ''artificiall women'' (sig. F6ᵛ·), ''Puppits'' (sig. F6ᵛ·), or things so deformed they are hardly credited with life. There is considerable violence in this rhetoric: anger at women who exercise independence, anger at women who assume male prerogatives, anger at women who will not hold the shapes men have constructed for them. The violence hints not only, as Louis Adrian Montrose has argued, at male anxiety about the rule of a female sovereign (1983, 75–85; see also Erickson in this volume), but at a more widespread gender tension (Newman, 1986, 91–2). Moreover, this rhetoric has a clear policing effect. It attempts to make certain behaviors unthinkable for ''good'' women and to marginalize and make monsters of those who do engage in such behavior.

The essentialism pervading the tracts – the insistence that some behaviors distort and falsify the *true* nature and the *true* position (inevitably a subordinate position) of certain social groups – resonates with the argument proposed perhaps most fully in Stephen Gosson's second tract, *Playes Confuted in Five Actions* (1582), that plays tell lies about reality and satanically distort the truths of nature. In this tract one can see very clearly how a connection is forged between lying fictions and lying actors and upstarts, and in Stubbes's hands the chain is extended to include lying women. One can also begin to see how authority is evoked to hold in place Gosson's particular construction of the world. Of the drama Gosson writes: ''Plays are no Images of trueth, because sometime they handle such things as never were, sometime they runne upon truethes, but make them seeme longer, or shorter, or greater, or lesse than they were, according as the Poet blowes them up with his quill, for aspiring heades, or minceth them smaller, for weaker stomakes" (1582, sig. D5–D5ᵛ·). Plays, enacting fabulous events ransacked out of old romances or concocted from thin air, make actors double liars: they present lies about reality and they counterfeit their true persons in the assumption of a fictional role. The transgression of gender categories by actors is, for Gosson, as for others, especially troubling. "Garments are set downe for signes distinctive betwene sexe and sexe, to take unto us these garments that are manifest signes of another sexe, is to falsifie, forge, and adulterate, contrarie to the expresse rule of the worde of God" (sig. E3ᵛ·). Stubbes, who, in *The Anatomie of Abuses*, steals great chunks of Gosson's tract, takes Gosson's rhetoric about male actors dressing as women and uses it to attack women who dress mannishly or outlandishly: "Our apparell was given us as a signe distinctive to discern betwixt sex and sex, and therefore one to weare the Apparel of another sex, is to participate with the same, and to adulterate the veritie of his own kinde" (sig. F5ᵛ·). It is, I think, significant that women and actors are constructed, interchangeably, in the same rhetoric of contamination and adulteration. They erase boundaries; they usurp privileges; they threaten the self-evidence of established categories of gender and rank. And, perhaps because of their very changeability, they provoke a troubling desire, debauching those who gaze on them too greedily.

In attacking plays as lies and actors as counterfeiters, Gosson marshals a host of classical and biblical authorities who supposedly support his position. In this, he simply makes use – as do a number of writers arguing for and against the theater – of the tactics regularly employed in Elizabethan polemical debate. Ingeniously, he also tries to enlist the authority of Queen Elizabeth on the antitheatrical side by constructing the battle over the theaters as a contest between God and the devil, Protestantism and Catholicism. He argues that the devil, faced with the virtue of Queen Elizabeth and the success of the Protestant Reformation, has to work more craftily than ever before. The devil's best instruments for sowing social discord are bawdy Italian books and stage plays. God is represented as desiring the banning of both. Of course, it wasn't God, but important figures in the City of London, who wanted the theater abolished.[11] The City was quite clear about its distaste for this upstart institution located just beyond the perimeter of its actual control. From this liminal zone the City constantly feared the outbreak of subversive or disruptive activity. This continued to be so right up to the time when a Puritan parliament closed the theaters. Before that neither the monarch nor the Privy Council responded affirmatively to pleas from the City to shut the theater, though great care was taken to license and censor stage productions. Moreover, Elizabeth, James, and Charles, each of whom resisted City pressure to suppress the theater and to varying degrees extended their own patronage to it, themselves employed highly theatrical pageants, processions, and allegorical tableaux as part of the arts of statescraft.[12] Perhaps more surprisingly, the City, site of much of the outcry against the public theater, cultivated with great enthusiasm the theatrical pageantry of the Lord Mayor's show.[13] These facts suggest that while Gosson may talk about the stage as an object of struggle between God and the devil, the real contest of authorities was more mundane. Everyone recognized the theater as a powerful and potentially dangerous force; the real questions were: who would control this power and which theatrical practices would be stigmatized, which ruled legitimate?

Sir Philip Sidney gives answers more complex than Gosson's simple desire to abolish the public theater by royal fiat, but even in his urbane tract, *An Apology for Poetry*, a defense of the stage is mounted in terms which reveal fears about the usurpation of privilege by the unworthy. Ironically, Gosson had dedicated his first attack on the theater to Sidney, trying to enlist the authority of this important Protestant aristocrat behind his cause. It may have been this treatise which prompted the composition of the quite antithetical *An Apology for Poetry*, in which Sidney defends poetry and the theater from the charge that poetic fictions are lies (Ringler, 1942, 117–24; Kinney, 1974, 44). "Now for the poet," Sidney writes, "he nothing affirms, and therefore never lieth" (p. 123). Instead, poetic fictions go beyond the world of fact and the arid prescriptions of philosophy to show what might and should be. Sidney thus counters Gosson's charge that plays are lies, but implicitly he surrenders into the hands of an elite the authority over this power of constructing what might and should be. Early in the treatise Sidney mystifies the idea of a poet, calling him a Godlike maker with access to a golden world of Platonic ideas (pp. 99–101). This does not sound much like the grubby hack work characterizing most theatrical writing. And in a wonderful instance of the latter end of a tale forgetting its beginning, Sidney's opening, expansive defense of the freedom of the poet as maker leads eventually to his *ex cathedra* imposition of rules of decorum and just imitation within which the freedom of the true poet must be exercised.

Moreover, when he talks of the theater directly, Sidney is quite critical of the classically imperfect fictions of the popular stage which fail to observe the unities or a proper decorum in the separation of kings from clowns, base scurrility from chaste delight (pp. 133–7). True poets and true poetry are thus constructed as being quite different from what passes for such in the popular realm. Fittingly, he ends his discussion of the stage thus:

> But I have lavished out too many words of this play matter. I do it because, as they are excelling parts of Poesy, so is there none so much used in England, and none can be more pitifully abused; which, like an unmannerly daughter showing a bad education, causeth her mother Poesy's honesty to be called in question.
>
> (p. 137)

The image constructs the popular theater as a wayward woman, obviously requiring surveillance, and hints that even the best of women, Poesy herself, is not entirely honest (i.e. can produce a bastard). The popular, the feminine, the theatrical – they all seem to have slipped beyond the control of the true poet, the classically trained male aristocrat, whose "defense" of poetry thus becomes a rather partial affair, at least where Poesy's highly stigmatized theatrical daughter is concerned. What the Sidney example allows us to see is that debates over the intrinsic morality of theater often mask political questions about *whose* theatrical practices will be declared legitimate and *who* will exercise control over theatrical representations. Sidney's contortions in saving theater, but not popular theater, from stigmatization are simply a case in point.

To sum up: the antitheatrical literature shows the enormous pressure placed on certain ideological positions by changing social conditions and practices. The tracts form a highly political discourse which, in the service of various interests, attempts to hold in place a static conception of the social order and an essentialist view of human subjectivity. While the theater is clearly the *institution* most identified with threats to the traditional social order, the tracts also attack other practices and groups held to threaten that order. As we have seen, for example, the denigration of actors often turns into the denigration of women. Other modes of polemical writing employ many of the same tropes of antitheatrical discourse and employ the same tactic of slipping from one object of attack to the next. For example, when Thomas Tuke, in his treatise opposing the use of cosmetics (1616), is in the midst of writing about the inherent duplicity and seeming of women, he suddenly swerves into a vituperative account of the duplicity and inherent theatricality of the Catholic religion. Castigating women who use cosmetics, Tuke recounts how certain Spanish priests give women permission to paint. He explodes:

> Surely it is a doctrine that doth well enough become the Jesuites, who as they are the gret Masters of lying, equivocation, and mentall reservation, so doe they make no difficultie, to teach that it is lawfull to belie the face, and the complexion. Secondly, it well enough beseemes the Church of Rome, who as shee is the Mother of spiritual fornications, magicke, sorcerie and witchcraft, so hath God given her over to defile herselfe with corporall polutions and fornications, not only to give allowance to publike Stewes and Brothel-houses, but that the Masse it self (which is the master peece of the Papacie) sholde be made the baude to much uncleannesse, as is well knowne by their Masses at midnight, and their morning Matins before day. And therefore this old Romish Jesabel, as she hath painted her owne face with the faire shew of many goodly ceremonies, of antiquity and succession, and multitude of her professors, thereby to set the world at a gaze, so in this particular also she doth tollerate the abuses of her children.

(sig. H1^{v})

The painted woman and the Catholic Church – itself personified as a painted woman – are interchangeably constructed. The duplicity of women is encouraged by priests because the whole Catholic religion is one of false piety and organized deception. Exactly what was supposed to go on at those midnight masses and daybreak matins, Tuke only intimates – clearly sexual depravities of some sort. This is the exact kind of double purpose repeatedly attributed to the theater, where, it was alleged, under the guise of entertaining or even educating the audience, actors, like priests, debauched and corrupted that audience, making the women prey to young gallants and making men effeminate.

Elsewhere Tuke has recourse to an extended metaphor which wonderfully reveals both the logical incoherence and the political purpose of much of this polemic. Overtly, Tuke is one who abhors all painting, acting, and artifice. Yet when he describes how a husband should wean a woman from painting, he does so in these terms:

> Dost thou not see that painters, when they goe about to make a faire picture, doe new apply these colours, and then others, wiping out the former? Be not thou more unskilfull then painters. They begin to paint the shape of the bodies on tables, do use so great paines and care; and is it not meet that wee should trie all conclusions, use all meanes, when we desire to make soules better? . . . If by degrees thou shalt thus reforme thy wives mind, thou shalt be the best painter, a faithfull servant, an honest husbandman.

> (sig. F2)

Tuke's rhetoric is fascinating, since, while condemning one form of painting (cosmetics), he condones another (the fashioning of a wife's soul to conform to her husband's wishes). The key point, of course, is who does the fashioning, for it is inherently an exercise of power. Women are not to do it themselves, for that shows their alliance with the devil, but men are free to shape this weaker sex as they may wish, for that is merely the natural order of things. In short, they wear the label of "painter" with a difference.

Shakespeare's *Much Ado About Nothing*

Shakespeare's play does not participate in the overtly polemical rantings of the antitheatrical or antifeminist tracts. From a common-sense perspective, this may seem to place the play "above ideology." From another perspective, it is precisely the work's distance from overtly polemical intentions which makes it an effective producer and disseminator of ideology, that is, of understandings of relations to the real so effectively naturalized that their constructed and interested character is obscured.

In regard to its representations of theatricality, one might expect *Much Ado* to be unequivocally positive. After all, the work itself is a play. But, just as support for the theatricality of *certain* groups can be found in the antitheatrical tracts, making them speak, as it were, against themselves, so Shakespeare's play speaks against itself in several important senses. Although *Much Ado* is a play, and although it dramatizes a world permeated with theatrical practices, it also eventually returns control over theatricality to "the better sort" and disciplines those who illegitimately aspire to wield such power. Read in relationship to the antitheatrical tracts, the play thus appears to police its own protheater tendencies by acknowledging the validity of much antitheatrical polemic and reproducing its writing of the social order, especially its fear of the dangerous duplicity of women and those who aspire to positions beyond their station. And yet, even as it enacts the disciplining of upstarts and the policing of theatrical power advocated by the antitheatrical tracts, the play as a material phenomenon – as produced on the Elizabethan public stage, rather than a modern one – literally involved men of low estate assuming the garments of women, playing the parts of aristocrats, and gaining economic power from the sale of dramatic illusions. This is a particularly egregious instance of the ideological function of the dramatic narrative coming into sharp, if often unacknowledged, conflict with the ideological implications of the material conditions of Elizabethan theater production. Moreover, the play also speaks against itself in regard to its presentation of the relationship between truth and illusion. While it circulates the idea that in some absolute sense a true reading of the world is possible, a reading which eludes the "distortions" and mediations of dramatic illusion, that view is countered by the dramatization of a world in which truth is discursively produced and authorized and so remains unknowable outside a set of practices, including theatrical practices, which secure one understanding of the world at the expense of another.[14] To tease out these contradictions and to consider their ideological implications is the purpose of what follows.

At its center *Much Ado* seems to dramatize the social consequences of staging lies. Don John precipitates the play's crisis by having a servant, Margaret, impersonate her mistress, Hero, in a love encounter observed by Hero's husband-to-be and Don John's brother. These theatrics make Hero appear a whore and lead directly to her denunciation in the church. This deception is clearly coded as evil: it is engineered by a bastard, involves the transgressive act of a servant wearing the clothes of one of higher rank, and leads to the threat of death for several of the play's characters.

Before discussing this evil trick further, however, I want to note the many other instances of theatrical trickery in this play and the changes Shakespeare made in his source material which radically compounded the amount of theatricality in the play as a whole. For example, while all the sources contain the trick at the window, none contains the Benedick and Beatrice subplot which depends on Don Pedro's theatrical deceptions of each of them (Prouty, 1950, 1). Moreover, while the source stories have two men, usually friends, vying for the Hero figure (Prouty, 1950, 34), Shakespeare substitutes rivalry between Don Pedro and his bastard brother – not for actual possession of the woman – but for power, though the control of women is a chief way of establishing masculine power in the play. This rivalry is largely carried on through competing theatrical tricks. If Don Pedro, the seeming agent for comic union, uses theatrical deception to promote marriages, Don John uses it to thwart his brother's fictions and to contest his brother's power.

The result of these changes is a series of highly overdetermined theatrical situations which betray a deeply conflictual psychic-social zone. None of the play's impersonations and playlets is unproblematical. When Don Pedro impersonates Claudio at the masked ball, for example, he doesn't unproblematically further Claudio's desires. Instead, his action opens the door for Don John's meddling and for a number of "mistakings." Moreover, even Don Pedro, the initiator of so much of the play's disguise and theatrical cozenage, cannot see through the pageant staged at Hero's window.

In trying to make sense of the play's treatment of theatricality, twentieth-century humanist criticism has typically made two moves: one involves drawing clear moral distinctions between "good" and "bad" theatrical practices; the other involves reassuring readers that the play offers ways to cope with – to see through – omnipresent theatrical deception. Richard Henze (1971) typifies the dominant critical position in discriminating between one form of theatrical deception which "leads to social peace, to marriage, to the end of deceit" and another which "breeds conflict and distrust and leads even Beatrice to desire the heart of Claudio in the marketplace" (p. 188). Later I will examine the implicit assumptions lying behind the disappointed phrase, "even Beatrice," but for the moment I wish simply to point out that most readings of the play use the two brothers to figure good and evil theatricality. Indeed, most readings of the play depend, crucially, on maintaining differences in the motives of the two men and in the social consequences of their practices. Similarly, many readings insist on Shakespeare's insistence that beneath the world of unstable appearances there is a world of essences to which man has access if he has, paradoxically, either faith or careful noting skills. Those possessing faith, an essentially mystified notion encompassing both intuition and religious belief, can comprehend the truth which can't be seen, but which lies behind the distortions produced by deceivers. Thus Beatrice sees beyond the appearance of Hero's guilt; and Dogberry and Verges, God's naturals, intuitively know a thief despite misunderstanding utterly his actual language. On the other hand, illusion can also be pierced by careful noting, a pragmatic and practical skill, one paradoxically more congruent with the dawning scientific age than the waning age of faith. Thus the Friar is said to take careful note of Hero in the church and by her blushes and behavior is able to pierce the lies of Don John's fictions. Henze, again, presents a characteristic summation of the dominant critical position: "This combination of intuitive trust and careful observation seems to be the one that the play recommends" (1971, 194).

I wish to challenge the focus of this criticism, first by substituting a political and social for a moral analysis of the play's theatrical practices and, second, by looking, not at how the individual subject can discern truth, but at the role of authority and authoritative discourses in delimiting what can be recognized as true. My intent is to examine both the play's ideological function in Elizabethan culture and also the displacement of political questions in much of the criticism through which that play is currently reproduced.

It is easy to provide a moral reading of Don John. He is the play's designated villain, its exemplification of the evil dramatist; and his chief deception – the substitution of Margaret for Hero at the bedroom window – is clearly a malicious act. Yet a characterological focus on Don John as origin of evil can obscure the extent to which the assumptions about women upon which his trick depends are shared by other men in the play. The trick at the window silently assumes and further circulates the idea that women are universally prone to deception and impersonation. This is a cultural construction of the feminine, familiar from the antitheatrical tracts, which serves the political end of justifying men's control and repression of the volatile and duplicitous female. Don John depends on the currency of this construction of women in Messina, and he is not disappointed. Faced with Don John's accusations, many men – including Hero's father – quickly conclude she has merely been impersonating virtue (Berger, 1982, 306). In short, Don John lies about Hero, but his lie works because it easily passes in Messina as a truthful reading of women.

Moreover, while Don John is the play's villain, he is also the bastard brother of the play's highest-ranking figure. This fact is ideologically significant because it locates the "natural" origins of social disruption in those who do not legitimately occupy a place in the traditional social order. Certainly, in the ideological economy of the play it is useful that the dangerous and threatening aspects of theatricality be located in and exorcised by the punishment of a scapegoat figure. While many figures *within* the play make Hero the scapegoat for their fears, for the audience the scapegoat is Don John, the illegitimate intruder among the ranks of the aristocracy. Thus, much as in the antitheatrical tracts, women and "bastards" (those who have no legitimate social position or have forsaken that position) are figured as the natural and inevitable source of social disruption and evil. Moreover, the very fact that Don John is a bastard further implicates women in crime. As Harry Berger writes: "The play's two scapegoats are a bastard named Trouble and a woman named Hero, and his bastardy tells us where the blame lies: like Edmund, no doubt, he is a testimony both to his father's prowess and to his mother's sin – a by-product of the frailty named Woman" (1982, 311).

Thus Don John is both a testimony to woman's weakness and a social outsider, someone tolerated within Messinian society only on the say-so of his legitimate brother. He is, moreover, punished for usurping an activity – the manipulation of the world through theatrical fictions – which is from first to last in this play associated with aristocratic male privilege. While women are characterized as deceivers, literally, as Balthasar's song more accurately declares, it is "Men [who] were deceivers ever" (II. iii. 60), especially men in power.[15] Don Pedro is, after all, the play's chief dissembler. It is he who first employs theatrical deception in his plan to woo Hero for Claudio, and he who then goes on to arrange the playlets by which Benedick and Beatrice are made to fall in love. When Claudio first approaches Don Pedro about marrying Hero, for example, the Prince volunteers in his own person to negotiate the contract between his retainer and his old friend's daughter. Moreover, while the Hero figure in the sources is of humble origins, this is not true of Shakespeare's Hero (Prouty, 1950, 43–4). Don Pedro is thus not in the unusual position of sanctioning a marriage across class lines, but instead promotes a union between social equals and so strengthens the existing social order.

His actions in regard to Benedick and Beatrice are more complex, and I will discuss them further below, but what they achieve is the disciplining of social renegades and their submission to the authority of Don Pedro and to the institution of marriage which it seems his special function to promote. Benedick, of course, openly scoffs at marriage throughout a good portion of the play; and Beatrice turns down a marriage proposal – however seriously meant – from Don Pedro himself. Through his staged pageants, Don Pedro asserts control over these two renegades and checks the socially subversive impulse their refusal to marry implies. What Don John by his deceptions thus usurps is the prerogative of theatrical deception by which his legitimate brother controls Messina. If Don Pedro is the one first to make use of impersonation and theatrical tricks, Don John is the copycat who imitates the initial trick of his brother and then makes that brother the victim/audience of the trick at the bedroom window. If Don Pedro exercises power by arranging marriages, Don John counters that power by spoiling marriages and does so using the very tools of theatrical deception employed by Don Pedro. The bastard's acts thus appropriate a power the play seeks to lodge with the legitimate brother. At play's end, it is this aggression for which the worst punishment is promised.

Further, the very *way* the various deceptions of the two brothers are materially represented on the stage has specific ideological consequences. Don John's crucial deception is his substitution of maid for mistress at the bedroom window. This trick involves a transgression against hierarchy in which, as on the public stage itself, an inferior assumes the borrowed robes of a social superior. This action is not dramatized. Consigned to the realm of the "unseen," its consequences disappear utterly – like a bad dream – at play's end. By contrast, Don Pedro's two most elaborate deceptions, the playlets put on for Benedick and Beatrice, *are* dramatized and are presented as part of the natural prerogatives of Messina's highest-ranking visitor. The result is to naturalize Don Pedro's practice so that, as in all ideological effects, the contingent passes as the inevitable. By contrast, the bastard's acts are represented as evil and so outside the natural order that they are assigned to the unreality of the unseen. The consequence is to produce moral differences between similar activities in ways that obscure the social differences justified and held in place by moral categories. As in the antitheatrical tracts, a key question turns out to be: whose fiction-making activities are to be construed as legitimate? And, as in those tracts, the answer involves matters of gender and rank as much as moral motive. Much modern criticism of the play, by focusing so resolutely on the morality of deception, has been complicit in allowing to pass unnoted the function of moral categories in reproducing existing power relations and social arrangements.

This criticism has also been obsessed with the problem of how one can "see through" the many theatrical practices in *Much Ado* to a truth not obscured by lies. This play, more than most, seems to engender in readers fears about never getting to "the real," but of being trapped in competing and manipulative discursive constructions of it. Focusing on getting outside of discourse, through either the empiricism of careful noting or the transcendentalism of faith, short-circuits a political analysis of how truth effects are produced through discourse, and of the social origins of those dissenting perspectives through which "truth" is exposed as somebody's truth.

The utopian nature of the desire to escape discourse is perhaps best seen by looking at the play's handling of Dogberry and Verges who, with their apparently intuitive recognition of villainy, are crucial to any reading which insists on the ultimate transparency of the world to the faithful and/or the astute. First of all, there is something improbable about their rescue of Messina from illusion. For three-quarters of the play illusions seem impermeable. Don Pedro and Claudio fall victim to them, as do the witty and skeptical Beatrice and Benedick. The world is only righted by two lower-class figures who flounder mightily in the Queen's English, and who capture the villains virtually by instinct rather than by any rational understanding of what was overheard or said or done by anyone. Moreover, it seems that the gift of intuition is bought at the price of speech and rationality. Dogberry and Verges exist almost outside of language, and this placement denies them any real social power. Constructed as God's naturals, these lower-class figures conveniently solve society's problems without ever threatening its central values or power relations or providing an alternative understanding of the social order (Krieger, 1979, 61). Pathetically eager to please their betters, they are obsessively preoccupied with that phantom, Deformed, whose chief crime, besides thievery, seems to be that he "goes up and down like a gentleman" (III. iii. 117–18) and spends money beyond his ability or desire to repay it (V. i. 294–9). Dogberry and Verges are as concerned as their betters to discipline upstarts. Unlike the more rebellious, clever, and even dangerous lower-class figures in some of Shakespeare's plays – Pompey, Jack Cade, Feste, Pistol – Dogberry and Verges perform a sentimental, utopian function. They keep alive the dream of a world where good and evil are transparent to the eye of innocence, and inferiors correct the "mistakings" of their betters without ever threatening the essential beliefs of those betters.

The utopian impulse simply to escape the world of deception and mediation not only finds its logical end in the garbled speech of Dogberry and Verges, but is also strongly countered by other aspects of the play's action which point to the conclusion that in a thoroughly dramatistic universe one can escape neither from discourse nor from the play of power which authorizes the truth of one construction of the world over another. In Elizabethan culture and in this play, a chief form of power is, of course, theatrical power. The role of theatrical functions as instruments of power and as a means of compelling belief in a particular view of truth is most graphically shown in Don Pedro's successful manipulation of Benedick and Beatrice. Readers often point out that these two are depicted as showing a keen interest in one another from the play's opening moments and as, perhaps, having once been romantically involved. By contrast, I want to focus on the role of Don Pedro's pageants in producing their love. While a modern discourse of love understands it as an essential, private, inwardly produced emotion which serves as the motive for marriage, in the Renaissance many upper-class marriages had other motives, political, economic, or social. In *Much Ado*, through the actions of Don Pedro, one can see how the investment of established authority in marriage is used to reproduce existing social relations (both gender and class relations) and to control threats to the social order. Far from *discovering* Benedick and Beatrice's preexistent love, Don Pedro works hard to *create* it. When the two of them "fall in love," they do not obey a spontaneous, privately engendered emotion so much as reveal their successful interpellation into particular positions within a gendered social order.[16] In this play, Don Pedro is the agent of such interpellation. He never indicates that he sees a repressed attraction between Benedick and Beatrice, nor does he present his fictions as simply revealing the truth. Instead, his object is to create love where its existence seems impossible and thus to control the social world around him. He places both Benedick and Beatrice as subjects of a love discourse in which a role for each to play is clearly marked, the role of the "normal" male and female.

The two playlets, however, though having the same general aim of making social renegades conform, also produce gender differences in the process. To be a "normal" male is not the same as being a "normal" female. In discussing Beatrice before Benedick, Leonato and his friends construct her as a vulnerable, pitiful victim. Her tears, her sleeplessness, her indecision – all are dwelt on in loving detail. The role mapped for Benedick is to be her rescuer, to become more "manly" by accepting his duty to succor women as well as to fight wars. And Benedick takes up his assigned place in the gendered social order by vowing to put aside his pride and accept her love. He presents his change of heart as a species of "growing up". As he says, "A man loves the meat in his youth that he cannot endure in his age" (II. iii. 218–19), and the misogyny he had embraced is an example of such meat now displaced by the maturer pleasure of peopling the world and receiving a woman's adoration. By contrast, the conversation staged for Beatrice only briefly focuses on Benedick's suffering. He is presented as the good man any woman would be a fool to scorn, but most of the attention focuses on how unnatural her pride, her wit, and her independence are. Her great sin is to be "so odd, and from all fashions" (III. i. 72), that is, so quick in mocking men who are to be revered, not exposed to ridicule. Tellingly, Beatrice shows her successful interpellation into the gendered social order by vowing to tame her "wild heart" to Benedick's "loving hand" (III. i. 112) – like a bird or an animal being domesticated. He becomes the protector and tamer, she the tamed repentant. And while Beatrice's character continues to show traces of the merry-shrew schema which served as Shakespeare's basic model, the two interior plays decisively mark the turn in the subplot toward marriage and the partial righting of the social order by the interpellation of social renegades into gendered and socially less iconoclastic subject positions.

The whole feat constitutes a remarkable display of power on Don Pedro's part. Using theatrical means, he offers Benedick and Beatrice understandings of self and other that serve his own ends. That Benedick and Beatrice accept his fictions as truth depends on a number of factors, including the authority of those promulgating this vision of the truth. Benedick and Beatrice believe the lies being voiced in the two eavesdropping encounters first because it is their friends who speak these lies. And while the cynical Benedick can imagine his friends as deceivers, he cannot think this of the grave Leonato: "I should think this a gull but that the white-bearded fellow speaks it. Knavery cannot, sure, hide himself in such reverence'' (II. iii. 115–17). Age has authorizing force. Further, Don Pedro's constructions are taken as true because they have the authority of cultural stereotypes. He writes Benedict and Beatrice each for the other in terms that resonate, as I have argued, with cultural definitions of "man-in-love" and "woman-in-love." Similarly, Don Pedro and Claudio believe the deception at Hero's window, not only because they trust the testimony of their eyes, but also because what Don John tells them has the truth of stereotype as well. Hero is the whore whose appetites are disguised by the illusion of virtue. Moreover, once Don Pedro and Claudio doubt Hero, it is their authority which plays a large part in making Leonato doubt his own daughter in the church. Those further down the social scale have less legitimating power. When in I. ii. Antonio tells Leonato that a serving man has heard the Prince say he wants to marry Hero, Leonato asks at once: "Hath the fellow any wit that told you this?" When Antonio replies "A good sharp fellow" (I. ii. 15–16), Leonato still decides to "hold it [the report] as a dream till it appear itself" (18–19). Nothing could cause such skepticism – in a play in which everyone is remarkably credulous – except the lowly social status of the reporter.

Consequently, although critics have been quick to deny that theatrical fictions create Benedick and Beatrice's love, the work can be read otherwise as encoding the process by which the powerful determine truth and the way in which belief depends upon the degree to which a fiction chimes with the common sense of the culture. Told by several people that Don Pedro wooed Hero for himself, Claudio responds: "'Tis certain so. The Prince woos for himself. / Friendship is constant in all other things / Save in the office and affairs of love" (II. i. 156–8). This truism makes it easy to believe the truth of a particular tale of violated friendship. The more a fiction draws on conventional schemata, the more it appears true to life.

In such a context the play reveals how hard it is for marginal figures to counter common sense or to overturn the constructions of the powerful, though social marginality is more likely than either careful noting or faith to be the cause of one's ability to see the arbitrary nature of power's truths. In this play, women are clearly marginal to the male order. When Hero hears herself named whore at her wedding, she does not contest that construction of herself; she swoons beneath its weight. It is as if there were no voice with which to contest the forces inscribing her in the order of "fallen" women. Even the friar, another figure marginal to the real power in Messina, cannot directly contest the stories endorsed by Don Pedro. He must work by indirection, knowing all the while that his fictions may not alter the fixed views of Claudio and Don Pedro and that Hero may live out her life in a convent. In this context, when existing authority so clearly predetermines what will count as truth, the use of the powerless Dogberry and Verges to rescue the world seems all the more a kind of wish fulfillment or magical thinking: an attempt to reconcile the recognition of power's power to determine truth with a view of a world where truth stands outside its discursive production in a social field.

Beatrice's role in the church is more complex. Drawn to the pattern of the witty shrew, Beatrice for much of the play does not see the world as others see it. Early in the play she is depicted as resisting the patriarchal dictum that the natural destiny of all women is marriage; similarly, her response to the revelations about Hero reveals she does not accept the misogynist dictum that all women are whores. It is precisely Beatrice's iconoclasm which Don Pedro's playlet seems designed to contain. Iconoclastic voices such as hers need to be recuperated or silenced. In the church, however, no recuperation of her position seems possible. She refuses Don John's assimilation of Hero to the stereotype of whore, but she cannot by her voice triumph over Don Pedro's authority. This, of course, is why she is driven to demand that Benedick "Kill Claudio" (IV. i. 285), a statement which has led to her denunciation in a good deal of criticism (recall Henze's "even Beatice" [1971, 188] which, by implicitly constructing women as peacemakers and repositories of good sense, writes their anger as more transgressive than men's), but which can be read as an acknowledgement that in a world where power resides in the words of powerful men, the violence their speaking can do can be successfully countered – not by the speaking of women – but by the literal violence of the sword.

Of course, at this juncture another ideological fissure opens in the play. When Benedick and Beatrice are depicted as standing out against marriage, they figure a challenge to the social order. When led to confess love for one another, they take up their places within that gendered order. But pretty clearly for Don Pedro their doing so was not supposed to threaten the patriarchal system. The wife was to be the tamed bird, submissive to her husband's hand, and the bonds between men were not seriously to be disturbed, as we see in Claudio's offer to marry and then promptly to escort Don Pedro on the next stages of his journey. He may be about to become a husband, but that seems not to disturb the primacy of his role as attendant upon the Duke. But, ironically, the bond with a woman *does* disrupt Benedick's bonds to men. The subject position of "lover" into which Don Pedro was so eager to maneuver his friend comes into conflict with the claims of male friendship, producing disequilibrium in the social order. At first, Benedick as lover offered no threat to Don Pedro. His perfume, his shaving, his seeking out of Beatrice's picture – all his actions reveal him very much the stereotypical and somewhat comic lover. He is exhibiting the appropriate masculine behavior Don Pedro and Claudio both intended to elicit and undergoing a rite of passage which marks him as "of the company of men" in a new way. Beatrice's "Kill Claudio," however, forces the issue of competing loyalties, revealing the potential contradictions in Benedick's position. And when Benedick is depicted as choosing faith in Beatrice over loyalty to Claudio and Don Pedro, these former friends are at first simply incredulous. They cannot credit this disruption of the patriarchal order.

The ending of the play "takes care" of this problem. As is the case with many of Shakespeare's comedies, the ending of *Much Ado* has a strongly recuperative function as it attempts to smooth over, or erase, the contradictions or fissures which have opened in the course of the play. In several obvious ways the ending seems to affirm the "naturalness" of a hierarchical, male-dominated social order and to treat challenges to that order, and to the privileges of its beneficiaries, as mere illusions or temporary aberrations. For example, the tension between male–male and male–female bonds simply disappears with Borachio's confession. There is no duel, and in the final scene the renewed friendship of Claudio and Benedick, affirmed by the exchange of cuckold jokes, is as prominent as their simultaneous marriages. Further, the transgressive appropriation of theatrical power by the bastard Don John collapses with equal suddenness. He is, as we learn by report, captured and held for punishment, but he is allowed no moment on the stage, a fact once more contributing to our sense that the threat he poses has no ultimate reality.

Less obvious, but equally necessary to a conservative righting of the social order, is the process by which act V of *Much Ado* relegitimates theatricality as a vehicle for the exercise, by aristocratic males, of power. When Don Pedro became the credulous audience to his brother's fictions, it is as though – in the play's economy of power – he loses the ability to control the world of Messina. Not only Benedick and Beatrice, but Antonio and Leonato as well, slide outside his control. Violence threatens on several fronts, and the Friar's feeble fictions affect very little. Even with Borachio's confession, no marriages occur. It is as if the world of Messina cannot be "well" until the power of fiction making has been relodged with duly constituted authority. This occurs when the patriarch, Leonato, takes up the task of righting the social order through a series of fictions to be enacted at Hero's tomb and at a second wedding. Hero, having died for the imagined crime of the independent use of her sexuality, is reborn when rewritten as the chaste servant of male desire. While it is often argued that through the second wedding Claudio is being taught to have faith in womankind, despite appearances (Dennis, 1973, 231–35), I read the wedding as a lesson in having faith in the authority of social superiors, a lesson to which Claudio is already predisposed. He has always been ready to take Don Pedro's advice, especially about love (Berry, 1972, 169), and the gift of Hero at play's end implies simply that rewards will continue to flow from such obedience. What he gets is the still-silent Hero, the blank sheet upon which men write whore or goddess as their fears or desires dictate.[17] The figure of the compliant woman becomes the instrument through which men (Claudio, Don Pedro, Antonio, and Leonato) reconcile their differences.

But while Hero is regranted the status of goddess, the antifeminism which caused her original denigration surfaces again in the horn jokes that figure so prominently in the play's final moments. "There is no staff more reverent than one tipped with horn" (V. iv. 121–2). As the antitheatrical tracts insist, women are duplicitous; they marry men to make them cuckolds. Admittedly, Claudio also says Benedick may prove a "double dealer" (V. iv. 112), but from line 44, when Claudio first mentions Benedick's fear of horns tipped with gold, the scene returns again and again to the threat men face in entrusting their honor to women in marriage. At the same time that the play quietly revalorizes the exercise of theatrical power by aristocratic males, it continues to locate – now less in bastards, but still in women – the threat of dangerous and unsanctioned theatricality. Moreover, while Beatrice is not "silenced" at the end of the scene, she is emphatically less in charge than in earlier scenes, and her mouth is finally stopped with Benedick's kiss. Thereafter it is he who dominates the dialogue and proposes the dance with which to "lighten" the men's hearts before they marry, as if the prospect is one which has made those hearts heavy.

A final word about the scene and its legitimation of aristocratic, male theatricality. Crucial to this project, as I see it, is the erasure of any lingering suspicion that the fictions of a Don Pedro or a Leonato tamper with nature, rather than express it more fully. Only then can dramatistic and essentialist views of the world be held in tenuous reconciliation. In fact, the final moments of the play can be read as advancing the proposition that, while illusion is everywhere, good fictions merely reveal a preexistent truth of nature (Beatrice and Benedick's love, Hero's chastity), while evil fictions (Hero's promiscuity) which distort nature melt like manna in the sun and their perpetrators disappear. Consequently Benedict and Beatrice must both learn of Don Pedro's tricks and also affirm, willingly and freely, the reality of their love for one another. At first they demur. What leads to their capitulation is the production of love sonnets each has written. What their hands have penned, their hearts must have engendered. And yet, of course, the sonnet form in the 1590s was the most highly conventional genre imaginable. In it one finds already written the text of love. Having been constructed by Don Pedro as lovers, Benedick and Beatrice *must* write sonnets, their production attesting less to the preexistence of their love than to their successful interpellation into a gendered-social order. And yet, by happy sleight of hand, what is their *destiny* within that order is made to seem their *choice*.

Shakespeare's romantic comedies often provide such utopian resolutions to the strains and contradictions of the period. The comic form, however, was not to serve Shakespeare, or, more properly, his culture, much longer in the form apparent in the high or romantic comedies. In 1604, in writing *Measure for Measure*, he creates a comic authority figure, the Duke, who increasingly uses the arts of theatre to order a disordered society. Yet in the end no one is convinced that the Duke's visions merely reveal a preexisting social reality. (Does Angelo love Mariana and just not know it?) The ending of that play makes much clearer than does *Much Ado* that when power's fictions fail to be persuasive, coercion will enforce their truth. Eventually, in a play like *King Lear*, the potential moral bankruptcy of authority and its power to compel – if not belief – at least compliance are openly acknowledged: "a dog's obeyed in office" (IV. vi. 155–6).

Much Ado hints at these things, but only obliquely. It polices its positive depiction of omnipresent theatrical practices by creating a villainous and illegitimate fiction-maker who simply tells lies. The play thus seems irreproachably conservative in its insistence that the power of theatrical illusion-mongering belongs in the hands of the better sort and that their fictions simply reproduce the truths of nature. And yet, as I have argued, the play differs from itself in ways that allow other readings – readings which reveal the constitutive, as opposed to the reflective, power of discursive practices, including theatrical practices, and of the role of authority, not nature, in securing the precedence of one truth over other possible truths. Moreover, under the pressure of a political analysis, the play's production of heroes and villains reveals itself as a strategy for holding in place certain inequalities of power and privilege. But in approaching the self-divisions and contradictions of this work, the contemporary critic has in one respect less access to these aspects of the play than did the Elizabethan theater-goer. We watch *Much Ado* within institutions which are citadels of high culture and which by and large employ middle-class actors of both sexes. People sitting in the new and culturally contested institution of the Elizabethan public theater watched a fiction in which the theatrical practices of a bastard and a woman wearing her mistress's clothes were roundly castigated, even while the agents of representation were most certainly men of mean estate who for their own profit assumed the clothes of women and of noblemen on the stage. As Robert Weimann argues in this volume, a contradiction opens within the material conditions of stage representation between what is being represented and who is doing the representing. For all its affinities with the antitheatrical tracts, in terms of its reproduction of a conservative understanding of the social order, *Much Ado* transgresses that order as the antitheatrical literature could not. This does not place the play ''above ideology,'' merely at a place in Elizabethan culture where — as text *and* stage play – it exhibits with particular force the contradictions of the social order of which it was both product and producer.

Notes

1. Rossiter (1961, 67) is typical of most of the play's thematic critics when he says: ''Deception by appearance in love is patently what most of *Much Ado* is 'about'.''
2. Huston (1981, 2), for example, sees many of Shakespeare's early comedies as dramatizing and celebrating the artist's playful ordering of the world through dramatic art. In *Much Ado*, however, Huston argues: ''Shakespeare may be dramatizing reservations he is beginning to feel about his art and about the relationship between it and reality. He may be dramatically confronting the problem of recognizing that there are limits to his assimilative powers, that reality may sometimes successfully resist his attempts to play with it, even in art'' (p. 142).
3. I draw here on Althusser's argument (1971, 127–86) that institutions such as the family, the educational system, and modes of entertainment help to reproduce the conditions of production by interpellating individuals as subjects of specific ideologies. While Althusser is often seen to focus exclusively on the *success* of these predominantly nonrepressive institutions in serving the interests of the state, he is very clear that the ideological state apparatuses ''may be not only the *stake*, but also the *site* of class struggle'' (p. 147). In short, they can provide sites for resistance to ruling ideologies.
   Crewe (1986) has argued that at least one Elizabethan writer, George Puttenham, held the view that the nature and origin of theater was to promote the hegemony of a ruling class and to make the lower orders governable.
4. Cohen (1985, esp. 136–85) argues, for example, that the emergence of the public theater in the Elizabethan period largely served the interests of a neofeudal

aristocracy and an imperfectly absolutist state, but that (1) the numerous popular elements in the drama made it also a site for subversion of dominant ideologies, and that (2) the tension between the essentially artisanal mode of theater production and the aristocratic ideologies it circulated created further ideological volatility. By contrast, a critic such as Greenblatt, at least in some of his writings (e.g. 1985), sees the power of the Elizabethan state constituted largely through its production *and containment* of subversion, with the theater playing a role in this process. Drama, in such a view, can never elude its function as servant of the state and become a site for genuine contestation. See also Bristol (1985); Dollimore (1984); Montrose (1980); and Weimann (1978).

5. For a useful overview of some of the issues involved in Renaissance antitheatrical discourse, see Barish (1981, 80–190).

6. Recently, Martha Rozett (1984, 15–25) has argued that in the 1570s, 1580s, and 1590s, the audiences for theater and for sermons overlapped. Preacher and playwrights were therefore in competition with one another for ''spectators.'' This helps explain both the pleas for the banning of Sunday playing and Northbrooke's concern that theatergoing interfered with religious observances.

7. Attacks on the theater as a seat of idleness were also connected to official moves to reduce the number of holidays and holy days associated with medieval catholicism and popular culture, since the theater to some extent offered a substitute for those repressed social rituals (Montrose, 1980, 60) and interrupted the clean distinction between work days and a properly observed Sabbath.

8. For an introduction to the social changes in the period, see Stone (1965, 1966, 1972) and Wrightson (1982).

9. Moretti (1982, 20–1) and Montrose (1980, 53–7) discuss changes in the way people understand themselves to be actors and the changed material circumstances that correlate with those changed understandings. Righter (1962) explores the difference between medieval theater, which saw itself as a direct expression of God's truth, and Renaissance theater, which increasingly presented man-made fictions for commercial consumption.

10. This preoccupation with feminine dress is also reflected in the Tudor sumptuary laws which in 1574 explicitly began to include prescriptions for women's apparel. The official policing of women's dress thus came about within two years of the opening of the theaters and the first wave of antitheatrical writings.

11. Ringler (1942, 26–8) argues that the City probably paid for Gosson's first tract and Anthony Munday's *A Second and Third Blast of Retrait from Plaies and Theaters*, and also undoubtedly blocked the public printing of Thomas Lodge's *A Reply to Gosson's Schoole of Abuse*. Kinney (1974, 17), however, argues that Gosson probably was *not* supported by the City since his fortunes did not at once improve and because there is no clear link between his case and that of Anthony Munday. To me the evidence in Gosson's case in inconclusive.

12. See Bergeron (1971) for a general discussion of the nature of civil pageantry in this period and of the iconography used to honor Elizabeth and James. See Yates (1975, 29–87) for detailed consideration of representations of Elizabeth as Astraea, and Goldberg (1983, 29–33) for an examination of the differing ways in which Elizabeth and James used and participated in pageants, progresses, and masques.

13. For a good discussion of the representation of the City in the pageantry of the Stuart Lord Mayor's show, see Paster (1985).

14. I am specifically indebted to Michael Foucault's investigations (1980) of the interconnections between power and knowledge.

15. All quotations from Shakespeare's plays are taken from the revised Pelican edition (Harbage, 1969).

16. For an important discussion of the discursive production of desire and of gendered subjectivities, see Henriques *et al.* (1984), esp. 203–63.

17. Cook (1986, 192) argues that Hero's silence elicits male fears that women are not readable and calls forth their repeated rewritings of her. For a view of Beatrice quite different from my own, see the rest of Cook's article in which she presents Beatrice as inscribed in a male-subject position and so as posing no threat to the masculine social order.

Works cited

Althusser, Louis (1971) *Lenin and Philosophy and Other Essays*, trans. Ben Brewster, New York, Monthly Review Press; London, New Left Books.

Barish, Jonas (1981) *The Antitheatrical Prejudice*, Berkeley, University of California Press.

Berger, Jr, Harry (1982) "Against the Sink-a-Pace: Sexual and Family Politics in *Much Ado About Nothing*," *Shakespeare Quarterly*, 33, 302–13.

Bergeron, David M. (1971) *English Civic Pageantry 1558–1642*, London, Edward Arnold.

——— (ed.) (1985) *Pageantry in the Shakespearean Theater*, Athens, University of Georgia Press.

Berry, Ralph (1972) *Shakespeare's Comedies: Explorations in Form*, Princeton, Princeton University Press.

Bristol, Michael D. (1985) *Theatre and Carnival: Plebeian Culture and the Structure of Authority in Renaissance England*, London and New York, Methuen.

Cohen, Walter (1985) *Drama of a Nation: Public Theater in Renaissance England and Spain*, Ithaca, NY, Cornell University Press.

Cook, Carol (1986) "'The Sign and Semblance of Her Honor': Reading Gender Difference in *Much Ado*," *Publications of the Modern Language Association*, 101, 186–202.

Crewe, Jonathan (1986) "The Hegemonic Theater of George Puttenham," *English Literary Renaissance*, 16, 71–85.

Dennis, Carl (1973) "Wit and Wisdom in *Much Ado About Nothing*," *Studies in English Literature, 1500–1900*, 13, 223–37.

Dollimore, Jonathan (1984) *Radical Tragedy: Religion, Ideology and Power in the Drama of Shakespeare and his Contemporaries*, Chicago, University of Chicago Press; Brighton, Harvester.

Foucault, Michel (1980) *Power/Knowledge: Selected Interviews and Other Writings*, ed. Colin Gordon, New York, Pantheon Books.

Fraser, Russell (1970) *The War Against Poetry*, Princeton, Princeton University Press.

Goldberg, Jonathan (1983) *James I and the Politics of Literature: Jonson, Shakespeare, Donne, and their Contemporaries*, Baltimore, Johns Hopkins University Press.

Gosson, Stephen (1579) *The Schoole of Abuse, Conteining a Plesaunt Invective against Poets, Pipers, Plaiers, Jesters, and Such Like Caterpillers of a Commonwelth*, London, STC 12097.

——— (1582) *Playes Confuted in Five Actions*, London; repr. 1972, New York, Johnson Reprint Corporation.

Greenblatt, Stephen (1980) *Renaissance Self-Fashioning from More to Shakespeare*, Chicago, University of Chicago Press.

——— (1985) "Invisible Bullets: Renaissance Authority and its Subversion, *Henry IV* and *Henry V*" in Dollimore, Jonathan and Sinfield, Alan (eds) *Political Shakespeare: New Essays in Cultural Materialism*, Manchester, Manchester University Press; Ithaca, NY, Cornell University Press, 18–47.

Harbage, Alfred (gen. ed.) (1969) *William Shakespeare: The Complete Works*, Baltimore, Penguin.

Henriques, Julian, Hollway, Wendy, Urwin, Cathy, Venn, Couze, and Walkerdine,

Valerie (1984) *Changing the Subject: Psychology, Social Regulation and Subjectivity*, New York, Methuen.

Henze, Richard (1971) "Deception in *Much Ado*," *Studies in English Literature, 1500–1900*, 11, 187–201.

Hill, Christopher (1964) *Society and Puritanism in Pre-Revolutionary England*, New York, Schocken Books.

Hooper, Wilfred (1915) "The Tudor Sumptuary Laws," *English Historical Review*, 30, 433–49.

Huston, J. Dennis (1981) *Shakespeare's Comedies of Play*, New York, Columbia University Press.

Kinney, Arthur (1974) *Markets of Bawdrie: The Dramatic Criticism of Stephen Gosson*, Salzburg Studies in English Literature, 4, Salzburg, Institüt fur Englische Sprache und Literatur.

Krieger, Elliott (1979) "Social Relations and the Social Order in *Much Ado About Nothing*," *Shakespeare Survey*, 32, 49–61.

Lodge, Thomas (1579–80) *A Reply to Gosson's Schoole of Abuse*, London, repr. 1973, New York, Garland Publishing Company.

Montrose, Louis Adrian (1980) "The Purpose of Playing: Reflections on a Shakespearean Anthropology," *Helios*, n.s. 7, 51–74.

———— (1983) "'Shaping Fantasies': Figurations of Gender and Power in Elizabethan Culture," *Representations*, 2, 61–94.

Moretti, Franco (1982) "'A Huge Eclipse': Tragic Form and the Deconsecration of Sovereignty," in Greenblatt, Stephen (ed.) *The Power of Forms in the English Renaissance*, Norman, Oklahoma, Pilgrim Books.

Munday, Anthony (1580) *A Second and Third Blast of Retrait from Plaies and Theaters*, London, STC 21677.

Newman, Karen (1986) "Renaissance Family Politics and Shakespeare's *The Taming of the Shrew*," *English Literary Renaissance*, 16, 86–100.

Northbrooke, John (1577) *A Treatise wherein Dicing, Dauncing, Vaine Playes or Enterluds . . . are reproved*, London, STC 18670.

Paster, Gail (1985) "The Idea of London in Masque and Pageant," in Bergeron, David M. (ed.) *Pageantry in the Shakespearean Theater*, Athens, University of Georgia Press, 48–64.

Prouty, Charles T. (1950) *The Sources of "Much Ado About Nothing"*, New Haven, Yale University Press.

Righter, Anne (1962) *Shakespeare and the Idea of the Play*, London, Chatto and Windus.

Ringler, William (1942) *Stephen Gosson: A Biographical and Critical Study*, Princeton, Princeton University Press.

Rossiter, A.P. (1961) *Angel with Horns and Other Shakespeare Lectures*, ed. Graham Storey, London, Longman.

Rozett, Martha Tuck (1984) *The Doctrine of Election and the Emergence of Elizabethan Tragedy*, Princeton, Princeton University Press.

Sidney, Sir Philip (1595) *An Apology for Poetry or The Defence of Poesy*, ed. Geoffrey Shepherd (1965), London, Thomas Nelson.

Stone, Lawrence (1965) *The Crisis of the Aristocracy, 1558–1641*, Oxford, Clarendon Press.

———— (1966) "Social Mobility in England, 1500–1700," *Past and Present*, 33, 16–55.

———— (1972) *The Causes of the English Revolution, 1529–1642*, London, Routledge & Kegan Paul.

Stubbes, Phillip (1583) *The Anatomie of Abuses*, London, STC 23376.

Tuke, Thomas (1616) *A Treatise Against Painting and Tincturing of Men and Women*, London, STC 24316.

Underdown, David (1985) *Revel, Riot, and Rebellion: Popular Politics and Culture in England 1603–1660*, Oxford, Clarendon Press.

Weimann, Robert (1978) *Shakespeare and the Popular Tradition in the Theater: Studies in the Social Dimension of Dramatic Form and Function*, ed. Robert Schwartz, Baltimore, Johns Hopkins University Press.

Whigham, Frank (1984) *Ambition and Privilege: The Social Tropes of Elizabethan Courtesy Theory*, Berkeley, University of California Press.

Wrightson, Keith (1982) *English Society, 1580–1680*, New Brunswick, Rutgers University Press.

Yates, Frances A. (1975) *Astraea: The Imperial Theme in the Sixteenth Century*, London, Routledge & Kegan Paul.

8

"Which is the merchant here? and which the Jew?": subversion and recuperation in *The Merchant of Venice*

Thomas Moisan

As a *locus* in which to ponder the ideological function of the Shakespearean text, *The Merchant of Venice* is an obvious, and obviously problematic, choice. At a glance, the *Merchant* seems to inscribe and affirm an ideological calculus that fused the interests of the state and the assertions of a providentialist Christianity with the prerogatives of an increasingly capitalist marketplace. We can perceive this calculus allegorized in the central action of the play and ratified in the ultimate thwarting of the Jewish usurer Shylock, the redemption of the Christian merchant Antonio, and the triumphs – forensic and domestic – of the bountiful aristocrat Portia, and we can see it reflected and legitimated in the sundry polarities the play has often been said to be – to use Frank Kermode's rather equivocal quotation marks – "'about'": the Old Law versus the New Law, Justice versus Mercy, Vengeance versus Love (1961, 224).[1] At the same time, however, the considerable residue of qualification that attends even the most compelling efforts to schematize the play in this way has made it no easy matter to say what the *Merchant* is "about;"[2] and in the degree to which the play leaves us, for example, feeling troubled over the treatment of Shylock, or appears to blur the distinctions on which the polarities above depend, leading us, in effect, to ask with Portia, "Which is the merchant here? and which

THOMAS MOISAN is an Associate Professor of English at Arkansas State University. He has published articles on Chaucer, Shakespeare, Henry King, and Robert Herrick, and is currently completing a study of the relationship of textuality and the self in Herrick's verse, *Robert Herrick and the Argument of his "Book"*.

the Jew?'' (IV. i. 170), we may wonder whether the *Merchant* invokes the ideologically sanctioned mythologies of the time only to question and subvert them.

In part, of course, it can be argued that the contradictions we experience in the *Merchant* are evidence, not of its subversive design, but of its mimetic fidelity, and that the dissonances we detect in it are but echoes of the tensions and stresses of the society it reflects, a society in transition, confronting – or being confronted by – what Louis Adrian Montrose calls ''the ideologically anomalous realities of change'' (1980, 64). ''Taken on its own terms,'' Jonathan Dollimore reminds us, ''an ideology may appear internally coherent. When, however, its deep structure is examined it is often discovered to be a synthesis of contradictory elements'' (1984, 20). Thus, in the inclination we feel to ask ''Which is the merchant here? and which the Jew?'' we may merely be responding to the traces in the play of a debate within the times over whether Old Religion and New Business were fully compatible, and whether the ''thrifty'' pursuit of trade and the ''prodigal'' indulgence of greed were fully distinct. On the other hand, to the extent to which we see in the *Merchant* a movement toward reconciliation and harmony – a thesis argued most fully by Lawrence Danson some years ago (1978, esp. 1–21, 170–95) – the play can be said to ritualize the ideological synthesis being wrought from the contrarieties of its society.

We find the *Merchant* scanned in these terms quite cogently in an essay published several years ago by Walter Cohen (1982). For Cohen the *Merchant* enacts a largely successful, and deeply comic, mediation between two differing conceptions of socioeconomic relations: the one rooted in English history and reflective of contemporary anxiety over the emerging economic order, the other derived from Shakespeare's Italian sources and reflecting both a less troubled view of the capitalist system and a more confident differentiation between the figure of the usurer, who incarnates, Cohen would suggest, ''a quasi-feudal fiscalism'' in decline, and that of the merchant, who embodies, in Cohen's words, ''an indigenous bourgeois mercantilism'' on the ascent (1982, 771). In Cohen's reading the workings of dramatic form and ideological synthesis are persuasively integrated. Even as the central action of the play, Cohen argues, upholds a ''formally dominant Christian, artistocratic ideology,'' we see in ''the subversive side of the play'' evidence of ''an internal distancing,'' a distancing, however, which may complicate but does not annul that harmonic ''movement'' Cohen sees in the play ''towards resolution and reconciliation'' (pp. 779–81). In this way *The Merchant of Venice* can be seen to negotiate among the heterogeneous impulses and interests that characterized the ''public'' of the public theater. At the same time, the *Merchant* can also be taken to exemplify what might be called the emerging ''containment'' theory of Renaissance drama, to wit, that the Shakespearean stage offered a platform on which cultural heterodoxy could be at once expressed, engaged, and contained, a forum, Cohen observes, for ''communal affirmation and social ratification, [and] a means of confronting fear and anger in a manner that promoted reassurance about the existence and legitimacy of a new order'' (p. 783; see also Montrose, 1980, 62–4; Greenblatt, 1981, 40–61).

Still, that there is a ''movement'' in *The Merchant of Venice* ''towards resolution and reconciliation'' has not been, the annals of criticism would show, a truth universally acknowledged. To be sure, a play which has as much conflict in it and yet ends as happily as the *Merchant* does would seem to have something to do with resolution and reconciliation, and, certainly, the subject of harmony is much in the night air of Belmont in act V. Yet whether the play actually produces a harmonious resolution and reconciliation or merely invokes harmony by the power of dramatic *fiat* and in the interest of ideological conformity or capitulation is not an easy matter to settle, though it is an important one to consider if we are to assess the nature of the accommodation the *Merchant* reaches with its society.

At this point it might be useful to think of what it is we experience in, to use Cohen's words, that ''internal distancing'' at work in the play. For Cohen this distancing is evident in the articulation the *Merchant* accords sentiments that would qualify or subvert the ideological prescriptions the action, or fable, of the play would appear to embrace. Ultimately, though, I would suggest that in the ''internal distancing'' we perceive in it, the *Merchant* asserts its ''play-ful'' alterity, distancing itself simultaneously, on the one hand, from the ideological implications of its fable, and on the other, from the very questionings and subversive sentiments to which it gives notice. We get a hint of this distancing in the tendency of the play to leave unresolved dialogic exchanges in which it permits the mythologies it inscribes to be interrogated. We sense it more pointedly, though, in the, literally, ''anti-literal'' skepticism we hear displayed in it toward ''words'' and ''texts,'' a skepticism through which the play pretends to dissociate itself from the very textuality that nourishes and complicates it. In this way the play implicitly underscores its theatricality and resolves, and ''recuperates,'' the ''confusions'' in its text by posing – or imposing – a comic, a comically dramatic, solution.

What follows, then, is an attempt to read *The Merchant of Venice* in and, in a sense, out of the discourse of its times. First, and at the risk of viewing the play from the kind of distortingly narrow, overly economic, overly Anglicized, perspective that Cohen warns against – and avoids (pp. 768–70) – I will look at some of the ways in which the play participates in and interrogates the economic mythologies of its times by affiliating itself with the texts in which these mythologies are shaped, rehearsed, and questioned. From there, however, I would like to speculate on how the play strives to extricate itself from the complexities and contradictions of the times which its text, and textuality, have ''uncovered.''

1

In what sense, though, would *The Merchant of Venice*, with its eponymous setting and Italian literary pedigree, have held up a mirror to its English audience? Quite apart from the topicality commentators have detected in it,[3] of interest to us here is our awareness that the *Merchant* evokes the growing "trafficking" of the English nation in trade, or, rather, the growing identification of England and its institutions *with* trade and capitalist enterprise. We hear this prominence of trade and investment recorded not a little sardonically in the impecunious Thomas Dekker's observation in "The Guls Horn-Booke" (1609) that the theater "is your Poets Royal Exchange," and that the poets' muses "are now turned to Merchants" (pp. 246–7). We find it noted more positively in contemporary *sententiae* fusing the pursuit of trade and the interests of the state. Thus, for Bacon ("Of Vsurie," 1625 [1966]) the "Customs of Kings or States . . . Ebbe or flow with Merchandizing" (p. 170), an opinion seconded and elaborated upon by John Stow in *The Survey of London* (1603 [1912]), when he pauses in his account of London's past to recount the benisons produced by London's mercantile present, remarking that

> truly merchants and retailers do not altogether *intus canere*, and profit themselves only, for the prince and realm both are enriched by their riches: the realm winneth treasure, if their trade be so moderated by authority that it break not proportion, and they besides bear a good fleece, which the prince may shear when he seeth good.
>
> (p. 495)

In sum, the business of Britain is business, and what's good for business is good for Britain.

At the same time, as we know, such assertions do not infrequently bear the refrain that what is good for business and Britain is probably not displeasing to God either. It is in God's name that profit often gets pursued, and it is as a providential sign of God's favor that the attainment of profit often gets justified. Certainly we find this providentialist and Calvinist-based mucilage spread quite profusely and adhesively in contemporary accounts of exploration of the New World, in which the propagation of God's word and the true faith is invoked both as a necessary and sufficient condition for the successful pursuit of commercial gain and national enhancement, and, at times, as a happy consequence of that pursuit. "Godlinesse is great riches," Hakluyt declares at the outset of his *Divers Voyages* (1582 [1850, 8]), his implicit confusion of riches spiritual and material a characteristic illustration of the idiom in which the desire for gain and a concern for salvation could without the slightest betrayal of cynicism be reconciled as part of the same ideological "project."

Nor is this coupling of the propagation of faith and trade any less pronounced – though it sounds less ingenuous – in the accounts of the English Merchant Adventurers' dealings with the Old World, a recurrent theme of which, understandably, is the abundance of blessings that will accrue to all parties concerned through an expansion of English trading rights on the continent. Hence, in a letter from one such Adventurer (*c.* 1565) we find the Earls of East Friesland being advised that with a strong English trading presence in their realm, "God shall be known, praised and feared, and his whole Gospel and

commandments taught and preached, to the comfort of all Christian nations"
(Ramsay, 1979, 113), and, it should be added, to the intended discomfort of the
Pope, the Turks, and any other infidels who might have political or religious,
or, of course, commercial, designs on that part of Europe.

To an audience inured to such texts, *The Merchant of Venice* might well have
seemed a transparent allegory of its times. It establishes the merchant in the
figure of Antonio as a friend of the state (IV. i. 1–34), it trots out a biblical
precedent for the association of profit by "venture" with the blessings of divine
providence (I. iii. 86–8), and, in the rather "providential" restoration of
Antonio's fortunes after his deliverance from the merciless Jew (V. i. 273–9),
it might well appear to subscribe to the notion that "Godlinesse is great riches."
Indeed, Cohen has alluded to act V in particular as an "aristocratic fantasy" in
which the "concluding tripartite unity of Antonio, Bassanio, and Portia enacts
precisely [an] interclass harmony between landed wealth and mercantile capital,
with the former dominant" (1982, 772, 777). If, for the moment, we accept
Sidney's contention in his *Defence of Poesie* (1595 [1968]) that the mimetic role
of poetry is to show not "what is, or is not, but what should, or should not be"
(p. 29), then we might say that the *Merchant* realizes its mimetic function by
dramatizing a vision of how the established social order and religious values
could be reconciled with the new economics.

Central to this vision, however, and deepening the involvement of the
Merchant in the economic discourse of its time is the triumph the play enacts
over usury in the figure of the usurer Shylock. That usury was at once a
widespread practice and significant concern in Shakespeare's society, and that
the resources of usurers were sought, not only by profligate young gentlemen
and capital-hungry merchants, but by Parliament and the Queen herself, are
facts well-established and oft remarked.[4] The purpose of underscoring them
here is to recall the degree to which a work like the *Merchant*, "indebted" as
it is to its Italian sources, could still integrate these sources with more localized
and contemporary materials both to create a fulcrum for the expression of
communal concerns and frustrations, and also, and more interestingly, to create
the illusion that whatever the socially and economically diverse elements of
Shakespeare's audience did *not* have in common, they at least shared a common
enemy in the form of usury and its personification.

In no small part, of course, the domestic appeal of the *Merchant* would have
lain in the domestication of its villain, Shylock, who – whatever kinship he may
share with his thinly drawn counterpart in the putative source story, *Il Pecorone*,
or with Marlowe's exotically evil and extravagant Machiavel, Barabas – should
have been quite recognizable to any in Shakespeare's audience who had read or
heard their share of the myriad of anti-usury harangues in circulation at the time.
To those so fortunate the penalty ultimately imposed upon Shylock – harsher
than that suffered by Fiorentino's usurer in *Il Pecorone*, and harsh enough to
have occasioned a good deal of critical rationalization[5] – may well have
seemed just what they had come to believe a usurer conventionally deserved,
including the obligation to be converted and saved in spite of himself.[6]

Certainly those in the audience who were versed in the anti-usury tracts of the times, and had heard interest taking excoriated by Henry Smith in *The Examination of Usury* (1591) as "biting usury" (p. 8), or had read in Thomas Lodge's *Alarum Against Usurers* (1584) that usurers possessed "the voracitie of wolves" with which to devour men's bodies and souls (p. 77), should have read the string of daimonic and "currish," wolverine epithets liberally bestowed upon Shylock in the play (I. iii. 106; II. ii. 22–6; II. viii. 14; III. i. 19–20; III. iii. 7; IV. i. 128; IV. i. 283) as merely a standard part of his job description.[7] Those, meanwhile, familiar with the tract wishfully entitled *The Death of Usury, or, The Disgrace of Usurers* (1594) would have read that when in days of yore "an usurer came to be knowne, his houses were called the devils houses, his fields the devils croppe" (p. 34), and may well have heard a familiar resonance in Jessica's preelopement complaint that "Our house is hell" (II. iii. 2).

Stephen Greenblatt has suggested that Jessica's description of her father's house as hell is an apt metonym for the peculiar social isolation of the Jew in the modern European society from which, and for which, he earned capital (1978, 295). We find this conception of the usurer's social alienation no less evident in the diatribes against the Jewish moneylender's Christian counterpart in Shakespeare's England. Cut off from the society his profession would undermine, the usurer – Henry Smith maintains (1591, 35) – will be cut off from posterity as well, a fate, we will recall, Shylock is spared only when, in the spirit of Christian forgiveness, Antonio compels Shylock to "re-inherit" his daughter and make her and her Christian husband his heirs (IV. i. 384–6). In his moral isolation the usurer is prone, Smith contends, to vices such as revenge, vices which may eventually work against the usurer's economic self-interest (pp. 6–7).[8] We are reminded of this especial, and ultimately self-destructive, perversity, of course, in Shylock's unwillingness to accept any compensation for the forfeiture of Antonio's bond except the penalty of flesh stipulated in the contract. "You'll ask me why I rather choose to have / A weight of carrion flesh, than to receive / Three thousand ducats," Shylock tauntingly declares. "I'll not answer that! / But say it is my humour, – is it answer'd?" (IV. i. 40–3).[9]

Nor, we might surmise, would Shakespeare's audience have had Shylock answer in any other way. For there must have been a certain rhetorical convenience and moral self-assurance in being able to cast the argument against usury in the terms of polar oppositions of good and evil that transcend purely economic considerations. Indeed, the pressure of ideology may manifest itself most strongly in the attempt evident in the rhetorical structure of the play to universalize its central conflict and suppress its more parochial economic antecedents. In the exchange with which the play opens, after all, Antonio is permitted to reject the insinuations of Salerio/Solanio that he is the total *homo economicus*, whose mind is "tossing on the ocean" with his investments (I. i. 8–45), and he implies both by his words here and by his actions shortly hereafter that, for him at least, it is not money that makes the world go round. For his part, Shylock may be sincere in attributing at least a part of his hatred of Antonio to the abuse he has suffered from Antonio on the Rialto (I. iii. 101–24), to the resentment he justifiably feels on behalf of his race (I. iii. 43–7), and to his perception of the hand Antonio's friends may have had in the elopement of Jessica and Lorenzo (III. i. 22–3), and we may well see in his enmity the traces of the economic rivalry in Venice between the Jewish moneylender and the up-and-coming Christian entrepreneur and banker (Cohen, 1982, 770–1). Yet as he proceeds in his bloodlust, Shylock acts in a way that would have confirmed the anti-usury polemicists of Shakespeare's audience in their darkest beliefs about usurers: he becomes that most reassuring of villains, the villain who pursues his villainy because "it is my humour," because he would "choose" it over, not only a more virtuous, but even a more lucrative alternative.

That Shylock should "choose" to do wrong reminds us, though, of the simultaneously most damning and yet socially and ideologically most reassuring charge to be leveled at usurers in Shakespeare's time, namely that usurers are heretics, willful choosers of the wrong course and, therefore, most deserving of unqualified reproach. "[O]ne saith well," Henry Smith observes, "that our Vsurers are Hereticks, because after manie admonitions yet they maintaine their errours, & persist in it obstinately as Papists do in Poperie" (1591, 2). In fact, we find this association of usury and heresy made quasi-official by that great collector of commonplaces and regurgitator of Elizabethan orthodoxy, Francis Meres, whose entries for "Vsurie" in his *Palladis Tamia* (1598) are followed immediately by those for "Heresie, Heretickes," which, doubtless by no accidental coincidence, are immediately followed by "Death" (pp. 322–7).

This association of usury with heresy and with choosing the wrong course is of "interest" on several counts. On the one hand, the connection between usury and heresy might suggest that the rhetoric was in place by which the usurer could be singled out, not simply as an economic scoundrel and renegade, but as an enemy of God and, therefore, a threat to the state, and our recognition of this possibility deepens our perception of the audience's perception of Shylock. On the other hand, the connection of usury with choosing enables us to see a link between Shylock and the unhappy "choosers" of the casket scenes, and suggests a sense in which both elements of the rather exotic source tradition behind the *Merchant*, both the flesh-bond and the caskets stories, could be said to respond to the domestic experience and economic concerns of Shakespeare's audience.

Here we might recall that oft cited passage from *The Schoole of Abuse* (1579) in which Stephen Gosson pauses in his drama-bashing long enough to bestow unwonted praise upon a play called *The Jew*, which Gosson describes as "representing the greedinesse of worldly chusers, and bloody mindes of usurers" (p. 30). Now, how indebted Shakespeare is to this play, if he is indebted at all, and whether Gosson's "worldly chusers" and "bloody minded usurers" refer to different characters or are merely different tags for the same character, are matters quite unsettled (Brown, 1955, xxix–xxxi; Bullough, 1964, 445–6). Still, we might observe that in the anti-usury parables to which Shakespeare's audience was likely to have been exposed two character types recur, the "bloody minded usurer" and the "wordly chuser," the figure, that is, whose craving for the riches and vain delights of the world creates the conditions in which the usurer thrives. We find evocations and validations of this antimaterialist sentiment in the unlucky choices of Morocco, who assays his choice of caskets by reckoning the things of this world he desires, and Aragon, who chooses by considering the things of this world he deserves. *"All that glisters is not gold,"* reads the not very consoling scroll Morocco finds in the death's head "awarded" him for choosing the golden casket (II. vii. 65), a truism Thomas Lodge invokes in his *Alarum Against Usurers* when he recounts how "a young Gentleman," smitten with promises of easy credit and easier living, listens to the blandishments of a wicked usurer, a "subtill underminer," and, "counting all golde that glysters," succumbs (p. 45).

Indeed, the wisdom of such antimaterialist apothegms is most volubly articulated, and heeded, by the one happy casket chooser, Bassanio, whose casket-selection musings resonate with the kind of *sententiae* one finds in Lodge or other anti-usury writers. Not for Bassanio is it to assume "all golde that glysters." Rather, "The world is still deceiv'd with ornament" (III. ii. 73). Obviously knowing something that eluded Morocco, Bassanio immediately rejects the allure of riches and beauty metonymized in the "crisped snaky golden locks" beneath which lurks "[t]he skull that bred them in the sepulchre" (92–6). Ornament "is but the guiled shore / To a most dangerous sea" (97–8), with "gaudy gold, / Hard food for Midas" (101–2), and silver but a "pale and common drudge / 'Tween man and man" (103–4).

Surely, though, there is at least a hint of incongruity in hearing this vein of rhetoric from Bassanio, whose tendency toward materialism and consumption has been deemed conspicuous enough to trouble a number of critics,[10] and whose reasons for seeking funds might well have reminded Shakespeare's audience of the idle borrowers condemned by the anti-usury authors, who seek loans, not to survive, but, as the author of *The Death of Usury* insists, "to consume in prodigall maner, in bravery, banketting, voluptuous living, & such like" (1594, 32). Bassanio may well love Portia for her "wondrous virtues," but, as we know, in limning her praises to Antonio, he notes first that she is "a lady richly left, / And she is fair" (I. i. 161–2). And, skeptical as Bassanio may later show himself to be toward "damned show," we recall that, by his own admission, it was precisely for the sake of "showing a more swelling port / Than my faint means" would permit that Bassanio "disabled mine estate" (I. i. 123–5) – even as his continued pursuit of financing will come close to disabling Antonio's estate and Antonio himself!

Surely there is an incongruity here, and it is an incongruity which reflects, not simply the hybrid traces of Shakespeare's sources,[11] but an ambivalence we find in Shakespeare's culture toward wealth and the "venturing" for it in trade. As we noted before, to those engaged in exploration for profit, there may have been something at once instructive and reassuring in Hakluyt's dictum that "Godlinesse is great riches." Yet for every suggestion that God and Plutus may not be incompatible, we hear the dissonant reminder that they are not identical either. "[S]hall we conclude," Lodge asks, not unrhetorically, "because the usurer is rich, he is righteous? because wealthie, wise? because full of gold, therefore godly?'' (1584, 71). Indeed, we overlook the full rhetorical agenda of texts celebrating the benefits of trade if we fail to hear in them an attempt to calm the fears and quiet the antimaterialist objections the ''prodigal'' pursuit of profit had engendered. Thus, Stow (1603), we will recall, trumpets the blessings trade has brought to the many, even as he acknowledges the great riches that have accrued through trade to the few, and even as he adds the rather anti-laissez-faire proviso that merchants' business ''be so moderated by authority that it break not proportion'' (p. 495).

In a sense, contemporary attacks upon usurers are a reflection of the success of such utilitarian rationalizations as Stow's. For if it is granted that the fruits of trade enhance the ''commonweal,'' then it only follows that the ills attendant upon the increases in trade and venture capitalism should be treated, not as inherent in the system, but as excesses or abuses, or even subversions of the system. Thus, it is quite consistent with the times that Bassanio, who so incarnates the entrepreneurial spirit of the age,[12] and whose very choice of the lead casket is encoded as an act of ''hazard,'' should dissociate himself from the ornamental riches with which ''the world is still deceiv'd,'' and the obsession which usurers and other breakers of economic proportion exploit.

As we know, however, usury and trade existed in a relationship that was far more ambiguous than anti-usury tracts might imply, indeed, a relationship that might be said to have been more symbiotic than inimical. Bacon puts the complexity of the relationship squarely when he observes (in ''Of Vsurie,'' 1625) that, while the first ''Discommoditie'' of usury is that ''it makes fewer Merchants'' since, obviously, it diverts money from trading to trading in money, the first ''Commoditie'' of usury is, paradoxically, that it makes more merchants and ''aduanceth'' trade, since ''it is certain, that the Greatest Part of Trade is driuen by Young Merchants, upon Borrowing at Interest'' (pp. 170–1).

This embarrassing interrelationship is a fact that not even avowedly anti-usury discourses can fully suppress. So it is that we hear the author of *The Death of Usury* labor to give the most moral, anti-usury, reading to the law enacted by Elizabeth which voided the ban imposed by Edward VI upon the practice of usury, and which formally reinstated 10 per cent as the maximum interest rate.[13] The law, the author maintains, could not be construed as condoning usury, but, instead, ''leaves it after a sort to the curtesie and conscience of the borrower'' – rather as if interest payments were to be regarded as something no more coercive than tipping! Why did Elizabeth enact this statute if it was not the intent of her government to encourage the practice of usury? Our author notes that when, under Edward VI, usury was prohibited ''this inconvenience came, fewe or none would lend because they might have no allowance, whereupon her Maiestie to avoyde this euill, made this remissiue clause'' (1594; see also Smith, 1591, 30). Having rationalized the government's unapprovingly permissive policy on usury, the same author wonders why the usurer does not simply follow the example of a number of merchants and invest his money in trade where, with the likelihood of fewer risks and greater profits, ''it will be lesse noted, and himself better esteemed'' (p. 27). Which is the merchant here, and which the usurer?

Indeed, to keep the distinction straight, and to cope with the disquieting realities of the economic system, we find polemicists engaging in the sorts of polarization evident in the surface of the *Merchant*. Merchants follow a career, Lodge hastens to affirm, ''both auncient and lawdable, the professors honest and vertuous, their actions full of daunger, and therefore worthy gaine; and so necessary this sorte of men be, as no well governed state may be without them'' (1584, 43). The blame for whatever is ''wrong'' with the system, then, is left for the usurer to absorb, whose function is rather that of the scapegoat: he embodies the enemy within that must be exorcised by being externalized and, literally, alienated.[14] What better figure to fill this role than, of course, the Jew, whose vices can be, as we suggested before, familiarized, but whose identity by type is comfortably different and distanced. Shakespeare's Shylock, rooted as he is in older and foreign literary and dramatic forms, is an appropriate focus for the domestic anxieties of Shakespeare's audience, not in spite of his difference, but, rather as Stephen Greenblatt has argued, because of it (1978, 295–6).

2

To enumerate ways in which a play ''reflects'' the discourse of its times is not the same, unfortunately, as saying how the play responds to that discourse, a truth one feels embarrassingly keenly in the case of *The Merchant of Venice*. It may be fair to suggest that what we encounter in the play is ''merely'' a mirroring both of the myths by which the age read itself and of the anxieties those myths could not entirely dispel. Yet in holding up the mirror to its age *so* faithfully, does the play affirm the myths it enacts, or does it subvert them by mirroring their qualifications as well? Or, rather, does it affirm the myths it dramatizes *by* mirroring their qualifications, by admitting them as qualifications which ultimately can be contained and ''lived with''?

Recently, Greenblatt has explored this *tertium quid* in texts where the play of ideology much more clearly assumes the form of a conflict between authority and forces threatening to undermine that authority (1981, 40–2). In the *Merchant* what is questioned is not authority as such, but whether the accommodation of Christian orthodoxy and economic reality the play inscribes is entitled to the moral authority to which it appears to lay claim. The play allows this questioning to be voiced, and voiced forcibly, only to contextualize it in such a way that its implications are deflected or muted, or, as Cohen has observed, repressed.

Certainly, for example, we feel the justice of Shylock's enraged defense of his humanity (III. i. 47–66), and we recognize as valid both in that speech and in others by Shylock the doubt being cast upon the Venetian Christian' presumptions of moral superiority. Yet, as Cohen remarks, though Christians may well be abusive slaveholders, we encounter no Christian slaveholders within the fiction of the play (1982, 774), and, a point so often noted, when push comes to shove, we know who cannot be dissuaded from killing whom, and who is capable of mercy – at least on some terms. And even though, as could be rightly objected, Gratiano shows himself (IV. i. 360–3, 375, 394–6) to be one Christian in whom the quality of mercy appears quite strained – perhaps, even, drained – still, it could also be urged that Gratiano is interestingly differentiated from his fellow Christians, who, it would seem, find him not worth listening to (I. i. 114–18).

Again, what is worth noticing is not that the *Merchant* should mute or repress contradictions and qualifications, but that it should call them into play at all only to repress them, illuminating them only to cover them, or, perhaps, "re-cover" them. For an example we might consider the curious resonances in the play of the idea of "prodigality." The word "prodigal" occurs several times, twice on the tongue of Shylock (II. v. 15; III. i. 39–40), who employs it as a term of derision for Christians whose "prodigality" clearly differentiates them from the "thrift" Shylock tends to associate with his own endeavors (I. iii. 45, 85, 172; II. v. 54). Like "thrift," "prodigal" is a word prodigally used in anti-usury tracts, and is employed to castigate, or warn, those "worldly choosers" whose wasteful ways and love of material things make them the prey of the likes of Shylock (*The Death of Usury*, 1594, 32; Lodge, 1584, 50, 51, 53, 56, 62, 75). On the one hand, there is, doubtless, a purposeful irony in having Shylock condemn the Christians for the sort of fiscal irresponsibility off which he "thrives;" to paraphrase Antonio, not only can the devil cite Scripture, but he seems to have done his share of reading in anti-usury tracts as well. Moreover, that Shylock should find prodigality contemptible obviously gives prodigality something to commend it, and we feel invited to associate the word with those antipenurious, anti-Shylockean virtues that schematic interpretations of the play generally place on the Christian side of the ledger: love, mercy, liberality. On the other hand, however, in the degree to which Shylock's words recall the antimaterialist rhetoric of the age, they remind us that in some sense Shylock's charges against the Christians are true, that Bassanio in particular is conspicuously, perhaps, culpably, "consumptive," and we may hear in his words an evocation, rather muffled, of that anxiety over wealth which is a part of the cultural context of the play.

At the same time, it is difficlt for us, and was likely to have been even more difficult for Shakespeare's audience, to hear the recurrent references to "prodigal" without thinking of the parable from Luke 15 with which "prodigal" has become synonymous. An allusion to the parable occurs in the chattering Gratiano's description of the once finely fretted merchant ship returning from its voyage "like the prodigal . . . / With over-weather'd ribs and ragged sails – / Lean, rent, and beggar'd by the strumpet wind!" (II. vi. 17–19). Dangling here in the idle Grantiano's idle simile, the parable of the prodigal son looms over much of the play, though it is a reference Shakespeare seems quite pointedly to have kept in the background. It informs the story in *Il Pecorone*, in which the surrogate Antonio is the adoptive father of the Bassanio figure and plays the part of the all-forgiving, self-sacrificing father when the son twice "hazards" – and loses – all he has (Bullough, 1964, 466–7, 469). It informs the *Alarum Against Usurers*, in which Lodge offers a variation on the parable, having the father at first forgive the son, only to disown him later when the prodigal proves unregenerate (1584, 56–7). In the *Merchant*, traces of the parable suggest themselves in the opening exchange between Antonio and Bassanio, only to remain submerged within the notoriously elliptical and elusive relationship between these characters. For Shakespeare to have made those traces more distinct would have strengthened the connection between Bassanio and the wastrel youths pilloried in the anti-usury tracts of the day, and, implicitly, would have given a sharper resonance to the antimaterialist evocations in Shylock's invective.[15] As it is, however, the parable of the prodigal son presents itself in the play as an analogy left teasingly inchoate, with our sense of its nonpresence keen enough for us to notice its suppression.

Still, is such suppression evidence that the *Merchant* participates in the religioeconomic mythology of its times, or that it parodies it? In reifying in its own text the rationalizations and contradictions we encountered in other texts of the times, is the *Merchant* exorcising these qualifications, or, rather, is it underscoring their persistence? As Norman Rabkin demonstrated several years ago, critical commentary on the *Merchant* documents nothing more clearly than the resistance we encounter if we seek answers to these questions in the text of the play (1981, 28–9). In fact, what the text of the play may lead us to infer is that "texts" themselves are not to be trusted. "Texts," the play insists, can mislead and can be misread. Scripture we may think is authoritative, but, as Antonio warns Bassanio, it can be cited by the devil "for his purpose" (I. iii. 93); *sententiae*, "Good sentences," no matter how "well pronunc'd," Portia reminds Nerissa, are far easier to pronounce than to follow (I. ii. 10–20); words are "tricksy," Lorenzo declares, and can be summoned to "Defy the matter" by any number of fools like Launcelot Gobbo, "who hath planted in his memory / An army of good words" for the purpose (III. v. 59–64); while "deliberate fools" can, like Morocco and Aragon, display their foolishness in the very deliberateness with which they puzzle over texts, showing that they "have the wisdom by their wit to lose" (II. ix. 81). Indeed, if we read E.F.J. Tucker's reading of the play aright, what Portia's climactic judgement against Shylock enshrines most of all is the principle that for the law to be properly applied it must be understood in its spirit or intent, rather than read for the "letter" of its text (1976, 100–1).

How do these expressions within the play of skepticism toward texts affect our reading of *The Merchant of Venice*? Collectively, they would appear to support the argument that the play allegorizes the triumph of love, mercy, divine justice, and other *desiderata* over the various mean-spirited and short-sighted impulses emblematized in a narrow, close-reading legalism. Bassanio, for example, does not have to ponder closely the wordings on caskets, since he has higher, intuitive impulses to guide him – not to mention, of course, the subliminally helpful hints and "mood music" provided by Portia! On the other hand, the antiliteralism we come upon in the play at times serves the ideologically salutary purpose of upholding orthodoxy against the subversive, and subversively unanswerable, "misuse" of the texts and authorities by which orthodoxy is normally enforced: Scripture, the law, formulations of the "best interests" of the "commonweal." Antonio issues his admonition about Scripture, after all, when Shylock proves uncomfortably adept at biblical exegesis, with Antonio's words, as A.D. Nuttall has put it, suggestive of "a man who is holding fast to a conviction that his opponent must be wrong but cannot quite see how" (1983, 128). Analogously, Lorenzo lodges his complaint against "tricksy" words and fools just after Launcelot has appealed to the laws of supply and demand to argue that Jessica's conversion to Christianity will raise the price of pork (III. v. 19–23). The "word" must be suspect if it allows a Jew to use Scripture to justify usury and a fool to use the economic calculus of the times to suggest that, at least in one respect, the interests of Christianity and the economic interests of the commonwealth are not identical!

Yet in underscoring the equivocality and ambiguity of texts and "the word," *The Merchant of Venice* distances itself from the very textuality which nourishes it and the texts which it evokes and by which its discourse is enriched and complicated: the Italian *novelle* that are the immediate source of its fable, anti-usury diatribes, accounts of commercial exploration and exploitation, parliamentary decrees and edicts of law, and, the most authoritative and yet misreadable text of all, Scripture. In calling attention to the ways in which texts can be misused to yield subversive generalizations, the *Merchant* would have its audience believe that it is something other than, more than, another text, and would persuade us that the way to true harmony and resolution lies in the playful particularity of its dramatic action. In this way the *Merchant* as a piece of *theater* distances itself from the subversive resonances it yields as a *text*. At the same time, however, by its very ludic nature the *Merchant* can pretend merely to "play" with the religioeconomic mythology its fable inscribes. In the degree to which the *Merchant* asserts its independence of the very textuality it evokes, its playwright can invoke the indemnity of Sidney's poet, who, Sidney glibly reminds us, cannot ever be said to lie, because he "nothing affirmeth" (1595, 29).

We find this curious negotiation between text and play epitomized at the outset of act V, in the exchange in which Jessica and Lorenzo lyrically recount some of the assorted amorous misadventures that occurred on just "such a night" as the moonlit one they are enjoying at Belmont (V. i. 1–24). It is a passage which can be cited to confirm the darkest misgivings that can be, and have been, entertained about the "prodigal" and "unthrift" manner in which Lorenzo and Jessica contrived to "steal from the wealthy Jew" (Moody, 1964, 46–7; Burckhardt, 1968, 224). It is a passage which, if read darkly, provides an ironic prelude to that "aristocratic fantasy" played out in the rest of this the concluding scene of the play. How we interpret this exchange depends very much on the degree of proximity we posit between Jessica and Lorenzo and the roster of literary amatory "unthrifts" whom they invoke and with whom they "playfully" associate themselves, or, rather, each other: Troilus and Cressida, Thisbe and Pyramus, Dido and Aeneas, Jason and Medea. To measure Jessica and Lorenzo by the texts in which they would inscribe themselves is not only to deepen our suspicion that Jessica and Lorenzo themselves either are not or will not be or do not deserve to continue to be happy, but also to bring the world of the play closer to the ambiguous light shed upon its proceedings by literary allusion and analogy. In the immediate context the intrusion of the dramatic action, in the person of Stephano arriving to announce the imminent return of Portia (V. i. 25), prevents Lorenzo and Jessica from fully shaping their own history to the specifications of the doleful texts they have been reciting. In this way they are permitted to maintain their theatrical "otherness" from the textual patterning by which they make it very tempting to read them. Hence, with no little tension, the world of texts is kept playfully separate from the world of the theatrical fiction.

Here, to be sure, it could be argued that the playfulness we have been claiming for the *Merchant* is but the rhetorical signature of its own textuality, with the distancing effect this playfulness produces nothing other than that parodic distance which Pierre Macherey contends must ever mark the relationship of "literary language" to the ideological discourses it evokes, that inherent distantiation through which "literary discourse merely mimics theoretical discourse, rehearsing but never actually performing its script" (1978, 59). At the same time, though – even as we must question whether "literary language" can in fact be so essentially distinguishable from other discourses as Macherey would maintain[16] – we are no less likely to recognize in the *Merchant* the symptoms of the curious dualism with which the public stage of Shakespeare's day "represented" the world of, and to, its public, and with which it negotiated – and accommodated – the ideological currents and cross-currents of the time. As Louis Montrose has demonstrated, Shakespearean drama in particular calls upon the affiliative power inherent in theater to "re-present" to the audience a "paradigm" of its culture even while calling attention, self-reflexively, to the devices, conventions, and forms that inscribe the experience of theater as but illusion, and its business but "play" (1980, 66; also 1981, 33). This dualism entails, of course, a certain artistic – and political – convenience, for even as it proclaims the mimetic power of drama to suggest and portray resemblances to "real life," it insists upon the figurative character of those resemblances and, thus, enables the playwright to claim limitations upon his responsibility, his accountability, for literal truth. "What childe is there," asks Sidney in his response to Gosson's attack, "that coming to a play, and seeing *Thebes* written in great letters upon an old doore, doth beleeve that it is Thebes?" (p. 29). Sidney's "question" is, in fact, an assertion of an artistic license which the more wary upholders of orthodoxy should have found disquieting: the license to be taken seriously but not literally, and, therefore, not *too* seriously!

In no form are this reflexivity and playing at representation so overt as in comedy, and in no Shakespearean comedy is the tension that this playing embodies – and the convenience it affords – more evident than in the *Merchant*, where, I have tried to suggest, we are treated to an exposition and interrogation of the prevailing religioeconomic mythologies of the day, even as we feel a pull toward the reassuring particularity only a dramatic solution and resolution can provide. Indeed, nothing better attests to the will and power of dramatic art to divert attention from the ideological contradictions it reflects to its own playful alterity than the sense that has permeated a good deal of criticism on the *Merchant* that "somehow," through some combination of conventions comic, festive, and carnivalesque, the play manages to transcend the issues its text problematizes to render a dramatically, theatrically, satisfying experience. "The happy ending," C.L. Barber observes, with a keen and generous appreciation for this festive *difference*, "which abstractly considered as an event is hard to credit, and treatment of Shylock, which abstractly considered as justice is hard to justify, *work* as we actually watch or read the play because these events express relief and triumph in the achievement of a distinction" (1959, 170). The *Merchant* "works" – and worked – and achieves its "triumph," of course, precisely in the degree to which it works upon its audience, and critics, to relax their discriminations and equate the illusion of a "distinction" with its "achievement."

Now, as Robert Weimann has shown, no figure in Shakespearean drama so well incarnates in action and speech the playfully representative force of Shakespearean drama as does the fool (1978, 30–48, 133–51), and so, to italicize the peculiarly playful relationship of the *Merchant* to the religioeconomic vision its fable enacts, we might conclude by looking once again at that exchange in act III (v. 19 ff.) in which the fool, Launcelot Gobbo, opines on the economic ramifications of Jessica's conversion. Cohen has observed how in general Launcelot's penchant for the verbal malapropos gives voice to "an alternative perspective on the related matters of Christian orthodoxy and social hierarchy" (1982, 780), and the truth of that observation is in no way belied by Launcelot's performance here. Yet what is most exemplary in what Lawrence Danson calls Launcelot's "wonderful confusion of carnal matters and spiritual" (1978, 97) is the complexity of response it elicits from us. Practiced as we have become in making sense of what we take to be the ostensible non-sense and inversions of sense that dot Launcelot's "normal" discourse, we have no difficulty in grasping an ulterior pertinence in the apparent im-pertinence of Launcelot's juxtaposition of things spiritual and porcine. After all, Launcelot is not the first character in the play, we are likely to recall, who has shown himself to be a *homo economicus* in matters related to Jessica; and whatever incongruity we may feel in hearing Jessica's conversion turn Launcelot's thoughts to pork is only a comic reprise of the incongruity we may have felt in hearing from Solanio that Jessica's elopement turned her father's thoughts to ducats (II. viii. 12–22). Still, even as Launcelot's reasoning reassuringly parodies the materialism we associate with and hear burlesqued in Solanio's burlesque of Shylock, it reminds us that it is not only the Jew and usurer who brings an economic algorithm to his reading of experience, and that the line in the play distinguishing the "thrift" of the usurer from the values of the Christian community is not so very reassuringly or consistently sharp.

At the same time, however, the associations called into play by Launcelot's words are kept at a playful distance by the comic theatricality of his character. Yet this distancing is double-edged. On the one hand, Launcelot's generic "foolishness" permits the play to articulate elements of social criticism without appearing to engage or take them seriously. Indeed, Launcelot's comicality enables the *Merchant* to glance yet glance but teasingly at assumptions left unquestioned by its fable: that godliness and riches are linked, that Christianity and the economic interests of the commonwealth are in harmony. On the other hand, though it may distance itself from the kinds of question and questioning Launcelot's words may suggest, the *Merchant* leaves these same assumptions ultimately unaffirmed. Lorenzo deals with Launcelot's provocative – and provoking – thesis, we will recall, not by refuting it, but by changing the subject and grumbling about "tricksy words" in the mouths of fools. Like the exchange between Jessica and Lorenzo, the dialogue here is significantly disengaged. Above all, in having economic theory uttered from the mouth of a fool, the *Merchant* glances reflexively and parodically at the very sort of discourse in which it has involved itself and immersed us. In the playfulness of Launcelot the *Merchant* asserts its own playfulness and illuminates the dramatic tension in which it holds the competing impulses of recuperation and subversion.

Notes

1. For another synopsis of the polarities through which the play is often schematized, see Greenblatt (1978), 293–4. All references to the *Merchant* are to the Arden edition, edited by Brown (1955).
2. Consider the note of qualification obtruding in Barbara Lewalski's contention that the conversion imposed upon Shylock at the end of the play is a prefigurement of the final conversion of the Jews: "because Antonio is able to rise at last to the demands of Christian love, Shylock is not destroyed, but, albeit rather harshly, converted" (Lewalski, 1962, 334).
3. For a summary and discussion of a number of the topical possibilities, see Brown (1955), xxi–xxvii.
4. See Draper (1935), 39–45; Brown (1955), xliii; also, *Acts of the Privy Council*, December 5 and 24, 1598, cited in Harrison (1931), 324–6.
5. In the source story from *Il Pecorone*, "[t]he Jew, seeing that he could not do what he had wished, took his bond and tore it in pieces in a rage." See Bullough (1964), 474.
6. Thus, in the concluding remarks in Thomas Lodge's *Alarum Against Usurers* (1584), the moneylenders are exhorted to "harden not your hearts, but be you converted . . . and turne, turne, turne unto the Lord, (I beseech you) least you perish in your own abhominations" (1584 [1853] 79). See also the penitence of the usurer at the conclusion of Lodge's *A Looking Glasse, for London and England* (1598 [1963, 69]).
7. See Lodge (1584 [1853], 77; Smith (1591), 8; also Brown (1955), xxiv.
8. Smith goes so far as to maintain that were there no usury, there would be no "revenging," and that "they which brought in Vsurie, brought in a law against themselves" (pp. 6–7).
9. In his insistence upon the letter of the bond, Shylock follows the example of the usurer in *Il Pecorone* (Bullough, 1964, 471), but in the defiance with which he

teasingly defends his right to the pound of flesh, he seems akin to the moneylender in Alexander Silvayn's *The Orator* (trans. L.P., 1596), who, having speculated on various reasons why "I would not rather take silver of this man, then his flesh," shrugs them off, and "will onelie say, that by his obligation he oweth it me" (Bullough, 1964, 484).

10. In, perhaps, the most virulent expression of anti-Bassanian sentiment among critics, A.D. Moody observes of Bassanio that "[i]t would not be inappropriate if his name came to be suggestive of baseness, in the sense of 'opposed to high-minded'; and perhaps also to suggest the bass, 'the common perch', which catches the shallow and callow aspect, and also 'a voracious European marine fish', which catches the more serious underside" (1964, 23–4). A.D. Nuttall puts the case of Bassanio's apparent materialism in more silken accents when he notes, "There is a certain repellent ingenuousness about Bassanio. He can trust his own well-constituted nature. It would never allow him to fall in love with a poor woman; for, after all, poor women are not attractive" (1983, 122).

11. In *Il Pecorone*, after all, we also find an interesting admixture of *Eros* and commerce, though it could be argued that the *Merchant* is an inversion of the fable of its source. For in *Il Pecorone* what begins as a commercial venture turns into an erotic adventure; in the *Merchant* what we would presume to be an amatory quest seems persistently mixed with material considerations.

12. To take but one example, Bassanio's very appeal to Antonio for a renewal of his loan appropriates the vocabulary of investment. Were Antonio to give Bassanio the funds with which to replace the money Bassanio has already wasted, Bassanio promises either "to find both, / Or bring your latter hazard back again," while the thought of his courtship of Portia "presages me such thrift / That I should questionless be fortunate" (I. i. 150–1, 175–6).

13. For a brief discussion of this statute, see Draper (1935), 41.

14. For two quite complementary discussions of Shylock as the figure of the scapegoat, see Girard (1978), 108–14; and Barber (1959), 177–84.

15. Indeed, had Shakespeare given greater definition to the analogy between Bassanio and the prodigal son, he might have affiliated the fable of the play with a concern evident in the anti-usury complaints of the day, namely, that the profits of usurers were a threat to familial legacies and, thus, to nothing less than social continuity. Lodge, who may have been especially sensitive to the overthrows familial fortunes could suffer, exclaims that "Purchased arms now possess the place of ancient progenitors, and men made rich by young youth's misspendings doe feast in the halls of our riotous young spend thrifts" (1584, 48).

16. At the heart of Macherey's position on the nonideological nature of "literary language" is the assumption that "literary language" is essentially nonrepresentational. Indeed, to Sidney's self-exculpatory claim that the poet never lies because he "nothing affirmeth," Macherey might well add that the poet – or playwright – can *only* lie whenever he seems to affirm. "Literature is deceptive," Macherey argues, "in so far as it is evocative and apparently expressive. . . . Making us take the word for the thing, or vice-versa, it would be a fabric of lies, all the more radical for being unconscious" (1978, 61).

Works cited

Bacon, Francis (1625) "Of Vsurie," in Bacon, Francis, *Essays*, Oxford, Oxford University Press, 1966.

Barber, C.L. (1959) *Shakespeare's Festive Comedy*, Princeton, Princeton University Press.

Brown, John Russell (ed.) (1955) *The Merchant of Venice* by William Shakespeare,

Arden edn, London, Methuen.

Bullough, Geoffrey (1964) *Narrative and Dramatic Sources of Shakespeare*, London, Routledge & Kegan Paul.

Burckhardt, Sigurd (1968) *Shakespearean Meanings*, Princeton, Princeton University Press.

Cohen, Walter (1982) "*The Merchant of Venice* and the Possibilities of Historical Criticism," *English Literary History*, 49, 765–89.

Danson, Lawrence (1978) *The Harmonies of The Merchant of Venice*, New Haven, Yale University Press.

The Death of Usury, or, The Disgrace of Usurers, London, 1594, STC 6443.

Dollimore, Jonathan (1984) *Radical Tragedy: Religion, Ideology and Power in the Drama of Shakespeare and his Contemporaries*, Chicago, University of Chicago Press; Brighton, Harvester.

Draper, John W. (1935) "Usury in *The Merchant of Venice*," *Modern Philology*, 33, 37–47.

Girard, René (1978) " 'To Entrap the Wisest': A Reading of *The Merchant of Venice*," in Said, Edward W. (ed.) (1980) *Literature and Society: Selected Papers from the English Institute*, Baltimore, Johns Hopkins University Press, 100–19.

Gosson, Stephen (1579) *The Schoole of Abuse, Containing a Pleasant invective against Poets, Pipers, Players, Jesters, and such like Caterpillers of a Commonwealth*, repr. 1841, London, The Shakespeare Society.

Greenblatt, Stephen (1978) "Marlowe, Marx, and Anti-Semitism," *Critical Inquiry*, 5, 291–307.

—— (1981) "Invisible Bullets: Renaissance Authority and its Subversion," *Glyph 8: Johns Hopkins Textual Studies*, Baltimore, Johns Hopkins University Press, 40–61.

Hakluyt, John (1582) *Divers voyages touching the Discouerie of America and the Ilands Adiacent*, ed. Jones, John Winter (1850), London, Hakluyt Society.

Harrison, G.B. (ed.) (1931) *A Second Elizabethan Journal: Being a Record of Those Things Most Talked of During the Years 1595–8*, London, Constable.

Kermode, Frank (1961) "The Mature Comedies," in Brown, John Russell and Harris, Bernard (eds), *Early Shakespeare*, Stratford-upon-Avon Studies, 3, London, Edward Arnold, 211–17.

Lewalski, Barbara (1962) "Biblical Allusion and Allegory in *The Merchant of Venice*," *Shakespeare Quarterly*, 13, 327–43.

Lodge, Thomas, (1584) *An Alarum Against Usurers*, repr. 1853, London, The Shakespeare Society.

—— (1598) *A Looking Glasse, for London and England*, vol. IV of *The Complete Works of Thomas Lodge*, 1883; repr. 1963, New York, Russell & Russell.

Macherey, Pierre (1978) *A Theory of Literary Production*, trans. Geoffrey Wall, London, Routledge & Kegan Paul.

Meres, Francis (1598) *Palladis Tamia*, London, facsimile repr. 1938, New York, Scholars' Facsimiles & Reprints.

Montrose, Louis Adrian (1980) "The Purpose of Playing: Reflections on a Shakespearean Anthropology," *Helios*, n.s. 7, 51–74.

—— (1981) " 'The Place of a Brother' in *As You Like It:* Social Process and Comic Form," *Shakespeare Quarterly*, 32, 28–54.

Moody, A.D. (1964) *Shakespeare: The Merchant of Venice*, Woodbury, New York, Barron's Educational Series.

Nuttall, A.D. (1983) *A New Mimesis: Shakespeare and the Representation of Reality*, London, Methuen.

Rabkin, Norman (1981) *Shakespeare and the Problem of Meaning*, Chicago, University of Chicago Press.

Ramsay, G.D. (ed.) (1979) *The Politics of a Tudor Merchant Adventurer: A Letter to the Earls of East Friesland*, Manchester, Manchester University Press.

Sidney, Sir Philip (1595) *The Defence of Poesie*, London, vol. III of *The Prose Works of Sir Philip Sidney*, ed. Albert Feuillerat, 4 vols, 1912, repr. 1968, Cambridge, Cambridge University Press.

Smith, Henry (1591) *The Examination of Usury*, London, STC 22660.

Stow, John (1603) *The Survey of London*, introd. H.B. Wheatley (1912), London, J.M. Dent.

Tucker, E.F.J. (1976) ''The Letter of the Law in *The Merchant of Venice*,'' *Shakespeare Survey*, 29, 93–101.

Weimann, Robert (1978) *Shakespeare and the Popular Tradition in the Theater: Studies in the Social Dimension of Dramatic Form and Function*, ed. Robert Schwartz, Baltimore, Johns Hopkins University Press.

9

Lenten butchery: legitimation crisis in *Coriolanus*

Michael D. Bristol

The general political form of the Coriolanus legend

Since antiquity, the historical fiction of Coriolanus, his rise to power, his expulsion by a tribunal of the people, and his tragic death, has provided material for a political theodicy. Much of the story is, of course, sheer invention (Lehman, 1952). Many of the details of the legend, however, do correspond to historically concrete elements within the Roman state, and, more broadly, to elements of political and social struggle that persist through the emergence of absolutist states and their successors in modern national sovereignties (Anderson, 1974a, 1974b; Guenée, 1985; Nicolet, 1980; Poggi, 1978; Richard, 1978; Strayer, 1970; Yavetz, 1969). The legend articulates a comprehensive vocabulary for the representation of the state. First, Rome is defined as a territory through the story of the war against the Volscians. Second, the internal administrative coherence of the *res publica* is accomplished through the interaction of three primary sociohistorical categories – Coriolanus, patricians, and plebeians and tribunate – that constitute a typology of political structure. State formation is conceived in terms of enmity and division. The solidarity of the whole is expressed through the compelling distinction between friend and foe (Poggi, 1978; Schmitt, 1976). But within that negatively determined solidarity, relations among men and women are differentiated according to a division of labor that is itself inimical

MICHAEL D. BRISTOL, Associate Professor of English at McGill University in Montreal, is currently working on a book tentatively entitled *The Politics of Literary Culture: Shakespeare as Institution 1946–1986*. He is the author of *Carnival and Theatre: Plebeian Culture and the Structure of Authority in Renaissance England* (New York and London, Methuen, 1985).

and invidious (Gramsci, 1957; Marx, 1973; Poggi, 1972). Because of this orientation toward struggle, negativity, and historically determinate action, the Coriolanus legend always exceeds the boundaries of any conservative project of simple apologetics for a given historical condition of the Roman *res publica* or for any of the institutions of political domination that claim succession from this origin.

The antagonism between Coriolanus and the tribunes who represent the common people suggests that something more fundamental is at stake in this narrative material than a difference of opinion over Coriolanus' fitness or unfitness to rule. That difference of opinion could presumably be settled by an appeal to a normative order of some kind. It is, however, the nature and purpose of that normative order, and not merely the appropriate role of one individual within an agreed-upon political structure, that is the central issue inscribed within the material. The historical fiction is, then, always at hand as a parable for what Jürgen Habermas calls legitimation crisis (1975, 1979). Such a crisis typically involves conflict at the deepest levels of social reality.

Legitimation crisis is a phenomenon that divides society over issues much more basic and enduring than factional strife over division of the spoils. First, there is likely to be profound divergence over the question of the derivation of authority and the source of social initiative. Second, there will be a general contestation of the allocation of authority and of the predominant mode of social organization. Third, the ethical horizons of social organization, the purpose or general *telos* of economic and political praxis, informs the other levels of the conflict by generating opposed general metaphors of social existence or "images of the good life" (Habermas, 1979; Jameson, 1981; McCarthy, 1978; Wallerstein, 1974; Walzer, 1976). What makes the Coriolanus legend so effective as the metaphorical embodiment of the general form of legitimation crisis is the distinctive role taken by the plebs or citizens (Nicolet, 1980; Richard, 1978; Scullard, 1935; Treggiari, 1969; Yavetz, 1969). This anonymous, collective player in the drama of political struggle represents not only a full and coherent alternative political culture, but also the will to power of that political culture.

Coriolanus, as the protagonist in the legend that bears his name, objectifies the principle of charismatic authority (Weber, 1947, 358 ff.). His claim to political and ethical priority rests on his exceptional powers as a military leader, most specifically his extraordinary personal valor and technical skill in combat. He is the embodiment of an ideal of *virtus*, manly excellence or prowess; the complementary and offsetting ideal of *pietas* comes into play only at the last minute and then in an oddly displaced and distorted form. His charisma rests exclusively on his quasimagical capacity for violence rather than on any prophetic or persuasive gifts, but it is a genuine charisma in that it derives from collectively sustained values. The sudden emergence of a charismatic figure within the *mise-en-scène* of a lawfully constituted political structure is inherently destabilizing; it is certainly ominous in that such a figure can act as the center for politically radical mass movements. In the Coriolanus material, however, it is the party in power, the patricians, who embrace Coriolanus, whom they see as a useful and reliable instrument for the defense of their own class interests.

Opposition to the principle of charismatic authority comes from the institution of the tribunate. That opposition is not merely negative, an intransigent resistance to a resented arrogation of civil authority. It is, on the contrary, an opposition founded on an opposing view of authority as derived from the force of social tradition and customary practice (Weber, 1947, 341 ff.). As E.P. Thompson has pointed out, a plebs is not a working class in the modern sense (1968, 1974). On the other hand, it is not an unorganized population of helots either, and still less a mob or rabble (P. Burke, 1978; Davis, 1975; Harrison, 1984; Richard, 1978). The plebs, or their cognates in the early modern period – Shakespeare's "citizens" – is a complex ensemble of producing classes. It is also a political entity, nominally excluded from the function of rule but nevertheless a collective agent within the dynamic of political life (Bristol, 1985). The plebs characteristically views authority as derived from local custom and from settled ways of doing things. As "theoreticians" or "onlookers" vis-à-vis official politics, the common people tend to view the objectively topmost positions not as a pervasive and ordered hegemony, but as a finite, rigorously bounded and precarious setting forth of an ideology of order and mastery surrounded by a "sea of productive labor." This implies a severe curtailment of the centralized function of state power in favor of a general dispersal of authority. Law takes precedence over decree, but custom takes precedence even over law on this view. The plebs thus acts on the conviction of its own prior authority, its expropriation by an elite, and on the need for redressive action to restore an original state of affairs when its constituencies had not yet become "the unprivileged" (Davis, 1975, 152 ff.).

Opposition over the derivation of authority is elaborated in the further opposition over the allocation of authority and the general form of social organization. In these terms, Coriolanus stands for a principle of hierarchically ordered and centrally administered social structure. It is unfortunate that so much of the critical literature on the best known of all the versions of the Coriolanus legend tends to collapse the terms hierarchy and order into a single category. This obscures the highly specialized character of the type of orderliness favored by Coriolanus. It also denies the possibility of other types of ordering principle and even of the broad range of hierarchizations available within social practice. Coriolanus' allegiance is not to "hierarchy" in general, but specifically to a vertical command structure of an exclusively military type. The general rationale for his vision of *l'état policier* is, not surprisingly, the idea that the mass of common people is lawless, predatory, and incapable of ordered social relations in the absence of a severe and rigorously enforced external discipline (Poggi, 1978, 5 ff.; Schmitt, 1976). This is the justificatory ideology of the regime of *Herrschaft* or lordship, which depicts itself as the exclusive source of order set over against internal as well as external foes (Le Roy Ladurie, 1979, 299–302).

The tribunate opposes this ideology not with an idea of subversion or derangement, but with an alternative (though not widely acknowledged) conception of social order based on solidarity, a regime of *Genossenschaft* in which the members of a group participate on a more or less equal footing (Durkheim, 1935; La Capra, 1985; Le Roy Ladurie, 1979; Poggi, 1972). Within this regime, of course, temporary pragmatic hierarchies may be recognized, but these differentiations are made for functional reasons, and do not symbolize a permanent and ideal framework of categories. Since there is no speciality of rule it can hardly be neglected. From this perspective it is possible to develop a full and cogent critique of the command structure advocated by Coriolanus, one that goes beyond the observation that he is too proud or that his adventurism might prove too costly. For it is central to the project of any command structure to forbid any countervailing system of imperatives, and specifically to deny the pertinence and the validity claims of any dispersed communal authority. However, if such a logic of domination is actually implemented, then it is clear that the existence of a "rabble" is one of the more important consequences of its functioning, since the command structure itself would entail the suppression of self-regulating norms and practises that promote and sustain communal solidarity. Rigid insistence on a vertical chain of command creates a situation where the only thing that matters is who's on top. Common people, normally organized in corporate bodies, sink into the condition of rabble as the result of material deprivation and of cultural violence (Durkheim, 1935). Plebeian culture has resources that enable it to resist such a process of internal colonization and the suppression of their own diffuse authority by the figure of the greater personality or *Führer*. The self-exclusion of the great public figure from the body of the people evokes "choric recrimination" (Styan, 1976, 102). Such anger and violent recrimination speaks to social and cultural norms deeply embedded in the practical consciousness of the plebs. The plebeian forms of *Genossenschaft* thus imply an absolute and radical reversal of the terms order and disorder, in which it is maintained that any hypostasis of the topmost positions in the form of an external disciplinarity is a fundamental derangement in the direction of an endless chain of violent actions.

The most fundamental opposition, then, between Coriolanus and his opponents is at the level of the generative metaphor, *telos*, or goal-value of social life. For Coriolanus, the fundamental *raison d'être* of social life is the state of affairs known as war. The body politic is thus envisioned as perpetually constrained by conditions of austerity and athletic self-discipline oriented toward the geopolitical Other in a posture of aggression (Jorgensen, 1956; Schmitt, 1976). This condition is not thought of as a "necessary evil," or even as the means toward some end such as, let's say, peace; it is, on the contrary, an end in itself, and in fact the only possible state of political well-being. This then gives rise to the cognate therapeutic metaphor in which injury and destruction are recuperated by images that refer to the discharge of excessive and superfluous political matter, or to the surgical elimination of pathological growth. The durable ideological appeal of this notion is itself part of the Coriolanus material, in that the legend suggests that the plebs is willing to follow Coriolanus into battle against the Volscians. However, a fundamental misunderstanding takes place as soon as this campaign has ended.

The plebs views war as at most an instrumental and purely temporary value. It constitutes a transient condition of political arousal, not a state of social health. For the plebs the governing metaphor of social life cannot be war; it can only be subsistence, the constellation of homeostatic processes of production, reproduction, and renewal most often represented by images of a living organism. This orientation gives rise to the speech type of popular culture, an idiom that grants special importance to what Bakhtin has called the "lower bodily stratum," and to those processes that mark the individual body as open, unfinished, and traversed by the activities of social production (Bakhtin, 1968, 368 ff.). One reason for the success of Menenius' speech to the angry plebeians is his ability to make use of their own characteristic idiom of the "grotesque body" and to appeal directly to the distinctive goal-values of plebeian culture by positing social health as homologous with the visceral satisfaction of bodily needs. His speech is, of course, tendentious, shaped by an ideology fundamentally alien to the aspirations of the social horizons of the plebs, but the legend suggest that an intervention of this type can be effective, at least in the short run, as a strategy of containment. The very effectiveness of the intervention tacitly acknowledges, however, that the plebeians have a distinctive outlook or world-view and that their consciousness is not merely an absence of political ideas, but a full and coherent mode of being-in-the-world, as well as a mode of being-with-others.

The opposition between Coriolanus and the tribunate is, of course, mediated by the framing social reality of the *res publica* as a lawfully constituted form of social life that finds its origins in the historical expulsion of the Tarquins, and the rejection in principle of absolute, individual rule. It is this "state" that suffers through legitimation crisis. In the distinct works that concretize the materials of the legend it is the *res publica*, an entity with a historically specific constitution that emerges from the turbulent cross-currents that threaten both its territorial integrity and its internal cohesion. The achievement of a constitutional settlement brings with it a more or less stable legitimation of an ensemble of power relations. In itself, however, a constitution does not resolve the conflicts built into the division of social labor. Active and open conflict is suspended and deferred; sociocultural and discursive antagonism persists, however, and one or another party to the ongoing process of legitimation may at any time withhold consent. Ideas of chronic social antagonism and incipient crisis are intrinsic to the Coriolanus material, and for that reason the story retains its potentially explosive character.

Shakespeare's *Coriolanus* and the politics of carnival

Shakespeare's full-scale dramatization of the Coriolanus legend begins with a scene depicting the community of citizens decisively entering into the sphere of political action that Fernand Braudel refers to as *l'histoire événementielle* (1977). The common people are always present as part of the nearly immobile level of history, the slow unfolding of material culture and everyday life (Braudel, 1981, 23–5). The emergence of the body of citizens into the more eventful dimension of history takes the dramatic form of a crowd or chorus surging onto the stage to enact their anger, their desire for social and economic restitution, and the will to power of a heretofore mute constituency. It has frequently been asserted that the common people are presented unsympathetically in this and subsequent scenes (Ide, 1980; MacCallum, 1967; Pettet, 1950; Rabkin, 1967; Rossiter, 1961; Simmons, 1973; Zeeveld, 1962). Stated in this form, the proposition is logically incoherent, since the quality of sympathy refers to intersubjective relations, but not to discrete objects or representations. If the claim is made in the more precise form – the plebeians are represented in a manner intended to evoke antipathy, then the ideologically contingent nature of the assertion becomes immediately apparent (Charney, 1963; Dollimore, 1984). The quality of sympathy or of antipathy would depend far less on the dramatic rhetoric as such, and far more on the prevailing social outlook of those present at the moment of reception.

Sympathy is, of course, a relative form. The response of shared feeling is likely to be governed by collective predispositions, often unconscious, much more than by a purely neutral and disinterested reaction to artistic language and mimetic action. The intersubjective condition of sympathy corresponds to a particular social experience, namely that of class-conscious solidarity. In reading *Coriolanus* it is, of course, extremely pertinent to ask who feels sympathy or its lack and for what reason. But this question requires that general criteria of "social goodness" or "social badness" be made explicit. The tendency to view the crowd of citizens unsympathetically reflects a specific ideological orientation. If this is not simply an unreflective elitism, it is most likely to be an orientation in which the dominant criterion of "social goodness" is a comprehenive order in which integration of disparate interests and rationalization of authority, power, and wealth are achieved by means of an uncontested hegemony. In this orientation, toleration for conflict and thus sympathy for those who appear to initiate it is extremely low. The ambient level of social violence ideally approaches zero by virtue of a rationally integrated apparatus that maintains a monopoly of coercive force. The idea of society or collective life is thus collapsed into the idea of the state as the indispensable objectification and agency of social order, the only possible barrier to the condition of interminable civil war. Within this tradition, spontaneous popular initiative can only be interpreted in one way, that is as an instance confirming a particular social dread, the war of all against all.

It may well be that Shakespeare's own ideological alignments fall within this tradition and that *Coriolanus* is precisely what traditional historicism has always claimed, that is, a theodicy of the absolutist state (Phillips, 1940; Honig, 1951; Rossiter, 1961; Simmons, 1973). If this is the case, then it seems that criticism might assume responsibility for making explicit both the grounds of this orientation and its consequences for social practice. This might entail the abandonment of a hermeneutics that simply keeps faith with tradition in favor of a critique of that tradition in which the authoritarian character of valued literary material is contested rather than simply confirmed as ''beyond ideology'' (Adorno, 1967; Gadamer, 1976; Giddens, 1977; Habermas, 1971; Hjort, 1985; McCarthy, 1978). There is, however, another way to challenge the confirmatory ideology of normal literary criticism, and that is to show how *Coriolanus* might be read as situated within an alternative political culture such as the one objectified in the crowd scenes and in the speeches of the unnamed citizens. Such a reconsideration would entail a more sympathetic view of the plebeians, not so much with the intention of assessing the justice of their claims, but rather with the aim of elucidating a distinctive political discourse. This seems particularly appropriate in light of the outbreaks of popular unrest during the early years of James I's reign, and more generally of the conditions of incipient revolution throughout the period (Charney, 1963; Dollimore, 1984; Goldberg, 1983; Sharp, 1980; Stone, 1972; Walzer, 1976).

In *Coriolanus* the ambient condition of political uncertainty and of gathering resistance to lawfully constituted authority is expressed in a complex and ambivalent rhetoric based on the traditional *topos* of the body politic (Cavell, 1984; Danson, 1973; Gurr, 1975; Hale, 1971). The image of the body is, of course, a familiar topic in the critical discussion of *Coriolanus*. The play is saturated with concrete situations in which the fate and condition of bodies is of paramount importance. Both literal and symbolic implications of the analogy between the private individual body and the body politic are elaborated in nearly every scene.

Menenius' great rhetorical set piece on the belly and the other members restates a commonplace of Renaissance political rhetoric that correlates the natural body and its functions with the body of the community and its social processes. The analogy suggests an organic view of society in which every member has an ascriptive status and function; social well-being depends on each member fulfilling his own duties and obligations. The fable of the belly itself derives ultimately from Aesop (Muir, 1952). Equally pertinent, however, is the image of the community of believers as articulated in *First Corinthians*:

> For as the body is one, and hath many members, and all the members of that body, being many, are one body, so also is Christ. For by one Spirit are we all baptized into one body. . . . If the foot shall say, because I am not the hand, I am not of the body; is it therefore not of the body? And if the ear shall say, Because I am not the eye, I am not of the body; is it therefore not of the body?

> (12:15–19)

Obviously physical health depends on the unity and coordination of the whole body; similarly the health of a community depends on a stable and harmonious division of labor and on the appropriate distribution of subsistence. In the normative use of this metaphor, harmony and orderly differentiation require the clear subordination of the ''lower organs'' to the higher faculties of reason and spiritual understanding. The belly cannot be in charge, and when the fable is used by such writers as Sidney, William Camden, or Edward Forset the political discordancy among the lower faculties of the body is reconciled by the superior agency of the head (Hale, 1968). *Coriolanus* can be read exclusively in light of such a normative tradition, but the text reveals that the lower bodily stratum continues to assert itself against the imperatives of vertical order and control.

The language of Coriolanus accords particular prominence to images of the viscera, digestion, mouth, tongue, food and eating, as well as to instances of thrashing, wounds, injury, and violent death. This constellation of images constitutes the system of the "grotesque body" (Bakhtin, 1968; Cavell, 1984; Bristol, 1985; Stallybrass and White, 1986). The visceral or lower-bodily orientation provides for the elaboration of an ethos in which abundance of material life and the continuity of processes of production and reproduction are both the primary agencies *and* the fundamental criteria of social well-being. The abundance of the material principle is the characteristic goal-value of plebeian culture, a horizon present throughout *Coriolanus* as a general speech type containing and surrounding other class discourses. Menenius appropriates this speech type in his "fable of the belly" performance, and again in his conference with the tribunes when he characterizes himself as a "humorous patrician . . . that converses more with the buttock of the night than with the forehead of the morning" (II. i. 47–53). No genuine political accommodation can be reached, however, by the superficial exchange of ideological currency. The imagery or language of the grotesque body is more than simply a novel and picturesque vocabulary; it corresponds to the way the body is actually lived.

The grotesque body is lived "together with others;" it is most fully expressed in the energetic confusion of the popular festive crowd, in feasts, and in the life of the public square (Bakhtin, 1968, 1981). This is, of course, exactly what Coriolanus himself finds most intolerable. Since Coriolanus lives his own body in accordance with the canons of a radical, voluntaristic, and proprietary individualism, the intimacy and physical actuality of the collective, grotesque body can arouse only disgust. His sense of the integrity of the private body, and the plebeians' demand for familiarity and crude contact, are mutually incompatible modes of social existence. That incompatibility is objectified in Coriolanus' response to the customary demand that he show his wounds in public. "I cannot / Put on the gown, stand naked, and entreat them, / For my wounds sake, to give their suffrage" (II. ii. 138–9). His personal modesty and physical reticence that confine acknowledgement and disclosure of the body to private, domestic space are a deliberate expression of contempt and mockery for the values of plebeian culture. These attitudes represent his refusal to understand the compelling ethical force of tradition and the equally compelling value of solidarity expressed by the public exposure of his body. His calculated self-exclusion from the experience of the grotesque body corresponds to a commitment to the ruthless suppression of the political culture of the plebs. Unlike Menenius, who seeks an ideological appropriation of plebeian culture and its integration with the *res publica* on terms favorable to his own party, Coriolanus seeks the comprehensive disciplinary control of popular energy. The implicit aim of his political sensibility would be a form of authoritarian populism based on terror and coercion. He is, however, unable to achieve such a dispensation; his intentions are thwarted by the actions of the aroused citizens, who make of him the exemplary victim of a popular festive scenario of crowning and uncrowning (Bakhtin, 1968, 275).

In the context of early modern Europe, the central event of popular festive life is the battle of Carnival and Lent. The battle, as it was enacted in the traditional scenarios in streets and public squares, articulates various symmetrical oppositions, beginning with the contrast between fat and lean, that is, between two different, seasonal cuisines. Carnival celebrates meat; Lent celebrates fish. The pattern of abstinence from meat and the shift to a diet of fish during Lent is a religious and spiritual discipline, a "burying of pagan ways" as part of the purification of the spirit in preparation for Easter (Le Roy Ladurie, 1979, 285). But the relationship of Carnival to Lent, or *Carême-carnaval*, has secular importance as well.

The battle of Carnival and Lent dramatizes permanent conflicts within the practical experience of the early modern European economy. During Carnival, surplus livestock that cannot be wintered is slaughtered and preserved; meat is consumed in abundance and butchers enjoy prosperity. As Carnival ends and Lent begins, butchers are required to close their shops. This coincides with travel into the countryside to begin purchase of cattle for the spring. While the butchers are inactive fishmongers claim their market. In due course, however, the butchers return and all the dogs "howl for joy" at the renewed abundance of meat. The annual ceremonial combat opposes two complementary social elements – Carnival/Lent; butchers/fishmongers; war/peace – that coexist in dynamic equilibrium. These contrasts between different times of year, different sources of wealth and abundance, different métiers, represent the complexity of social life as a dialectical tension between the persistent drive toward material abundance and the requirements of social discipline. Closely connected with this is a corresponding dialectic between violence in the form of Carnival butchery and social peace in the form of the Lenten Truce of God.

In the recurrent rhythms of Carnival's battle with Lent, the figure of Carnival is closely identified with butchers and thus with the complex and ambivalent interconnection of slaughter with the abundance of the material principle (Bristol, 1985). The interval of abstinence and intensified social discipline known as Lent is the period during which the butchers' shops are closed. This interval is framed by two periods of climactic ascendancy for butchers, first in the Carnival feasting itself, and then, after the Easter Sunday observances, in the triumphal return of the butchers and the annual compensatory expulsion of Lent.

> Then pell-mell murder in a purple hue,
> In reeking blood his slaughtering paws imbrue:
> The butcher's axe (like great Alcides' bat)
> Dings deadly down, ten thousand thousand flat:

Each butcher (by himself) makes marshall laws,
Cuts throats, and kills, and quarters, hangs, and draws.
(Taylor, 1630, 19)

This is, in fact, celebratory imagery of renewed material abundance, but it suggests the very deep ambivalence and complexity that must be acknowledged in and through the productive processes that sustain collective life. The forms of *Carême–carnaval* can be regarded, not as the discharge of accumulated energy, but as the collective balancing and coordination of antagonistic elements within productive life and the channeling along familiar lines of chronic and irreducible social violence. The apparent lawlessness of these proceedings can also be read as an alternative law of coexistence. In this model of being-with-others, *Carême–carnaval* requires that every moment of ascendancy be checked, that every claim of domination be thrashed and regularly expelled. The aim of this social process is not the definitive resolution of conflict through rationalized administration, but the dynamic reenactment of traditional allocations of wealth and authority that nevertheless permits customary practice to be altered. The process is "conservative" in the sense that there is a diffuse collective will to conserve social wealth, established communal autonomy, and other elements that make up the horizons of the "good life."

Coriolanus follows the normal pattern of crowning and uncrowning/expulsion until halfway through the action, at which point the patterns of *Carême–carnaval* are disrupted. Unlike the expulsion of the butchers, who are scattered and dispersed into the countryside, only to return later to reassert the "bodily-material principle," Coriolanus' expulsion is made permanent, his attempted return at the head of a hostile army is prevented by the intervention of his mother. In order to understand this general pattern of political action, it is useful to compare Coriolanus with the ominous figure of the Lenten Butcher.

The categorical framework of *Carême–carnaval* maps the sociopolitical order into opposing domains depicted agonistically. The abundance of the material principle as manifested in the forces of production is projected as the Carnivalesque figure of the Butcher. Over against this is the principle of social discipline and restraint objectified in the Lenten Fishmonger. Obviously the kingdoms of Carnival and Lent must remain separate and the inhabitants of each domain kept apart. Nevertheless within the social landscape of Elizabethan and Jacobean England there is actually such a person as a Lenten Butcher. Such a figure transgresses the boundaries between Carnival and Lent. Equally important, he appears both within the criminal underworld as the supplier of contraband flesh, and also within the sphere of legally privileged economic monopoly. The Lenten Butcher who is granted a royal "license to kill" is permitted to practise his trade in accordance with secular imperatives that override the religious prohibition against the consumption of meat. The figure of the Lenten Butcher cuts across the boundary between Carnival and Lent, between law and its transgression. A Lenten Butcher does his work in Sir Francis Drake's ship at Deptford, my Lord Mayor's barge, and divers secret and unsuspected places, and there they make private shambles with kill-calf cruelty and sheep slaughtering murder, to the abuse of Lent, the deceiving of the informers, and the great griefe of every zealous fishmonger.

(Taylor, 1630, 13)

Under this institutional sanction, violence not only persists without periodic remission, it is in fact invested with immense preemptive authority "for reasons of state." The secular demands that require, for example, that naval vessels be provisioned during the lenten period lead to a general curtailment of the traditional *Carême–carnaval* alternative. The grotesque ambivalence of the Carnival Butcher gives way to the principle of selectivity and rationally administered violence that finds its source not in the "abundance of the material principle" but in the *projets de grandeur* of the state apparatus.

In *Coriolanus* the conquest of *res publica* by charismatic authority and rationally administered violence embodied in the ascendancy of a Lenten Butcher is averted by Coriolanus' extraordinary act of self-cancelation. Legitimation then takes the form of a class compromise, in which the party in power is able to reestablish dominance over the popular element. The *res publica* – or is it only the party in power? – is saved from utter and calamitous defeat at the hands of military absolutism. And the threat of calamity provides the means for incorporating and channeling the energy of popular initiative. The outcome is clear, though not, I think, exactly what we are to make of it. Is this an authentic and exemplary resolution of crisis? Is it a case of making the best of a bad situation? Or is it an instance of the thwarting of a genuine collective will by a dominant minority, using a general strategy of dramatized crisis, sacrifice, and the claims of a "national emergency" to control and redirect the energy of a popular majority?

Coriolanus and the patterns of ideological mobilization

To interpret *Coriolanus* is to engage in critical reflection on the legitimation problem of the modern state, especially if the state is seen as a constellation of balanced interests challenged on the one hand by the "*Führer* principle," or cult of personality, and, on the other, by a radical collective will that threatens a general appropriation of the means of production. That discussion does not, it would appear, permit ideological neutrality. Furthermore, the general institutional setting in which that discussion takes place is one in which there has already been a general appropriation of Shakespeare for the "national interest." For this reason, orientations that entail a strong critique of the existing sociocultural order, or that are subversive in some other way, are the only ones likely to appear overtly ideological. Normal readings are not particularly likely to reveal themselves as tendentious. In general, however, normal readings assume that the state must exist as the uncontested principle of sovereignty; "social goodness" is possible only within such a political formation and criticism is limited to the adjustment of contending interests and the therapeutic elimination of "social badness."

It would not be difficult to demonstrate the general recruitment of Shakespeare for the purpose of fostering the diffuse mass loyalty necessary for the continuing legitimation of state power and the class interests represented by that power (Dollimore, 1984). There are of course overt and external forms of appropriation, for example in the use of Shakespeare's plays in the English system of state examinations (Dollimore and Sinfield, 1985, 134–57; Wayne, this volume). Just as direct is the expression of diffuse sentiments about the need to promote the heritage of "western values" as the *raison d'être* of literary scholarship generally and Shakespeare studies in particular. The expression "western values" is, however, a way of coding an intensified cold-war militancy. If one poses the question "western values as opposed to what?" then the point of these descriptions of the critical vocation becomes clear. Western values are to be contrasted with Soviet values, and indeed, in the US, Education Secretary William Bennett has declared that this contrast is to be enshrined in a national curriculum (Bennett, 1985a, 1985b; Fiske, 1985). The purpose of this project is, forsooth, that more people will support the President's foreign policy.

The recruitment of Shakespeare is mediated by a disciplinary ideology that sets forth a constellation of interests and goal-values which either directly underwrite the aims of a general mobilization or channel oppositional energies so as to curtail any possibility of effective dissemination. Space does not permit a full elaboration of that disciplinary ideology here, but any account of its salient features would certainly include the following points. To begin with, there is a high value accorded to the integrity of the dramatic work of art and to the achievement of a higher order of resolution within those works of historically specific conflicts. This view leads to the endlessly recurring universalistic claim that Shakespeare is "beyond ideology." Although this has the occasionally useful effect of offering resistance to entrenched doxological formulations, it also carries with it the desire to escape from the nuisance of real history. By transcending history both Shakespeare and the scholarship that would contemplate his work are excused from participation in historically contingent political life. Closely connected with the consensus as to the integrity of the dramatic work of art is the view of Shakespeare's authority in terms of an ahistorical conception of the "exceptional subject." This entails a view of the cultural producer as a singularity; the producing subject is characterized as a proprietary, autonomous, and voluntaristic self, distinguished from ordinary men and women. In the case of Shakespeare, the thematics of a contemporary achievement ideology finds an abundant reservoir of examples in the complex structure of his works. Value-laden propositions can then be authorized by attribution to this exceptional individual who is carefully set apart from anything that resembles a collective will. One important consequence of this is the shift from politics to sensibility. Criticism discovers in Shakespeare a higher loyalty to the human imagination and to universalistic higher-order integration. This corresponds to criticism's renunciation of partisan political engagement (Gilbert, 1968).

Within the range of interest generally authorized by a disciplinary ideology, contending voices can certainly be heard. It is even possible to challenge the disciplinary ideology itself. However, what I hope to indicate in the following remarks is that most of the spectrum of legitimate contention rehearses the stance of civil and vocational privatism that either endorses the goal-values of the existing political structure and of the sociocultural order that supports it *or* confines the function of critical intervention to relatively narrow channels. I shall try to develop this by considering two kinds of normal readings of *Coriolanus*: first, readings mainly concerned with analysis of Coriolanus' character, and second, "balanced views" of the forces at play within the text.

There is no doubt that the Coriolanus that is represented in the Shakespearean text is a fascinating character. Like other Shakespearean tragedies, *Coriolanus* can certainly be read exclusively in light of the pathos of the exceptional subject. The case of Coriolanus is, like a number of others, sufficiently complex to have generated abundant controversy. One type of reading in this tradition concentrates on developing some basis for sympathetic identification with Coriolanus, or at least respect for the worthiness of his character (Bradley, 1912; Ide, 1980; MacLure, 1955; Rossiter, 1961). Alternatively, a reading might seek to give an account of his character in which his strengths are somehow compromised by one or more personal shortcomings, so that he fails to convey to his antagonists any sense of his true value (Adelman, 1978; Berry, 1973; Cavell, 1984; Sicherman, 1972). Or his character may be depicted as containing a deeper inner contradiction of some kind, so that the virtues he possesses are themselves the cause of his undoing (Cantor, 1976; Honig, 1951; McCanles, 1967). The tension between tragic and ironic reading represents a concern with the question of Coriolanus' personal fitness to rule, the nature of his ideals, and the pattern of his motivations. Whatever specific judgements may be rendered on this question, however, all these accounts of the "exceptional subject" rehearse the stance of civil/vocational privatism (Habermas, 1975; McCarthy, 1978). Critical intervention confines itself to an evaluation of leadership qualifications and to assessments of leadership performance. Neither the goal-values of institutions nor their organizational structure is called into question. The channeling of interpretation and criticism into controversy over highly visible individual personalities is a powerful way to sustain consensus in relation to broader issues of institutional structure and public policy.

Balanced views of *Coriolanus* are typically more concerned with Shakespeare as the source of a complex and aesthetically satisfying elaboration of conflict than they are with description of a singular character. One pattern of balance depicts the common people in light of their genuine need for subsistence over against the potential for "greatness" embodied in Coriolanus (Cantor, 1976; Charney, 1963; Paster, 1981; Rabkin, 1967; Simmons, 1973). The tragedy lies in the failure of these two elements to achieve reconciliation. "If he cannot help being greater than they are – and in his greatness alone – they cannot help being less. Thus, although we would not have the community die for Coriolanus, it survives diminished, starved by feeding" (Paster, 1981, 143). On this view,

Coriolanus serves as the sacrificial victim for the sake of a circumscribed communal harmony which no doubt would have been much richer had Coriolanus himself been able to call forth a more stable and generous collective will. But Paster gives no account of a community's need for heroes, nor does she explain how singular instances of greatness enhance communal well-being or promote "social goodness." In fact, the "great individual" may be fundamentally incompatible with genuine solidarity; the connection of towering personalities with pathological forms of social life is certainly familiar in contemporary political experience (Suvin, 1980). In the darker version of balanced reading neither Coriolanus nor the common people deserve any sympathy, since they represent equally ignoble forms of narrow self-interest (Goldberg, 1983; Goldman, 1972; Kott, 1966). In every case, however, the equation of complexity and artistic sophistication with balance entails a prior, usually implicit distribution of values that constitutes the spectrum necessary for discovering the balanced position (Ryan, 1982). In the variations on the balanced position, the extremes of the spectrum turn out to be the opposing claims of individual achievement or "greatness" on the one hand, and a diffuse, leveling collective will on the other. The balance point will always take the form of a class compromise usually endorsed only conditionally as a necessary evil. As with the civil privatism of interpretation of Coriolanus' character, balanced readings constitute a gesture of political renunciation. Since neither side is ever seen to embody a plenitude of social goodness, disengagement and critical appreciation of complexity "beyond ideology" are to be preferred to active participation in discursive will formation (Habermas, 1971, 1975).

In my opinion it is extremely difficult to foster and sustain an alternative political culture within the dispensation of diffuse mass loyalty and civil/vocational privatism (Habermas, 1975). And in the absence of an effectively organized alternative political culture it is difficult to see how to articulate an oppositional or subversive discourse in the elaboration of our cultural history. Simply to say "forbidden things" about Shakespeare or to connect his work to an ideologically subversive discourse remains bound up in the politically weak and practically insignificant corporate goal-values of pluralism unless the critique of tradition breaks out towards an active constituency (Erlich, 1986; Jameson, 1981; Mitchell, 1986; Ohmann, 1976; Rooney, 1986). Nevertheless, I think there is some real point in rearticulating the institution of Shakespeare as a strategic encounter with the hegemonic cultural order. But such a rearticulation must transgress the frame of the play itself, moving from specifically literary interpretation to a consideration of the effective history of the Shakespearean canon (see Cartelli in this volume). And it must, in addition, come to terms with the political and social foundations of critical scholarship by examining the terms of a "post-war settlement" of institutional claims.

Although a full account of such a postwar settlement is beyond the scope of an essay of this length, a brief sketch may suggest why critical scholarship is likely to result in legitimation rather than in practically effective critique. To begin with, the agencies of national publicity – newspapers, magazines, radio and television – are powerfully oriented toward legitimation rather than critique. Thus even a debacle like Watergate may be editorially processed so that it "proves that the system works." In the university, on the other hand, critique is permitted, but only insofar as it is mandated by the imperatives of pluralism. Marxist or socialist opposition to the existing sociocultural order is thus limited to the status of an "approach" or a "point of view"; such opposition must submit to the discipline of "objective revisionism" – in other words theory is not to be translated into a practical program (Erlich, 1986; Jameson, 1981). Universities thus remain depoliticized. The critical authority of scholarship has no direct bearing on the public sphere. Finally, the working-class movement, partly through self-policing, partly through statutory repression, renounces its own distinctive political goal-values in the form of a socialist alternative and confines its activities to struggling for a greater share in the North American standard of living. The weakening or depoliticizing of these large institutional structures has made the task of general ideological mobilization very much easier for the hegemonic sociocultural order. In the light of these massive constraints the prospect of rallying effective cultural opposition appears disheartening, to say the least. But it is only in an accurate appraisal of the tactical situation that a practically significant deployment of the possibilities of tradition can begin.

Works cited

Adelman, Janet (1978) "'Anger's My Meat': Feeding, Dependency, and Aggression in Coriolanus," *Shakespeare, Pattern of Excelling Nature*, ed. Bevington, David and Halio, Jay, Newark, University of Delaware Press.

Adorno, Theodor (1967) "Culture Criticism and Society," *Prisms: Cultural Criticism and Society*, trans. Samuel and Shierry Weber, London, Verso.

Anderson, Perry (1974a) *Lineages of the Absolutist State*, London, New Left Books.

—— (1974b) *Passages from Antiquity to Feudalism*, London, Verso.

Bakhtin, Mikhail (1968) *Rabelais and his World*, trans. Hélène Iswolsky, Cambridge, Mass., MIT Press.

—— (1981) *The Dialogic Imagination*, trans. Michael Holquist and Caryl Emerson, Austin, University of Texas Press.

Bennett, William (1985a) "Lost Generation: Why America's Children are Strangers in their Own Land," *Policy Review*, 33, 43–5.

—— (1985b) "To Reclaim a Legacy," *American Educator*, 21 (1), 1–4.

Berry, Ralph (1973) "Sexual Imagery in *Coriolanus*," *Studies in English Literature 1500–1900*, 13, 301–16.

Bradley, A.C. (1912) "*Coriolanus*: British Academy Lecture 1912," in *A Miscellany* (1929), London, Macmillan.

Braudel, Fernand (1977) *Afterthoughts on Material Civilization and Capitalism*, trans. Patricia Ranum, Baltimore, Johns Hopkins University Press.

—— (1981) *The Structure of Everyday Life: The Limits of the Possible*, trans. Sian Reynolds, New York, Harper & Row.

Bristol, Michael D. (1985) *Carnival and Theatre: Plebeian Culture and the Structure of Authority in Renaissance England*, London and New York, Methuen.

Brower, Reuben (ed.) (1966) *Coriolanus* by William Shakespeare, Signet edn, New York and Scarborough, Ontario, New American Library.

Burke, Kenneth (1966) "*Coriolanus* and the Delights of Faction," in Burke, Kenneth, *Language as Symbolic Action*, Berkeley, University of California Press.

Burke, Peter (1978) *Popular Culture in Early Modern Europe*, New York, New York University Press.

Cantor, Paul A. (1976) *Shakespeare's Rome: Republic and Empire*, Ithaca, NY, Cornell University Press.

Cavell, Stanley (1984) " 'Who Does the Wolf Love?' *Coriolanus* and the Interpretations of Politics," *Shakespeare and the Question of Theory*, ed. Patricia Parker and Geoffrey Hartman, London, Methuen.

Charney, Maurice (1963) *Shakespeare's Roman Plays*, Cambridge, Mass., Harvard University Press.

Danson, Lawrence K. (1973) "Metonymy and *Coriolanus*," *Philological Quarterly*, 52, 30–42.

Davis, Natalie Z. (1975) *Society and Culture in Early Modern France*, Stanford, Ca., Stanford University Press.

Dollimore, Jonathan (1984) *Radical Tragedy: Religion, Ideology, and Power in the Drama of Shakespeare and his Contemporaries*, Chicago, University of Chicago Press.

Dollimore, Jonathan and Sinfield, Alan (eds) (1985) *Political Shakespeare: New Essays in Cultural Materialism*, Manchester, Manchester University Press; Ithaca, NY, Cornell University Press.

Durkheim, Emile (1935) *The Division of Labor in Society*, New York, Free Press.

Erlich, Bruce (1978) "Structure, Inversion, and Game in Shakespeare's Classical World," *Shakespeare Survey*, 31, 53–63.

—— (1986) "Amphibolies: On the Critical Self-Contradictions of 'Pluralism'," *Critical Inquiry*, 12, 521–50.

Fiske, Edward B. (1985) "Reagan's Man for Education," *New York Times Magazine*, 22 December, 30–1, 56, 58–60, 63, 68.

Gadamer, Hans-Georg (1976) *Philosophical Hermeneutics*, Berkeley, University of California Press.

Giddens, Anthony (1977) *Studies in Social and Political Theory*, London, Hutchinson.

Gilbert, James Burkhart (1968) *Writers and Partisans: A History of Literary Radicalism in America*, New York, John Wiley.

Goldberg, Jonathan (1983) *James I and the Politics of Literature*, Baltimore, Johns Hopkins University Press.

Goldman, Michael (1972) *Shakespeare and the Energies of Drama*, Princeton, Princeton University Press.

Gramsci, Antonio (1957) "The Modern Prince: Essays on the Science of Politics in the Modern Age," in Gramsci, Antonio, *The Modern Prince and Other Writings*, trans. Louis Marks, New York, International Publishers.

Guenée, Bernard (1985) *States and Rulers in Later Medieval Europe*, trans. Juliet Vale, Oxford, Basil Blackwell.

Gurr, Andrew (1975) "*Coriolanus* and the Body Politic," *Shakespeare Survey*, 28, 63–9.

Habermas, Jürgen (1971) *Knowledge and Human Interests*, trans. Jeremy Shapiro, Boston, Beacon Press.

—— (1975) *Legitimation Crisis*, trans. Thomas McCarthy, Boston, Beacon Press.

—— (1979) "Legitimation Problems in the Modern State," in Habermas, Jürgen, *Communication and the Evolution of Society*, trans. Thomas McCarthy, Boston, Beacon Press.

—— (1985) "Neo-Conservative Culture Criticism in the United States and West Germany: An Intellectual Movement in Two Political Cultures," in Bernstein, Richard J. (ed.) *Habermas and Modernity*, Cambridge, Mass., MIT Press.

Hale, David G. (1968) "Intestine Sedition: The Fable of the Belly," *Comparative*

Literature Studies, 5, 377–87.

—— (1971) "*Coriolanus*: The Death of a Political Metaphor," *Shakespeare Quarterly*, 23, 197–202.

Harrison, J.F.C. (1984) *The Common People: A History from the Norman Conquest to the Present*, London, Flamingo.

Hawkes, Terence (1986) *That Shakespeherian Rag: Essays on a Critical Process*, London, Methuen.

Hjort, Anne Mette (1985) "The Conditions of Dialogue: Approaches to the Habermas–Gadamer Debate," *Eidos*, 4, 11–37.

Honig, Edwin (1951) "*Sejanus* and *Coriolanus*: A Study in Alienation," *Modern Language Quarterly*, 12, 407–21.

Ide, Richard (1980) *Possessed with Greatness: The Heroic Tragedies of Chapman and Shakespeare*, London, Scolar Press.

Jameson, Fredric (1981) *The Political Unconscious: Narrative as a Socially Symbolic Act*, Ithaca, NY, Cornell University Press.

Jorgensen, Paul A. (1956) *Shakespeare's Military World*, Berkeley, University of California Press.

Kott, Jan (1966) *Shakespeare Our Contemporary*, trans. Boleslaw Taborski, New York, Anchor Books.

La Capra, Dominick (1985) *Emile Durkheim: Sociologist and Philosopher*, Chicago, University of Chicago Press.

Lehman, Alan D. (1952) "The Coriolanus Story in Antiquity," *The Classical Journal*, 47 (8), 329–36.

Le Roy Ladurie, Emmanuel (1979) *Carnival in Romans*, trans. Mary Feeney, New York, G. Braziller.

MacCallum, M.W. (1967) *Shakespeare's Roman Plays, and their Background*, London, Macmillan.

McCanles, Michael (1967) "The Dialectic of Transcendence in *Coriolanus*," *Publications of the Modern Language Association*, 82, 44–53.

McCarthy, Thomas (1978) *The Critical Theory of Jürgen Habermas*, Cambridge, Mass., MIT Press.

MacLure, Millar (1955) "Shakespeare and the Lonely Dragon," *University of Toronto Quarterly*, 24, 109–19.

Marx, Karl (1973) *Grundrisse: Introduction to the Critique of Political Economy*, trans. Martin Nicolaus, New York, Vintage Books; Harmondsworth, Penguin.

Mitchell, W.J.T. (1986) "Pluralism as Dogmatism," *Critical Inquiry*, 12, 494–503.

Muir, Kenneth (1952) "Menenius' Fable," *Notes & Queries*, 198, 240–2.

Nicolet, C. (1980) *The World of the Citizen in Republican Rome*, trans. P.S. Falla, Berkeley, University of California Press.

Ohmann, Richard (1976) *English in America: A Radical View of the Profession*, New York, Oxford University Press.

Paster, Gail Kern (1981) "To Starve with Feeding: The City in *Coriolanus*," *Shakespeare Studies*, 11, 135–43.

Pettet, E.C. (1950) "*Coriolanus* and the Midlands Insurrection of 1607," *Shakespeare Survey*, 3, 34–42.

Phillips, James Emerson (1940) *The State in Shakespeare's Greek and Roman Plays*, New York, Columbia University Press.

Poggi, Gianfranco (1972) *Images of Society: Essays on the Sociological Theories of Tocqueville, Marx, and Durkheim*, Stanford, Stanford University Press.

—— (1978) *The Development of the Modern State: A Sociological Introduction*, Stanford, Stanford University Press.

Rabkin, Norman (1967) *Shakespeare and the Common Understanding*, New York, Free Press.

Richard, Jean Claude (1978) *Les Origines de la plèbe romaine: Essai sur la formation du dualisme patricio-plébéien*, Rome, Ecole Française de Rome.

Rooney, Ellen (1986) "Who's left out? A rose by any other name is still red; or, The Politics of Pluralism," *Critical Inquiry*, 12, 550–64.

Rossiter, A.P. (1961) *Angel With Horns*, ed. Graham Storey, London, Longmans, Green.

Ryan, Michael (1982) *Marxism and Deconstruction: A Critical Articulation*, Baltimore, Johns Hopkins University Press.

Schmitt, Carl (1976) *The Concept of the Political*, trans. George Schwab, New Brunswick, Rutgers University Press.

Scullard, H.H. (1935) *A History of the Roman World From 753 to 146 B.C.*, London, Methuen.

Sharp, Buchanan (1980) *In Contempt of All Authority: Rural Artisans and Riots in the West of England, 1586–1660*, Berkeley, University of California Press.

Sicherman, Carol (1972) "*Coriolanus*: The Failure of Words," *English Literary History*, 39, 189–207.

Simmons, J.L. (1973) *Shakespeare's Pagan World: The Roman Tragedies*, Charlottesville, University Press of Virginia.

Stallybrass, Peter and White, Allon (1986) *The Politics and Poetics of Transgression*, London, Methuen.

Stone, Lawrence (1972) *The Causes of the English Revolution: 1529–1642*, New York, Harper & Row.

Strayer, Joseph R. (1970) *On the Medieval Origins of the Modern State*, Princeton, Princeton University Press.

Styan, J.L. (1967) *Shakespeare's Stagecraft*, London, Cambridge University Press.

Suvin, Darko (1980) "Brecht's *Coriolan*, or Stalinism Retracted: The City, the Hero, the City that does not need a Hero," *Fiction and Drama in Eastern and Southeastern Europe*, Columbus, Slavica.

Taylor, John (1630) *Iacke a Lente*, London, facsimile edn, in *The Works of John Taylor, The Water Poet*, ed. Charles Hindley (1872), London, Reeves & Turner.

Thompson, E.P. (1968) *The Making of the English Working Class*, Harmondsworth, Penguin.

—— (1974) "Patrician Society, Plebeian Culture," *Journal of Social History*, 7, 382–405.

Treggiari, Susan (1969) *Roman Freedmen During the Late Republic*, Oxford, Clarendon Press.

Wallerstein, Immanuel (1974) *The Modern World System: Capitalist Agriculture and the Origins of the European World Economy in the Sixteenth Century*, New York, Academic Press.

Walzer, Michael (1976) *The Revolution of the Saints: A Study in the Origins of Radical Politics*, New York, Atheneum.

Weber, Max (1947) *The Theory of Social and Economic Organization*, trans. E.M. Henderson and Talcott Parsons, ed. Talcott Parsons (1964), New York, Free Press.

Wolf, Eric R. (1982) *Europe and the People without History*, Berkeley, University of California Press.

Yavetz, Z. (1969) *Plebs and Princeps*, Oxford, Clarendon Press.

Zeeveld, Gordon W. (1962) "*Coriolanus* and Jacobean Politics," *Modern Language Review*, 57, 321–34.

10

The failure of orthodoxy in *Coriolanus*

Thomas Sorge

The use of analogies is characteristic of various sixteenth-century discourses, providing for a proliferation of the conjunctions *as* and *like*. The compilation of commonplaces in Francis Meres' *Palladis Tamia*, for example, in which similes abound, points towards both a long tradition of analogic, pre-Cartesian thought inherent in corporative societies and its unprecedented plenitude and omni-presence in Elizabethan culture. It is as if a given idea, observation, or tenet could not rest convincingly on its own feet, as if solitary signifiers were suspected of being unable properly to carry the weight of the argument or thought without the support of a plethora of analogies that later ages might consider redundant. There seems to have been only a brittle divide between the confident assertion of a universal wholeness into which the individual view fitted neatly and the self-conscious conjuring up of a totality of correspondences without which the case in point might appear untenable. This was especially true at a time when organicist thinking, though rarely openly challenged, was becom-ing so seriously undermined that analogies, by definition not quite congruent with what they refer to, could not infrequently produce a superfluity of meaning which influenced the original set of ideas or purposefully served as a stratagem in narrative discourse. Francis Meres, while quite innocent of having made use of the latter possibility, in his eagerness to assemble as many quotations as he could, as well as some observations of his own, under one *locus communis* invited (perhaps unwittingly) a heightened sense of discernment in his readers by offering them some strange, even contradictory examples. Thus, under the

THOMAS SORGE is Lecturer in English Literature at Humboldt University, Berlin (GDR). He has published articles on *Hamlet, Julius Caesar, Coriolanus, The Merchant of Venice*, and *Henry V* in *Shakespeare Jahrbuch*, all of them enquiries into political and ideological issues of Shakespeare's time. Sorge's current work is on the dominant concept of the 'common weal' as it is transformed in dramatic art.

heading of *Matrimoniall Society*(!), the wife's obedience is emphasised by the
following analogy:

> The Viper being the deadliest of all serpentes, desireth to engender with the
> Sea Lamprey, & by hissing doth bring ye Lamprey out of the vast ocean, &
> so the Lamprey engendereth with ye poysonfull viper; so a wife must beare
> with her husbande, though he be rough and cruell. . . . Hee doth strike thee,
> thou must beare him: he is thy husband; he is a drunkard, but he is ioyned
> by nature unto thee. He is fierce and implacable, but he is thy member, and
> the most excellent of all thy members. But as the Viper doth vomite out his
> poyson for the reverence of engendering: so a husband must put awaie all
> fierceness, roughnes, cruelty, and bitternes towardes his wife for the
> reverence of union.
>
> (Meres, 1598, 132–3)

As can be seen, the moral of these lines becomes ambivalent by the very simile
that is devised to support it: the irreconcilability of harmony of affection with
the concept of patriarchal domination and violence (Sinfield, 1983) is
reproduced in the contradiction between vehicle and tenor. Similarly, in another
passage, the state of a 'drunkard', with the conventional pejorative connotation,
seems to take on a positive implication when applied by Meres as follows:

> As wine doth first serve and obey the drinker, but by little and little mixing
> it selfe with the bloud in the veynes, dooth rule over the drinker, and makes
> him a drunkerd: so he that comes to the government of a Common-wealth,
> at the first applieth himselfe to the humours of the people, but afterwardes hee
> draweth them to his purpose, and makes them his subjects and vassals.
>
> (Meres, 1598, 226)

Obedience, elsewhere achieved through sobriety and reason, can here be interpreted as a consequence of vice. Equally treacherous – in respect of the intended
message – must have been, for example, Henry Smith's comparison of wife and
husband, 'partners, like two oares in a boate', when the wife is in the same
breath likened to an 'under-officer in [her husband's] common-weale' (Smith,
1597, 30).

Of course, the ideological inconsistency unveiled by calling attention to these
discrepancies may seem barely perceptible or perhaps innocuous. Let us
therefore look at analogies which effectively amplify (in the sense of
Renaissance rhetoric) and reinforce major tenets of Renaissance political
thought. The simile of corporate, prebourgeois society which compares the
human body and the body politic is probably the most common and widespread
such analogy in the sixteenth century (Hale, 1971b). Although it had been
frequently used for a variety of political purposes, the body analogy predominantly served as a privileged signifier to support hierarchies favouring rulers and
those groups and classes benefiting from an immobile, rigidly stratified social
structure (Allen, 1957). This had been true from the time of Plato and is
especially true for the Elizabethan and Jacobean period in England. To be sure,

discussions about changes in the body politic and alternative views of the same did not just disappear under the pressure of such powerful means of indoctrination as the *Exhortation concerning Good Order and Obedience to Rulers and Magistrates*, which declared that it was 'God's ordinance, God's commandment, and God's holy will, that the whole body of every realm, and all members and parts of the same, shall be subject to their head, the king' (*Certain Sermons* . . ., 1908, 121). On the contrary, the ever increasing volume of Tudor and Stuart propaganda can be seen as an effort to counter the advent and dispersal of new models of state organization arising out of the interest in Greek and Roman history, or to quell the spread of Calvinist, Huguenot, and monarchomachist writings (Talbert, 1962, 39) which despite differing and often (for the situation in England) irrelevant political objectives, carried potentially subversive implications. The Tudor administration thus embarked on the difficult task of monopolizing the persuasiveness of body imagery in a sociopolitical environment in which the most divergent forces extensively employed this analogy; and the very fact that the organic simile served the call for obedience to the otherwise not very compatible governments of Edward, Mary, and Elizabeth did not make this task easier to achieve. The analogy certainly had not yet lost its appeal, but it became increasingly available to a host of social groups that tried to claim it as their own signifier. As the anthropomorphic perception of nature and society essentially belonged to prefeudal and feudalistic formations (Barkan, 1975), the waning of the original breeding ground of the analogy led to its involvement in a variety of new but ultimately alien contexts and uses. Thus, the repetition of corporeal analogies does not indicate their easy applicability to the enforcement of Tudor discipline: rather, the repetition suggests that the government's specific – and I would add 'specious' – interpretation of such imagery could hold sway only as long as it was noisily reiterated. There is a tension between the material and the end to which it is used, a superfluity of meaning that constantly threatens to contradict the overall project of law and order it is supposed to support. The uneasy relationship of the body image to the absolutist aim of domination and subjection provides a good example of how Tudor ideology was both temporarily victorious and ultimately self-defeating.

A proposition like this of course immediately raises the question why the body analogy had become so privileged a signifier in Tudor thought if it was so inherently self-contradictory. Finding support in Terry Eagleton's contention that 'the problem of class hegemony can only be resolved if we recognize that any dominant ideology incorporates within itself (*not without ceaseless struggle*) the codes and forms whereby subordinate classes "practice" their relations to the social formation as a whole' (Eagleton, 1980, 152, emphasis added), I would answer that the concept of a both rigidly stratified and interdependent community, the idea of an interplay of separate corporations within an organic, body-like system which confirmed the autonomy of the separate entity at the same time as it expressed its socioeconomic nexus, strongly appealed to members of different social standing at the very moment the underlying structures were in decay. The fears induced by unprecedented social change and

mobility helped the wide acceptance of an image of harmony which in reality
enforced the power of the crown, the magistrates, and even of such relatively
modern institutions as the Merchants Adventurer.[1]

But what made the analogy of the human body to the political organization of
England even more effective was its roots in medieval communal ritual and its
connection with 'the age-old communal spirit of the country village and . . . the
related tradition of Christian communism' (Ferguson, 1965, 369). Although its
referential quality as a representation dates back to ancient Rome and Greece,
the *experience* of social life as corporeal, as a lived reality, can still be traced
alongside the emergence of such inherently corporative thought as can be found
in, for example, Augustine, Boethius, Aquinas, John of Salisbury. While the
medieval church and secular rulers expounded corporative theory, the life
rhythm of self-contained village communities (still very much sealed off against
outside influences) *was* in fact still very much an organic one. The universalism
of the Middle Ages implied particularism as its necessary counterpart, thus
incorporating its components only superficially, without for a long time
seriously affecting their interior constitutions. 'Communal property . . . [as] an
old Teutonic institution which lived on under the cover of feudalism' (Marx,
1867 [1976, 885]) provided for the basis of a community life of which the main
feature was not stress on hierarchy and the dominance of certain members of
this social body but mutuality, interdependence, and unity of aims. As the usual
life rhythm embodied these values, there was no vital need to encode them in
a special representational system of signifiers set over against the 'real' life
process. The anthropomorphic character of primitive societies (Eliade, 1961) in
which rituals and symbols form an important part of everyday activity, rather
than a reflection of it, can serve to illuminate the nature of much of town and
village life up to the Tudor period. Of course we have to take account of the
relatively advanced economy of medieval England which hardly permitted
unadulterated communal rituals. But the coexistence of representational and
ritual modes in even a moderately developed medieval town such as Bristol
shows clearly the link between popular communal interests and the latter mode:

> In ritual and festival the body politic appeared as a world of reciprocal
> relations – of harmonies and correspondence – not of absolutes. For taken
> together, events like St. Clement's and St. Katherine's emphasized the social
> limitation on authority, not the sovereignty of those who exercised it.
>
> (Sacks, 1986, 155)

Similar remnants and echoes of the anthropomorphic quality of communal life
are preserved, for instance, in the Corpus Christi celebrations (James, 1983;
Kinser, 1986), although the ostentatiousness and sophistication of ritual display,
as well as the advanced economy of late medieval towns in England, pointed
towards a representation of wholeness which no longer existed outside the
festivities and processions. The formation of town elites, the exclusion of seg-
ments of the population from the ceremonies, the growing imposition of order
and the consequent advent of the Lords of Misrule and other kinds of inversion

(Phythian-Adams, 1972) marked the waning of what Lotman calls the symbolic sign system and the simultaneous increase of analogic use of body imagery (Lotman, 1981; Barkan, 1975). But just as the Elizabethan platform stage and its popular drama were far from being completely representational (Weimann, 1978), neither, to a large extent, was popular consciousness (Thomas, 1971). Thus the manipulative effect of body imagery in Tudor propaganda was considerably enhanced by residual ritualistic connotations that tended to evoke a communal wholeness and include the addressee in an organic social fabric which no longer existed in reality. In sum, then, organic imagery was retained in dominant political discourse of the sixteenth century not only because it belonged to the inventory of a 'theoretical apparatus inherited from an earlier era' with which 'men of insight' necessarily had to work (Ferguson, 1959, 175), nor only because it mirrored the historic settlement between crown and middle class in the sixteenth century. It was also, perhaps primarily, retained because of the aforementioned specific aura and popular appeal which rendered it exceptionally useful as a rhetorical device in official propaganda.

The corporeal analogy gestured towards something which was, however, at the same time denied by the pragmatic use of that analogy for the self-preservation of the dominant social hierarchy. Precisely because of this tension, the foregrounding of which could not be avoided, the ruling ideological efforts constantly ran the risk of inviting unwelcome discussion and erosion of the historical conjuncture with the orthodox signified. Besides Henry VIII, James I, and their many major and minor mouthpieces, other forces, groups, and individuals of different persuasions made use of this metaphor for their purposes. It thus became evident that its referential employment more often than not entailed distortions and ambiguities that sometimes even threatened to explode its coherence. The incisive, almost accusing, tone of *A Supplication of the Poore Commons* belies the alleged inferiority of the members to the kingly head:

> *Remembre* that your office is to defende the innocent & to punysh the oppressor. . . . *Contrariwyse*, if you suffre his pore membres to be thus oppressed, loke for none other then the ryghtefull judgment of God. . . . *Indanger not your solle* by the sufferyng of us. . . . *Let us be* unto your Highnes, as the inferior membres of the bodye to their head.
>
> (*A Supplication* . . ., 1546 [1871, 81], emphasis added)

Clearly, the supplicants' demand described a situation which did not fit the organic simile, and they consequently hastened to prevent Henry from understanding the implications only too well: 'We speake not this because we thinke by this, that we may rebel against you, our naturall Prince' (p. 83). And Edward Forset, anxious to please the new Stuart regime, embarrassingly brands the commonwealth of Elizabeth a monstrosity because 'Brittannia one body needing but one head' obviously had one head too many before James's accession (Forset, 1606, 58). Writing under the pseudonym 'R. Doleman' (1594), the Jesuit Robert Parsons claimed that 'as the whole body is of more authority then the only head, and may cure the head if it be out of tune, so may the weal-publique cure or cutt of their heades, if they infect the rest' – an interpretation which actually renders the simile absurd and inapplicable so that its author is forced to provide an explanation to bridge the divergence:

> seeing that a body civil may have divers heades, by succession, and is not bound ever to one, as a body natural is, which body natural, if it had the same ability that when it had an aking or sickly head it could cut it of and take an other, I doubt not, but it would so do.

> ('Doleman', 1594, 38)

Another good example is found in John Ponet's *Short Treatise of Politique Power* (1556), which postulates that 'Commonwealths and realmes may live, whan the head is cut of, and may put on a newe head, that is, make them a newe governour' (Ponet, 1556, D7ʳ·), while further on in the treatise the analogic confusion is complete: 'If our eie, foote, or hande offende us, let it be taken from the rest of the bodi. . . . By . . . eie, foote and hande, is understanden the headdes and rulers, and not the other membres and subjectes' (Ponet, 1556, sig. G4ᵛ·–5).

The non-hierarchical dimension of the body imagery surfaced throughout the sixteenth century, but it was often contained by texts and contexts that tried to diminish its influence on the consciousness of the addressee. First, antimonar-chical and anti-Tudor literature from abroad, in which the well-being of the body politic was argued to be dependent on the dismissal of the doctrine of civil obedience, etc., could be rather effectively suppressed by stigmatizing such texts as the work of foreign and religiously deviant enemies of the English nation. Second, certain petitions and treatises blaming the rulers and the rich for the plight of the people and reminding the head of its responsibility for the body – such as Thomas Starkey's *Dialogue* or Robert Crowley's *Informacion and Petition*[2] – were not meant to reach the ears of the multitude. Sir Thomas Smith's *Discourse of the Common weal*, a singularly pragmatic and clear-sighted analysis written in 1549 (but not published until 1581), was meant to be read solely by Cecil (Smith [ed. Dewar, 1969, xxiv, 12–13]). The mere capacity of the subordinate classes to reason about matters of government, their ability to compare and evaluate (even if they did not thereby reject the doctrine of obedience), was considered dangerous:

> what a perilous thing were it to commit unto the subjects the judgment, which prince is wise and godly and his government good, and which is otherwise; as though the foot must judge of the head; an enterprise very heinous, and must needs breed rebellion.

> (*Certain Sermons* . . ., 1908, 593)

It was one thing to say in Parliament that the impoverished 'weak feet' were oppressed by the rich and 'too heavy body' in order to make reluctant MPs see that it was to their advantage and security if they assented to an increase in poor relief, but it was quite another matter to make the lower classes aware of their power in the body politic, 'for if the feet knew their strength as we know their oppression, they would not bear as they do' (D'Ewes, 1682, 490). The organic analogy is here, in fact, cynically used to perpetuate the degradation of the poor although the Menenius-like speaker temporarily demands more succour for them. Third, even if the wider public was informed that the disease of a social body might very well originate in a tyrannical head or in other privileged members, closure was achieved, nevertheless, by embedding the argument in religious discourse through which the responsibility for oppression, poverty, and tyranny was laid upon the conscience of the individual. Here Crowley's *Way to Wealth* (1550) provides a notable example: the sermon first introduces the complaint of a 'poore man' about 'idle bealies' that will devour 'al that we shal get by our sore labour' and ruin the commonwealth, a state of affairs for which he is amply pitied by Crowley, but the final verdict – 'thi sinnes have deserved this oppression' – undermines any subversive consequences that might arise from the initial analysis (Crowley, 1872, 133, 138).[3] Ideological closure of the multidimensional body analogy was more difficult to contrive, however, in drama or in protodramatic dialogic writings. Thus in William Averall's *A Mervailous Combat of Contrarieties* (1588), the Tongue, endowed with the attractiveness of the Vice convention, succeeds in rallying Hande and Foote against their oppressors, Belly and Backe. Tongue's striking arguments, revealing a deep disharmony in the body, are rendered even more persuasive by the infighting between Belly and Backe who accuse each other of the very misdemeanours Tongue mentions. At last, Tongue is very unconvincingly branded as a traitorous troublemaker and labelled the only obstacle for Belly's being 'by nature a friend unto' the members. As she – of course Tongue must not be masculine – cannot be beaten by arguments, Averall simply reduces her to silence in order to achieve eventually the outward harmony of members necessary to defend the realm against Spain. The subsequent 'Application, briefly declaring the Summe of this Dialogue' fits uneasily with the rather inconclusive meaning of the dialogue itself and does not dispel the reader's impression that there are serious disturbances within the body politic only superficially covered up by the appeal for unity against the outside threat.

The ample, almost excessive use of organic imagery for the most diverse political interests (Hale, 1971b; Talbert, 1962; Allen, 1957), occasions, and events strongly contributed – despite persistent propagandistic efforts – to the erosion of the seeming 'naturalness' of ruling-class uses of that imagery; and so the gap between ritualistic connotations and pragmatic referential use was widened further still.[4] The simile of human body and body politic thus, on one level, could be regarded as a commonplace in the sense that it was a battleground where competing interests fought for the supremacy of the particular meaning they gave to the simile. Tudor and Jacobean propaganda might seem to hold considerable sway in so far as the government was best able to sustain high-volume battle cries, but knowledge of terrain often proved more effective than noise. Given the ritualistic, communal dimension of the social body, attempts to claim the analogy in favour of order and discipline against the interests of the

community (which was, after all, largely made up of the subordinate classes)
turned out to be a questionable enterprise in the long run. The 'concern with
conflicting aspects of certain ideas, with the conflicting relevance of certain
commonplaces, and with the conflicting interpretation of events' (Talbert, 1962,
145) is characteristic, for example, of Samuel Daniel's art; and the subversive
potential of politically accentuated plays – even if they presented the issues from
different perspectives without providing subversive solutions – is verified by,
among other things, Fulke Greville's preference for closet drama over plays for
the popular theatres, in which the social composition of the audience entailed
political risks (Norbrook, 1984, 169).

*

Shakespeare's *Coriolanus* not only ran these risks but was designed to generate
them. Although much criticism has made Coriolanus the sole focus of its
concerns (for a critique of such criticism, see Bristol in this volume), the play
is not organized solely around a central character. Its structure is incapable of
ensuring the highest tragic effect at the moment of the fall of the hero. Its
concern with the clash of political forces, rather than the exploration of
characters, corresponds with its topical sociopolitical context, the Midlands
rising of 1607–8 (Pettet, 1950). Like *Julius Caesar*, it presents three models of
government – the rule of one, the rule of the few, the rule of the many – to be
evaluated by the audience, and by offering a choice of models, it potentially
challenges authority's representation of monarchy as the only form of rule
beneficial for England.

But the play does more than confront the audience with different political
structures; after all, the figures who speak for aristocracy and democracy in
Coriolanus do not directly give sufficient information about the real social fabric
of and the priority of interests within these forms of government: what is at stake
in Rome (as in England) is not *primarily* a certain political form but the much
more important issue of the fabric of social relationships. The body analogy, for
that matter, with its potential to show various interplays of different members,
is very well-suited to serve as the focus of a demonstration of how the inhabitants
of Rome conduct their affairs among one other. In response to D.G. Hale's view
that 'the analogy itself fails' because (the purpose of playing allegedly being to
hold a mirror up to nature) 'the nature reflected in the glass of *Coriolanus* is not
ordered and structured, with the members functioning for the well-being of the
whole body' (Hale, 1971a, 201), I would maintain that the failure of the analogy
is less an index to the inadequacy of the body image for mirroring the real
political situation than an occasion of audience insight into the way different
forces in the drama apply the body image for their own objectives. The analogy
is first and foremost a rhetorical figure by means of which particular interests
are pursued, no matter whether reality is thereby reflected accurately or
otherwise.

A suitable starting point to substantiate this view is Maurice Charney's observation that when 'Coriolanus does use figures of speech, he inclines to similes rather than metaphors'. This, I would add, is characteristic not only for Coriolanus but for the whole play; and as similes 'do not suggest new areas of meaning, but give points already stated an added force and vividness' (Charney, 1970, 75), there is reason to assume that the linguistic structure of the play lends itself to reinforcements of the protagonists' already stated and all too well-known positions. The language of the play does not explore, it underpins the arguments of the conflicting sides. Sometimes signifiers even become meaningless or unimportant: Coriolanus' tirades against the people, for instance, are noteworthy because of their 'expletive force' – it is as though he feels secure in his posture and claims as long as he foams and rails at his opponents. Menenius, a populist, and equally verbose, is also shown to be capable of ranting when he wishes, especially when things do not work in his favour, as they do not in I. i. 158 ff. ('Thou rascal, that art worst in blood to run').[5] His fable of the belly is the most obvious rhetorical ploy to make the citizens see the way the patricians would like them to see. Again, there is nothing new for the audience and for the citizens about the fable's narrative or intent: Menenius himself says that they may 'have heard it, / But since it serves my purpose[!], I will venture / To stale't a little more' (I. i. 89–91); he decides to tell this story because the citizens had so far refused to agree that the patricians cared for them 'like fathers' (I. i. 76). Thus, the general knowledge of what he is going to narrate and thereby amplify is the precondition for how it is subsequently received: the dramatic structure of this scene serves to make the Elizabethan audience become aware of how the Roman citizens see through the representations of their superiors, of how the rhetorical arsenal of the rulers is no longer effective in manipulating the subordinate classes. And with the fable of the belly as its centre, the first scene anticipates in the fable's futile repetitiveness the desperate and fruitless attempts of the patricians to turn their strongest man, Coriolanus, into an acceptable representation throughout the whole play.

Menenius' story can quite correctly be termed, as Stanley Cavell terms it, 'a sort of play-within-a-play', but not one which makes the people 'halt moment-arily, . . . turn aside from their more practical or pressing concerns' (Cavell, 1983, 15). It is, rather, a very deliberate and politically important attendance on Menenius' performance in order to free themselves from the representations of the rulers by testing the validity of these representations. In fact, the encounter with Menenius is not the citizens' first halt in the development of the whole scene; the opening of the play shows them on their way to secure their interests 'with staves, clubs, and other weapons' (stage direction before I. i.), but already the first line marks a suspension of this movement: 'Before we proceed any further, hear me speak' (I. i. 1). The following discussion efficiently introduces the audience to the conflict as seen from the plebeians' perspective and is meant to show both their resolve and their deliberation; 'hunger for bread' is the motive, not 'thirst for revenge' (I. i. 23, 24) and even 'the services' of Cajus Marcius are fairly considered (31–45). Clearly, this is not a mindless, demoralized rabble. And what is already noticeable is the capacity of the First Citizen to puncture the self-assured epithets of the patricians:

> *Second Citizen*: One word, good citizens.
> *First Citizen*:   We are accounted poor citizens, the patricians good.
>
> (I. i. 13–15)

The ensuing depiction of the patricians' covetousness calls their goodness sufficiently into question.

While the first halt reveals the motives of the mutiny, the second stop of the plebeians starts with their friendly readiness to talk to Menenius, who is seen as 'one honest enough' (I. i. 52). Again, they stress the causes of their unrest (I. i. 78–85), which are even more creditable because of their concurrence with widespread contemporary complaints about usury and engrossing. As these arguments clearly refute Menenius' claim that the oligarchy 'care for you like fathers' (I. i. 76), and as he equally clearly does not want to confirm the accusations, he decides to tell the citizens a tale, which in a veiled form does nothing but repeat his former allegiations that the patricians have 'most charitable care' (I. i. 64). But in order to make his fable an obvious parallel to the situation in Rome, he starts his tale with an account of the complaints of the members against the belly. Unfortunately, this harbours an opportunity for the citizens to identify with the content of the account and is likely to endanger the intended impact of the belly's answer. Indeed, the attitude of the First Citizen ('Well, sir, what answer made the belly?'; 'Your belly's answer – what?', I. i. 105, 113) is not that of a child eager to know the end of a table but of someone convinced that the arguments put forth by the members are difficult to defeat: 'What *could* the belly answer?' (I. i. 123, emphasis added).[6] Menenius gives the answer only about forty lines later. It seems as if he realizes after the First Citizen's first question (I. i. 105) that the plebeians are not yet in the mood to be taken in by the belly's moral and that humorous deviations are needed (like imitating the belching of the belly) to make them more amenable. But however unstable the citizens' opinions later appear to be, they here cannot be swayed by listening to Menenius ('You must not think to fob off our disgrace with a tale'; I. i. 92–3). His attempts to crack jokes, which reveal a great deal of uncertainty in the face of his audience's imperviousness, are cut short by the First Citizen, who, while his language changes from prose to verse, then takes the initiative ('this fellow speaks'; I. i. 119) and mockingly parades some of the conventional similes that were part of the conventional law-and-order rhetoric (king / head, counsellor / heart, arm / soldier; I. i. 114–18). Suddenly the roles have been reversed; Menenius is now the listener and asks questions while the First Citizen seems to be perfectly capable of continuing the narrative. The effortless reversal of narrator and listener underscores the impression that the fable is known to belong to the patricians' arsenal of propaganda, and the First Citizen's final question ('How apply you this?'; I. i. 146) again does not reveal an eagerness to know the moral of the story but suggests an understanding of the essential incompatibility of the intended moral and the reality of Rome. Moreover, a second look at the way the First Citizen parades the conventional rhetoric of the fable's underlying analogy shows how he turns the tale in the plebeians' favour by stressing that the different members are after all oppressed 'by the cormorant belly' (I. i. 120) – a move which forces Menenius both to interrupt him and to beg for more time and 'Patience awhile' (I. i. 125) before he can tell them the belly's already well-known answer. And it is no surprise that the answer eventually comes as an unsatisfactory anticlimax (*'First Citizen*: It was an answer'; I. i. 146) which needs further comment as well as the exhortation of the plebeians to 'digest things rightly / Touching the weal o'th'common' (I. i. 149–50). But here the chosen verb ('digest') is most ambiguous because it carries the above-mentioned role reversal between Menenius and the First Citizen over into the former's language: for a moment the plebeians themselves can be associated with the digesting belly. Thus, Menenius' tale proves full of pitfalls, and in dismantling its manipulative representation, the citizens have gained a first victory, which partly explains why Menenius loses his composure.[7]

That Menenius has used histrionic skills to present himself as a populist is made more obvious by his later, Coriolanus-like outbursts of anger (e.g. I. i. 156–62;[8] IV. vi. 96–9) and by his sober and grave appearance among the other patricians (e.g. II. ii.). By contrast, Cajus Marcius proves absolutely incapable of presenting himself to the people as an acceptable ruler. In a critical situation when conventional means of manipulation fail to achieve their intended effect, the patricians fail to produce a creditable leader. And, what is worse, in foregrounding his contempt of the people, Coriolanus assumes a subversive stature because he exposes the nature of the ruling oligarchy by rendering their more conciliatory façade transparent. Not unlike Petruchio in *The Taming of the Shrew*, who makes a mockery of the conventions of the wedding ceremony and embarrasses the rich burghers of Padua by rejecting the solemn ritual that usually conceals their money matches (III. ii.), Coriolanus rejects any representation of himself that is more palatable to the multitude and therefore indispensable for the maintenance of oligarchic rule: his 'heart's his mouth' (III. i. 255) – that is exactly what is wrong with him from the patricians' point of view (and, for that matter, an unobtrusive comment on the disarray in his body, too).

Coriolanus fails to see the essentially ritualistic connotations of the people's demand that he show them the wounds on his body and put on humble garments to demonstrate that he is, after all, part of the social body of Rome. He construes the request as nothing but an encroachment upon his privacy and temporary employment of alien signifiers – in short, as a contemptibly histrionic 'part / That I shall blush in acting' (II. ii. 144–5). Coriolanus will be nothing but Coriolanus, but his disdain of acting at the same time implies that he ascribes to words a remarkable importance: 'In III. i. . . . Coriolanus seizes upon the humble "shall" as if it were a menacing entity . . . he is "fleeing from words" . . . rather than realities' (Charney, 1970, 78); or words, we might say, are literal realities for him and mostly regarded as hostile unless they originate from his own mouth. The uttering of alien words and the performing of a part (III. ii. 109) for him mean adopting a 'harlot's spirit' (III. ii. 112), and he fears that this may infect his mind so that it will remain corrupted ever after: 'And by my body's action teach my mind / A most inherent baseness' (III. ii. 122–3). For Coriolanus, playing a part has strongly feminine and harlot-like (and thus revolting) overtones (he 'blushes in acting'); even in his adolescence when he might have been allowed to 'act the woman in the scene' (II. ii. 96) without dishonour, he manfully lived up to his designation. There is a strange literalness which drives him to fashion himself after what he is called – a man, a warrior, his mother's son, a boy. This collapsing of the signified into the signifier can be found in contemporary literature, for example, in Henry Smith's sermon 'A Preparative to Marriage', which likewise employs the analogy of the stage actor in a pejorative sense:

> Likewise the woman may learne her duties of her names. They are called goodwives, as goodwife A and goodwife B. Every wife is called a good wife, therefore if they be not good wives, their names doe belie them, and they are not worth their titles, but answere to a wrong name, as players doe upon a stage.
>
> (Smith, 1597, 33)

In the same way, Coriolanus feels compelled to behave according to his name and sex; while his wife stays at home, he roams about abroad, while she is tender and silent, he is harsh and noisy.

> God hath made the man to travell abroad, and the woman to keep home: & so their nature, and their wit, and their strength, are fitted accordingly; for the mans pleasure is most abroad, and the womans within. . . . As it becommeth her to keepe home, so it becommeth her to keepe silence, and alway speake the best of her head . . . sometimes she must observe the servants lesson, *Not answering againe*, and holde her peace, to keepe the peace . . . silence oftentimes doth keep the peace, when words would break it.
>
> (Smith, 1597, 27, 35, 36)

Accordingly, Virgilia – the 'gracious silence' – is reprimanded because she does not 'rejoice in that absence wherein he won honour' (I. iii. 3–4), and she is almost as thoroughly silenced as her husband wants the people to be. Coriolanus, however, again goes to extremes that are subversive because they render absurd the division of roles between husband and wife. While he seems to have very little in common with Virgilia and certainly hardly anything to say to her, his relationship to Cominius reveals a strong emotional dimension:

> Oh! let me clip ye
> In arms as sound as when I woo'd; in heart
> As merry as when our nuptial day was done
> And tapers burn'd to bedward.
>
> (I. vi. 29–32)

His behaviour towards Aufidius shows an even stronger confusion of the qualities of lover, warrior, and enemy, resulting in the end in a love match, as it were, with the enemy and against his family as part of Rome. The conventionally different spheres of life of the sexes, as prescribed in Smith's *Preparative*, have been moved so wide apart as to become hostile to each other, thus foregrounding the dilemma of their original division.

A similar development could be argued for in connection with the citizens and Coriolanus whose final, desperate attempt to reduce them to silence means making war against them.[9] But Coriolanus has overstrained himself. His decline begins after he ostentatiously banishes Rome. To get to Aufidius he has to put on a disguise – the very humble clothing he was loath to wear in Rome, and his dialogue with Aufidius' servants in IV. v. is conducted on an equal footing, which was formerly unbearable to him; at last he must consciously become an actor. And it is he who at the end of the play is reduced to a womanly silence by Volumnia, who had fashioned him and may consequently dismantle her creation so that he forgets his part like a 'dull actor' (V. iii. 40) and eventually, as the stage direction indicates, 'holds her by the hand silent' (V. iii. 183).

Coriolanus is a play in which an oligarchy tries to make the central character act in its and his own interests but sees him finally, after a prolonged reluctance to act at all, act against them. Analogous with this failure of their most renowned representative to make himself palatable to the people is the failure of the fable of the belly to serve as a rhetorical means capable of contributing to persuade the people to remain obedient. But the play is also about the emergence of a new, fairly self-contained social body that finds its centre in the citizens. While the body analogy as a means of manipulation in favour of the ruling class loses influence, its hidden ritualistic history of communal harmony (i.e. not the biased representation of the Tudor concept of harmony as it was idealized by Tillyard) comes to the fore and provides a basis on which a competing body ('*Coriolanus*: two authorities are up'; III. i. 108) with its own 'mouths' and 'hands' (III. i. 269–70) is being formed. It is a body for which Coriolanus is but a 'disease that must be cut away' (III. i. 292); it makes itself recognised by the audience less by a detailed description than by its visual, gestural impact and its stress on custom and ritual. (Again, see Michael D. Bristol's contribution to this volume.) Though it is frequently denounced as a monstrosity by its opponents, this newly emerging body has few if any grotesque features. It rather moves within the province of time-worn communal, organic thought, and posits the body analogy in opposition to the Tudor and Jacobean ideology of civil obedience and order. It is not an organism that by its grotesqueness would still remain defined in a dependent juxtaposition to the body ruled by the Patricians.

*

Only a few decades after *Coriolanus* was first staged, radical forces in the English revolution made use of the body analogy in their own interests. Henry Denne, for instance, a Baptist much maligned and persecuted by moderates and law-abiding magistrates as well as a leading Leveller insurgent (even if he 'recanted to avoid being shot'; Hill, 1972, 102), defended his radical project against orthodox attacks by declaring its subversive aim as in fact a harmonizing one:

> It hath been . . . mine endeavour . . . to give unto every limb and part not only his due proportion but also his due place, and not to set the head where the foot should be, or the foot where the head. I may peradventure to many seem guilty of that crime . . . to turn the world upside down.
>
> (Denne, 1645, quoted in Hill, 1972, 12)

The ancient notion of an organic community life, which covertly informed the body imagery throughout its period of predominantly orthodox usage, was strongly seized on by the Digger Gerard Winstanley, whose strivings for social equality and common ownership of land were indivisibly intertwined with surviving agrarian community traditions and nourished by prehierarchical Christian belief:

> not any one according to the Word of God (which is love) . . . ought to be lord or landlord over another, but whole mankind was made equal and knit into one body by one spirit of love . . . even [as] all the members of man's body, called the little world, are united into equality of love to preserve the whole body.
>
> (Winstanley, 1649 [1973, 133])

Doubtless Shakespeare's plays on the whole do not have the revolutionary zeal which informs Winstanley's use of the body analogy. Apart from generic differences, the theatre around 1600 essentially belongs to that transitional period leading, on a very abstract level, to the classic system of representation (Foucault, 1970, chs. 2 and 3) – a process which to a large degree entails calling into question the older order of sign and thing. On a more concrete level, this means that the priority is to present and discuss the various issues of social change rather than to call for single-minded action as many of the mid-century pamphleteers did. And as the Renaissance provided for an abundance of significations, of 'relationships so numerous, so intertwined, so rich' (Foucault, 1965 [1973, 18]), so the dissolution of medieval society with its separate corporations permitted certain areas of contact for a host of ideological forces that were only superficially or insufficiently sanctioned by the ruling authorities. Seen in the context of Renaissance thought and society the question of containment of radical forces seems curiously beside the point here; the ideological impact of the mere presentation of different political outlooks in Shakespeare's *Coriolanus* may easily be underestimated if seen from the perspective of a modern media society submerging its population in all sorts of information. But the historically new habit of examining the validity of conventional signs such as the image of the body politic by comparing them with the things they are referred to is part of the intellectual equipment seventeenth-century Englishmen needed in order to pursue their interests. This crucial disposition of the mind is sometimes strengthened in most contradictory ways. Menenius, for example, seeks to turn the citizens away from their objectives by trying to force the moral of his fable on them. He employs an analogy that formerly, to use Foucault's line of thought again, was situated *among* the things rather than in representational opposition to them and was therefore a truth in itself. But the irony is that in order to persuade the citizens he has to relate the fable and its central image to the state of affairs in Rome, i.e. he has to use it as a representation. Thus, the plebeians (and with them the audience) are virtually invited to compare and find out that the analogy is not an equivalent representation: the members/ citizens starve, not the belly/patricians. Menenius' effort is self-defeating and in fact helps bring about a critical mental attitude which he had set out to avoid. And while on the one hand the body analogy is unfit adequately to reflect the social conditions of the time, it can serve, on the other hand, as has been argued above, to project the aspirations of the most varied ideological forces.

Notes

1. Wheeler (1601) provides ample evidence of the use of harmonious, organicist thought in defence of the privileges of the company of Merchants Adventurer.
2. The former was destined for Henry VIII, the latter addressed to Parliament. For a discussion of Crowley, see Elton (1979), 32.
3. For similar examples, see Latimer (1844–5).
4. Another significant influence is provided by the emerging conflict between harmony and hierarchy within established referential frameworks. See Sinfield (1983).
5. All references are to the Arden edition of *Coriolanus* (Brockbank, 1976).
6. In his 1953 'Study of the First Act of Shakespeare's *Coriolanus*', Bertolt Brecht pointed out that 'Shakespeare gives the plebeians good arguments to answer back with. And they strongly reject the parable for that matter' (Brecht, *Versuche*, 15 [Berlin, 1957], trans. John Willett, in Brecht, 1964, 253).
7. Menenius is an up-stage character who has appropriated the dramaturgical equipment of down-stage characters, i.e. of fools and of representatives of the lower classes, or holders of positions noticeably lower than those of the main-plot characters. Rather than interpreting this anomaly as evidence for a benevolent portrayal of Menenius, I would maintain, again, that his inconsistent make-up points towards a contradiction between his intent and his behaviour.
8. Both Menenius and Coriolanus call the plebeians 'rats' (I. i. 161, 248).
9. See, for example, his intent to 'pluck out / The multitudinous tongue' (III. i. 154–5). Notice also that he wants to take the people's votes (their 'voices') in II. iii. and at the same time despises the ritual procedure which he has to undergo if he wants to get those voices: the ritual act (the uttering) for him means nothing but the dispersal of stinking breath (see Gordon, 1975). Again, representational and ritual elements contradict each other.

Works cited

Allen, J.W. (1957) *A History of Political Thought in England*, London, Methuen.
Averall, William (1588) *A Mervailous Combat of Contrarieties*, London, STC 981.
Barkan, Leonard (1975) *Nature's Work of Art: The Human Body as the Image of the World*, London and New Haven, Yale University Press.
Brecht, Bertolt (1964) *Brecht on Theatre*, ed. and trans. John Willett, London, Methuen.

Brockbank, Philip (ed.) (1976) *Coriolanus* by William Shakespeare, Arden edn, London, Methuen.
Cavell, Stanley (1983) ' "Who does the wolf love?" Reading *Coriolanus*', *Representations*, 3, 1–20.
Certain Sermons or Homilies Appointed to be Read in Churches in the Time of the Late Queen Elizabeth of Famous Memory (1908), London, Society for the Promotion of Christian Knowledge.
Charney, Maurice (1970) 'The Dramatic Use of Imagery in Shakespeare's *Coriolanus*', in Phillips, James E. (ed.) *Twentieth-Century Interpretations of 'Coriolanus': A Collection of Critical Essays*, Englewood Cliffs, NJ, Prentice-Hall.
Crowley, Robert (1872) *The Select Works of Robert Crowley*, ed. J.M. Cowper, London, Early English Text Society, Extra Series no. 15.
D'Ewes, Simonds (1682) *The Journals of all the Parliaments during the Reign of Queen Elizabeth, both of the House of Lords and House of Commons*, London, facsimile edn (1973), Shannon, Irish University Press.
'Doleman, R.' [= Parsons, Robert] (1594) *A Conference About the Next Succession to the Crowne of Ingland* [Antwerp], S.T.C. 19398.
Eagleton, Terence (1980) 'Text, Ideology, Realism', *Literature and Society*, ed. Edward W. Said, Baltimore and London, Johns Hopkins University Press, 149–73.
Eliade, Mircea (1961) *Images and Symbols*, trans. P. Mairet, London, Harvill Press.
Elton, G.R. (1979) 'Reform and the "Commonwealth-Men" of Edward VI's Reign', *The English Commonwealth 1547–1640*, in Clark, P., Smith, A.G.R. and Tyacke, N. (eds) Leicester, Leicester University Press.
Ferguson, Arthur B. (1959) 'Fortescue and the Renaissance: A Study in Transition', *Studies in the Renaissance*, 6, 175–94.
—— (1965) *The Articulate Citizen and the English Renaissance*, Durham, NC, Duke University Press.
Forset, Edward (1606) *A Comparative Discourse of the Bodies Natural and Politique*, London S.T.C. 11188.
Foucault, Michel (1965) *Madness and Civilization: A History of Insanity in the Age of Reason*, trans. Richard Howard, New York, Pantheon; (1973) Vintage Books edn, New York, Random House.
—— (1970) *The Order of Things: An Archaeology of the Human Sciences*, New York, Pantheon.
Gordon, Donald J. (1975) 'Name and Fame: Shakespeare's *Coriolanus*', in Orgel, Stephen (ed.) *The Renaissance Imagination: Essays and Lectures by D.J. Gordon*, Berkeley and London, University of California Press, 203–19.
Hale, David G. (1971a) 'The Death of a Political Metaphor', *Shakespeare Quarterly*, 22, 197–202.
—— (1971b) *The Body Politic: A Political Metaphor in the Renaissance*, The Hague and Paris, Mouton.
Hill, Christopher (1972) *The World Turned Upside Down: Radical Ideas in the English Revolution*, London, Temple Smith.
James, Mervyn (1983) 'Ritual, Drama and Social Body in the Late Medieval English Town', *Past and Present*, 98, 3–29.
Kinser, Samuel (1986) 'Presentation and Representation: Carnival at Nuremberg, 1450–1550', *Representations*, 13, 1–41.
Latimer, Hugh (1844–5) *The Sermons of Hugh Latimer*, ed. G.L. Corrie, London, Parker Society.
Lotman, Juri (1981) 'Zeichen und Zeichensystem in Bezug auf die Typologie der russischen Kultur (11. bis 19. Jahrhundert)', *Kunst als Sprache*, Leipzig, Reclam.
Marx, Karl (1867) *Capital: A Critique of Political Economy*, trans. Ben Fowkes [1976], I, Harmondsworth, Penguin.
Meres, Francis (1598) *Palladis Tamia, Wit's Treasury*, facsimile edn (1973), introd.

Arthur Freeman, New York, Garland.

Norbrook, David (1984) *Poetry and Politics in the English Renaissance*, London, Routledge & Kegan Paul.

Pettet, E.C. (1950) '*Coriolanus* and the Midlands Insurrection of 1607', *Shakespeare Survey*, 3, 34–42.

Phythian-Adams, Charles (1972) 'Ceremony and the Citizen: The Communal Year at Coventry 1450–1550', in Clark, P. and Slack, P. (eds) *Crisis and Order in English Towns*, London, Routledge & Kegan Paul.

Ponet, John (1556) *A Short Treatise of Politique Power: And of the True Obedience which Subjects owe to Kings, and other Civil Governours* (Antwerp), facsimile edn (1970), Menton Scolar Press.

Sacks, David Harris (1986) 'The Demise of the Martyrs: The Feasts of St Clements and St Katherine in Bristol, 1400–1600', *Social History*, 11, 141–69.

Sinfield, Alan (1983) *Literature in Protestant England 1560–1660*, Beckenham, Croom Helm.

Smith, Henry (1597) *The Sermons of Maister Henrie Smith*, London, S.T.C. 22722.

Smith, Thomas (1581) *A Discourse of the Commonweal of this Realm of England*, ed. Mary Dewar (1969), Charlottesville, Va., University of Virginia Press.

A Supplication of the Poore Commons (1546) ed. J.M. Cowper (1871), London, Early English Text Society.

Talbert, Ernest William (1962) *The Problem of Order: Elizabethan Political Commonplaces and an Example of Shakespeare's Art*, Chapel Hill, University of North Carolina Press.

Thomas, Keith (1971) *Religion and the Decline of Magic: Studies in Popular Beliefs in Sixteenth and Seventeenth Century England*, London, Weidenfeld & Nicolson.

Weimann, Robert (1978) *Shakespeare and the Popular Tradition in the Theatre: Studies in the Social Dimension of the Dramatic Form and Function*, ed. Robert Schwartz, Baltimore and London, Johns Hopkins University Press.

Wheeler, John (1601) *Treatise of Commerce*, London, S.T.C. 25331.

Winstanley, Gerrard (1973) *The Law of Freedom and Other Writings*, ed. Christopher Hill, Harmondsworth, Penguin.

11

Speculations: *Macbeth* and source

Jonathan Goldberg

This paper (or so its title suggests) poses a plurality of speculations against a presumed singleness of source; it glances, thereby, at a dispersal of origins. Source – in its heterogeneity – is its concern, aimed ultimately at locating Shakespeare's relation to *Macbeth*. But, it can be assumed, there is no immediate path to the author as source of the text except through a relay of mediations, and, by the end, even the supposed ultimate source – the author – must be considered within a heterogeneous dispersal.[1]

That dispersal might be termed *history*, and this essay aims at a description of the place of *Macbeth* within some familiar historical determinations – its sources in Holinshed's *Chronicles*, its relation to the rule and rhetoric of James I, its proximity to Jonson's *Masque of Queens*. Yet, in alluding to such historical determinations as heterogeneous, determinations become indeterminate. It is with the openings within the hegemonic that this essay is concerned, and its trope for such situations is specular and speculative: to imagine that within the language of hegemonic imposition and superimposition, duplication opens a specter of uncontrolled resemblance rendering difference problematic, rendering, that is, determinate differences indeterminate.

Like Stephen Greenblatt in "Shakespeare and the Exorcists," in this essay

JONATHAN GOLDBERG is Sir William Osler Professor of English Literature at The Johns Hopkins University. Among his books are: *Endlesse Worke: Spenser and the Structures of Discourse* (Baltimore and London, Johns Hopkins University Press, 1981); *James I and the Politics of Literature* (Baltimore and London, Johns Hopkins University Press, 1983); and, most recently, *Voice Terminal Echo: Postmodernism and English Renaissance Texts* (London and New York, Methuen, 1986). He is currently editing Milton (with Stephen Orgel) for Oxford University Press, and writing about Shakespeare and cultural graphology. Another version of his essay in this volume appeared in *Post-Structuralist Readings of English Poetry*, ed. Christopher Norris and Richard Machin (Cambridge, Cambridge University Press, 1987).

in "the elephants' graveyard of literary history" (as he characterizes source study; 1985, 101), I am guided by the thesis that "history cannot be divorced from textuality, and all texts can be compelled to confront the crisis of undecidability revealed in the literary text" (p. 102). Greenblatt terms this a "subversive" hypothesis (subversive of the territorial claims of history and literature), and I, too, am interested in examining the limits of subversion, the modes of representing officially discountenanced positions. In Greenblatt's study of the relationship between Samuel Harsnett's *A Declaration of Egregious Popish Impostures* and *King Lear*, the source practices a version of the exorcism it denounces; exorcists are exposed as theatrical imposters. Shakespeare welcomes what Harsnett has debunked, and the theater accrues a demonic power more frightening than Harsnett could imagine. For Greenblatt, this exchange crosses and establishes the borders between the source and literacy representation; it displays an institutional economy. "The official church dismantles and cedes to the players the powerful mechanism of an unwanted and dangerous charisma; in return the players confirm the charge that these mechanisms are theatrical and hence illusory" (p. 116). As described, this exchange characterizes a "cultural poetics" (p. 103) that is apparently a closed system, an economics, thus, in which there is no waste. Yet Greenblatt adds a paradoxical twist to this paradigm: the theater practices an evacuation even more excessive than the official one and, at the same time, a surplus value – literariness – is founded in that self-revealed lack, the depiction of evil. Paradoxically, then, the theater's loyal gesture has a subversive edge; indeed, on that margin, it establishes its position.

What Greenblatt salvages from the elephants' graveyard is nothing less than the saving powers of theater, of Shakespearean theatricality in particular. His *King Lear* answers to "our need . . . our desire for spectacular impostures" (p. 123). He wittily complains that deconstruction "is not satanic enough" (p. 102). His criticism is properly satanic; from nothing, he produces the satisfaction of needs and desires. "If I have any fear, it is not of falling into hell, but of falling into nothing," Greenblatt quotes from John Wesley; in Greenblatt's recuperation of the source in Shakespeare, we do not fall into an abyss, but, instead, into a satanic recouping of loss. Thus, for Greenblatt, *King Lear* offers the equivalent of devil worship: "the force of evil in the play is larger than any local habitation or name" (p. 122), and we are made to love what that theater produces: "The force of *King Lear* is to make us love the theater, to seek out its satisfactions, to serve its interests, to confer upon it a place of its own, to grant it life by permitting it to reproduce itself over generations" (p. 122).

The inversion that Greenblatt practices may resituate the literary, but it does not ultimately call into question the value system upon which it rests. Greenblatt's *King Lear* is, in many ways, perfectly recognizable: good and evil are not in question (nor is the greatness of *King Lear* or Harsnett's stylistic poverty); nor is there any question of the human desires that the play engages. Not surprisingly, then, the play's "subversion" (its demonism) is congruent with the demonism officially exorcized. And theatricality takes on a transcendental function in its very negativity: the "life" breathed into the corpse of the elephantine source.

Greenblatt insists in the opening pages of "Shakespeare and the Exorcists," upon the modesty of his project: "for me the study of literature is the study of contingent, particular, intended, and historically embedded works; if theory inevitably involves the desire to escape from contingency to a higher realm, a realm in which signs are purified of the slime of history, then this paper is written *against theory*" (1985, p. 101). Yet, it could be argued, I think, that with "theatricality" Greenblatt has found that "universal, encompassing, and abstract problematic," which, he says, might be called theory, and which, if it is, he opposes. While the rhetoric of specificity has a Foucauldian ring, the practice of "cultural poetics" has its transcendental value (theatricality) and its metaphysical and humanistic investments. The situation in his text reveals, despite itself, a will to totalization. These are, of course, the charges that Derrida (1978) leveled at Foucault in "Cogito and the History of Madness."

I review Greenblatt's argument here to distance myself from a method which my own work certainly shares in some of its concerns and presuppositions, but also because Greenblatt's argument does not seem to me to go far enough in distinguishing itself from more conventional literary criticism. It seeks to preserve the very notion of literariness it calls into question; its subversion is most like that deconstructive reversal that does not, in fact, throw logocentric suppositions into question. Unlike Greenblatt, then, my concern in the pages that follow is with an *uneconomic* expenditure, with "an excess in the direction of the non-determined" (Derrida, 1978, 57). The direction I take, as these phrases indicate, is Derridean; it is also, I would argue, political.

The argument that I make depends upon the notion that dominant discourses allow their own subversion precisely because hegemonic control is an impossible dream, a self-defeating fantasy. That defeat is marked by the self-division in Greenblatt's essay. More usually, that fantasy, I would argue, attaches itself to source, to the belief in an ultimate, and ultimately authoritative, origin. What I trace is an absolutist fantasy, and one that not only kings indulge. For literary critics, of various kinds, are prone to its lure as well, when they suppose, for example, that there are certain unquestionable facts, rather than allowing that what counts as factual is itself a discursive formation; or when they imagine for the text and its author some autonomy of intention. Greenblatt, for instance, assumes a literary intentionality in the Shakespearean text; I do not, but regard the literariness of his texts as a literary-critical invention. Greenblatt opens his essay (1985) with a characteristic gesture toward the unquestioned reality of dates and facts, the local event that locates the Shakespearean text within a cultural economy. "Between the spring of 1585 and the summer of 1586, a group of English Catholic priests led by the Jesuit William Weston, alias Father Edmunds, conducted a series of spectacular exorcisms" (p. 101). I mean to call into question the methods of literary critics, and the practices of textual, historical, and formalistic criticism. The method that I offer instead owes much to poststructuralism and, in this paper, to the work of Jacques Derrida. For it is his inquiries (1976, 304, 152–7; 1982) into questions of origin that inform my own.

Derrida stages a version of that inquiry in his examination of Foucault's reading of Descartes. For my purposes here, it is unnecessary to decide who reads Descartes correctly (I would argue in fact that such a decision is not possible). The argument hinges on whether a passage in Descartes introduced by "sed forte" is a feigned objection (in Derrida's account, 1978) or a determining marker (as it is for Foucault, 1979). Greenblatt would follow Foucault, I believe, in assuming that a text could be so historically saturated that a reading could reveal the historicity of the text. Derrida's alternate reading, even if only entertained hypothetically, shatters this notion of the historic decisiveness of any textual mark. The Foucauldian intervention in Descartes depends upon the possibility of constructing history as the history of meaning. It depends upon history as a rational concept. Whereas, for Foucault, the Cartesian text has all the force of an originary moment, a decisive break, for Derrida, the Cartesian text – as text – cannot be reduced to a historical determination; in its heterogeneity it opens an interval between history and historicity-in-general. In his reading, Foucault has mistaken one for the other.

To invoke the name of Derrida in support of an argument that seeks to recover history – even history as a discursive formation – points to the central methodological issue of this paper. Derrida has far too easily been dismissed as unconcerned with history (Edward Said's denunciations are perhaps the most familiar), whereas history is for him a problematic matter precisely because it has been tied to certain metaphysical notions that will not bear close scrutiny. These include the idea of the present moment as one of complete self-presence, the idea of a past moment as one of sheer literality, and the idea of the future as the necessary outcome of such prior moments. As I have argued (1985):

> history, as the word says, means narrative, and narrative means representation tied to principles of beginning and end that are part and parcel of the view of the world that rests upon concepts like Being and Presence, and such distinctions as inside and outside or body and spirit. *Différance*, Derrida writes, can replace the notion of origin or ground and, so doing, would open up a question that he terms *historial*. That neologism, as much as *différance*, is an attempt to provide terms for that for which there are no terms. (p. 5)

As Derrida says in *Positions* (1981), history is a term, like "writing," whose force he requires, although its metaphysical, ontological investments must be called into question. What is needed is "a history that also implies a new logic of *repetition* and the *trace*, for it is difficult to see how there could be history without it" (p. 57). Indeed, Derridean "history" requires the full range of his nonconceptual concepts if it is to be reinscribed. To quote myself again: "History is the meeting of articulation, difference, and writing; history crosses paths with trace and supplement. These terms are not all the same, although their motion and meeting testify to the endless play in time of *différance*" (1985, 7). The historic interval, or spacing, is a setting aside that refuses self-identity; the historical "moment" must be "marked twice" (Derrida, 1981, 65). It is neither unitary nor homogeneous.

Derrida's highly condensed statement suggests a number of things:

1. That the historical moment – as a differential moment – must differ from itself and must defer its identity;

2. That the critical activity of delineating a "moment" itself occupies a differential relation to the moment marked, and which it inevitably re-marks;

3. Thus, the necessity of double-marking refers both to the "original" historical moment, itself traversed by and constituted by difference, and to any subsequent moment of re-marking the "original;"

4. Such re-marking therefore characterizes historicity-in-general, spacing, differance, etc., all testifying to the failure of self-coincidence which produces textuality and temporality;

5. Re-marking also defines the deconstructive project as a form of historicity, and, indeed, as the attempt to re-mark the difference between history and historicity-in-general;

6. Re-marking, then, is the "new concept of history" (Derrida, 1981, 59) because it marks the break with the old metaphysical concept in an overturning that is not a reappropriation, since it permits the dissemination of the mark into the determined (historical) field without confining the mark to such determinations.

Parker (1981) offers a brilliant summary of these arguments, emphasizing the Derridean sense of history as refiguration, a temporality at one with deferral.

> Such a form of temporality elides the very "firstness" of the "prior" event, placing in question the possibility of an event that could be isolated in its self-contained moment of occurrence; as a *mélange* of proleptic and metaleptic relationships, deferred action would suggest that if our present understanding "normally" is dependent on the past as its determining ground, then the future would be equally predictive of the "pastness" of the past. (p. 70)

Hence, in the essay that follows, history is limited by texts whose very determinations are indeterminate, texts, that is, which are determined precisely by their double marking – the overdetermination that renders any text a duplicate, a copy with no original. The issue of success/succession in *Macbeth* provides an image of this, indeed of the entire mirror structure that produces the Otherness of Others, or of other moments (the past, the future), in short, the Otherness-of-the-present or of the self as it (fails to) coincide(s) with itself.

Derrida sums up his historical concerns in *Positions*: "Must I recall that from the first texts I published, I have attempted to systematize a deconstructive critique precisely against the authority of meaning, as the *transcendental signified* or as *telos*, in other words history determined in the last analysis as the history of meaning, history in its logocentric, metaphysical, idealistic . . . representation" (1981, 49–50). The statement comes, as is well known, in the midst of Derrida's most extended confrontation with Marxist critics, and in the midst of a struggle to define his political position. In "Between Dialectics and

Deconstruction: Derrida and the Reading of Marx,'' Andrew Parker has, once again, brilliantly explored these issues. His call, "to construe the political *other-wise*" (1985, 147), I take to be exemplary. If Derrida objects to Marxists, as he does to Foucault, for their metaphysical investment, for their belief in Marxism as a decisive and grounded discourse (and, it must be noted, these accusations do not keep Derrida from endorsing certain Althusserian arguments, or, indeed, from being willing to call himself a materialist), his critical "position" represents a politics that insists on the (inevitably limited) recognition involved in taking positions. It is the usual complaint to regard Derrida's refusal to be "for" or "against" as an implicit endorsement of the status quo; it is, however, Derrida's argument that taking such a position (taking sides) in no way alters the dualistic, logocentric suppositions upon which position taking is posited. That is, in effect, the argument that I rehearsed above in relation to Greenblatt's essay, which ends by denouncing political totalitarianism and yet by endorsing what might be called a literary totalitarianism.

I would argue, then, that to think of history as heterogeneous dispersal, as I attempt to do in this paper, is a political act precisely because it calls into question those modes of "logocentric, metaphysical, idealistic . . . representation" that ascribe determinate force to hegemonic rhetoric and that assume that ideological inscriptions really have the power they claim. It is instead the argument of this paper that ideology is haunted by what it excludes, subverted by what it subordinates. Yet the argument does not assume the possibility of some other mode of discourse (an Althusserian dream of science, for instance, "outside" of ideology), for to do so would be to replace one form of idealism with another. And thus, in this paper, the terms which must be used – referring us to texts and authors and events – can only be taken as tropes, speculations with counters that discourse fills, but which cannot be contained; halls of mirrors in which resemblance does not halt. In that respect, this paper might be called "The Mirror of Kings." Although the argument I make seems to me congruent with the thesis of *James I and the Politics of Literature* (1983), there is a shift of emphasis in this paper. In that book I was interested in mapping strategies of representation shared by Jacobean authors and their monarch. This paper looks at the dark side of representation. The emphasis now is on the *re* in representation, the haunting specter of duplication that unmoors texts and events from a positivistic view of history or literature. What is *real*, then, is the *re*, perhaps itself a recovery of the nothing into which things slide. Latin *rem* lies behind French *rien*.

*

"Shakespeare deals freely with his source," so Frank Kermode writes (1974, 1308), considering the relationship of *Macbeth* to Holinshed. "The actual words of Holinshed are closely followed, notably in IV. ii, but Shakespeare deals freely with his source, making Duncan old and venerable, instead of a young and weak-willed man. This is part of the general blackening of Macbeth's character.'' Geoffrey Bullough (1973) marvels at "Shakespeare, with that wonderful memory ever ready to float up, albeit unconsciously, associations from reading or hearsay" (p. 444). Thus, these critics affirm, Shakespeare moves freely in Holinshed, drawing on many narratives to fashion his "composite picture," as Bullough calls it (p. 448);[2] and whereas, in Holinshed, Duncan is both a good king and a weak one, and Macbeth is, at first loyal and then traitorous, Shakespeare – so the common line has it – recombines and simplifies his materials to offer a saintly king and his villainous murderer, and thereby makes differences clear-cut. Holinshed's narrative, because it motivates Macbeth's rebellion by allowing for defects in Duncan's rule (Duncan bars Macbeth's right to succeed to the throne, after all), takes an about-face when Macbeth turns tyrant; his earlier service to the king is labeled "counterfet" (Bullough, 1973, 498). Shakespeare, according to Kermode, does not have Holinshed's problem; his Macbeth is "blackened" from the start. The start? Where does a "composite" text begin?

Such a question, I would argue, must be raised, and with it the common assumptions about Shakespeare, implicit in these descriptions of the relationship of *Macbeth* to Holinshed, can begin to be investigated. For the assumption about the autonomous imagination of the author is allied to a description of a text remarkable for its moral clarity and its political conservatism – a description that may reveal more about the critics than about the play.

To test these commonplaces, let us take as an example Duncan's musing on the treacherous Thane of Cawdor:

> There's no art
> To find the mind's construction in the face:
> He was a gentleman on whom I built
> An absolute trust   (I. iv. 11–14)

These lines, cut short by the entrance of Macbeth, are generally seen as an index to the innocence of Duncan's mind. What is their source? In Holinshed, Duncan's words are spoken by a witch. She prophesies that the "trustie servant" of King Natholocus, who has come to her on his ruler's behalf, will murder his monarch. The king, she says, will be killed by one "in whome he had reposed an especiall trust" (Bullough, 1973, 478).

Duncan's lines, especially as they have been read most usually, suggest clear-cut moral differences. Yet that other habit of Shakespearean composition, its "free" association, might lead one to ask if it is significant that Duncan voices lines spoken elsewhere by a witch. The question resonates if one allows another echo to sound, the reverberations of the witches' greeting of Macbeth – "All hail Macbeth! hail to thee, Thane of Cawdor! / All hail, Macbeth! that shall be King hereafter" (I. iii. 49–50) – reverberations that come to occupy Duncan's mouth. Just a few lines after the witches' all-hailing, messengers from the king arrive, bid to "call" Macbeth "Thane of Cawdor: / In which addition, hail, most worthy Thane" (105–6); a scene later, Duncan names the king to be, "Our eldest, Malcolm; whom we name hereafter" (I. iv. 38). The text of *Macbeth* is itself "composite," redistributing the witches' lines.

Is it to be accounted to the *free* dealing of the author's mind that Duncan's lines have their source – in Holinshed, in the play – in the mouths of witches? We might notice, too, that where Duncan swerves from the lines in Holinshed describing a king *reposing* his *special* trust, he substitutes the *activity* of *building* an *absolute* trust, and recall that Shakespeare drops Holinshed's description of Macbeth as master-builder of Dunsinane, virtually the only incident from Macbeth's career not duplicated in the play, and allows Duncan instead to comment on the architecture of Inverness, thus permitting Duncan's to be the constructing mind. In short, the absolute differences and moral clarity that critics have found to be Shakespeare's are, at least in these instances, Duncan's. Monarch of the *absolute*, Duncan constructs differences against the demonic source of his lines, spoken by a witch and to a figure that serves as a model for Macbeth. Duncan's musings on the betrayal of the Thane of Cawdor have always been allowed the ironic echo that extends to the newly named Thane, Macbeth; the lines, I would suggest, might also be thought of as self-reflective. "There's no art / To find the mind's construction in the face;" has not criticism – with scarcely an exception – succumbed to Duncan's glassy surface?[3]

That surface is cut into again if we return to the source of Duncan's lines in Holinshed. For Holinshed also describes King Duff as one "having a special trust in Donwald" (Bullough, 1973, 481), the loyal retainer that slays him. Holinshed's King Duff is a haunted and sleepless figure who sends his trusty servant to try to discover the cause of his disease. Donwald, the servant, finds a witch "rosting upon a woodden broch an image of wax at the fier, resembling in each feature the kings person" (p. 480). The king's illness is the result of this demonic voodooism, spectral identification, and he is restored to health as soon as Donwald destroys the waxen image. It scarcely needs mention that Holinshed's King Duff is – except for the line that Duncan speaks – a version of Macbeth. Does the specter of identification drawn from the composition of Holinshed in *Macbeth* signify in the play? Both Duff and Donwald are versions of Macbeth. Duncan is a further spectral emanation of a source less intent on *absolute difference* than on resemblance. After King Duff is cured, he celebrates his recovery by making a "spectacle" (p. 481) of hanged rebels. Among them are Donwald's kin, and the loyal retainer who cured the king by destroying his specter turns on the king who has made the spectacle. So, *Macbeth* opens with reports of Macbeth fixing a rebel head upon the battlements (I. ii. 23) and closes with his severed head displayed by Macduff (V. ix. 20); a plot inscribed and generated within specularity: in each instance, a supposedly saintly king has let another do his dirty work.

As another example of specular contamination, consider this episode from Holinshed: King Kenneth, successor to King Duff and murderer of his son and heir, suffers guilt and sleeplessness; he is told by prophetic voices that he will die and that the heir he has named will not succeed to the throne. His murder is accomplished by Fenella, avenging the death of her son, another child killed by the guilty monarch. Knowing "that the king delighted above measure in goodlie buildings'' (Bullough, 1973, 486), she constructs an elaborate tower covered with engraved flowers and other images. ''In the middest of the house there was a goodlie brasen image also, resembling the figure of king Kenneth'' (p. 487) holding in his hands a golden apple which, if plucked, activates crossbows aimed at the taker. The king succumbs to the lure and is killed. Whose career is this in *Macbeth*, Macbeth's . . . or Duncan's?

Macbeth looks in his conscience, torn by demonic representations and by Duncan's furthering of their designs; in soliloquy, he produces the saintly king – as a mirror. ''This Duncan / Hath borne his faculties so meek, hath been / So clear in his great office, that his virtues / Will plead like angels'' (I. vii. 16–19). Duncan's polished surface: is it the representation of an absolute power or the mirror of resemblance?

Duncan articulates, constructs, absolute difference, but equivocation arises from the source. ''People wished,'' Holinshed writes,

> the inclinations and maners of these two cousins to have beene so tempered and enterchangeablie bestowed betwixt them, that where the one had too much of clemencie, and the other of crueltie, the meane vertue betwixt these two extremities might have reigned by indifferent partition in them both. (Bullough, 1973, 488)

So, Lady Macbeth fears her husband ''is too full o' th' milk of human kindness'' (I. v. 17); so, as Harry Berger (1980) has persuasively argued, the opening scenes of the play enact an elaborately concealed hostility between Duncan and Macbeth, scenes, that is, of rivalry between characters who represent (in Holinshed's words) the ''indifferent partition'' that ''reign[s]'' in *Macbeth*.[4] ''Have we eaten on the insane root, / That takes the reason prisoner?'' (I. iii. 84–5), Banquo asks after the witches appear. The ''insane root'' lies in the source; in Holinshed, Duncan disables the rebels by feeding them a poisoned brew that puts them to sleep. ''Look up clear,'' Lady Macbeth counsels her husband (I. v. 71), and he looks in a mirror, to find Duncan, ''clear in his great office'' (I. vii. 18). Succession in the play can never take place except in a mirror. Macbeth invents the sainted king; he is not visible in the lines he speaks. After Macbeth kills him, he reports that Duncan's silver skin was breached with golden blood (II. iii. 110).[5] Such images are the obstacles that Macbeth finds in his path; they are also the source of his own legitimation when he comes to occupy Duncan's place. Macbeth succeeds as the king of the image repertoire in *Macbeth*.

Thus, when one looks to the most apparently straightforward scene of the transmission of source – the recasting of Holinshed's conversation between Macduff and Malcolm in IV. iii., what one discovers is that something has come between the source and the scene. What blocks the way of transmission is the text of *Macbeth* itself; Malcolm and Macduff repeatedly echo words and phrases that have come before, words most often heard in Macbeth's mouth. Resemblance, not difference, dominates the text; Macbeth attempts unpartnered to occupy alone what occupies him, to the end ''wrought / With things forgotten'' (I. iii. 151).

"People wished the inclinations and maners of these two cousins to have beene so tempered and enterchangeablie bestowed betwixt them," so Holinshed writes; is that desire, articulated in the source, also Shakespeare's? The chance and wayward associations of his "wonderful memory"? The floating of his unconscious? A conscious design? To consider these questions, another source must be considered, the occasion of the play, for it is equally a critical commonplace to see the author of *Macbeth* succumbing to the exigencies of history, and to regard the play as a royal compliment: Edward the Confessor touches for the King's Evil as James, reluctantly, did; Banquo fathered James's line.[6] Moreover, the text of *Macbeth* that we have derives from a court performance. Could Shakespeare have represented the contaminations of spectral resemblance before James I? Intentionally? Secretly? These questions about source lead to what Fredric Jameson might call the *political unconscious* of the play, a determined heterogeneity rather than the freeplay of the mind.[7] What, we need to ask, are the political conditions of representation in which *Macbeth* is located?

The text of *Macbeth* offers one index to these conditions, for it is, as Stephen Orgel (1983, 43) has remarked, a palimpsest, combining at least two versions of the play; one version dates from the time of the Gunpowder Plot, and is alluded to, for instance, by the Porter's use of *equivocation* in the play (II. iii.; and also, at V. v. 43, by Macbeth); another version is several years later, and is marked by the additions of songs from Middleton's *The Witch*, a play presumed to postdate Jonson's 1609 *Masque of Queens*. From act III on, if not before, the text of *Macbeth* shows signs of tampering: transposed scenes, cut lines, wholesale interpolations of songs and dances. The menacing powers of the witches are trivialized, and to reduce the impact of their show of kings they propose to "cheer . . . up" Macbeth:

> Come, sisters, cheer we up his sprites,
> And show the best of our delights.
> I'll charm the air to give a sound,
> While you perform your antic round;
> That this great King may kindly say,
> Our duties did his welcome pay.
> (IV. i. 127–32)

Who is "this great King" to whom compliment is paid, if not the monarch in the audience? The text alludes to the presence of King James in this compliment as well as in the formal accommodations that make the text of *Macbeth* masquelike. But even these trivial lines of jaunty welcome to the king enact a curious play of resemblance. The editor of the Arden edition of *Macbeth*, for example, takes "this great King" to refer to Macbeth. One king slides into the other, a type of diffusion that can be remarked elsewhere in the latter half of *Macbeth*, in the withdrawal of Lady Macbeth and her replacement with Lady Macduff, or in the English scenes with their echoes of Scottish horror; we see less of Macbeth as the play proceeds, and hear more of him. The presence of

King James in the text of *Macbeth*, however much it disturbs the original and irrecoverable designs of the play, also seems to be written within them. Might we say that the earlier relationship between Macbeth and Duncan is reenacted between Macbeth and King James? That there is room in the text for only one king? That these two monarchs are haunted by spectral identification? A mirror, literally, provides an answer to these speculations. In the show of kings, Macbeth looks into the mirror in which James I is reflected:

> . . . the eighth appears, who bears a glass,
> Which shows me many more; and some I see,
> That two-fold balls and treble sceptres carry.
> Horrible sight!
>
> (IV. i. 119–22)

Disturbing the notion of clear-cut difference in this confrontation is, once again, the problem of source, for the show of kings is provided by the "filthy hags" (115), and however much their subsequent jauntiness seems to diffuse the spectacle, it retains its disturbing power. Steven Mullaney (1980, 41) has written wonderfully about this moment, about the alliance of the demonic to a linguistic excess. As he says, in that mirroring moment

> genealogy and prophecy are made manifest in the visible display, but there is another genealogy in the air as well, one heard rather than seen. Juxtaposed to the projection of James's line, the witches' riddles complicate its complimentary gesture with what amounts to a genealogy of treason and equivocation.[8]

If earlier Duncan spoke witches' words, here the king is transported on stage in the witches' show, caught within speculation. If earlier Duncan bestowed gifts and titles to "name" a "hereafter" already named, here James is asked to "kindly say" that the witches' "duties did his welcome pay." The king lives to bestow, as James indicated when he titled his treatise on kingship the *Basilikon Doron*, the royal gift. His gift was his presence and the heir he produced; presentation that is re-presentation. There is an economy of speculation.

Is the show of kings subversive? Do its spectral identifications implicate Shakespeare in a revolutionary politics? Could such a politics evade the reflections of a mirror that catches the king on stage and off? Is there an autonomous realm available for representation that would not be caught within representation? That realm of autonomy, Franco Moretti (1982, 9) suggests, is coincident with sovereignty imagined as "a power . . . having its origin *in itself*." When James represented that power, as in the sonnet prefatory to the *Basilikon Doron*, he declared himself a god by announcing that "God gives not Kings the stile of *Gods* in vaine"; the king who gives all has been given his power as a *style*, and as an echoing name. The king stands *in the place* of the "heavenly King," his "Lieutenant." Duncan dresses Macbeth in borrowed robes as well, making a voodoo version of himself. "Remember," James (1616 [1918, 39]) counseled his son and heir, "the throne is Gods and not yours, that ye sit in." Presenting himself, claiming all his kingdom as his own – the kingdom was his body and his wife, he declared on more than one occasion – James also saw himself as representation, a king on stage, whose behavior offered a living "image" of himself. Royal existence is representation. "Let your owne life be a law-booke and a mirrour to your people" (p. 30), James urged his son in the book in which he similarly presented himself, counseling him to present himself as the "vive image" of his "vertuous disposition" (p. 51). Offering himself to parliamentary inspection, the king was fond of declaring that his breast was a crystal mirror, both a reflecting surface and a transparent one. What could one's "owne life" be in such formulations of identity – even absolute identity – as reflection? Wouldn't this hall of mirrors include the notion of "a power . . . having its origin *in itself*" – whether we were to attach that idea of autonomy to the king or to the sovereign author of *Macbeth*? Could there be an end to these speculations, or a source?

Ben Jonson's masques for King James frequently depend upon such absolutist assertions and they are our best guide to the conditions of absolutist representation in the Jacobean period. When Jonson wrote a masque celebrating James's birthday in 1620, the king was cast as Pan, for Pan means "all": "Pan is our all, by him we breathe, we live, / We move, we are" (Jonson [1969], lines 170–1). Yet, included in the spectacle that Jonson offered the king were disturbing reflections of himself and his courtiers, particularly in the figure of a court ape outrageously parodying the court. Jonson showed James how to view the attack by reprimanding the parodist in the masque. "Your folly may well deserve pardon because it hath delighted," he is told; "but beware of presuming, or how you offer comparisons with persons so near deities. Behold where they are that have now forgiven you, whom should you provoke again with the like, they will justly punish that with anger which they now dismiss with contempt" (131–6). The court and its parodist face each other in this moment to regard one another within the spectacle of "comparisons" and resemblances; the derisory spectacle is to be seen with derision. James must forgive all if all reflects him and if he is the ultimate source of all representation. In Jonson's masques, the representation of the king's claims to totality offers the possibility of endless replications within the system of reflecting power in which the king was placed.[9]

This can be demonstrated, too, in *The Vision of Delight* (1617), a masque, as its title suggests, about vision. For in it, the spectacle of the king's Arcadia on stage, the image of the realm perfected, is presented by the antimasque figure of Fant'sy. Fant'sy's realm is, in the antimasque, the suspect terrain of wayward dreams:

> Dreams of the maker and dreams of the teller,
> Dreams of the kitchen and dreams of the cellar;
> Some that are tall, and some that are dwarfs,

Some that are haltered, and some that wear scarfs;
Some that are proper and signify o' thing,
And some another, and some that are nothing.
(55–60)

What sort of dream does Fant'sy present when the antimasquer presents the king, and offers this climatic vision of his realm in the masque proper:

Behold a king
Whose presence maketh this perpetual spring,
The glories of which spring grow in that bower,
And are the marks and beauties of his power.
(189–92)

Is this vision of majesty a tall dream, too? Are not the confusions of Fant'sy's antimasque speech also to be found in the mirror image of the king and his imagined Arcadian state? What kind of spectacle does he present, one that signifies one thing, or many . . . or even nothing? The impropriety of making Fant'sy the purveyor of the royal image dallies with double meanings and with the subversions that lurk in the mirror of resemblance.

Pan's Anniversary and *The Vision of Delight* can be offered as examples of the proximity of royal compliment and its subversion that Jonson managed before his monarch's eyes. We can come closer to the source of *Macbeth* if we look at the Jonsonian masque that stands somewhere behind the masquelike movement that the play ultimately takes. *The Masque of Queens* is particularly apt for consideration here because, like *Macbeth*, central to its concerns is a contention between royal and demonic powers and, specifically, the question of the source of power.

Jonson's *Masque of Queens* is palpably dualistic in design. It opens with "a foil or false masque" (12) in which eleven witches invoke their Dame. She arrives and the witches join together as "faithful opposites" (120) to "disturb" the entertainment – and, more frighteningly, to oppose the accomplishments of an "Age of Gold" (129) and return all things to chaos. The Dame proposes their plans in these words:

Let us disturb it then, and blast the light;
Mix hell with heaven, and make Nature fight
Within herself; loose the whole hinge of things,
And cause the ends run back into their springs.
(134–7)

Gathering together the elements necessary for their powers, the Dame attempts to raise a spirit to accomplish their task. She fails, and in the midst of their frenzied dances, loud music and a sudden change of scene usher in Perseus, the figure of Heroic Virtue, announcing the arrival of Fame; she, in turn, brings on a consort of twelve heroic queens, who end the masque in dancing. Virtue has triumphed over vice; as Jonson notes at the climactic change of scene, the hags vanish "scarce suffering the memory of such a thing" (337).

"Scarce suffering" – barely permitting, but yet, not entirely effacing. For, as is apparent even in a brief summary of the action of the masque, the forces of good and evil bear a striking resemblance – 12 hags, 12 queens – and the structure of the two halves of the masque is also broadly parallel – invocations, arrivals, dances. Dualism would seem to be a mirror effect. In *Queens*, moreover, language passes through the mirror, overriding differences. Although ostensibly the two parts of the masque are related only by opposition, and although the second half of the masque removes all traces of the first, the language of the masque is seamless. Its central trope, in fact, involves sources and origins, suggesting an overriding power. Jonson announces that the argument of the masque is "true fame bred out of virtue" (6); yet breeding, arrival, origination are everywhere apparent in the masque, throwing the relationship between the two parts into question. Does the second come from the first? Has the Dame's unsuccessful attempt to raise a spirit issued in the arrival of Heroic Virtue? Is there a beginning principle?

Here in any event is the seamless thread: the witches arrive, claiming they "come . . . from" a landscape replete with death (45–54), and as they try repeated charms, naming all their instruments (owls, baying dogs, toads, voodoo images, and the like), they raise their Dame. More invocations follow, filled with snatchings, gatherings, pluckings, choosing, biting, sucking, getting, and making – a depletion and a dismemberment of nature to reconstitute it in the specter they would raise. The earth is made a grave, they bury (230) what they have gathered and seek to make it rise again, reconstituted. Here, the language of birth that underlies all these activities is made explicit:

> Dame earth shall quake,
> And the houses shake,
> And her belly shall ache
> As her back were brake
> Such a birth to make
>
> (240–4)

At first they are unsuccessful – "our labor dies! / Our magic feature will not rise" (269–70) – and they attempt again their "magic birth" (298). Instead, the House of Fame rises "in the place of" (338) the witches' hell, as the stage direction indicates. Perseus declares himself the "parent" (356) of Fame; Fame arrives acknowledging her "father" (431) and announcing that she will "draw . . . forth" (439) the twelve queens, who sing in celebration of "Fame that's out of Virtue born" (487) and "this famous birth" (500).

These continuities would seem to confirm the Dame's design, mixing hell with heaven, loosing the "whole hinge of things," and making endings fetch their origins in chaotic beginnings – the scarce-remembered, almost vanished traces of a design which the masque replicates even as it replaces it. If we ask why this specter of resemblance should be in the masque, the answer, we may assume, has to do with absolutist power. Power in the masque is figured as origin giving. Perseus is both parent and strength (356); like the witches, he makes life from death: "When Virtue cut off Terror, he gat [i.e. begat] Fame. / . . . when Fame was gotten Terror died" (351–2). As much as the witches, he needs to dismember to make. Powers of making depend upon depletion – and this, too, is how the masque itself is constructed, "scarce suffering" the memory of the displaced hags, but not entirely effacing them. Jonson's making is thus also in question. Although Perseus points to the columns of the House of Fame as "men-making poets" (362), the poet of the masque is at pains to disavow his powers, telling his reader (Prince Henry) that the masque's invention comes from the queen (9–10); that the decorum of the masque derives from Horace (7–8); that the queens and witches are drawn from the storehouse of classical and contemporary books that he has perused; that even the spectators give life to his designs: "a writer should always trust somewhat to the capacity of the spectator, especially at these spectacles" (95–6).

The privileged spectator here is the king, of course, and the spectacle is designed to mirror and bring forth his mind. Hence, when Perseus presents the twelve queens, he ends with the king, and although Bel-Anna (Queen Anne's role in the masque) is the highest of queens, she must submit "all her worth / To him that gave it," the one who has "brought forth / Their names to memory" (402–4). The pronoun may refer to the poet; a few lines later, it means the king, source of all "increase" (410), conferring the bounty on all which is "contracted" (412) within himself. The king, Perseus says, will "embrace" the "spectacle" (414–15). From a "spectacle of strangeness, producing multiplicity of gesture" (17–18), as Jonson describes the antimasque of witches, arises "the strangeness and beauty of the spectacle" (466), the genuine masque of queens. What the text produces is referred to the king's eye.

What lives in the king's eye here, as in *Macbeth*, is genealogy, what he produces; here, as in *Macbeth*, the king lives to bestow, to give gifts which are contracted within him and which are extended without. Royal absolutism is coincident with full ownership and extension over all so that nothing and no one has autonomy except the king; yet this means that, like Duncan, his absolutism also signifies opacity. The king who gives all is appropriated by what he appropriates. Building and constructing all in his all-embracing view, his power is his blindness. His power lies in a mirror whose reflections cannot be controlled: speculative investments that may deplete the all-giver. Duncan and Macbeth meet for the first time in the play, and Duncan voices the depletion involved in giving, the horrific sense that their exchanges are spectral identifications, transfers like the voodoo magic between the king and his replica:

> O worthiest cousin!
> The sin of my ingratitude even now
> Was heavy on me. Thou art so far before,
> That swiftest wing of recompense is slow
> To overtake thee: would thou hadst less deserv'd,
> That the proportion both of thanks and payment

> Might have been mine! Only I have left to say,
> More is thy due than more than all can pay.
> (I. iv. 14–21)

The more he gives, the less he has; his wish: "would thou hadst less deserv'd."
A few lines later, Duncan attempts to name the "hereafter" despite Macbeth's
success, "so far before."

*

On August 27, 1605, in the course of a visit James and his family made to
Oxford, they were welcomed to St John's College by a learned show, a Latin
entertainment hailing the fulfillment of fate's prophesied genealogy (the line of
Banquo) embodied in the king and queen and their heirs. The lines were spoken
by three woodland creatures, "quasi Sibyllae," they are called, boys
masquerading as numinous female powers, all-hailing their monarch (Bullough,
1973, 471):

> Fame says the fatal Sisters once foretold
> Power without end, great Monarch, to thy stock . . .
> And thus we greet thee: Hail, whom Scotland serves!
> Whom England, Hail! Whom Ireland serves, all hail![10]

So, too, the witches greet Macbeth, so Duncan gives addition to the new Thane
of Cawdor. Banquo wonders if the witches can speak true, but the echoes go
back further. The witches' all-hailing inaugurates Macbeth's career by
appropriating a moment of royal compliment. From the start, the mirror of representation respects no boundaries; the show of kings staged for the mutual
benefit of Macbeth and King James occurs *within* these representations. There
is no source, not even a sovereign author, outside of representation, no end or
beginning to these speculations.

*

Within *Macbeth*, the menacing heterogeneity of uncontrolled duplication that
threatens the autonomy of power is embodied in the witches. In the anxiety about
women in the play we might find a further reflection of the disturbing questions
raised about the sources of the Shakespearean imagination.[11] Jonson's *Masque
of Queens* is instructive in that regard as well, for in order to represent sovereign
power, woman's control over nature and birth are ascribed to the king. Perseus
declares his power – to give birth – and refers it to the king's bounty. Yet, what
is presented to the monarch's eyes is a pageant of armed women to replace the
army of hags, a haunting version of the king's declaration of patriarchal
appropriations. Questions about a power that "lies like truth" (*Macbeth*, V. v.
44) menace men's words and their assertions of authority. Kings and authors,
then, are menaced.

In *Macbeth*, the heterogeneity of the female as Other is implicated in scenes of writing and reading that may reflect on the Shakespearean signature and its sources. "The King hath happily receiv'd, Macbeth, / The news of thy success" (I. iii. 89–90), Rosse reports, describing Duncan as reading:

> and when he reads
> Thy personal venture in the rebels' fight,
> His wonders and his praises do contend,
> Which should be thine, or his   (90–3)

Contention over ownership of the text, however, is, as Rosse goes on to say, "silenc'd," rendered undecidable; the text that Duncan attempts to master instead masters him, news of success that cannot be controlled:

> silenc'd with that,
> In viewing o'er the rest o' th' selfsame day,
> He finds thee in the stout Norweyan ranks,
> Nothing afeard of what thyself didst make,
> Strange images of death.   (93–7)

Within the *selfsame* ("th' selfsame day") a specter of swallowed difference rises;[12] Duncan discovers Macbeth "in the rebels' fight," "in the stout Norweyan ranks," and he finds himself implicated in Macbeth's acts. They meet in "strange images of death" which neither monarch nor his general fears. And so Rosse's report of the king and Macbeth locked in contention for the interpretation of a text ends with Duncan's submission to what "came post with post" (I. iii. 98), the news of Macbeth's success and the specter of succession passing from king to rebel: the king impressed with the letter. Two scenes later, the scene of reading is repeated, literally. Macbeth sends his wife a letter, which he has "thought good to deliver thee," as if he were giving birth to the word as his child. "Lay it to thy heart," he orders (I. v. 10–14). Lady Macbeth looks in her heart, and finds Macbeth "too full o' th' milk of human kindness" (17); whose milk does she find in the word, hers or his? King James declared that his gifts to the nation were their very "nourish-milke" and that he was the kingdom's "loving nourish-father" (1616 [1918, 24]); the patriarch as male mother, greedily sucked dry. Reports of Macbeth's success, Rosse says, were "pour'd . . . down before" (I. iii. 100) the king, delivering what they "bear":

> As thick as hail,
> Came post with post; and every one did bear
> Thy praises in his kingdom's great defence,
> And pour'd them down before him.
>   (I. iii. 97–100)

And in his letter to his wife, Macbeth relates and conflates the earlier scene, "came missives from the King, who all-hail'd me, 'Thane of Cawdor'; by which title, before, these Weird Sisters saluted me." The letter circulates, and male attempts to appropriate power encounter a heterogeneity in their attempted representations; an alliance between women and their words. Macbeth's letter suppresses the success the witches have promised to Banquo, just as the play organizes itself around the conflict between Macbeth and Macduff, and the succession from Duncan to Malcolm. Its mirroring structure represents an absolutist fantasy surpassed by the witches' show.[13]

The hypermasculine world of *Macbeth* is haunted – as is *The Masque of Queens* – by the power represented in the witches; masculinity in the play is directed as an assaultive attempt to secure power, to maintain success and succession, at the expense of women. As is typical of many of Shakespeare's tragedies, the play is largely womanless and family relationships are disturbed; Duncan and Banquo both have heirs, but no wives; Macbeth and Lady Macbeth have no surviving children. The one fully gratuitous act of Macbeth's is the murder of Lady Macduff and her children, an act in which Macduff is fully complicit; he has abandoned his wife, and she accuses him of betrayal. He allies himself with Malcolm in a scene in which the future monarch displays his credentials first by presenting himself as excessively libidinous – and Macduff willingly responds as a virtual procurer to satisfy his lust – and then as excessively chaste; either way, masculinity and power are directed against women. When Macbeth is finally defeated, he is replaced by two men who have secured power in the defeat of women. Indeed, Macduff has not only abandoned his wife and family, his very birth represents a triumph over his mother's womb, the manifest fantasy of being self-begotten that also deludes Macbeth in his final encounter. To mark the new powers in Scotland, the battle concludes with Siward's celebration of the ritual slaughter of his son. It is not Macbeth alone who opposes generativity or wishes to eradicate its source. Good and bad Scots alike are bent on securing power, and that means to seize fully the terrain of women. For Scotland is a bleeding mother in the play, and their aim is to "bestride our downfall birthdom" (IV. iii. 4). "It cannot / Be call'd our mother, but our grave" (165–6), Rosse goes on to say. Birth and death are, in these paradigmatic utterances, man's downfall, the limits of beginning and end; they survive his successes, unlimited limits. The seizure and defeat of women is a bid for immortality, for a power that will never fade.

The shape of that fantasy is revealed in the mirror scene; a line of kings propagated in the mirror. Males produce males, just as Banquo and Duncan seem capable of succession without the interference of women. "Look in thy glass, and tell the face thou viewest / Now is the time that face should form another;" so the third sonnet opens on the prospect of a duplication of images that might be called – if we follow Luce Irigaray (1977, 189) – a determining patriarchal fantasy, the glassy façade of "the sovereign authority of pretense."[14] Macbeth looks in the mirror and sees his reflection in the line that extends to James; not in the mirror is Mary Queen of Scots, the figure that haunts the patriarchal claims of the *Basilikon Doron*, the mother on whom James rested his claims to the throne of England – and whom he sacrificed to assure his sovereignty.

Men may look in the mirror, may have their being in the mirror; but in

Macbeth, the specter of duplicates is in other hands. The spectacle of state here, or in *The Masque of Queens*, is the witches' show. All masculine attempts at female deprivation – including Lady Macbeth's desire to unsex herself – are robbed of ultimate success. Mortality cannot be killed. What escapes control is figured in the witches; emblematically bearded, linguistically ambiguous, they represent, in Harry Berger's brilliant phrase (1982, 52), the textual "display of withheld surplus meaning." Their words stretch out "to th' crack of doom" (IV. i. 117), an ultimate fissure in which both Macbeth and Malcolm have their place hereafter.

Confronting source – and end – the play registers an excess, unsettling in its indifferent and repetitive production, one king after another, a Malcolm for a Macbeth, raised on the body of woman, embodied in the text. The partnership of indifference begins (and ends) in rivalry over the letter, Duncan's reading of Macbeth, Lady Macbeth's reading of Macbeth's letter, or Banquo's confrontation with the witches:

> You seem to understand me,
> By each at once her choppy finger laying
> Upon her skinny lips: you should be women,
> And yet your beards forbid me to interpret
> That you are so.   (I. iii. 43–7)

Their beards and fingers on their lips forbid interpretation and point beyond an order of words and utterance to an excess at the source. Generators of the text, they suggest that the male fantasy of *Macbeth* may have as its counterpart the fantasy of the autonomy of the artistic imagination – Prospero's fantasy in *The Tempest*, for instance, when he displays his power in a masque whose deities are all female – and they caution the critic who would describe the play as the free workings of a mind playing with its sources.[15] At the furthest reach of speculation, they intimate that the mirrors in *Macbeth* represent a meeting of authority and author swallowed in its source. That textual situation might be named Volumnia.

Notes

1. The assumption here overlaps Michel Foucault's argument (1977) that the author must be replaced by the "author-function" as limited and made possible by historical formations. Among the signs of the dispersal of the dramatic author in Shakespeare's time are his failure to publish his plays and the evidence of ongoing revision (rather than a stabilizing of an authoritative authorial text) in at least some of the texts gathered in the 1623 Folio; in the case of *Macbeth*, as discussed below, the Folio text is not entirely Shakespearean, a condition that did not keep Heminge and Condell from publishing it. For some incisive probing of this issue, see Orgel (1981). All references are to the Arden edn of *Macbeth* (Muir, 1982).

2. Booth (1968) also argues for Holinshed's "composite" composition. His thesis is that Holinshed attempts "to contain all accounts in one account" (p. 45) and that "the *Chronicles* are the work in English literature that most fully shares the most peculiarly Shakespearean of Shakespeare's traits – the ability constantly to shift the

perception of a reader or audience from one set of principles for judgment to another'' (p. 72). There are differences between the authors, however, that Booth fails to register. Holinshed is a relentless explainer; however multiple his perspectives he rationalizes each stage in his story; the explanations may not add up, but they are supplied. Shakespeare, on the other hand, omits such things as Holinshed's explanation of Scottish laws of succession and Lady Macbeth's ambition to be queen. Booth's description of *Macbeth*'s relationship to Holinshed echoes the commonplaces, adding to them the New-Critical idea of textual complexity as the Shakespearean version of Holinshed's composite complexity: ''in *Macbeth* Shakespeare omits all indication that Duncan was ever a bad king or Macbeth a good one. He does, however, create a deeper and more intense conflict in his audience by causing its members to sympathize with and share the consciousness of a moral monster'' (p. 80).

For a tabulation of Shakespeare's borrowings from Holinshed, see Law (1952).

3. A notable exception is Berger (1980), to which I am deeply indebted in this discussion.

4. Without making anything of it, Dover Wilson (1947) notes a version of this when he remarks that Holinshed's phrase for Duncan, ''too much of clemencie,'' ''came to be associated in his [Shakespeare's] mind with Macbeth himself.'' More exactly, Lady Macbeth transfers it to her husband. Harding (1969, 246–7) notes that the source for Lady Macbeth's milk in Holinshed lies in the rebels' characterization of Duncan as a milksop.

5. Cf. Berger (1980), 16: ''From the moment in 1.7 when Macbeth approaches the murder as a real possibility, we see his attachment to the figure of Duncan increase.'' Construction continues, too, in Macduff's naming Duncan ''The Lord's anointed Temple'' (II. iii. 67), ''a most sainted King'' (IV. iii. 109). No one speaks about Duncan in these terms before his death, and the king is represented as rebel-besieged; tense in his relations to them – and to those, like Macbeth, dependent upon his generosity; preemptory in naming his heir.

6. Such connections are noted by Kermode (1974) and Muir (1982). They are part of a long tradition of reading *Macbeth* in conjunction with James I fully exemplified by Paul (1950) and Clark (1981). Such views are answered forcefully by Hawkins (1982), who argues against the notion of the monolithic historical background, suggesting instead that Jacobean society was an ambiguous amalgam of tense political relationships and systems; for him, Banquo, Duncan, Macduff, and Malcolm all have political and moral weaknesses, and Macbeth is not entirely a villain. The play is equivocal throughout, as was contemporary politics. Hawkins's skeptical and empirical view does not credit the power of symbolic discourse in political behavior, and the ambiguities he details are perhaps more rational than the equivocations in *Macbeth*.

The choice of reflecting James in Edward the Confessor must be set in the context of James's repeated disgust and sarcasm at the practice of touching; see Willson (1956), 172–3. That Banquo is hardly innocent in the play has been observed by critics from Bradley (1904 [1956, 379–87]) on.

7. At the very least, if we account for the composition of *Macbeth* in terms of the operation of Shakespeare's unconscious associations, we should recognize that the unconscious is a historical phenomenon that never operates freely, and is intimately bound to social structures (e.g. the family, the state) that promote and limit autonomy.

8. On the political significance of the witches, see the suggestive essay by Stallybrass (1982), which acutely situates the witches in opposition to patriarchal rule as an antistate and an antifamily. I am particularly indebted to him for suggesting that the dilemma they pose is ''solved'' by the attempt to form families without women (p. 198). The ''normality'' of this patriarchal fantasy, and its historical refigurations,

is the subject in Sedgwick (1985).

9. I consider this moment in the masque from a slightly different perspective in *James I and the Politics of Literature* (1982), 130–1. All masque citations from Jonson (1969). The trope of this essay, and my treatment of the masque, depend upon Orgel (1975, 77) who describes the form as "the mirror of the king's mind."

10. The relation of this entertainment to *Macbeth* was noted by Chambers (1930) and is conjectured in Nichols (1828, I, 543). Bullough's text translates a page appended to Matthew Gwinne's *Vertumnus*; it may not represent the exact form of the entertainment, which is discussed by Nichols (pp. 543–5). Sir Isaac Wake (1607) gives his account of the royal visit; his description of the entertainment explicitly mentions Macbeth, whereas Gwinne's text alludes solely to the prophecy to Banquo. Wake introduces his account of the entertainment with the story of "tres olim Sibyllae occurrisse duobus Scotiae proceribus *Macbetho & Banchoni*, & illum praedixisse Regem futurum, sed Regem nullum geniturum, hunc Regem non futurum, sed Reges geniturum multes" (p. 18).

11. The subject of masculinity and femininity in the play has been discussed often; see, e.g., Harding (1969); Berger (1980), 26–8, (1982), 64–74. Gohlke (1980) argues that the play centers on the eradication of the feminine and male fantasies of self-authorship but tends to essentialize and sentimentalize the idea of the feminine, a view that can be corrected, as Jones argues (1981, 255–61), only by attention to the historical particularities that would underlie psychic formations.

12. On the question of same and different in Shakespeare, see Fineman's (1980, 89, 103–4) acute development of René Girard's terms. For a rather mechanical treatment of doubling and a brief consideration of Macbeth's relationship with his wife as a son-mother pairing, see Rogers (1970), 48–51.

13. Studying the limiting aspects of masculinity, Asp (1981, 165) suggests that Macbeth's inhuman project may be related to the sexually undifferentiated witches; the end of the play, in this view, replicates its initial stereotypes, a view also suggested by Felperin (1977). Horwitch notes (1978, 371) that Malcolm confesses to Macbeth's crimes in IV. iii. and "may be seen as, potentially, a Macbeth in embryo." It is surely to the point that his ultimate position, replicating Duncan's, as Macduff mirrors Macbeth, is offered as a success that the witches have pre-ordained for the line of Banquo.

14. See also Irigaray (1983), a selection from *Amante marine: de Friedrich Nietzsche*, for an extraordinary discussion of patriarchal appropriations of the maternal. My use, like Irigaray's, is Lacanian – inflected, I hope, with the historical particularities involved in Renaissance constructions of the feminine.

15. The question of textual autonomy can be approached from many directions. It is surely no accident that *Macbeth* was early appropriated for the New Criticism by Brooks (1947) as a particularly *dense* text apt for close readings; not surprisingly, such readings have been intensely conservative. Valuable along these lines, however, is Stein (1951) with its emphasis on Macbeth's linguistic insecurity.

As Moretti (1982, 32–4) argues, soliloquy (particularly in *Macbeth* and *Hamlet*) represents an excessive blockage of political process, the excrescence of ideological mystification that I have called, following him, an absolutist fantasy. Mullaney (1980, 42–5) argues that the linguistic excess in *Macbeth* imbricates treason – an uncontrollable ambiguity rather than the New-Critical kind. Finally Greenblatt (1982, 1985) seeks to describe Shakespearean autonomy as an improvisatory effect accomplished within the institutional / ideological space determined by social fictions and discourses. In their various ways, these critics move toward a demystification of autonomy and a description of the achievement of an autonomy effect.

If, as I suggest, Shakespeare represents the textuality of his plays through women, and allies his author function with them, Greenblatt's (1980) study of the *submission* of Desdemona, an absorption of text and role that does not exclude her "downright violence" (I. iii. 249), might prove useful in exploring the nature and representation of Shakespeare's authorial autonomy.

Works cited

Asp, C. (1981) " 'Be bloody, bold and resolute': Tragic Action and Sexual Stereotyping in *Macbeth,*" *Studies in Philology,* 78, 153–69.

Berger, Jr, H. (1980) "The Early Scenes of *Macbeth*: Preface to a New Interpretation," *English Literary History,* 47, 1–31.

—— (1982) "Text against Performance in Shakespeare: The Example of *Macbeth,*" *Genre,* 15, 49–79.

Booth, S. (1968) *The Book Called Holinshed's Chronicles,* San Francisco, Book Club of California.

Bradley, A.C. (1904) *Shakespearean Tragedy,* repr. 1956, London, Macmillan.

Brooks, C. (1947) "The Naked Babe and the Cloak of Manliness," in Brooks, C., *The Well-Wrought Urn,* New York, Harcourt, Brace, & World.

Bullough, G. (1973) *Narrative and Dramatic Sources of Shakespeare,* VII, London, Routledge & Kegan Paul.

Chambers, E.K. (1930) *William Shakespeare,* Oxford, Clarendon Press.

Clark, A.M. (1981) *Murder Under Trust or The Topical Macbeth,* Edinburgh, Scottish Academic Press.

Derrida, J. (1976) *Of Grammatology,* trans. G.C. Spivak, Baltimore, Johns Hopkins University Press.

—— (1978) "Cogito and the History of Madness," in Derrida, J., *Writing and Difference,* trans. A. Bass, Chicago, University of Chicago Press.

—— (1981) *Positions,* trans. A. Bass, Chicago, University of Chicago Press.

—— (1982) "Qual Quelle: Valéry's Sources," in Derrida, J., *Margins of Philosophy,* trans. A. Bass, Chicago, University of Chicago Press, 273–306.

Felperin, H. (1977) *Shakespearean Representation,* Princeton, Princeton University Press.

Fineman, J. (1980) "Fratricide and Cuckoldry: Shakespeare's Doubles," in Kahn, C. and Schwartz, M. (eds) *Representing Shakespeare,* Baltimore, Johns Hopkins University Press.

Foucault, M. (1977) "What is an Author?" in Foucault, M., *Language, Counter-Memory, Practice,* trans. D.F. Bouchard and S. Simon, Ithaca, Cornell University Press.

—— (1979) "My Body, This Paper, This Fire," *Oxford Literary Review,* 4, 9–28.

Gohlke, M. (1980) " 'I wooed thee with my sword': Shakespeare's Tragic Paradigms," in Kahn, C. and Schwartz, M. (eds) *Representing Shakespeare,* Baltimore, Johns Hopkins University Press.

Goldberg, J. (1983) *James I and the Politics of Literature,* Baltimore, Johns Hopkins University Press.

—— (1985) "Herbert's 'Decay' and the Articulation of History," *Southern Review,* 18, 3–21.

Greenblatt, S. (1980) *Renaissance Self-Fashioning: From More to Shakespeare,* Chicago, University of Chicago Press.

—— (1982) "*King Lear* and Harsnett's 'Devil Fiction'," *Genre,* 15, 239–42.

—— (1985) "Shakespeare and the Exorcists," in Jay, G.S. and Miller, D.L. (eds) *After Strange Texts,* University, University of Alabama Press.

Harding, D.W. (1969) "Women's Fantasy of Manhood," *Shakespeare Quarterly,* 20, 245–53.

Hawkins, M. (1982) "History, Politics and *Macbeth,*" in Brown, J.R. (ed.) *Focus on Macbeth,* London, Routledge & Kegan Paul.

Horwitch, R. (1978) "Integrity in *Macbeth*: The Search for the 'single state of man',"
Shakespeare Quarterly, 29, 365–73.

Irigaray, L. (1977) "Des marchandises entre elles," in *Ce sexe qui n'en est pas un*,
Paris, Minuit; trans. Claudia Reeder, in Marks, E. and de Courtivron, E. (eds) *New
French Feminisms*, New York, Schocken.

—— (1983) "Veiled Lips," *Mississippi Review*, 33, 93–131.

James I (1616) *Basilikon Doron*, in McIlwain, C.H. (ed.) (1918) *The Political Works of
James I*, Cambridge, Mass., Harvard University Press.

Jones, A.R. (1981) "Writing the Body: Toward an Understanding of *l'écriture
féminine*," *Feminist Studies*, 7, 247–63.

Jonson, B. (1969) *The Complete Masques*, ed. S. Orgel, New Haven, Yale University
Press.

Kermode, F. (1974) "Introduction" to *Macbeth*, in *The Riverside Shakespeare*, Boston,
Houghton Mifflin.

Law, R.A. (1952) "The Composition of *Macbeth* with Reference to Holinshed," *Texas
Studies in English*, 31, 35–41.

Moretti, F. (1982) "'A Huge Eclipse': Tragic Forms and the Deconsecration of
Sovereignty," *Genre*, 15, 7–40.

Muir, Kenneth (ed.) (1982) *Macbeth* by William Shakespeare, Arden edn, London,
Methuen.

Mullaney, S. (1980) "Lying like Truth: Riddle, Representation and Treason in
Renaissance England," *English Literary History*, 47, 32–47.

Nichols, J. (1828) *The Progresses of King James I*, London, J.B. Nichols.

Orgel, S. (1975) *The Illusion of Power*, Berkeley, University of California Press.

—— (1981) "What is a text?" *Research Opportunities in Renaissance Drama*, 24,
3–6.

—— (1983) "Shakespeare imagines a Theater," in Muir, K., Halio, J. and Palmer,
D.J. (eds) *Shakespeare, Man of the Theater*, Newark, University of Delaware Press.

Parker, A. (1981) "'Taking Sides' (on History): Derrida re-Marx," *Diacritics*, 11 (3),
57–73.

—— (1985) "Between Dialectics and Deconstruction: Derrida and the Reading of
Marx," in Jay, G.S. and Miller, D.L. (eds) *After Strange Texts*, University, University of Alabama Press.

Paul, H.N. (1950) *The Royal Play of Macbeth*, New York, Macmillan.

Rogers, R. (1970) *A Psychoanalytic Study of the Double in Literature*, Detroit, Wayne
State University.

Sedgwick, E.K. (1985) *Between Men: English Literature and Male Homosocial Desire*,
New York, Columbia University Press.

Stallybrass, P. (1982) "*Macbeth* and Witchcraft," in Brown, J.R. (ed.) *Focus on
Macbeth*, London, Routledge & Kegal Paul.

Stein, A. (1951) "*Macbeth* and Word Magic," *Sewanee Review*, 59, 271–84.

Wake, I. (1607) *Rex Platonicus*, Oxford.

Willson, D.H. (1956) *King James VI and I*, New York, Oxford University Press.

Wilson, J.D. (1947) "Introduction" to *Macbeth*, Cambridge, Cambridge University
Press.

12

Towards a literary theory of ideology: mimesis, representation, authority

Robert Weimann

At this stage of exploration and opening up of fresh vistas, the new historical and materialist criticism of Shakespeare deserves respect when, seeking to avoid self-congratulation, it is positively concerned to dispel any impression of undue conceptual unity or methodological coherence. This becomes obvious in at least three areas of theory against which the discursive acts and social functions of ideology in the Shakespearean theatre can helpfully be discussed. These areas involve: (1) the space of conflict and / or concurrence between mimesis and signification; (2) the uses of representation as a specifically theatrical type of historical activity; (3) the social and ideological uses of authority in this connection.

1

Let me begin with the observation that, in the new historical and materialist-cultural criticism, the role of mimesis in the ideological function of the Shakespearean text has hardly been considered. True, there appears to be some general consensus (widely reflected in these essays) that criticism needs to go beyond the position of Georg Lukács according to which the ideological uses

ROBERT WEIMANN is the author of a number of books and articles on literary theory, literary history, and Renaissance texts. His major books available in English include *Shakespeare and the Popular Tradition in the Theater*, ed. Robert Schwartz (Baltimore, Johns Hopkins University Press, 1978), and *Structure and Society in Literary History* (Baltimore, Johns Hopkins University Press, 1984). He is Vice-President of the Akademie der Kunste of the GDR and the Head of the English and American section in the Zentralinstitut für Literaturgeschichte of the Akademie der Wissenschaften of the GDR.

(and, for Lukács, the aesthetic values) of the text are first and foremost to be assessed in terms of its mimetic dimension and achievement. As against that, we are presented with a more balanced position, according to which the social function of the text draws its energy and power from its referential register as well as its capacities for production, mediation, and communication. The text is a product as well as a 'producer' of power, a reflection as well as an agent of social relations. Such a position, for instance, is neatly paraphrased by Don E. Wayne in this volume when he notes that Elizabeth forms of power are 'reflected, refracted, displayed, mediated, or even produced by . . . plays in concert with other contemporaneous social practices' (p. 52).

This, of course, is a formulation which is not designed to address theoretical issues: even so it may not be unfair to conclude from a position such as this that the ideological function of the text, the actually achieved effect of subversion or recuperation, appears to be linked with its capacity for reflection and, hence, mediation and communication of power. But then the question must be asked how and to what extent do these mimetic uses of power either conflict with or corroborate the uses, in language, of an ideological signified which is always already given? It will cause no surprise for us to come across the altogether different position which holds that art is no longer an imitation of nature or life when life itself is taken to be a symbolization. From a stance like this, the conclusion seems inevitable (and is, indeed, drawn) that the work of the mimetic critic must be conceived as altogether irreconcilable with that of the post-structuralist or semiotic critic.

In view of this dichotomy (which, I think, seriously interferes with a more balanced view of the functions of ideology in the theatre) my question is, how do we assess and grapple with both this presumed antinomy and the actual nonidentity between the referential and the signifying dimensions of the text? For the element of nonidentity seems vital: there is no point in minimizing the actually existing contradiction between mimesis and the sign. The question is, rather, how to accept this contradiction as inevitable and, perhaps, as a productive register of the power of ideology in a specifically theatrical context of dramatic signification and representation. In other words, the suggestion is that, far from obliterating or displacing this contradiction, we need to bring it out into the open, in order to use it with a view to stimulating a materialist and historicist understanding of the mimetic dimensions of the theatrical sign and the signifying dimensions of theatrical mimesis – 'mimesis' taken in both its discursive and its nondiscursive dimensions, in language as well as in action. It is at the crossroads of these two dimensions that, I think, the production and reception of theatrical texts can best be explored as to the strengths and limits of the ideological functions involved in them.

There is one further reason why this contradiction should be acknowledged but not be used to set up impenetrable barriers between semiotics and the study of referentiality. For it seems perfectly plausible to argue that both fields of study can, in different ways and degrees, attain to an awareness of history only to the extent that the communicative dimension of both representation and signification is given its due. To historicize the Elizabethan drama seems impossible without at least attempting to relate the text to the theatre and the society of which this theatre was and is, then and now, *both* a product (or mirror) and, as it were, a producer, communicator, and distributor of signs. I am using this formulation, in the sense that Karl Marx, in the *Grundrisse*, talks about art as one of the special modes of production (Marx, 1939 [1973, 409]) – a definition which appears particularly relevant when we come to consider the theatre not as a mere chronicle of the times or abstract of events but as a socially overdetermined and highly institutionalized space of cultural activities. Among these activities mimesis and signification do indeed loom largest: in the social process of the theatre they both involve the communication of ideological effects, and they do so through the theatrical use of signs which go to make up images, and the use of dramatic images which are made up of signs discursive and nondiscursive.

This of course is the hastiest of generalizations, one which needs to be discussed and taken further, not only because of its vital importance in terms of current literary theory but also because it so obviously involves considerations of cultural politics. If the newest historical-materialist criticism of the Shakespearean text wishes to sustain its impact, then it can only be helpful if American new historicism and British cultural materialism negotiate their differences (as well as areas of concurrence) in relation to the politics of deconstruction. From the point of view of theory, to focus on the links and gaps between mimesis and the sign is one way to redefine what, in either case (though for differing reasons), is a highly undeveloped awareness of the political ironies and paradoxes of the dominant tenets in poststructuralist criticism. What we need is clarification, but this clarification cannot very well be achieved unless we proceed to a more stringent critique of some of the unhistorical and formalist elements in the poststructuralist project.

2

My second question (which starts from and takes further the first complex) focuses on the relationship of representation and ideology. This of course is a vast question, and although it also involves highly controversial issues, perhaps it is useful to discuss some of the most basic premises on which the ideological uses of representation can be explored.

Normally, and the contributions to this volume form no exception, highly diverging positions can be noted. For instance, there is the position, or at least the implication, that the ideological function of the text can best be revealed and defined in terms of a nonrepresentational concept of writing and reading. As against this stance, there is the position (as outlined by Karen Newman in this volume) that 'our critical task is not merely to describe the formal parameters of a play, nor is it to make claims about Shakespeare's politics, conservative or subversive, but to reveal the discursive and dramatic evidence for such representations, and their counterparts in criticism, *as representations*' (p. 158, emphasis added).

Obviously, the Derridean critique of logocentrism and teleology and Foucault's searching genealogy of the sign are profoundly stimulating as some anti-idealistic alternative to Platonic and Aristotelian concepts of representation. Yet the question is: do they not remain unsatisfactory as soon as, in our case, the theatre is considered as a social, cultural, mimetic, and of course ideological institution in Elizabethan history? If this is so, the whole process of representation needs to be reconsidered beyond the Derridean terminology of presence and absence. Is it good enough to approach representation as representation or as the representation of difference? Or, rather is not the representation of difference a function of social conflicts in the sense that it is preceded by existential needs, desires, and appropriations?

It is most encouraging to find that, at least by implication, some such position is taken in several of the essays in this volume. Jean E. Howard, for instance, sees in the Shakespearean theatre an appropriation of theatrical power by unsanctioned social groups (see Chapter 7). But the question might be pondered: how do we define the ideological use of this power in terms of the specific theatrical forms and functions of representation itself? To appropriate the theatre as a commercial institution is one thing; it is quite another for unsanctioned social groups to develop and project some consciousness of the social location of their appropriation through representational action and discourse. As long as we do not follow those critics who would define representation as *eo ipso* some *Herrschaftseffekt*, some oppressive regime of social domination, the question needs to be asked how and in which ways the juridical appropriation of the Elizabethan theatrical institution was followed up by some contiguous representational activity which did not homogenize discursive space and which did not suppress discontinuity in favour of some stabilizing hierarchy.

Obviously, what we need is some reconsideration of 'representation' as the representation of 'difference' in both the social sense of class conflict, gender, and cultural heterogeneity *and* the linguistic sense of the discontinuity between signifier and signified. Such discontinuity might well be traced to the centre of the discursive processing of ideology in the theatre: the signifier as used in the language and representational action of those 'unsanctioned social groups' (i.e. the what and who is *representing*) might then be seen to be either more or less discontinuous with who and what is *represented* (i.e. the signified in the mirror held up to kings and princes or sanctioned norms of social behaviour). For instance, if, as Hamlet in his advice to the players suggests, this signified is identical with 'virtue' showing 'her feature, scorn her own image' (III. ii. 22–3), then the represented would be conceived prior to the act of representation itself. In that case, the contradiction might indeed be considerable between the represented and the representing standards of unsanctioned theatrical activity. The point, of course, which I would like to make is that ideology, once we look for it in the representational process itself, must be seen to be operative in conflicting ways, above all in the contradiction itself between who and what is representing and who and what is represented. (For a fuller development of this point, see Weimann, 1985.)

However, this emphasis on the social and existential correlative of representational action must not lead us to ignore or minimize the fictional status of theatrical discourse. To approach 'representations as representations' is to draw attention to the institutionalized status of Shakespeare's artificial persons and to emphasize the extent to which these signs and images of difference in language and society are sustained by cultural conventions as constituted and mediated by varying (and potentially conflicting) types of discourse. While it is immensely helpful not to underestimate the powers and privileges of this institutionalized language in the theatre, the question needs to be asked whether the ideological uses of representation can exhaustively be described in terms of its theatrical context alone. If, as I have suggested elsewhere (Weimann, 1978), there is a connection between the representational (as against the allegorical) mode of drama and the rise of political representation in the sixteenth and seventeenth centuries, then at least the possibility needs to be considered that representational uses of mimesis involve a new type of social delegation, generalization, and typicality – and if they do, we must ask to what extent.

The suggestion is that in talking about the uses of representation, over and beyond its linguistic and epistemological problematic, we must not forget about representation as an act of embodying and intercepting the desires, the privileges, the political unconscious of certain powerful groups of men and women. If, as René Girard has emphasized, the act of appropriation and, let me add, the material reproduction of life precede the problematic of the sign, then representation must be defined on several levels, including that of the world of history. Thus, the political idea of representativity, as it takes shape in Shakespeare's time, is intricately bound up with the decline of a society based on lineage. In the world of feudal relations, social interests were not primarily delegated and upheld in terms of juridically or politically asserted patterns of representativeness but in terms of family and dynastic loyalties. As long as these tended to be more directly translated into the use of force or noneconomic modes of constraint, the social uses of discourse were different and more limited, its ideological function more subservient to the dominant repertoire of a strictly controlled use of transcendental signifieds.

It is only with the advent of the printing press, the subsequent explosion of discursive activities, and as a consequence of the more highly abstract and self-authorized types of discourse associated with the Reformation, that modern forms and effects of ideology came to be widely appropriated in more easily accessible texts and through more highly variegated uses of language. As I have attempted to show in my *Shakespeare und die Macht der Mimesis* (Weimann, 1987), this state of affairs directly affects the institutionalized quality and function of discourse in the Elizabethan drama. From now on the representation and delegation of power find themselves confronted with a new (ideological) power of representation, in the sense that the discursive acts of writing and reading attain to a greater degree of autonomy. The relationship of signifier and signified becomes more dynamic, less predictable, and more indeterminate. Hence there is more space for ambivalence, in which ideology can be either hidden or undermined. At the same time, there is a proliferation of ideological effects which goes hand in hand with the Elizabethan theatre's relative independence of any of the ruling classes.

As soon as the appropriation of the theatre is viewed as constituting difference within as well as outside the act of representation, the question poses itself: on what ideological grounds, in terms of which legitimation gestures was it possible for these unsanctioned social interests in the public playhouses to authorize their own theatrical discourse? This question places ideology at the cross-roads of the institutional and the linguistic modes of appropriating cultural power and social influence, and it seeks to sound the political unconscious in the unformulated modes of existence and production in the late Tudor and early Stuart public theatre.

3

In approaching the uses of authority in the Shakespearean theatre the most immediate observation is that, characteristically, the reproduction of ideology is not something preordained or simply given. The whole process of authorizing discourse and action is, in the theatre, fundamentally different from what we have in the ruling institutions of political 'order'. There, we find a prominent Justice of the Peace, the indefatigable servant of the crown in Kent, William Lambarde, talking about juridical authority as 'already given' (Lambarde, ed. Read, 1962, 80). As against such preordained uses of authority, the theatre is a place of ideological production as well as reception, and the nature of this reproduction is inseparable from the element of indeterminacy in both the Elizabethan stage and the way that text and action, discursive and nondiscursive modes of mimesis, involve a constant interchange of used signs and unused significations. As Keir Elam has reminded us, a dramatic text is not simply a text which is written and then translated into the convention of theatrical production. Rather, 'the written text . . . is determined by its very need for stage contextualization, and indicates throughout its allegiance to the physical conditions of performance' (Elam, 1980, 209).

It is this interdependence of text and stage which makes it impossible for us to discuss the theatre's norms of cultural self-authorization without, at the same time, going into the peculiar authority which resides in the dramatic text itself. Peter Erickson, in this volume, has made the point (a point which he formulates with particular reference to patriarchal ideology) that in the Elizabeth theatre, ideological control 'has to be negotiated each time, and the outcome is variable and uncertain'. What is important about the operation of ideology in the Shakespearean theatre is, then, that there is 'genuine exploration and struggle rather than . . . the unfolding of a doctrinal formula' (Erickson, p. 117). This exploratory mode is intimately associated with the element of indeterminacy and unpredictability which results from the interaction of text and stage, when textualized, oral, physical, conventional, and naturalizing signs meet and constitute areas of difference and contradiction within representational practice itself.

Once this point of intersection is recognized as crucial in establishing the peculiarly unsanctioned and unstable norms of authority in the Shakespearean text in the theatre, it should not come as a surprise that 'authority' (the word occurs sixty times in Shakespeare's works) has to be approached as both an object and an agent of representation. As an object, it is part of the representation of power; but when this 'great image of authority' is represented as 'a dog's obey'd in office' (*King Lear*, IV. vi. 160–1), the difference, within the act of representation, emerges clearly: the authority of who and what is representing has become altogether different from, if not hostile to, what and who is being represented.

Thus, the question of authority in both the text and the theatre is inseparable from the rupture in representation, the difference among activities signifying and signified. But preceding the unstable determination of this rupture is the gesture of appropriation, the struggle of material interests in the very process of confirming or challenging ideological control beyond its customary space of closure and predetermination.

4

Finally, and in conclusion to these highly generalized theoretical notes on ideology in Shakespeare's text and theatre, I should like to say a word on the problematic of ideological criticism. At the height of Shakespeare's concern with authority, when 'madness in discourse' is taken to register a deep split between the authority of morality, belief, and tradition and the authority of the senses, of what Troilus can hear and see and experience in the Grecian camp, the appropriation of intellectual authority itself is dramatized and shown up as involving some bifurcation of ideology and 'experience'. While it may not be acceptable to regard this 'bifold authority' (*Troilus and Cressida*, V. ii, 143) as a valid definition of the dilemma of ideology in Shakespeare's text, yet this dilemma contributes to a sense of embarrassment and incompleteness as soon as the total effect of Shakespeare's text in the theatre is subsumed under the name and order of ideology. Once its stupendous importance is no longer in doubt, it may be necessary to face the limits of ideology and the limitations of a purely ideological criticism. To make this point is not some kind of revisionist gesture, but one which takes its point of departure from the subversive effects of the Shakespearean text. For the question is not fully answered yet: how, and by which strategies, did the Shakespearean theatre escape or displace the enormous pressures of the ruling-class ideology? Here, the use of theatrical game, sport, playfulness, riddle, the fool's impertinence, the antic disposition, the conventions of madness and song loom large, and particularly so if we wish to spell out and specify the means and effects of the appropriation of theatrical power. To be sure, such specification can no longer be obtained in terms of C.L. Barber's magnificent book on festive comedy (Barber, 1959), all the more so since 'festive release' cannot be defined in terms of any benign theatrical process and effect. On the other hand (and this refers to an important strand in the seminar discussion) any criticism, and especially a politically committed criticism, would as a matter of course condemn itself to a grim kind of puritanism if the sheer element of fun, release, reckless enjoyment were ever minimized or, even, by implication, theoretically ostracized. This is not to say that, for instance, the Brechtian concept of *Spass* (fun, pleasure) is, functionally, beyond ideology; the point is it cannot exclusively be defined in terms of ideological structures and categories, any more than other forms of corporeal activity, such as eating, laughing, smiling, and sneezing can be reduced to ideological gestures of subversion or rehearsal. This is why, I think, it is not an idealistic stance to begin again to talk about the enjoyment of Shakespeare's text: rather, any materialist criticism which obliterates this whole dimension must appear suspect. Ultimately, it may perhaps be said that one of the ways by which the Elizabethan theatre appropriated power was to challenge the representation of authority by an alternative authority of theatrical representation which derived at least part of its strength from vitalizing and mobilizing a new space for *Spass*, with all its irreverent and equalizing implications in the social process.

Works cited

Barber, C.L. (1959) *Shakespeare's Festive Comedy*, Princeton, NJ, Princeton University Press.
Elam, Keir (1980) *The Semiotics of Theatre and Drama*, London and New York, Methuen.
Girard, René (1961) *Deceit, Desire, and the Novel: Self and Other in Literary Structure*, trans. Yvonne Freccero (1965), Baltimore, Johns Hopkins University Press.
—— (1978) *'To double business bound': Essays on Literature, Mimesis, and Anthropology*, Baltimore and London, Johns Hopkins University Press.
Jenkins, Harold (ed.) (1982) *Hamlet*, by William Shakespeare, Arden edn, London, Methuen.
Lambarde, William (1962) *William Lambarde and Local Government: His 'Ephemeris' and Twenty-Nine Charges to Juries and Commissions*, ed. Conyers Read, Ithaca, NY, Cornell University Press, for the Folger Shakespeare Library.
Marx, Karl (1939) *Grundrisse*, trans. Martin Nicolaus (1973), Harmondsworth, Penguin, in association with New Left Review.
Muir, Kenneth (ed.) (1964) *King Lear*, by William Shakespeare, Arden edn, London, Methuen.
Palmer, Kenneth (ed.) (1982) *Troilus and Cressida*, by William Shakespeare, Arden edn, London, Methuen.
Weimann, Robert (1967) *Shakespeare and the Popular Tradition in the Theatre: Studies in the Social Dimension of Dramatic Form and Function*, ed. Robert Schwartz, Baltimore and London, Johns Hopkins University Press.
—— (1985) "Mimesis in *Hamlet*," in Parker, Patricia and Hartman, Geoffrey (eds) *Shakespeare and the Question of Theory*, New York and London, Methuen, 275–91.
—— (1987) *Shakespeare und die Macht der Mimesis: Autorität und Repräsentation im elisabethanische Theater*, Berlin, Aufbau.

Afterword

Margaret Ferguson

From the Janus-faced position of an afterword writer I want to reflect on a set of questions implied by the main title of this volume and explored, in fruitful but necessarily provisional ways, by many of the contributors. The questions are difficult and I don't have satisfactory answers to them. Indeed one of the results of working on this volume, of participating in the process by which this set of conference papers and responses to them have been revised for publication, is that I see more clearly now than I did a year ago the contours of what I don't know, or cannot articulate clearly, about my own political options and those available to members of that (possible) coalition of Shakespearean critics and teachers invoked by Walter Cohen in this book. I also see better, however, how the questions raised implicitly and explicitly by my co-contributors about the problem of political *agency* are related to questions currently being addressed by other left-wing intellectuals who are linked, across disciplinary and national boundaries, by the material and ideological contradictions of their position as oppositional educators whose political views entail a critical perspective on the educational institutions that trained them and within which most of them earn their living.

"Shakespeare Reproduced": the title plays on both the negative and the positive connotations of the term reproduction. At one end of the semantic spectrum repeatedly traversed in these pages, reproduction signifies a desideratum, the possibility of producing Shakespeare *differently*, as the editors write in their

---

MARGARET FERGUSON, Professor of English and Comparative Literature at Columbia University, is the author of *Trials of Desire: Renaissance Defenses of Poetry* (New Haven, Yale University Press, 1983) and coeditor, with Maureen Quilligan and Nancy Vickers, of *Rewriting the Renaissance: The Discourses of Sexual Difference in Early Modern Europe* (Chicago and London, University of Chicago Press, 1986).

introduction, by exploring "the ideological functions of texts at various historical junctures and in various cultural practices" (p. 4). Here reproduction is understood as refashioning, making new, or, more precisely, as the possibility of making original scholarly research and critical arguments work to change traditional ways of interpreting Shakespeare in academic writing, in teaching, and in theatrical production. At the other end of the spectrum, however, reproduction connotes mere mechanical repetition or worse, an effect of repetition that occurs despite the intention, on the part of an individual or group, to make a political difference. This negative pole of meaning has acquired a specific historical and political valence in recent years because of the centrality of the concept of reproduction in debates between radical social theorists about the ways in which capitalist societies maintain themselves over time. As a general term for the complex of economic, institutional, political, and ideological forces that work to preserve the *status quo*,[1] reproduction is a specter that haunts the editors of this volume and most of the contributors too, including me. The presence of that specter in these pages – and in those of two other recently published collections of political / critical essays on Shakespeare – is, however, not necessarily a cause for lament; on the contrary, one might argue that the very possibility of reproducing Shakespeare in the sense of producing him *differently* requires that we confront, as several of the essayists in this volume do explicitly, the question of how ostensibly oppositional critical or pedagogical practices may serve, in the long run or even the short, to further rather than disrupt the processes of social reproduction.

Let me try to illustrate this point with specific reference to the arena of pedagogical practice. I choose this focus for several reasons: first, because I agree with the editors that it may ultimately be more important, and also more difficult, to effect significant changes in the ways Shakespeare is taught than in the ways his texts are produced in academic critical writing, though there are obviously interesting and potentially fruitful relations between the two practices. Second, of the principal institutions through which Shakespeare's plays are disseminated in modern times – academic publishing, theater, film, television, and education – the last, as Alan Sinfield has argued, seems to place the most stringent constraints on acts of radical reinterpretation (Dollimore and Sinfield, 1985, 132). Third, most readers of this book, like most of the contributors, are likely to have extensive knowledge of how Shakespeare is commonly presented in the classroom. And finally, there is a large and provocative debate among contemporary social theorists about educational institutions as sites both for social reproduction and for effective political intervention. Even a bird's-eye view of these recent debates, which reflect fundamental tensions within and on the fringes of the traditions of western Marxism, will show their relevance to the theoretical and practical issues at stake in *Shakespeare Reproduced*.

The major participants in the education-as-reproduction debates may be roughly divided into two camps: on one side are theorists such as Louis Althusser, Pierre Bourdieu, and Jean-Claude Passeron in France, and Samuel Bowles and Herbert Gintis in the US. What links these writers, despite their significant theoretical differences, is their dark view of educational institutions as sites for reproducing both the capitalist division of labor (a constantly changing structure which includes not only a "diversely skilled" labor force but its stratification along lines of gender, class, and race) and also the ideological *relations* between dominant and subordinate groups.[2] The other camp includes a growing number of progressive educational theorists working in several countries: Michael W. Apple, Martin Carnoy, Stanley Aronowitz, and Henry A. Giroux for instance, in the US; Madeleine MacDonald and Michael Young in Britain; Rachel Sharp in Australia; Noëlle Bisseret, Christian Baudelot, and Roger Establet in France. These writers have during the past decade offered serious critiques of Althusser, Bourdieu and Passeron, and others (I shall call them the "severe reproduction theorists") who present, in their opponents' view, overly deterministic, functional, or totalizing theories of educational reproduction.[3] Members of this second camp, which I shall label the "contestatory" one, seek at once to define and to dramatize the possibilities for effective radical action, on the part of both students and teachers, within educational institutions. Without denying that the *main* function of such institutions is to reproduce the existing system of social relations, the contestatory theorists stress the "often contradictory conditions which tie education to an unequal society" (Apple, 1982, 8). Examining these contradictions in ways that make the concept of reproduction a double-edged sword, Michael W. Apple epitomizes the "contestatory" critical perspective when he argues (following Gramsci) that there are "countervailing tendencies and oppositional practices" occurring within educational institutions, and that such institutions may therefore work to reproduce forms of opposition as well as the existing (but not monolithic) system of capitalist social relations (Apple, 1982, 8).

It should be clear that participants on both sides of this debate start from assumptions that contrast sharply with those held by liberal educational theorists who have traditionally seen school reform – in curricular matters or admissions policies, for instance – as a way of directly effecting beneficent changes in the social distribution of power and knowledge.[4] Radical educational theorists, in contrast, characteristically assume that schools, and most projects of school reform as well, generally work in the interests of the state. What is at issue between different radical educators is how *successfully* schools serve as "ideological state apparatuses" (in Althusser's phrase) and, correlatively, how much opportunity schools provide, at specific historical moments, for effective contestation. It is fair to say that in their general view of schools as sites for social reproduction, though not in their valuation of that function, left-wing educational theorists have more in common with conservative educators than with most liberal ones: the right-wing authors of a recent *Commentary* article on higher education in the US, for instance, clearly articulate the idea that schools *should* serve the state. "Until recently," the *Commentary* authors write, "the university served as an important means of integrating the future leadership of American society and assimilating the upwardly mobile"; now, however (the article dates from October, 1986), university classrooms are being invaded by academics who foster "political estrangement and cultural segmentation." The article excoriates tenured left-wing teachers in various disciplines for their failure to perform their proper job, which is to "promote intellectual openness and tolerance through an honest reading of the West's achievements" (Balch and London, 1986, 50).

With such back-handed testimonials to the current effectiveness of radical pedagogy, do "contestatory" educational theorists need to listen to voices on the left which sound less sanguine? My sense is that they (we) do. In the North American academy, at least, the arguments of the "severe" reproduction theorists have hardly begun to be seriously debated; giving them a hearing may well clarify some of the choices realistically available to those of us who hope to produce Shakespeare differently in the classroom. Moreover, given the prevailing ideology of free will in the US, and the tendency which Gramsci saw as characteristic of traditional intellectuals to think of themselves as independent and autonomous, one should not underestimate the strategic importance of arguments that stress the ways in which oppositional pedagogical work may be "contained" or recuperated by the educational system itself and by the larger social system to which schools contribute. While such arguments have been attacked, by E.P. Thompson among others, for fostering and rationalizing an attitude of political anomie on the part of intellectual elites, the arguments can, it seems to me, be read more dialectically, and possibly more productively, than Thompson allows (Thompson, 1978, esp. 374–81).

Samuel Bowles and Herbert Gintis's study of "Capitalism and Education" in America (1977), for instance, poses a useful challenge to an assumption that evidently informs many contemporary discussions of the value of "opening the canon." The assumption is that the representation of works by women and ethnic-minority writers in traditional "great books" courses is somehow a sign of, or even a means to, more substantial *political* representation for members of such groups.[5] By providing a Marxist economic and historical account of the social function of educational reforms, Bowles and Gintis interrogate the political meaning of a pedagogical project such as opening the canon, and they thereby invite both liberal and radical teachers to ask whether their time is truly well spent on that kind of curricular work. "The major reform periods [in US education]," Bowles and Gintis argue, "have been preceded by the development of significant divergences between the ever-changing social organization of production and the structure of education. Each major reform period has been associated with the integration into the wage-labour system of new groups of workers" (Bowles and Gintis, 1977, 203). The increasing visibility of feminist criticism in mainstream journals and traditional humanities courses looks less clearly like a political advance in any real sense when we consider the statistics discussed by Andrew Hacker in a recent article on "Women and Work"; among those statistics is the startling one that women have, since 1980, taken 80 percent of the new jobs created in the US economy (Hacker, 1986, 26). Women's increasing presence in the labor force has not, however, brought substantial changes in the "gender gap" in pay rates: according to a Census Bureau report of 1984, "women as a group made $637 for every $1,000 earned by men." Moreover, a National Academy of Sciences study found that "as women enter a field, earnings tend to drop, not only for [women] but for the men who remain" (Hacker, 1986, 31). Such economic statistics cast an ironic light on feminist projects for "undoing the canonical economy," to borrow a phrase from the title of an influential essay by Christine Froula (1983). Such projects are arguably instances of what Bowles and Gintis call "pluralist accommodation" and define as a "reorientation of educational perspectives in the face of a changing economic reality." In periods of economic changes, Bowles and Gintis argue, "educators tend to alter their educational values and goals in 'progressive' directions – directions conforming to the new 'economic rationality' emerging in the social relations of production" (Bowles and Gintis, 1977, 205).

As I have suggested, Bowles and Gintis have been criticized for presenting an overly pessimistic account of the correspondences between "modern forms of capitalism, the functional requirements of the division of labor, and modern forms of schooling" (Apple, 1982, 8). Their analysis does indeed, as Martin Carnoy suggests, "lose sight" of a possibility other Marxist educators want to stress, namely that the educational "superstructure" may have a degree of autonomy from the economic base and may therefore, in Carnoy's view, "become a focus of revolutionary struggle" (Carnoy, 1982, 112). The notion of the "relative autonomy" of the superstructure" invoked by Carnoy against Bowles and Gintis has, however, been deployed by other severe reproduction theorists to arrive at conclusions no less apparently pessimistic than Bowles and Gintis's are about the possibilities of using the school as a site for effective political action. Althusser, indeed, in "Ideology and Ideological State Apparatuses," derives his bleak view of the school's reproductive functions precisely from an argument about that institution's "relative autonomy" from the economic base. The "reproduction of the skills of labour power," he maintains, "is achieved more and more outside production: by the capitalist educational system and other instances and institutions" (Althusser, 1971, 13). He further argues that education has replaced religion as the *dominant* "ideological state apparatus" in mature capitalist formations (p. 157).

Althusser's theory of reproduction has been criticized by the British sociologists of education, Michael Erben and Denis Gleeson, for advancing a "passive model of socialization" and for assuming "a reified model of a system tightly policed by a 'conspiracy' of apparatuses in dominance" (Erben and Gleeson, 1977, 74). Althusser's view of teachers particularly irritates his English-speaking critics, most of whom are themselves professional educators. Rachel Sharp uses the term "patronizing" (Sharp, 1980, 163) to describe the passage in which Althusser apologizes to the small group of "heroic" teachers who "attempt to turn the few weapons they can find in the history and learning they 'teach' against the ideology, the system, and the practices in which they are trapped" (Althusser, 1971, 157). Erben and Gleeson fault Althusser for failing to explain "how radicals emerge from . . . and engage with the 'crushing' influences of State Apparatuses''; the essay, they suggest, ''is likely to reinforce the idea that radical change is beyond [teachers'] frame of reference'' (1977, 74, 75).

Bourdieu and Passeron's *Reproduction in Education, Society, and Culture* (1977), like Althusser's essay, seems to foreclose the possibility that individual teachers or groups thereof can effect significant social change within or through the educational institution. Bourdieu and Passeron argue that the primary object of educational reproduction is the educational institution itself; they further argue that the (French) school system's apparent freedom to enforce its own standards and hierarchies is ''the quid pro quo of the hidden services it renders to certain [dominant] classes'' (Bourdieu and Passeron, 1977, 153). Those ''services'' include, first, imposing the cultural values, norms, and languages of a dominant group on children of all social classes. This function occurs through modes of pedagogic action and communication that Bourdieu and Passeron analyze under the rubric of ''symbolic violence'' and see as a necessary effect of the teacher's position of institutional authority. No matter what the ''content'' of the teacher's message, and no matter what *theory* of teaching she or he may hold (the authors refer scornfully to ''Socratic and neo-Socratic myths of non-directive teaching, Rousseausitic myths of natural educa-tion . . . [and] pseudo Freudian myths of non-repressive education'' (p. 13)), the structural form of the teacher–student relation within the educational institu-tion entails symbolic violence, that is, the exercise of power ''to impose mean-ings and to impose them as legitimate by concealing the power relations which are the basis of its force'' (p. 4). The school's second major function, closely related to the first, is to separate upper-class children from lower-class ones through institutional procedures which individual teachers have little power – as individual agents – to alter. Those procedures reproduce existing hierarchies of social class through an apparently neutral ''meritocratic'' system: children from privileged backgrounds, who enter school with more ''cultural and linguistic capital'' than their less privileged mates, are more frequently promoted to higher grades, and gain entrance to more prestigious schools, than their working-class counterparts do. The latter, in Bourdieu and Passeron's view, repeatedly learn from their school experience to regard themselves as academic failures. The school thus functions to transmute a ''social inequality into a specifically educa-tional inequality, that is, an inequality of . . . success'' that masks, behind the opposition between the passed and the failed, an unequal distribution of ''cultural capital'' and the inequality of ''chances of *access* to the highest levels of education'' (pp. 158–9).

Bourdieu and Passeron's account of the reproductive function of the educa-tional system, which is much more complex than I have indicated (not only in itself but in its historical relation to the events of May, 1968 in France), has obvious affinities to Foucauldian, new historicist, and Frankfurt school visions of the ways in which a given social system effectively ''contains'' forces that might challenge its legitimacy. And recent critiques of Bourdieu and Passeron's work offer suggestive parallels to some of the critiques mounted in this volume and elsewhere against the new historicists. Rather than rehearsing those critiques in detail (their outlines have already been suggested), I want to consider now some implications of the radical education debates for the pedagogical project of producing Shakespeare differently in the classroom – a project sketched by the editors in their introduction and adumbrated by many of these essays' revisionary readings and political contextualizations of Shakespeare's plays.

First, the debates invite us to think realistically about the limits of curricular change as a mode of political action. Such change, in and of itself, cannot do much to alter what many theorists take to be the school's major social function, namely the reproduction of a labor force stratified along lines of gender, class, and race. Because this kind of reproduction occurs mainly through procedures of credentialization that ratify students' unequal access to different levels of schooling, and to different types of school (vocational versus liberal arts, for instance), it is a phenomenon that college-level teachers may well not even notice, much less seek to criticize. We can, of course, choose to participate in struggles to change the procedures of credentialization characteristic of a particular educational system (and these of course vary significantly from country to country). If we live in the US, however, it's hard to see how participating in such struggles can be related directly to our work on Shakespeare; his texts are after all of minor importance in certification examinations such as the SATs. In Britain, where Shakespeare continues to be a major topic in A- and O-level examinations, radical Shakespeareans clearly have greater scope for intervening in those aspects of educational reproduction that partly determine the audience for liberal arts courses on Shakespeare.

A second general implication of the education debates is that changes in the *content* of the curriculum need to be correlated with changes in the *forms* of instruction – the forms which Bourdieu and Passeron analyze as the "symbolic violence" of "pedagogic communication" and which other radical theorists have termed "the hidden curriculum": a complex of ideological practices that work to legitimize bourgeois language uses and values and that thereby make the classroom a site for reproducing social relations of domination and subordination.[6] Arguing against Bourdieu and Passeron's account of how teachers are necessarily agents of such reproduction simply by virtue of their position of power and institutional authority, some radical theorists have sketched strategies for deconstructing the hidden curriculum which could usefully be deployed in classes on Shakespeare, and which, indeed, seem to follow logically from some of the interpretive strategies illustrated in this volume.

One frequently mentioned starting point for deconstructing the hidden curriculum is to render it *less* hidden by making the issue of pedagogical authority a topic for critical discussion – which need not entail the naive notion that teachers can or should somehow divest themselves of authority. The workings of the hidden curriculum can also begin to be deconstructed by pedagogical practices that stress, rather than occlude, the social differences that exist among one's students – differences in race, class, ethnicity, and gender which generate the disparate forms of "cultural capital" students bring to the school. Stanley

Aronowitz and Henry Giroux argue forcefully that the language uses and cultural experiences of students from subordinate social groups need to be "validated," but also critically challenged, in the classroom; these authors also urge that the "cultural politics" of the classroom be directly related to the formal curricula teachers develop or mediate (Aronowitz and Girouz, 1985, 156).

Acknowledging that such recommendations are much easier to make than to put into practice, I would nonetheless suggest that teachers of Shakespeare have unusually good opportunities for constructing passages between their formal subject matter and the question of their students' different formations as political subjects. Such passages would seem fairly easy to envision as extensions of lines of critical inquiry already drawn in this volume – in the essays on *The Tempest, The Merchant of Venice, Coriolanus*, and *Othello*, to mention only the most obvious examples. Karen Newman's critique of the modern Arden edition of *Othello* would be especially useful for a discussion of students' attitudes toward and experiences of racial prejudice. Showing how racist ideologies are perpetuated, and in interestingly contradictory ways, through a widely used edition, Newman notes that the most recent reprint of the Arden *Othello* portrays on its cover a "veritable negro" of exactly the physiognomy that Coleridge found "monstrous" and that M.R. Ridley, in his introduction to the Arden edition, assures us was *not* the physiognomy of Shakespeare's noble Moor. The material object of the Arden edition could indeed be fruitfully analyzed in the classroom as a locus of conflicting ideologies of race in recent US history: Ridley's introduction, written in 1958, distinguishes between "sub-human" and noble blacks by comparing Othello to a "negro conductor on an American Pullman car" who had "one of the finest heads I have ever seen on any human being" (quoted by Newman in this volume, p. 143). Newman's essay suggests how we might focus pedagogical attention on the historical *mediations* between the Shakespearean play's moment of production and its moment of reception by the modern student. Another way of focusing class discussion on such historical mediations, and of relating them directly to the students' more or less developed awareness of their different "cultural capitals," is suggested by Don E. Wayne's essay. His brief but provocative remarks on certain historical correspondences between the "successive waves of immigrant culture" in the US and the ways in which a play such as *The Merchant of Venice* was produced both in the theatres and in the schools of New York could be fruitfully pursued in a class on that play or even (more ambitiously) in a course entitled (say) "Shakespeare and the American Ideology of the 'Melting Pot.'"

The task of devising pedagogical strategies for countering the hidden curriculum is clearly larger and more complex than I have indicated. The radical education debates suggest not only the importance of that task but also its manifold difficulties, one of which is the fact that teachers generally have to rely on prepackaged curricular materials. College teachers of Shakespeare are obviously freer to depart from standardized materials than elementary-school teachers are, but that freedom is only relative: the one- or multi-volume editions of Shakespeare commonly used in college courses constitute a considerable obstacle to pedagogical innovations of the kinds proposed both by the editors and by me. If one works at an elite institution, one may have funds for photocopying historical materials to supplement the standard play editions – selections from the antitheatrical tracts discussed by Jean E. Howard, for instance, or from the *Discourse* on the "causes" of blackness by George Best that Karen Newman adduces in her essay on *Othello*. It is obvious, however, that new editions of the plays which printed such materials would substantially aid the task of historicizing and politicizing the teaching of Shakespeare either at the college or at the secondary-school level. It is also clear that alternative pedagogies of the kind implied by the deconstructive, feminist, and historicist approaches illustrated in this volume would be much easier to put into practice if we had texts of the plays themselves – or rather, *not* self-evidently themselves – which demystified the notion of the aesthetic object as the product of a unified intention. A school edition of *Hamlet*, say, which printed both the "bad" and the "good" quarto versions of the play along with the Folio text, would be a major material support for teachers seeking to counter the ideological reproduction of Shakespeare as an author whose genius, transcending the contaminations of ideology, makes him the "bearer of universal values."

The labor of (repeatedly) contesting the reproduction of that still powerful image of Shakespeare may seem politically nugatory or worse, a way of contributing, in a small way, to the reproduction of the existing socioeconomic order: that order includes a Shakespeare publishing industry which by its very existence seems to confirm and capitalize on Ben Jonson's famous dictum that Shakespeare wrote not for an age but for all time. If, however, we read that line in context – even the minute context of the poem in which it occurs – we may have an emblem for a strategy of interpretation which is well illustrated in this volume and which, I have been suggesting, might be productively deployed in the classroom too. That strategy seeks to disrupt the processes of ideological reproduction by splicing familiar texts with less familiar literary, historical, and political contexts. Consider what happens when we subject Jonson's familiar line to a simple version of that interpretive procedure:

> Triumph, my Britaine, thou hast one to showe,
> To whom all Scenes of Europe homage owe.
> He was not of an age, but for all time!

These lines, which show the famous image of an apparently transhistorical Shakespeare arising directly from a historically charged articulation of British imperialist pride, invite us to ask: what specific political or economic interests are served by the production of a transhistorical Shakespeare? To ask that question – a version of Marx's *cui bono?* – is to begin, at least, to interrupt the processes of ideological reproduction.

It is a peculiarity of ideology, Louis Althusser maintains, that "it imposes obviousnesses as obviousnesses," making us cry out "That's obvious! That's right! That's true!" (Althusser, 1971, 172). And it is also, according to

Althusser, "the peculiarity of ideology . . . that it is endowed with a structure and a functioning such as to make it a non-historical reality, i.e. an *omni-historical* reality" (p. 161). Insofar as the figure of Shakespeare continues to serve in modern English-speaking societies as a prime instance of, and support for, ideologies that relay the idea of an "omni-historical reality," it is worth continuing the struggle dramatized in this volume: the struggle to separate obvious Shakespeares from less obvious ones.

Notes

1. See the article on "reproduction" in *A Dictionary of Marxist Thought* (Bottomore, 1983) for a discussion of the different senses in which the term has been used in recent Marxist and feminist theory.
2. Carnoy (1982, 79–126) provides a useful account of these two distinct but related aspects of educational reproduction: the first has to do with the ways in which different types of schools and "tracking" systems within them serve to distribute individuals into "materially different social and economic positions" (p. 107); the second, with the ways in which students are socialized in the schools to follow "different rules of behaviour according to the type of job that they are likely to hold" (p. 92).
3. See Apple (1981, 1–31) for a survey of this general field of debate, which I have schematically simplified. My distinction between "severe" reproduction theorists and "contestatory" ones glosses over the ways in which these two positions are frequently held simultaneously (albeit with different emphases) in the work of individual authors. My way of mapping the field also fails to do justice to the opposition between theories that stress cultural forms of reproduction and those that stress economic forms.
4. Sinfield (in Dollimore and Sinfield, 1985, 146) observes that for many decades in Britain both the Labour Party and the Communist Party held a liberal view of education as an inherently beneficial means of developing human potential and as requiring reform chiefly in order to "equalise opportunities" for individuals to benefit from it.
5. I owe this point to John Guillory, who kindly allowed me to see a draft of his essay "Canonical and Noncanonical: A Critique of the Current Debate" (forthcoming in *English Literary History*).
6. So far as I know, the concept of the "hidden curriculum" was first elaborated by Ivan Illich (1971, 1973) to describe the ways in which the *structure* of schooling works to inculcate bourgeois norms, values, and dispositions: "The hidden curriculum teaches all children that economically valuable knowledge is the result of professional teaching and that social entitlements depend on the rank achieved in a bureaucratic process. The hidden curriculum transforms the explicit curriculum into a commodity and makes its acquisition the securest form of wealth" (Illich, 1973; quoted in Apple, 1977, 101). See also Aronowitz and Giroux (1985, 75 and *passim*); they define the hidden curriculum as "those classroom social relations that embody specific messages which legitimize the particular views of work, authority, social rules, and values that sustain capitalist logic."

Works cited

Althusser, Louis (1971) *Lenin and Philosophy and Other Essays*, trans. Ben Brewster, New York, Monthly Review Press.
Apple, Michael W. (1977) "Ivan Illich and Deschooling Society," in Young, Michael and Whitty, Geoff (eds) *Society, State and Schooling: Readings on the Possibilities for*

Radical Education, Falmer, Sussex, Falmer Press, 93–121.

—— (ed.) (1982) *Cultural and Economic Reproduction in Education: Essays on Class, Ideology and the State*, London, Routledge & Kegan Paul.

Aronowitz, Stanley and Giroux, Henry A. (1985) *Education Under Siege: The Conservative, Liberal and Radical Debate over Schooling*, South Hadley, Mass., Bergin & Garvey.

Balch, Stephen H. and London, Herbert I. (1986) "The Tenured Left," *Commentary*, 82 (4) (October), 41–50.

Baudelot, Christian and Establet, Roger (1975) *L'Ecole capitaliste en France*, Paris, François Maspero.

Bisseret, Noëlle (1979) *Education, Class Language, and Ideology*, London, Routledge & Kegan Paul.

Bottomore, Tom (ed.) (1983) *A Dictionary of Marxist Thought*, Cambridge, Mass., Harvard University Press.

Bourdieu, Pierre and Passeron, Jean-Claude (1977) *Reproduction in Education, Society, and Culture*, trans. Richard Nice (French edn, 1970), London and Beverly Hills, Sage.

Bowles, Samuel and Gintis, Herbert (1976) *Schooling in Capitalist America*, New York, Basic Books.

—— (1977) "Capitalism and Education in the United States," in Young, Michael and Whitty, Geoff (eds) *Society, State and Schooling: Readings on the Possibilities for Radical Education*, Falmer, Sussex, Falmer Press, 192–227.

Carnoy, Martin (1982) "Education, Economy and the State," in Apple, Michael W. (ed.) *Cultural and Economic Reproduction in Education: Essays on Class, Ideology and the State*, London, Routledge & Kegan Paul, 79–126.

Dollimore, Jonathan and Sinfield, Alan (eds) (1985) *Political Shakespeare: New Essays in Cultural Materialism*, Manchester, Manchester University Press; Ithaca, NY, Cornell University Press.

Erben, Michael and Gleeson, Denis (1977) "Education as Reproduction: A Critical Examination of Some Aspects of the Work of Louis Althusser," in Young, Michael and Whitty, Geoff (eds) *Society, State and Schooling: Readings on the Possibilities for Radical Education*, Falmer, Sussex, Falmer Press.

Froula, Christine (1983) "When Eve Reads Milton: Undoing the Canonical Economy," *Critical Inquiry*, 10, 321–47.

Hacker, Andrew (1986) "Women and Work," *New York Review of Books*, 33 (13) (August 14), 26–32.

Illich, Ivan (1971) *Deschooling Society*, New York, Harper & Row.

—— (1973) "After Deschooling What?" in Gartner, Alan, Greer, Colin, and Riessman, Frank (eds) *After Deschooling What?*, New York, Harper & Row.

MacDonald, Madeleine (1980) "Socio-cultural Reproduction and Women's Education," in Deem, Rosemary (ed.) *Schooling for Women's Work*, London, Routledge & Kegan Paul.

Sharp, Rachel (1980) *Knowledge, Ideology and the Politics of Schooling: Towards a Marxist Analysis of Education*, London, Routledge & Kegan Paul.

Thompson, E.P. (1978) *The Poverty of Theory and Other Essays*, London, Merlin Press.

Young, Michael F.D. (1971) *Knowledge and Control: New Directions for the Sociology of Education*, London, Collier Macmillan.

Young, Michael and Whitty, Geoff (eds) (1977) *Society, State and Schooling: Readings on the Possibilities for Radical Education*, Falmer, Sussex, Falmer Press.

Index

Adams, Joseph Quincy 64–5
Adelman, Janet 23, 219
Adorno, Theodor W. 213
Aers, David 27
Aeschylus 10
Aesop 141
Akrigg, G.P.V. 70, 137
Alarum Against Usurers, An (Lodge) 193, 195–9, 203–4
Allen, J.W. 226, 231
Althusser, Louis 3, 4, 27, 60, 100, 118, 136, 183, 247, 274, 277, 278, 281–2
Altick, Richard D. 77
Amery, Colin 73–4
Anatomie of Abuses, The (Stubbes) 166, 169
Anderson, Perry 21, 207
Ansruther, Ian 94
Antony and Cleopatra (Shakespeare) 23–4, 28, 156
Apology for Poetry, An (Sidney) 170–1, 192, 200–1
Apple, Michael W. 275, 277, 282
Aquinas, Thomas 228
Archer, William 96
Aristotle 113
Armstrong, Nancy 65
Arnold, Matthew 31, 52, 54, 56, 61, 64
Aronowitz, Stanley 275, 279–80, 282
Arts Council of Great Britain 72–6, 95
As You Like It (Shakespeare) 37, 55, 87, 125
Asp, C. 262
Augustine 228
Averall, William 231

Axton, Marie 137

Bacon, Francis 130, 149, 191, 196
Bakhtin, Mikhail 3, 29, 32, 211, 214–15
Balch, Stephen 275–6
Bamber, Linda 23
Barber, C.L. 24, 202, 204, 271
Barish, Jonas 184
Barkan, Leonard 137, 227, 229
Barker, Anthony 158
Barker, Felix 87
Barker, Francis 27–30, 106, 112, 114
Barrie, James Matthew 75
Barton, Anne Righter 119, 136–7, 184
Basilikon Doron (James I) 252–3, 259
Baudelot, Christian 275
Beckett, Samuel 10
Becon, Thomas 159
Behn, Aphra 154
Belasco, David 64
Belsey, Catherine 26–8
Bennett, Tony 107, 154
Bennett, William 218
Benson, Constance Featherstonehaugh 87
Benson, Francis Robert 92
Berger, Harry Jr. 113, 175, 250, 260–2
Bergeron, David M. 184
Berry, Ralph 219
Best, George 146–8, 150–1, 153–4, 158, 281
Bethell, S.L. 31
Bhabha, Homi 159
Billington, Sandra M. 16
Bisseret, Noëlle 275
Blanco, Carlos 65

Bodin, Jean 148, 159
Boethius 228
Bond, Edward 7
Boose, Lynda 160
Booth, Stephen 260-1
Bottomore, Tom 282
Bourdieu, Pierre 60, 274, 278-9
Bowers, Fredson 128
Bowles, Samuel 274, 276-7
Bradbrook, Muriel Clare 117, 135
Bradley, Andrew Cecil 24, 31, 219, 261
Brantlinger, Patrick 102-3
Brassington, William Salt 95
Braudel, Fernand 211-12
Braunmuller, A.R. 137
Brecht, Bertolt 50-1, 239, 272
Bridges-Adams, Walter 86
Bristol, Michael D. 13-14, 16, 32, 184,
   207, 209, 214-15, 232
Brockbank, Philip 239
Brooks, Cleanth 262
Brown, Ivor 92
Brown, John Russell 194, 203
Brown, Paul 16, 29, 65, 106, 112
Brown, Stephen J. 63, 65
Browne, Thomas 159
Bull, John 81-2
Bullough, Geoffrey 194, 199, 203-4,
   248-50, 257, 262
Bundy, Edgar 88, 92
Burckhardt, Jacob 28
Burckhardt, Sigurd 200
Burke, Edmund 55
Burke, Kenneth 149, 159
Burke, Peter 209
Burton, Richard F. 102

Camden, William 214
Cannadine, David 136
Cantor, Paul A. 219
Carnoy, Martin 275, 277, 282
Carr, Philip 96
Carroll, William C. 136
Cartelli, Thomas 12, 16, 19, 99, 220
Cavell, Stanley 213-14, 219, 233
Cawley, A.C. 158
Cecil, William (Lord Burleigh) 230
Certain Sermons or Homilies Appointed
   to be Read . . . 227, 229
Césaire, Aimé 112
Chambers, Edmund K. 262
Chandler, Wayne B. 160
Charles I (King) 169

Charney, Maurice 212-13, 219, 232-3,
   235
Chaste Maid in Cheapside, A
   (Middleton) 96
Chaucer, Geoffrey 16, 65
Chesterton, Gilbert Keith 95
Chitty, C.W. 158
Chow, Rey 160
Chronicles of England, Scotland and
   Ireland (Holinshed) 242, 247-50,
   260-1
Churchill, Jenny Jerome Spencer (Lady
   Randolph) 12, 69-70, 92, 95
Churchill, Peregrine 95
Churchill, Randolph S. 83, 85-6
Churchill, Winston Leonard Spencer 69,
   83, 85-6
Cinthio, Giraldi 152-3
Cixous, Hélène 24, 29
Clark, A.M. 261
Cody, 'Buffalo' Bill 77
Cohen, Walter 2, 5, 11-12, 16, 18, 22,
   32, 36, 111, 137, 183, 189-90, 192,
   194, 202, 273
Coleridge, Samuel Taylor 31, 143
Collard, A.O. 80-1
Columbus, Christopher 112
Comedy of Errors, A (Shakespeare) 71
Communist Party of Great Britain 282
Conrad, Joseph 103-4, 106, 108
Cook, Carol 184-5
Coriolanus (Shakespeare) 3, 13-14, 23,
   51, 207-21, 225-39, 280
Cornforth, John 95
Cornwallis-West, George 78
Cornwallis-West, Mrs George: see
   Churchill, Jenny Jerome Spencer
Country Life Illustrated 71-2, 74-5,
   95
Crewe, Jonathan 183
Crewe, Marquess of 76, 78
Cripps-Day, Francis Henry 92
Cromwell, Oliver 55
Crowley, Robert 230-1, 239

Daniel, Samuel 232
Danson, Lawrence 189, 202, 213
Dante Alighieri 65
Dasent, John Roche 158
Dash, Irene 24
Davidson, Michael 65
Davis, Natalie Z. 209
Death of Usury, The 193, 195-6, 198

Declaration of Egregious Popish Impostures, A (Harsnett) 243
Defence of Poesie, The (Sidney): *see Apologie for Poetry, An*
Dekker, Thomas 191
Denne, Henry 237–8
De Man, Paul 17
De Quincey, Thomas 55
Derrida, Jacques 14, 27, 29, 32, 60, 63, 147, 150, 244–7, 268
Descartes, René 225, 245
Devonshire, Duchess of 68–70
D'Ewes, Simonds 231
DeWitt, Johannes 71
Dickens, Charles 55
Dinesen, Isak 114
Dior, Christian 6
Doane, Mary Anne 159
Doctor Faustus (Marlowe) 81, 87
Dods, R.S. 73
'Doleman, R.': *see* Parsons, Robert
Dollimore, Jonathan 3, 22, 26–9, 31, 48, 51, 63, 65, 136, 184, 189, 212–13, 218, 274, 282
Drakakis, John 31, 48–51, 63, 65
Drake, Francis 217
Draper, John W. 203–4
Dreher, Diane Elizabeth 23–5
DuBois, Page 65
DuBois, W.E.B. 160
Duff (King) 249
Duncan I (King) 248–50
Dunn, Robert Paul 16
Durkheim, Emile 210

Eagleton, Terry 5, 27, 29, 32, 227
Earl's Court Exhibition 12, 77, 94, 96
East India Company 158
Edward the Confessor (King) 251, 261
Edward III (King) 127
Edward VI (King) 196, 227
Edward VII (King) 69, 70, 80
Eglinton Tournament 94
Elam, Keir 270
Elen, Gus 87
Eliade, Mircea 228
Elias, Norbert 61–2
Eliot, Thomas Stearnes 31, 52
Elizabeth I (Queen) 86, 116, 118, 128–32, 134–5, 137, 148, 167, 169, 184, 192, 227, 229
Elizabethan Stage Society 70–1
Elton, G.R. 239

Endgame (Beckett) 10
Erben, Michael 277
Erickson, Peter 12–13, 16, 23–5, 116, 136, 168, 270
Erlich, Bruce 220–1
Essex, Earl of (Robert Devereux) 134, 137
Establet, Robert 275
Evans, Malcolm 24, 26–7, 29–32
Examination of Usury, The (Smith) 193–4, 196, 203

Faerie Queene, The (Spenser) 127, 132, 136
Fanon, Franz 113
Fareon, George 92
Farrell, Kirby 16
Fastolf, John 36
Fedalto, Giorgio 160
Felperin, Howard 262
Fenner, George 159
Ferguson, Arthur B. 228–9
Ferguson, Margaret W. 15, 16, 273
Fiedler, Leslie 114
Fineman, Joel 24, 262
Fiorentino, Giovanni 192, 198, 203–4
First Performance of 'The Merry Wives of Windsor' 1599, The (Bundy) 88–90
Fiske, Edward B. 218
Fletcher, John 87
Forset, Edward 214, 229
Forster, Leonard 129, 137
Fortuny, Mario 92
Foucault, Michel 27–30, 33, 35, 38, 57, 60, 63, 184, 238, 244–5, 247, 260, 268, 278
Fraser, Russell A. 166
French, Marilyn 24–5
Freud, Sigmund 57, 156
Freund, Elizabeth 16
Frewen, Clara Jerome 95
Friedrich, Otto 47
Froula, Christine 277

Gadamer, Hans-Georg 213
Gardner, Helen 31
Garner, S.N. 161
Garner, Thomas 79
Garstow, George 87
Garter, Order of the 12, 125–9, 133–7
Gates, Thomas 113
Gaudet, Paul 16
Geertz, Clifford 60

George V (King) 82–3
George, Katherine 159
Gheerhaerts, Marcus 136
Gibbs, Philip 94
Giddens, Anthony 213
Gilbert, James Burkhart 218
Gintis, Herbert 274, 276–7
Girard, René 204, 262, 269
Girouard, Marc 94
Giroux, Henry A. 275, 280, 282
Gleeson, Denis 277
Goethe, Johann Wolfgang von 64
Goetze, Sigismund 95
Gohlke, Madelon: see Sprengnether
Goldberg, Jonathan 14, 16, 22, 24,
    33–7, 63, 160, 184, 213, 220, 242
Goldman, Michael 220
Gordon, Donald J. 239
Gosson, Stephen 159, 167–70, 184, 194,
    201
Gotch, J. Alfred 79
Goulden, Holly 16
Gradidge, Richard 73–4
Gramsci, Antonio 27, 208, 275
Green, William 126, 136–7
Greenblatt, Stephen 19, 33–8, 63, 114,
    129, 136–7, 149, 150, 156, 159, 167,
    184, 190, 197, 203, 242–5, 262
Greer, Germaine 136
Grenville, Richard 82
Greville, Fulke 232
Guenée, Bernard 207
Guest, Frederick Edward 93
Guillory, John 282
Guls Horn-Booke, The (Dekker) 191
Gurr, Andrew 213
Gwinne, Matthew 262

Habermas, Jurgen 13–14, 32, 208, 213,
    219, 220
Hacker, Andrew 276–7
Haigh, Christopher 136
Hakluyt, Richard 111, 146, 158–9, 191,
    195
Hale, David G. 213–14, 226, 231–2
Hall, Peter 49
Hall, Stuart 117, 135–6
Hamlet (Shakespeare) 24, 28, 55, 99,
    100, 225, 267, 281
Hamner, Robert 103
Harbage, Alfred 31, 136, 184
Harding, D.W. 262
Hardinge, Henry 76

Harrison, J.F.C 209
Harsnett, Samuel 243
Hartley, Jon 16
Hartman, Geoffrey 17
Hawkes, Terence 3, 24, 27, 31
Hawkins, John 148
Hawkins, M. 261
Hazlitt, William 7, 55
Hedrick, Donald K. 16, 112
Heinemann, Margot 19, 20, 31, 50–1
Helgerson, Richard 65
Henriques, Julian 184
Henry V (King) 36
Henry VIII (King) 229, 239
Henze, Richard 174
Herrick, Robert 188
Hibbard, G.R. 135–6
Hibbert, Christopher 113
Hicks, Seymour 87
Hill, Christopher 27, 166, 238
Hill, Errol 19, 31
Hitler, Adolf 103
Hjort, Anne Mette 213
Holderness, Graham 15, 27–8, 30–2, 65
Holinshed, Raphael 242, 247–50, 260–1
Homer 64
Honig, Edwin 212, 219
Honour of the Garter, The (Peele) 127,
    133, 137
Hooch, Pieter de 95
Hooper, Wilfred 167
Horwitch, R. 262
Howard, Jean E. 13, 16, 22, 38, 63, 65,
    163, 268, 281
Howe, Irving 64
Hudson, Edward 72
Huet, Marie Hélène 159
Hughes, Paul L. 148
Hulme, Peter 29, 30, 106, 109, 112–14
Hunter, G.K. 159
Hussey, Christopher 74, 76
Huston, J. Dennis 183

Iacke-a-Lente (Taylor) 215–17
Ide, Richard 212, 219
Idyllic Players 86, 88, 96
Illich, Ivan 282
Informacion and Petition (Crowley) 230
Irigaray, Luce 24, 262
Irving, Henry 64, 83
Irving, Robert Grant 76

James I (King) 169, 184, 229, 247,

251–7, 259, 261
James, Mervyn 228
Jameson, Fredric 208, 220–1, 251
JanMohamed, Abdul 114
Jardine, Lisa 25, 137
Jekyll, Gertrude 73
Johnson, Rosalind 159
Johnson, Samuel 31
Johnson, Walter 55
Jones, Anne Rosalind 262
Jones, Eldred 159
Jonson, Ben 47, 145, 149, 242, 251,
    253–7, 260, 262, 281
Jordan, Winthrop 145, 158, 160
Jorgensen, Paul A. 210
Julius Caesar (Shakespeare) 51, 87, 225,
    232

Kahn, Coppélia 23, 25
Kant, Immanuel 51, 53
Kavanagh, Patrick 16, 31
Keen, Maurice 128, 136
Kehler, Dorothea 16
Kennedy, John Fitzgerald 136
Kenneth I (King) 250
Kermode, Frank 31, 113, 188, 247, 261
Kettle, Arnold 63
King, Henry 188
King, Thomas 70
King Henry IV, Parts 1 and 2
    (Shakespeare) 27, 34, 36, 128
King Henry V (Shakespeare) 27, 34, 36,
    127–8, 136, 225
King Henry VI, Part 1 (Shakespeare)
    127, 130
King Henry VIII (Shakespeare) 35
King John (Shakespeare) 87
King Lear (Shakespeare) 24, 27, 28, 32,
    156, 182, 243, 271
King Richard II (Shakespeare) 27, 35
King Richard III (Shakespeare) 87
Kinney, Arthur 170
Kinser, Samuel 228
Kipling, Rudyard 101
Kiralfy, Imre 77–8
Kirwan, Patrick 86, 88, 92
Knapp, Stephen 65
Knight, George Wilson 31, 108, 110
Knights, L.C. 31
Kott, Jan 220
Kress, Gunther 27
Krieger, Elliott 177
Krieger, Murray 63

Kristeva, Julia 24, 29
Kuhn, Annette 135

Labour Party 21, 282
Lacan, Jacques 24, 29, 60, 262
LaCapra, Dominick 210
Lamb, Charles 55
Lambarde, William 270
Lamming, George 110–12
Larkin, James F. 148
Latham, Charles 72, 95
Latimer, Hugh 239
Law, R.A. 261
Lawson, Nigel 50
Leavis, F.R. 21, 31, 50, 52
Lehman, Alan D. 207
Leicester, Earl of (Robert Dudley) 137
Lelyveld, Toby 64
Lenz, Carolyn Ruth Swift 19, 22
Leo Africanus 148, 158–60
Le Roy Ladurie, Emmanuel 209–10, 215
Leslie, Leonie Jerome 95
Leslie, Michael 136
Leslie, William Seymour 95
Levin, Carole 134
Levin, Harry 47, 158
Lévi-Strauss, Claude 118
Lewalski, Barbara 203
Lieblein, Leanore 16
Livingstone, David 109
Lloyd George, David 76
Lockhart, J.G. 99, 113
Lodge, David 56
Lodge, Thomas 184, 193, 195–9, 203–4
Lok, John 159
London, Herbert I. 275–6
Longhurst, Derek 3, 16
Looking Glasse for London, A (Lodge)
    203
Lorimer, Robert 73
Lotman, Juri 229
Love's Labour's Lost (Shakespeare) 29
Lucas, E.V. 141
Lucas, John Seymour 83, 92
Luckhurst, Kenneth 77–8
Lugard, Frederick Dealtry 102
Lukács, Georg 265
Lutyens, Edwin Landseer 12, 72–82, 92,
    95
Lutyens, Emily Lytton 76–8
Lutyens, Mary 75
Lyons, Charles H. 158
Lytton, Victor, Earl of 77–8

Macaulay, Thomas Babington 55
Macbeth (Shakespeare) 14, 24, 26, 55,
    87, 156, 242–63
MacCallum, M.W. 212
McCanles, Michael 219
McCarthy, Joseph R. 19, 53
McCarthy, Thomas 208, 213, 291
McCoy, Richard 137
MacDonald, Madeleine 275
Macherey, Pierre 27, 201, 204
Machiavelli, Niccolò 129
Machin, Richard 242
McLaughlin, William 142
MacLure, Millar 65, 219
McLuskie, Kathleen E. 24, 26, 65
Manchester, Consuelo, Duchess of 70
Mandeville, John 148, 159
Manningham, John 70–1
Mannoni, Dominique O. 113
Marlowe, Christopher 87, 125
Marsh, Edward 95
Martin, Ernest 159
Martin, Ralph G. 69, 93
Marx, Karl 208, 228, 267, 281
Marxist criticism 2, 3, 11–12, 19–22,
    25–33, 35, 37–8, 50, 56, 221, 246–7,
    276–7, 282
Mary (Queen) 82–3
Mary I (Queen) 227
Mary, Queen of Scots 259
Masque of Blacknesse, The (Jonson) 145
Masque of Queens, The (Jonson) 241,
    251, 254–6, 260
Mazer, Cary M. 96
Measure for Measure (Shakespeare)
    182
Meisel, Martin 88
Menaechmi (Plautus) 71
Merchant of Venice, The (Shakespeare)
    13, 55, 64, 87, 125, 188–204, 225,
    280
Meres, Francis 194, 225–6
Merry Wives of Windsor, The
    (Shakespeare) 12, 87, 117–35
Mervailous Combat of Contrareities, A
    (Averall) 231
Michaels, Walter Benn 65
Middleton, Thomas 19, 96, 251
Midsummer Night's Dream, A
    (Shakespeare) 32, 37, 87, 125, 134
Milton, John 55, 65, 242
Mitchell, Julian 95
Mitchell, W.J.T. 65, 220

Moisan, Thomas 13, 16, 32, 188
Montrose, Adrian Louis 22, 34, 37,
    168, 184, 189–90, 201
Moody, A.D. 200, 204
Moretti, Franco 20, 184, 252, 262
Much Ado About Nothing (Shakespeare)
    136, 163–85
Muir, Kenneth 213, 251, 260–1
Mullaney, Steven 34–6, 137, 252, 262
Mulvey, Laura 159
Munday, Anthony 184
Murphy, Sophia 68–9

Neame, Alan 109
Neely, Carol Thomas 19, 22–5, 135
New Criticism 5, 17, 21–3, 52–5, 63,
    262
Newman, Karen 13, 16, 24, 143, 168,
    267, 280–1
Newton, Judith 135
Ngugi Wa Thiong'o 12, 101–7, 111,
    113–14
Nichols, John 262
Nicolet, C. 207–8
Norbrook, David 136, 232
Norris, Christopher 242
Northbrooke, John 165, 184
Novy, Marianne 25
Nunn, Trevor 49
Nuttall, A.D. 200, 204

O'Connor, Marion F. 12, 16, 65, 71
Ohmann, Richard 53, 56, 220
Oldcastle, John 36
Oliver, H.J. 133, 135
Orgel, Stephen 35, 63, 132–3, 145, 242,
    251, 260, 262
Orkin, Martin 158
Oroonooko (Behn) 154
Orwell, George 102
Othello (Shakespeare) 13, 23, 28, 121,
    136, 143–61, 280–1
Ovid 143
Oz, Avraham 16

Palladis Tamia (Meres) 194, 225
Pan's Anniversary (Jonson) 253–4
Parker, Andrew 246–7
Parsons, Robert 229–30
Passeron, Jean-Claude 274, 278–9
Paster, Gail Kern 184, 219
Patterson, Annabel 35
Paul, H.N. 261

Pecorone, Il (Giovanni Fiorentino) 192,
  198, 203–4
Peele, George 127, 133, 137
Peter Pan (Barrie) 75
Petrarchism 12, 129–32, 145
Pettet, E.C. 212, 232
Phillips, James Emerson 212
Phillips, L. March 74
Phythian-Adams, Charles 229
Plantyn, Christopher 158
Plato 108, 226
Plautus 71
Playes Confuted in Five Actions
  (Gosson) 168
Pliny the Elder 148
Poel, William 70, 83, 88, 90, 95–6
Poggi, Gianfranco 207–10
Pollard, David 16
Ponet, John 230
Pope, Alexander 7
Pory, John 148
Postlewayt, M. 154, 160
Pratt, Mary Louise 108, 158
Prouty, Charles Tyler 173, 175
Pseudodoxia Epidemica (Browne) 159
Ptolemy 146
Puttenham, George 183

Quality Street (Barrie) 75
Querini, Tomaso 155
Quilligan, Maureen 273

Rabkin, Norman 113, 199, 212, 219
Ralegh, Walter 82, 129
Raleigh, Walter 31, 146, 158
Reagan, Ronald 19, 59
Reese, M.M. 48–50
Reiss, Timothy J. 33
Revenge 12, 82–3, 91, 95–6
Rhodes, Cecil 12, 99, 106, 111, 113
Richard, Jean Claude 207–9
Richardson, Margaret 73, 95
Ridley, Jane 95
Ridley, M.R. 143–5, 155, 280
Righter, Anne: *see* Barton
Ringler, William 170, 184
Rogers, R. 262
Rollins, Hyder 159
Rooney, Ellen 220
Rosenfelt, Deborah 135
Ross, Lawrence 156
Rossiter, A.P. 183, 212, 219
Royal African Company 154, 160

Royal Shakespeare Company 7, 49
Rozett, Martha 184
Ruggiero, Guido 155
Ryan, Michael 220
Rymer, Thomas 143–4, 152–3, 155, 160

Sacks, David Harris 228
Said, Edward 161
Salisbury, John of 228
Sanderson, Michael 87, 96
Savage, Peter 73
Schmitt, Carl 207, 209–10
Schoole of Abuse, The (Gosson) 159,
  167, 194, 201
Scullard, H.H. 208
Sedgewick, Eve K. 15, 262
Senden, Caspar van 148
Serpieri, Alessandro 20
Shakespeare, William *passim, and see
  under titles of individual plays*
'Shakespeare's England' 12, 76, 91–2,
  94
Sharp, Buchanan 213
Sharp, Rachel 275, 277
Shepherd, Simon 20, 25
Shultz, George 99, 100
Sicherman, Carol 219
Sidney, Philip 170–1, 192, 200, 214
Siegel, Paul N. 32
Silvayn, Alexander 204
Simmons, J.L. 212, 219
Sinfield, Alan 3, 16, 27–9, 31, 48–50,
  136, 218, 226, 239, 274, 282
Smith, Hallet 113
Smith, Henry 193–4, 196, 203, 226,
  236
Smith, Thomas 230
Snowden, Frank M. Jr. 158
Soellner, Rolf 16
Sorge, Thomas 13–14, 20, 225
Southampton, Earl of (Henry
  Wriothesley) 137
Southern, Richard 70
Spenser, Edmund 65, 127, 132–3, 136,
  242
Spivak, Bernard 151
Sprengnether, Madelon Gohlke 23, 117,
  262
Spurr, David 114
Stallybrass, Peter 26, 158, 160, 214,
  261
Stamp, Gavin 76
Stanley, Henry Morton 106, 109–11, 114

Starkey, Thomas 230
Steadman, John M. 137
Stein, A. 262
Stone, Lawrence 147, 184, 213
Stow, John 191, 196
Strachey, William 113
Stratton, Arthur 79
Strayer, Joseph R. 207
Strong, Roy 126, 136
Stubbes, Philip 166, 168–70
Styan, J.L. 210
Sundelson, David 24
Supplication of the Poore Commons, A
   229
Survey of London, The (Stow) 191,
   196
Suvin, Darko 220

Talbert, Ernest William 227, 231
Tale of Two Cities, A (Dickens)
Tamar Can 149
Taming of the Shrew, The (Shakespeare)
   117, 235
Tay, William 65
Taylor, John 215–17
Taylor, Philip 64
Tempest, The (Shakespeare) 12, 37,
   99–101, 103–4, 106–13, 280
Tennenhouse, Leonard 34–8, 63
Tennyson, Alfred 82
Thatcher, Margaret 9, 19, 49, 50
Thomas, Keith 132, 149, 229
Thomas, Maxime de 92
Thompson, E.P. 118, 209, 276
Tillyard, Eustace M.W. 31, 48, 50, 57,
   63
Titus Andronicus (Shakespeare) 149
Todorov, Tzvetan 103, 112
Tokson, Elliot H. 19, 159
Towerson, William 159
Treatise of Commerce (Wheeler) 239
Treatise wherein . . . are reproved . . . ,
   A (Northbrooke) 165
Tree, Herbert Beerbohm 86
Treggiari, Susan 208
Trewin, John Courtney 93
Trilling, Lionel 54, 55, 64
Troilus and Cressida (Shakespeare) 51,
   271
Trousdale, Marion 63
Tucker, E.F.J. 199
Tuke, Thomas 171, 172
Twelfth Night (Shakespeare) 71, 87

Underdown, David 167

Vale, Juliet 127
Vale, Malcolm 136
Vanbrugh, Violet 87–8
Vermeer, Jan 95
Vertumnus (Gwinne) 262
Vickers, Nancy 273
Victoria (Queen) 68, 71–2, 76, 80
Vision of Delight, The (Jonson) 253–4
Volpone (Jonson) 149

Wake, Isaac 262
Walcott, Derek 111
Wallerstein, Immanuel 208
Walvin, James 160
Walzer, Michael 203, 213
Warfield, David 64
Watt, F.W. 65
Way to Wealth (Crowley) 231
Wayne, Don E. 11–12, 16, 21, 47, 57,
   76, 218, 266, 280
Weaver, Laurence 75
Weber, Max 208–9
Webster, John 142
Weimann, Robert 15–16, 20, 29, 30,
   32, 62–3, 184, 202, 229, 265, 268–9
Weldon, Harry 87
Wells, Susan 22, 32
Wesley, John 243
Westlake, John 16
Weston, William 244
Wheeler, John 239
Wheeler, Richard 24
Whigham, Frank 147, 164
White, Allon 214
White Devil, The (Webster) 142
Whitley, J.R. 77–8
Whitney, Geoffrey 142, 158
Whitworth, Geoffrey 88
Wild Goose Chase, A (Fletcher) 87
Williams, Linda 159
Williams, Penry 132
Williams, Raymond 26, 48, 52, 118,
   135–6
Williamson, J. Bruce 71
Willson, D.H. 261
Wilson, Elkin Calhoun 129–30, 137
Wilson, John Dover 31, 261
Winstanley, Gerard 238
Winter's Tale, The (Shakespeare) 24
Witch, The (Middleton) 251
Wittkower, Rudolph 158